Word for Windows™ 6

SELF-TEACHING GUIDE

Wiley SELF-TEACHING GUIDES (STG's) are designed for first time users of computer applications and programming languages. They feature concept-reinforcing drills, exercises, and illustrations that enable you to measure your progress, and learn at your own pace. Other Wiley Self-Teaching Guides:

DOS STG (covers versions 5 and 6), Ruth Ashley and Judi N. Fernandez
INTRODUCTION TO PERSONAL COMPUTERS STG, Peter Stephenson
OBJECTVISION 2 STG, Arnold and Edith Shulman, and Robert Marion
1-2-3 Release 4 FOR WINDOWS STG, Douglas J. Wolf
PARADOX FOR WINDOWS STG, Gloria Wheeler
Q&A 4 STG, Corey Sandler and Tom Badgett
PAGEMAKER 5 FOR WINDOWS STG, Kim Baker and Sunny Baker
NOVELL NETWARE 2.2 STG, Peter Stephenson and Glenn Hartwig
MICROSOFT WORD 5.5 FOR THE PC STG, Ruth Ashley and Judi Fernandez
WORD FOR WINDOWS 6 STG, Stephen Guild
MICROSOFT WORD FOR WINDOWS 2 STG, Pamela S. Beason and Stephen Guild
WORDPERFECT 6 FOR DOS STG, Neil Salkind
WORDPERFECT 5.0/5.1 STG, Neil Salkind
SIGNATURE STG, Christine Rivera
WINDOWS 3.1 STG, Keith Weiskamp
MASTERING MICROSOFT WORKS STG, David Sachs, Babette Kronstadt, Judith Van Wormer, and Barbara Farrell
GW BASIC STG, Ruth Ashley and Judi Fernandez
TURBO C++ STG, Bryan Flamig
SQL STG, Peter Stephenson and Glenn Hartwig
QUICKEN STG, Peter Aitken
HARVARD GRAPHICS 3 STG, David Harrison and John W. Yu
HARVARD GRAPHICS FOR WINDOWS STG, David Harrison and John W. Yu
AMI PRO 2 FOR WINDOWS STG, Pamela S. Beason and Stephen Guild
EXCEL 4 STG, Ruth K. Witkin

To order our STG's, you can call Wiley directly at (201)469-4400, or check your local bookstores.

"Mastering computers was never this easy, rewarding, and fun!"

Word for Windows™ 6

SELF-TEACHING GUIDE

Stephen Guild

John Wiley & Sons, Inc.
New York ▲ Chichester ▲ Brisbane ▲ Toronto ▲ Singapore

Publisher: Katherine Schowalter
Editor: Tim Ryan
Managing Editor: Jacqueline Martin
Editorial Production and Design: Impressions, a Division of
  Edwards Brothers, Inc.

Windows is a registered trademark of Microsoft Corporation. Designations used by companies to distinguish their products are often claimed as trademarks. In all instances where John Wiley & Sons, Inc. is aware of a claim, the product names appear in initial capital or all capital letters. Readers, however, should contact the appropriate companies for more complete information regarding trademarks and registration.

This text is printed on acid-free paper.

Copyright © 1994 by John Wiley & Sons, Inc.

All rights reserved. Published simultaneously in Canada.

This publication is designed to provide accurate and authoritative information in regard to the subject matter covered. It is sold with the understanding that the publisher is not engaged in rendering legal, accounting, or other professional service. If legal advice or other expert assistance is required, the services of a competent professional person should be sought. FROM A DECLARATION OF PRINCIPLES JOINTLY ADOPTED BY A COMMITTEE OF THE AMERICAN BAR ASSOCIATION AND A COMMITTEE OF PUBLISHERS.

Reproduction or translation of any part of this work beyond that permitted by Section 107 or 108 of the 1976 United States Copyright Act without the permission of the copyright owner is unlawful. Requests for permission or further information should be addressed to the Permissions Department, John Wiley & Sons, Inc.

Library of Congress Cataloging-in-Publication Data:

Guild, Stephen.
    Word for Windows 6: self-teaching guide / by Stephen Guild.
        p. cm. -- (Wiley self-teaching guides)
    Includes index.
    ISBN 0-471-30467-0
    1. Microsoft Word for Windows 2. Word processing. I. Title.
II. Title: Word for Windows six. III. Series
Z52.5.W655G85   1994
652.5'536--dc20   93-43048
                                                            CIP

Printed in the United States of America
10 9 8 7 6 5 4 3 2 1

To Pat, Darren, and Sue Anne

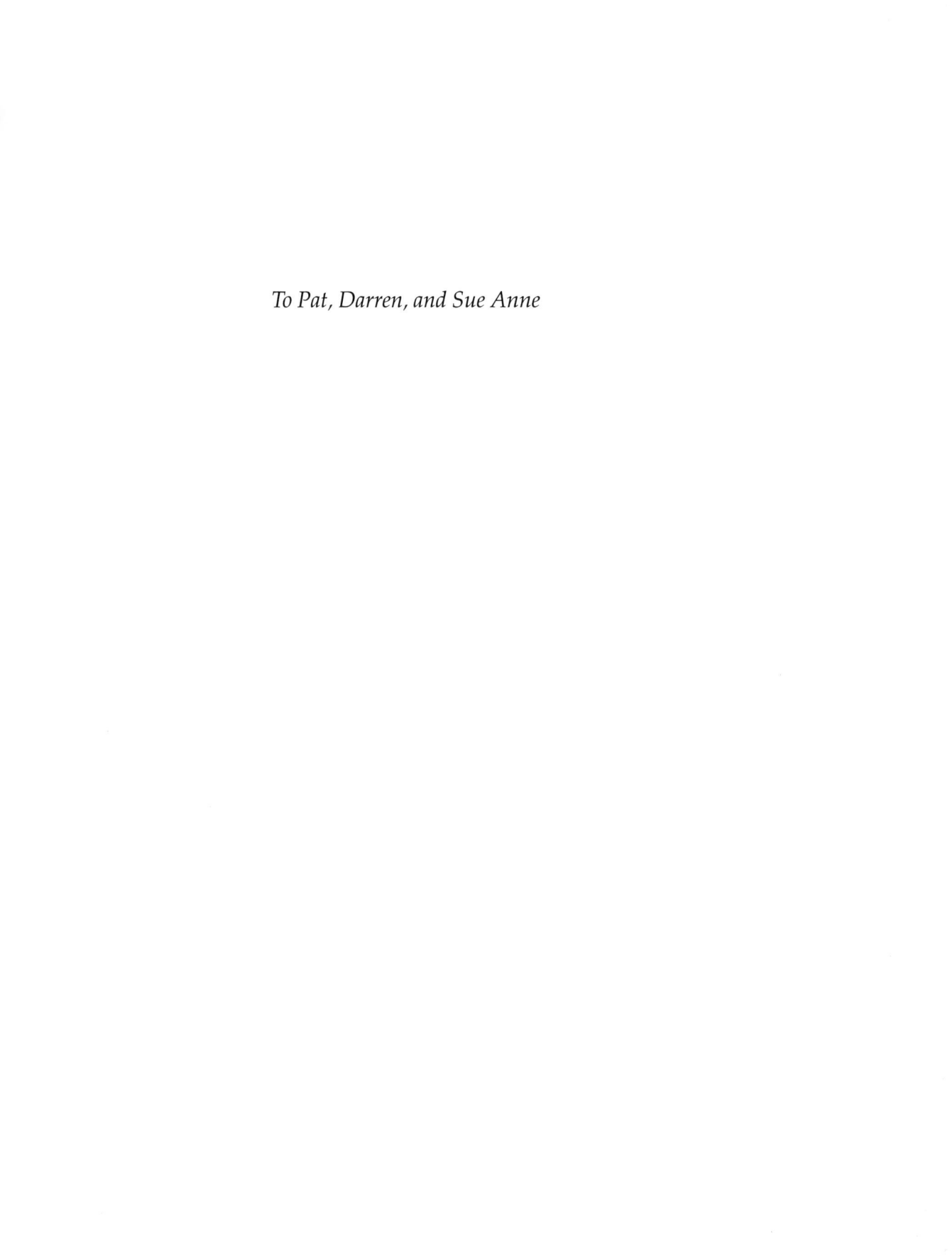

Contents Overview

1 Getting Started, 1
2 Creating, Saving, and Managing Files, 29
3 Basic Editing, 59
4 Power Editing, 83
5 Checking Spelling and Word Usage, 107
6 Character Formatting, 121
7 Paragraph Formatting, 137
8 Using Styles, 163
9 Page Layout and Frames, 193
10 Adding Pictures and Creating Drawings, 217
11 Charts and Equations, 241
12 Setting Up Tables and Forms, 257
13 Headers, Footers, and Footnotes, 291
14 Pagination and Printing, 307
15 Creating Form Letters and Address Labels, 327
16 Outlining and Numbering, 361
17 Finishing Touches, 383
18 Macros, Fields, and Linking, 411

Contents

1 Getting Started, 1

Word, Windows, and the Operating System	2
Starting Word	2
A Tour of the Word Screen	3
Using the Mouse	4
Using Keys	5
Choosing Commands	5
Using Dialog Boxes	7
Using Different Views and Modes	10
Setting Screen Preferences	16
Using Toolbars	19
Getting Help	23
Quitting Word	24

2 Creating, Saving, and Managing Files, 29

DOS Filename Rules	30
How Word Names Files	30
Documents and Templates	31
Using Word's Wizards	35
Entering Text	36
Opening Existing Files	36
Saving Word Files	38
Protecting Documents	42
About the Summary Info Dialog Box	43
Displaying Document Statistics	45
Using the Document Management System	45
Changing Startup Options and Paths	53
Changing the User Info Options	54

3 Basic Editing, 59

Scrolling Through a Word File	60
Moving the Insertion Point	61
Selecting: Telling Word Where to Make Changes	63

	Making Inserted Text Replace Selected Text	66
	Typing over Text	67
	Deleting Text	68
	Moving or Copying Text	68
	Cutting and Pasting Several Items at Once: Using the Spike	70
	Undoing a Change	71
	Working with Multiple Document Windows	72

4 Power Editing, 83

Searching for and Replacing Text and Formatting	84
Using AutoText Entries	90
Using Revision Marks	94
Comparing Versions	98
Using Annotations	99
Adding Bookmarks	103

5 Checking Spelling and Word Usage, 107

Checking Spelling	108
Using the Thesaurus	113
Counting Characters or Words in Your Document	114
Checking the Grammar in Your Document	115

6 Character Formatting, 121

What is Character Formatting?	122
About Fonts and Font Sizes	123
Using the Formatting Toolbar	124
Using the Font Dialog Box	126
Keyboard Shortcuts for Character Formatting	130
Changing the Case of Text	131
Inserting Symbols	132
Copying Character Formatting	132
Removing Character Formatting	133

7 Paragraph Formatting, 137

What Is a Paragraph in Word?	138
Selecting Paragraphs	138
Using the Formatting Toolbar and the Ruler	138

Using the Paragraph Dialog Box	140
Indenting Paragraphs	141
Setting Tabs	145
Aligning Paragraphs	149
Changing Line Spacing Within and Between Paragraphs	151
Adding Boxes, Lines, or Shading to Paragraphs	153
Creating a Dropped Capital Letter	155
Controlling Page Breaks in Paragraphs	156
Controlling Line Numbers in Paragraphs	157
Copying Paragraph Formatting	157

8 Using Styles, 163

What Are Styles?	164
Styles Provided with Word	165
Using the Style Gallery	165
Defining a Style	166
Creating a Paragraph Style	169
Creating a Character Style	171
Applying Styles	173
Displaying Style Names in the Document Window	175
Using AutoFormat to Apply Styles	177
Changing a Style	179
Setting Up a Chain of Styles to Format Sequential Paragraphs	181
Removing Additional Formatting from Styled Paragraphs	182
Returning Paragraphs to the Normal Style	183
Deleting Styles	183
Using Styles from Another Document	184
Styles and Templates	185
Printing a List of Styles	188

9 Page Layout and Frames, 193

Working with Sections	194
Changing Margins	196
Changing Page Size and Orientation	198
Setting Vertical Alignment	199

Creating a Default Document Format		200
Formatting Text in Columns		200
Using Frames		206
Adding or Removing Border Lines and Shading in Frames		212
Smoothing Out Ragged Margins with Hyphenation		213

10 Adding Pictures and Creating Drawings, 217

Inserting Pictures	218
Using the Drawing Tools	221
Editing a Drawing	223
Working with Pictures in Word	230
Using WordArt to Add Special Effects	236

11 Charts and Equations, 241

Creating Charts	242
Building Equations	251

12 Setting Up Tables and Forms, 257

Some Table Examples	258
Inserting a Blank Table	258
Using the Table Wizard	260
Displaying or Removing Table Gridlines and Cell Text Markers	261
Creating a Table from Selected Text	262
Entering Information in Table Cells	264
Formatting Tables	266
Adding Borders to a Table	272
Formatting a Table Using AutoFormat	273
Positioning a Table on a Page Precisely	274
Merging Table Cells	275
Adding Individual Cells and Rows and Columns to Tables	276
Deleting Individual Cells and Rows and Columns from Tables	277
Splitting One Table into Two	279
Copying and Moving the Contents of Cells	279

Converting a Table into Normal Text	280
Calculating in Tables	281
Using Tables to Create Forms	282

13 Headers, Footers, and Footnotes, 291

Adding Page Numbers	292
Adding Headers or Footers	293
Adding Footnotes or Endnotes	298

14 Pagination and Printing, 307

Controlling Pagination	308
Jumping to a Specific Page	311
Preparing to Print	311
Basic Printing	311
Printing Envelopes	318
Printing Labels	321
What If It Doesn't Print?	321

15 Creating Form Letters and Address Labels, 327

Merging Basics	328
Using Word's Mail Merge	329
Entering New Records in the Data Source Document	333
Sorting Data in Mail Merge Helper	335
Inserting Merge Fields	341
Deleting Merge Fields	343
Checking for Errors in the Data Records	343
Merging Data with the Main Document	344
Using Word Fields in Merging	346
Printing Merges	350
Merging to Create Form Letters	351
Merging to Create Sheets of Address Labels	352
Creating and Printing Addresses on Envelopes	356
Removing Merges from Main Documents	357

16 Outlining and Numbering, 361

Working with Outlines	362
Numbering Paragraphs	372

Adding Bullets to Paragraphs 374
Numbering Lines 376

17 Finishing Touches, 383
Creating a Table of Contents 384
Using Field Codes in a Table of Contents 387
Creating Lists of Figures, Tables, and Other Elements 389
Using Field Codes in Lists of Figures and Other
 Elements 390
Creating an Index 392
Updating a Table of Contents or an Index 397
Creating a Table of Authorities 398
Adding Captions and Labels to Figures and Tables 398
Creating Cross-References 401
Creating Master Documents 403
Formatting Master Documents 408

18 Macros, Fields, and Linking, 411
Saving Time with Macros 412
Creating Your Own Macros 412
Running a Macro 415
Assigning Macros to Toolbars, Menus, or Keys 417
Using Word's Supplied Macros 422
Troubleshooting and Correcting Macros 422
Using Fields 424
Inserting Fields 425
Displaying Codes or Results in Fields 427
Printing Field Codes 428
Editing and Deleting Fields 428
Jumping to Fields 429
Locking and Unlocking Fields 430
Exchanging Information with Other Applications 430
Editing Embedded and Linked Objects 432

Index, 437

Preface

Welcome to the *Word for Windows 6: Self-Teaching Guide*. The first version of Word for Windows introduced many Windows users to graphical word processing, but this new version makes Word even easier to use with more features and tools to simplify formatting, merging, and compiling large documents. Word for Windows 6 provides many helpful features, such as Wizards, to take the drudgery out of word processing. Whether you're already familiar with the previous version of Word for Windows or you're completely new to the program, the *Word for Windows 6: Self-Teaching Guide* will walk you through all the features of this latest version of Word. Using a practical, hands-on approach, this book explains each topic thoroughly and lets you test yourself at intervals, so you can learn at your own speed.

How to Use This Book

This book progresses from basic ideas to advanced topics, so we suggest that you read the chapters in order. Many chapters assume you've mastered the skills presented in previous chapters. Like other books in the Wiley Self-Teaching Guide series, this book is organized into a series of relatively brief lessons. Each lesson helps you master a particular aspect of Word. Although you should work through the lessons in order, you can pause between lessons at any time. You'll find a number of helpful features in this book:

- ▲ At the beginning of each chapter, you'll find a list of the chapter's major topics.
- ▲ In each chapter, Check Yourself exercises encourage you to practice what you've learned so far. Each exercise includes a brief description of the steps you should follow to complete the exercise.
- ▲ Throughout the chapters, brief Tip sections call your attention to important points, shortcuts, and cautions.

▲ At the end of each chapter, a Quick Command Summary lists and reviews the important procedures you learned in the chapter.
▲ Also at the end of each chapter, Practice What You've Learned exercises suggest additional steps you may wish to complete to review the chapter material.

The book is illustrated throughout with screen shots that show you how the Word window should look as you perform various tasks. Both the Check Yourself and the Practice What You've Learned exercises are painless because they list the steps needed to accomplish what you've been asked to do. You don't need to reread previous sections when you just need a reminder of which command to choose next.

What's in This Book

Chapter 1, "Getting Started," begins the "basics" portion of the book. This chapter explains how to use commands and dialog boxes, how to display a document in many different views, and how to get help.

Chapter 2, "Creating, Saving, and Managing Files," details everything you need to know about creating and managing files, including how to use the program's built-in file management system.

Chapter 3, "Basic Editing," starts the editing portion of the book. This chapter shows you how to move the insertion point; how to select text for further editing; how to cut, copy, and paste information; and how to work effectively with multiple windows and files.

Chapter 4, "Power Editing," introduces you to Word's sophisticated editing features that can significantly speed up your work: search and replace, glossaries, revision marking, document comparison, annotations, and bookmarks.

Chapter 5, "Checking Spelling and Word Usage," is just what you might expect from the chapter title: an explanation of how to use Word's spelling checker, thesaurus, and grammar-checking tools.

Chapter 6, "Character Formatting," begins the formatting section of the book. In this chapter you will learn how to change the appearance of characters with fonts and point sizes and attributes such as bold and italic. You will learn how to control the positioning of characters by making them superscripts and subscripts or condensing or expanding them.

Chapter 7, "Paragraph Formatting," explains how to change the look of complete paragraphs. You'll find out how to change indents, alignments, and line spacing, as well as how to set tabs.

Chapter 8, "Using Styles," shows you how to combine character and paragraph formatting to create and apply styles, which are the key to controlling the appearance of every Word paragraph. You'll learn how to use the styles already provided for you, how to create your own, and how to modify styles to get just the effect you're seeking.

Chapter 9, "Page Layout and Frames," shows you how to control margins and columns to change the appearance of all or part of your document and how to use frames to position text and graphics.

Chapter 10, "Adding Pictures and Creating Drawings," details ways to import and format graphics from a variety of applications and shows how to use the drawing tools in Word to create your own drawings.

Chapter 11, "Charts and Equations," explains how to use Microsoft Graph to create charts and how to create equations using the Equation Editor.

Chapter 12, "Setting Up Tables and Forms," illustrates how to use the table feature to easily control and manipulate a variety of sophisticated row-and-column arrangements.

Chapter 13, "Headers, Footers, and Footnotes," shows you how to position text, graphics, and page numbers in the top or bottom margins of your pages and how to insert, edit, and format footnotes.

Chapter 14, "Pagination and Printing," explains how to control where page breaks occur and how to print text and graphics. You'll also learn how to use Word's envelope printing feature.

Chapter 15, "Creating Form Letters and Address Labels," teaches you how to create form letters and address labels by merging data files with boilerplate letters and label formats.

Chapter 16, "Outlining and Numbering," shows you how to use Word's Outline view to create and number outlines for any document, how to add bullets or numbers to lists, and how to number lines in a document.

Chapter 17, "Finishing Touches," illustrates how to create tables of contents, indexes, and other lists that can be generated from entries within a document and how to use the master document feature to compile long individual sections or chapters into a single long document.

Chapter 18, "Macros, Fields, and Linking," is for the user who wants to use all that Word has to offer. You'll learn how to plan and record your own macros to automate tasks. You'll also get an introduction to the basics of using fields to insert a variety of information into a document, and you'll learn how to use links to connect Word and other applications and keep your documents updated.

Acknowledgments

I'd like to thank everyone who helped to make this book possible: the folks at Microsoft, who shared information and sent beta copies of the program; Tim Ryan, my editor at Wiley; Jacqueline Martin, who handled production; Jean Tucker, who copyedited the manuscript; and Impressions, who composed the book pages.

Getting Started

Most word processors share many common elements and procedures, but each has a slightly different approach to easing the task of text processing. To fully use Word's power, you need to know some basic procedures before you begin to explore the program. This chapter describes many of those basic techniques. If you're new to Word for Windows, you'll want to read it thoroughly before going on. In this chapter, you will learn how to:

- ▲ Start and quit Word
- ▲ Choose commands and use dialog boxes
- ▲ Switch between different views
- ▲ Use your toolbars
- ▲ Use Word's help system

Word, Windows, and the Operating System

When you use Word for Windows, you're really dealing with three layers of software, all running at the same time. Word runs on top of Windows, so you can use the Windows Control Panel to change the colors and other aspects of Word for Windows; you also use Windows to install fonts and printers. As in any other Windows application, you can change the size of the Word window, making it larger or smaller or shrinking it to an icon.

Windows in turn runs on top of your operating system, which controls the hardware (reading from and writing to disk, sending information to the printer, and so forth). Because Word and Windows interact with the operating system, you must follow the operating system's naming conventions when you name files created with Word. You should understand your operating system's tree structure and know how to use its pathname conventions when you refer to files in different directories or on different drives. For more information about your operating system, see the manuals that came with your computer.

Starting Word

After you've started Windows, you can start Word in four ways:

▲ Use the arrow keys to highlight WINWORD.EXE in the File Manager window, then press **Enter**; or use the mouse to double-click **WINWORD.EXE**.

▲ In the File Manager, use the arrow keys to highlight the name of any file created with Word for Windows, then press **Enter**; or use the mouse to double-click the name of a Word file. This starts Word and opens the document at the same time.

▲ Choose **File Run** from the Program Manager or File Manager's File menu, type **winword** in the dialog box, then press **Enter**.

▲ In the Program Manager, double-click the Microsoft Word for Windows icon (picture), which will be found in the Word for Windows 6.0 program group (or another program group if you've moved it).

Starting Word

If Windows is not yet running, you can start Word by typing **win winword** at the operating system prompt (usually C:\>). For this method to work, both the Windows and the Word for Windows directories must be in your path. (See your operating system manual for more information about paths.)

A Tour of the Word Screen

Word first opens in Normal view—the view you'll use most often. Take a look at Figure 1.1, which points out different parts of the Word window. You'll see these terms used throughout this book.

If you didn't open a specific document when you started Word, you'll notice that "Document2" appears in the title bar. This is Word's default name for a new document. You can enter text to create a new document, then save it with the name you want, or you can close this empty document and open another document that you've already created.

▼ *Figure 1.1. The Word Window in Normal View*

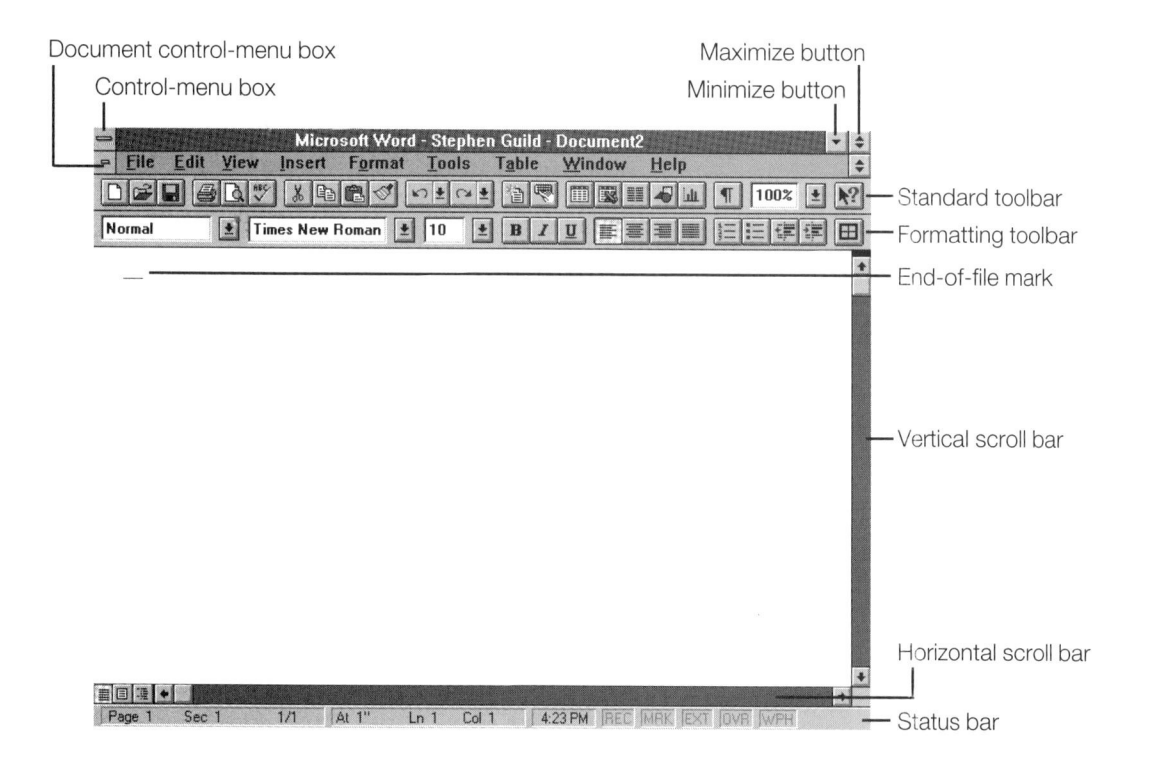

Using the Mouse

As in most Windows applications, you can use the mouse, the keyboard, or a combination of both to choose commands and perform common tasks. The mouse terms listed in Table 1.1 are used in this book.

The mouse pointer takes on different shapes depending on the kind of action that is being performed.

Since most Windows users have the mouse, we stress mouse techniques throughout this book. However, this chapter also explains keyboard techniques you can use with Word. Whenever there's a keyboard shortcut you can use, we'll be sure to tell you about it.

Table 1.1. Mouse Terms

Term	Meaning
Point	Slide the mouse on your desk to move the mouse pointer to a specific location in the Word window.
Click	Quickly press and release the mouse button while the pointer is at a specific location. For example, "Click the **OK** button" means that you move the mouse pointer to the OK button, then press and release the mouse button. You almost always click the left mouse button; the right mouse button is usually reserved for shortcut techniques.
Double-click	Quickly press and release the mouse button twice while the pointer is at a specific location.
Drag	Hold down the mouse button while you move the mouse. For example, "Drag the tab icon" means that you point to the tab icon, then hold down the mouse button while you move the mouse to drag the tab icon to a new location.

Using Keys

Because Word is a word-processing program, you'll obviously be using the keyboard to enter text. Usually, it's easiest to use a combination of keyboard and mouse techniques, choosing the fastest technique for the task at hand. However, if you don't have a mouse and you're not in a hurry, you *can* use the keyboard to do all tasks in Word.

When this book tells you to press two or more keys at once, the key combination is shown with a plus sign (+) between the key names. For example, "press **Ctrl+C**" means that you hold down the **Ctrl** (for Control) key while you tap the **C** letter key. We're using uppercase letters to show more clearly alphabetic keys in key combinations, but you don't need to press Shift to make the letter uppercase—the lowercase letter works just as well.

When you need to press and release keys in sequence, you'll see the key combinations written with commas between the key names. For example, "press **Alt, F, N**" means press and release the **Alt** key, press and release the **F** key, and then press and release the **N** key.

Choosing Commands

If you've used a Windows program before, you probably already know how to choose commands from menus. This section contains both mouse and keyboard instructions.

In this book, we combine menu names and command names when we refer to commands. For example, when we say "Choose the **File Open** command," we mean "Drop down the File menu, then choose the Open command." When a command is dimmed ("grayed") on a menu, that command is not currently available. In other words, you cannot choose dimmed commands.

To choose a command with the mouse:

1. Click the menu name to drop down the menu.
2. Click the name of the command you want.

If you drop down a menu and decide not to choose a command, just move the pointer off the menu, then click.

To choose a command with the keyboard:

1. Press **Alt, Letter** to drop down the menu. Each menu name has one underlined letter to indicate which letter to use with the Alt key. For example, the letter *F* in the File menu is underlined, so you would press **Alt, F** to drop down the File menu; the letter *o* in the Format menu is underlined, so you would press **Alt, O** to drop down the Format menu.
2. Press the underlined letter in the command name. For example, the letter *N* in the New command on the File menu is underlined. So, you drop down the menu, then press **N** to choose the New command.

Word has two exceptions to the underlined-letter procedure: the Control menu in the Word window's upper left corner and the Document Control menu in each document window's upper left corner. These menus are represented by icons rather than by menu names. The Word Control-menu icon is meant to look like the spacebar on the keyboard—to remind you that you use **Alt, Spacebar** to drop down that menu. The Document Control-menu icon is meant to look like a hyphen—you use **Alt, Hyphen** to drop down that menu.

If you drop down a menu, then decide not to choose a command, press the **Esc** (for Escape) key.

Using Shortcut Keys to Choose Specific Commands

Many commands also have a *shortcut key* combination displayed beside the command name on the menu. You can use this key combination to choose the command without first dropping down the menu.

For example, to choose **File Open** from the File menu, you could use the mouse to click the menu name and the command name as described earlier; press **Alt, F, O**; or press **Ctrl+O**, the shortcut key combination. You'll find that memorizing and pressing the shortcut keys for frequently used commands will speed up your work with Word.

Using Dialog Boxes

Some Word commands take effect as soon as you choose them. Other Word commands display dialog boxes to ask you for more information about what you want to do. Each command that displays a dialog box is followed by an ellipsis (...) in the menu.

When Word displays a dialog box, you have to close the dialog box before you can choose another command or type text in your document. If you try to do something outside of the dialog box, Word beeps to remind you to close the dialog box first.

Dialog boxes are filled with options you can choose to affect your document. Word has different types of dialog box options, as shown in Figure 1.2.

When you open a dialog box for the first time, you'll see that some options are selected, and sometimes you'll see a filename or a measurement in a box. These choices come from Word's default settings—the settings Word assumes you'll want to use most of the time. Word's default settings are part of the NORMAL.DOT template. (For more information on templates, see Chapter 2.)

You can accept the default settings in a dialog box by leaving them alone, or you can choose new options to affect the document or selected text. Choosing new options in a dialog box doesn't change the default settings—they'll reappear the next time you choose a command in a new document. (You can, however, modify many default settings with the Tools Options command.)

The rest of this section tells you how to choose different types of options. (If you open a dialog box to practice, click the **Cancel** button or press **Esc** to close the dialog box when you're finished.)

Choosing Options with the Mouse

To choose an option in a dialog box with the mouse:

1. Click the option. If the option is an option button or a command button, clicking chooses the option. If the option is a check box, this turns it on (inserts an X) or turns it off (removes the X). Clicking other types of options simply moves the insertion point to the option you click.

8 ▲ Word for Windows 6

▼ *Figure 1.2. The Dialog Box Options*

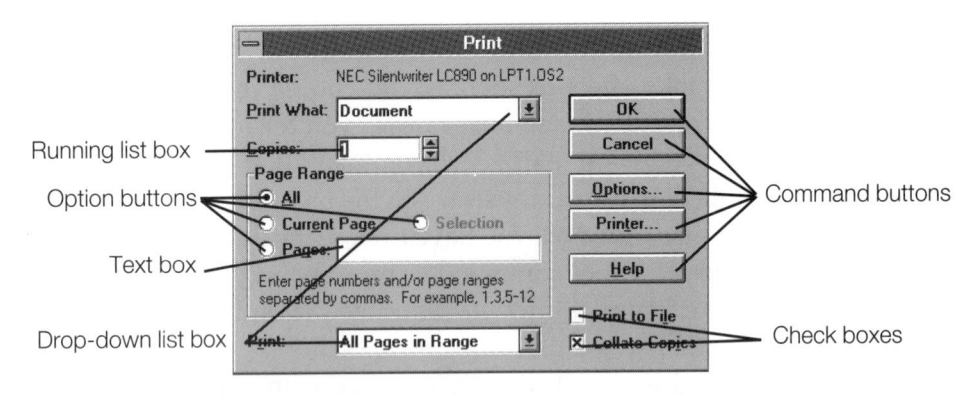

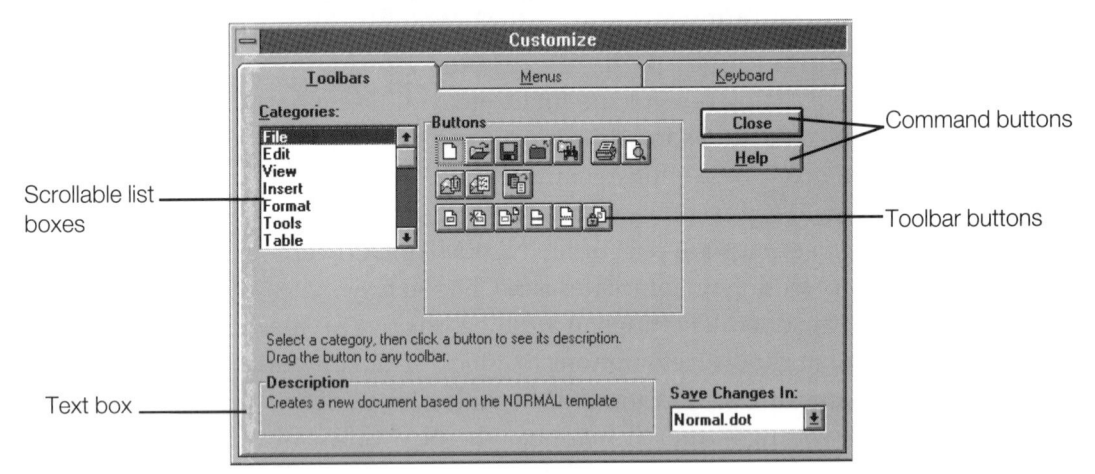

[Figure 1.2: Two dialog boxes illustrating the Print dialog and the Customize dialog, with labels pointing to: Running list box, Option buttons, Text box, Drop-down list box, Command buttons, Check boxes, Scrollable list boxes, Command buttons, Toolbar buttons, and Text box.]

2. Choose one of the following actions, if necessary:
   ▲ If the option is a scrollable list box, use the scroll bar to examine the list, then click a list item to select (highlight) it.
   ▲ If the option is a drop-down list box, point to the arrow and click to drop down the list, then click the item you want.
   ▲ If the option is a running list box, click the arrows until you see the item you want, or type in the box.
   ▲ If the option is a text box, type new text or edit the existing text.

Using Dialog Boxes

Some dialog boxes have tabs that you can click to display a different set of options.

Choosing Options with the Keyboard

To use keys to choose an option in a dialog box:

1. Move the focus to the option using one of the following methods:
   - ▲ Press **Tab** to move through the options from left to right. **Shift+Tab** moves in the opposite direction.
   - ▲ Hold down the **Alt** key and press the underlined letter in the option label.
2. Choose one of the following actions:
   - ▲ If the option is a scrollable list box or a running list box, use the up or down arrow key to highlight an item in the list. If the list has an attached text box, you can also type in the text box.
   - ▲ If the option is a drop-down list box, use the up or down arrow key to select an item from the list.
   - ▲ If the option is a text box, type new text or edit the existing text.
   - ▲ If the option is a command button and you've chosen all the options you want in the dialog box, press **Enter**.

TIP

In most dialog boxes with list boxes, you can also double-click a list item, which selects the list item, chooses the default command button (usually OK), and closes the dialog box, all at the same time.

If a dialog box is hiding a part of your document that you need to see, you can point to the title bar of the dialog box and drag the box to a new location. Here's the keyboard alternative for this method: Press **Alt+Spacebar, M** to choose the **Move** command from the dialog box's Control menu, use the arrow keys to move the dialog box; then press **Enter** to set its new position.

Using Different Views and Modes

Word provides several ways to view your documents. In the following sections, you'll learn about

▲ Normal view
▲ Page Layout view
▲ Draft mode
▲ Print Preview

Master view allows you to see all sections of a master document (a long report with several chapters, for example). Full Screen view displays your document without the title bar or other elements of a Windows screen. There's also another view, called Outline view, but we'll discuss this in Chapter 16.

Using Normal View

For most of your work with Word, you'll probably use Normal view. In this view, you can edit and format text and graphics and see most of the formatting as it will appear when printed. However, Normal view has its drawbacks: You can't see multiple columns of text or the proper page positions of frames or of headers and footers.

To display a document in Normal view, simply choose **View Normal** or click the **Normal** View button (the far left button on the toolbar at the bottom of your screen). Figure 1.3 shows a document in Normal view. Note that we've removed the Standard toolbar so that you can more easily see the document.

Using Page Layout View

Page Layout view shows you the finished document—with text, graphics, headers and footers, and footnotes in their correct positions—exactly as everything will appear when printed. When you work in Page Layout view, you can

Getting Started ▲ 11

▼ *Figure 1.3. A Document in Normal View*

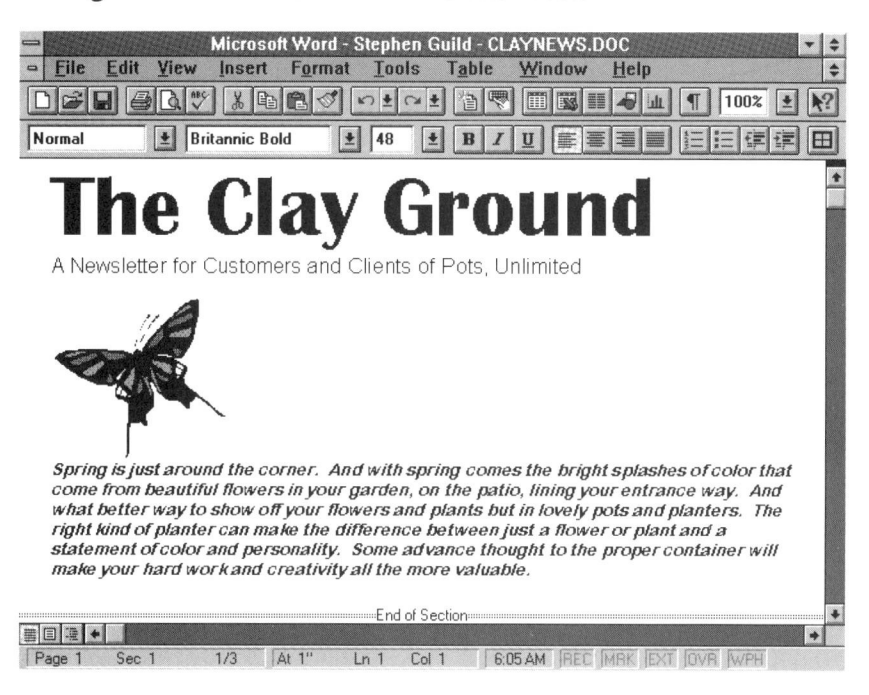

Using Different Views and Modes

▲ Reposition framed items
▲ Move, type, and edit headers, footers, and footnotes
▲ See the precise measurements of tab stops or indents in a column
▲ Scroll one page at a time
▲ Display the boundaries of individual blocks of text and graphics by choosing the General category in the Tools Options dialog box

To display a document in Page Layout view, choose **View Page Layout** or click the **Page Layout** View button (the second button from the left on the toolbar at the bottom of your screen). Figure 1.4 shows a document in Page Layout view. You'll learn more about using Page Layout view in Chapter 9.

Using Draft Mode

You can switch to Draft mode from Normal view to speed up your typing and editing. In Draft mode, Word displays all text in one font type and size, regardless of any other fonts or sizes you may

▼ **Figure 1.4. A Document in Page Layout View**

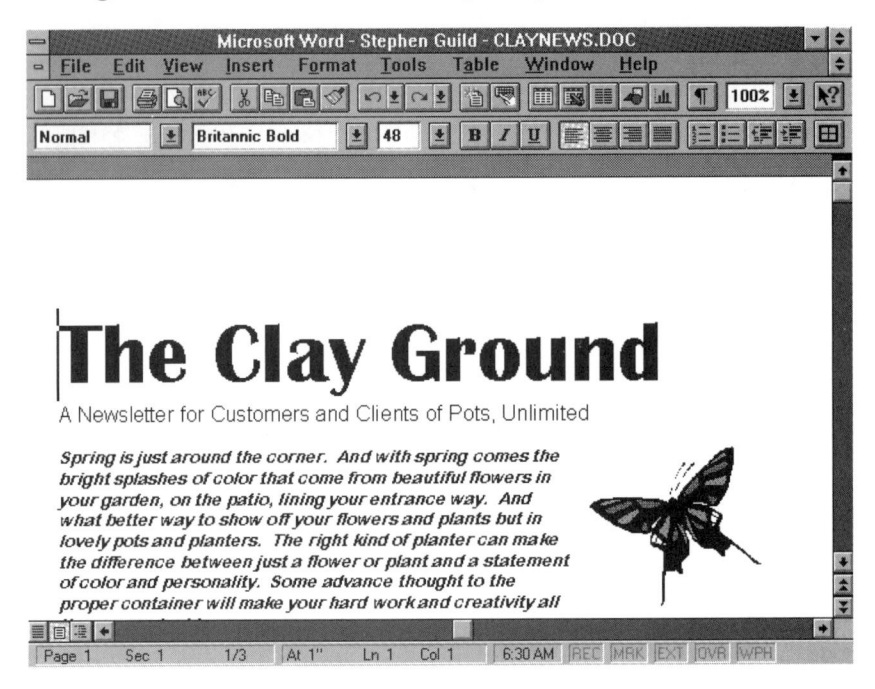

have applied. Formatted characters appear underlined and pictures appear as empty frames.

To switch to Draft mode:

1. Choose **Tools Options** and choose the **View** tab.
2. Click the **Draft Font** box.
3. Click **OK** or press **Enter**.

Figure 1.5 shows our sample document in Draft mode. To switch out of Draft mode (to return to Normal view), choose **Tools Options**, click the **Draft Font** box, and click **OK** or press **Enter**.

Magnifying or Reducing the Page Display

You can enlarge or reduce the view of your document in Word by using the View Zoom command. This doesn't change the document but displays text on the screen in a different size.

To magnify or reduce the view of your document:

1. Choose the **View Zoom** command.

▼ **Figure 1.5. A Document in Draft Mode**

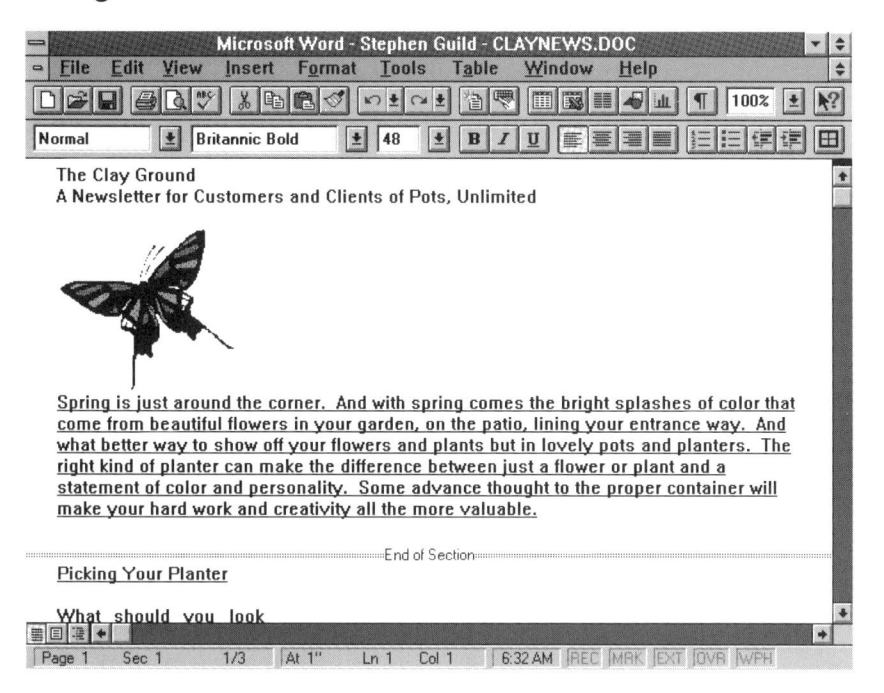

Using Different Views and Modes

2. Under Zoom To, choose one of the following options:

To	Do This
Display the page at twice the normal size	Click the **200%** button.
Display the page at normal size	Click the **100%** button.
Display the page at reduced size	Click the **75%** button.
Display the widest line on the page	Click the **Page Width** button.
Display the entire page at once	Click the **Whole Page** button.
Display multiple pages in the same document at once	Click the **Many Pages** button.
Display the page at a size you specify	Type **10%** to **200%** in the Percent running list box.

3. Click **OK** or press **Enter**.

You can also customize the toolbar to include buttons that show different views. Figure 1.6 shows a document in Normal view zoomed to 200%.

Using Print Preview

When you want to see what a document will look like on paper before you actually print, switch to Print Preview (shown in Figure 1.7). This view shows you a miniature version of your pages. To see full pages, make sure the Word window is full size when you use Print Preview.

In Print Preview you can use the mouse to change margins, indentations, column widths, tabs, and other formatting features controlled by the ruler. You'll learn more about using Print Preview in Chapter 9.

To switch to Print Preview:

▲ Choose **File Print Preview** or click the **Print Preview** button on the Standard toolbar.

▼ *Figure 1.6. A Document Zoomed to 200%*

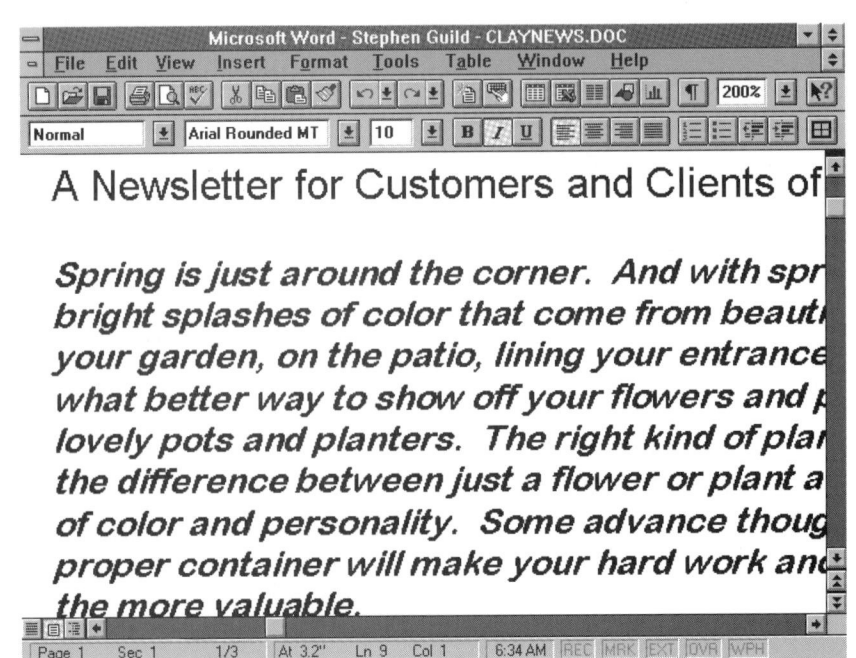

Using Different Views and Modes

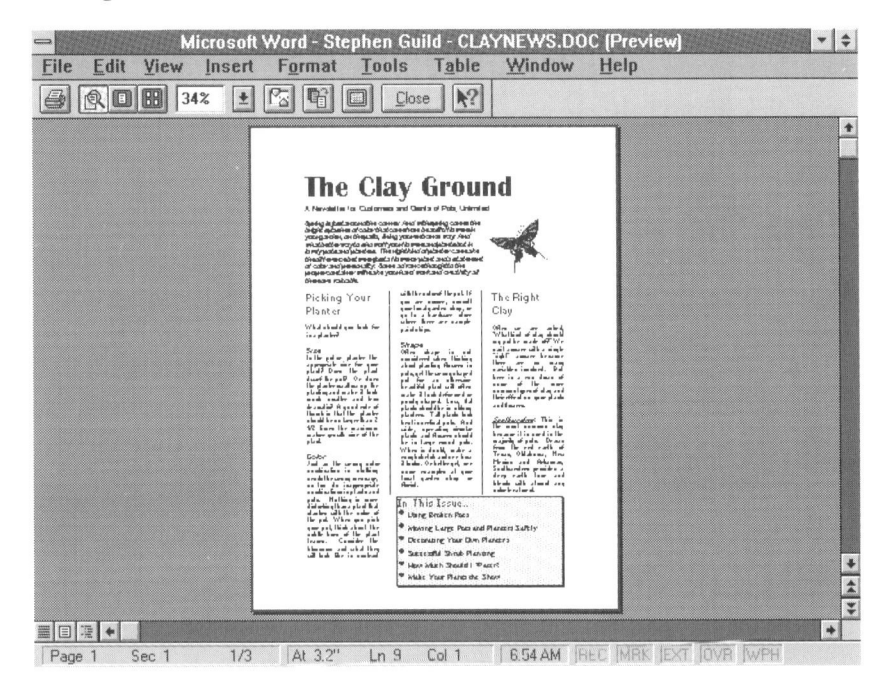

▼ *Figure 1.7. A Document in Print Preview*

When you first switch to Print Preview, Word displays the page that currently contains the insertion point.

To exit Print Preview:

▲ Click the **Close** button in the Print Preview window, or press **Esc**.

To use the mouse to display a different page:

▲ Click below the scroll box in the vertical scroll bar to display the next page, or click above the scroll box to display the previous page.

To use keys to display a different page:

▲ Press **Page Dn** to display the next page, or press **Page Up** to display the previous page.

You can also display up to twenty-one pages at a time by using the Multiple Pages button on the Print Preview toolbar.

To switch from a one-page display to a multiple-page display:

▲ Click the **Multiple Pages** button at the top of the window. Move the mouse pointer to indicate the number of pages you want to display. Word redraws the window to display the pages. Figure 1.8 shows Print Preview in a three-page display.

To switch from a multiple-page display to a one-page display:

▲ Click the **Multiple Pages** button at the top of the window. Move the mouse pointer to one page.

CHECK YOURSELF

Which commands allow you to change the display of your document?

▲ The Normal, Outline, Page Layout, Master Document, Full Screen, and Zoom commands in the View menu and the Print Preview command in the File menu (Outline view is discussed in Chapter 16.)

Setting Screen Preferences

The View tab in the Tools Options dialog box controls the parts of the window and the special characters that are displayed in the

▼ *Figure 1.8. Print Preview in Three-Page Display*

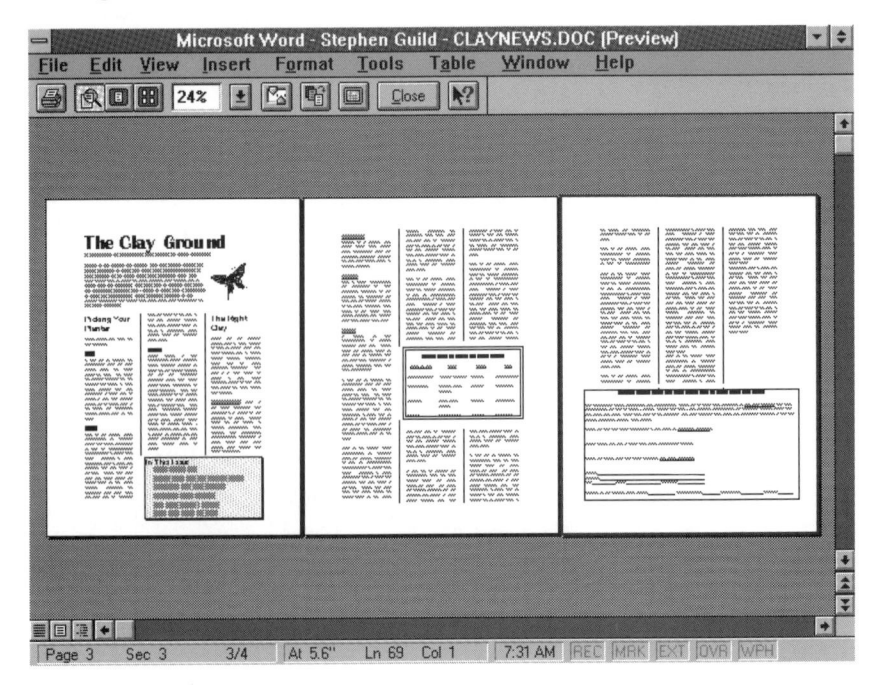

Word window. You can choose to display formatting characters and other options that are invisible by default. Most of the options in the View tab are toggles. To turn on an option, just click it to add an *X* to the accompanying check box. To turn the option off, click it again to make the *X* disappear.

Setting Screen Preferences

To control which characters and window parts are displayed:

1. Choose the **Tools Options** command, then (if necessary) choose the **View** tab at the top of the dialog box. The options displayed will depend upon whether you are working with a document in Normal view or Page Layout view.
2. Turn the options on or off.

Option	*Action*
Draft Font	Displays a document in Normal view in the draft font.
Wrap to Window	Wraps the text from one line to the next line within a window in Normal and Outline views.
Drawings	Displays drawing objects in Page Layout view.
Object Anchors	Displays the anchor symbol used to tie an object to text in Page Layout view.
Text Boundaries	Displays dotted lines around page margins, text columns, objects, and frames in Page Layout view.
Picture Placeholders	Displays rectangles instead of graphics. Turning off the display of pictures can significantly increase display and printing speeds when your document contains a lot of graphics.
Field Codes	Displays field codes instead of the results of fields. You can also toggle field codes on and off by pressing **Alt+F9**.
Bookmarks	Displays the square brackets around all bookmarks.

Option	*Action*
Field Shading	Displays shading in fields. You can choose **Never**, **Always**, or **When Selected** in the drop-down list.
Status Bar	Displays the status bar at the bottom of your screen. The status bar gives you information about the location of the insertion point, the size of the view, and various modes that you can turn on and off.
Horizontal Scroll Bar	Displays a horizontal scroll bar at the bottom of your screen, above the status bar. You need a horizontal scroll bar to view text that is wider than the window.
Vertical Scroll Bar	Displays a vertical scroll bar at the right of your screen. You need a vertical scroll bar to display text that is below or above the window.
Vertical Ruler	Displays a vertical ruler at the left of your screen in Page Layout view.
Style Area Width	Determines the width of the style bar at the left-hand edge of the screen.
Tab Characters	Displays an arrow symbol for each tab character (inserted when you press the **Tab** key).
Spaces	Displays a small dot for each space (inserted when you press the spacebar).
Paragraph Marks	Displays paragraph marks (¶), end-of-table-cell characters, and line break markers (↵). A paragraph mark is inserted every time you press the **Enter** key; end-of-table-cell characters

Setting Screen Preferences

Option	Action
	occur automatically in tables; and a line break mark is inserted when you press **Shift+Enter**.
Optional Hyphens	Displays optional and nonbreaking hyphens. Optional hyphens are usually inserted with Word's hyphenation feature; you can insert nonbreaking hyphens, which keep hyphenated words together, by pressing **Ctrl+Shift+Hyphen**.
Hidden Text	Displays hidden text with a dotted underline. (See Chapter 14 for more information about printing hidden text.)
All	Displays all nonprinting characters (paragraph marks, tab marks, space marks, and so on).

3. Click **OK** or press **Enter**.

Using Toolbars

Word comes with many different toolbars, which you can use to simplify and speed up your work. Each toolbar has buttons and, occasionally, drop-down lists that mouse users can click to choose commands quickly without dropping down menus. You can control the display of the toolbar by choosing View Toolbar.

Some of the toolbars available in Word are:

- ▲ Standard
- ▲ Formatting
- ▲ Borders
- ▲ Database
- ▲ Drawing
- ▲ Forms
- ▲ Microsoft

- ▲ Header and Footer
- ▲ Print Preview
- ▲ Outlining
- ▲ WordArt
- ▲ Mail Merge
- ▲ Macro

You can choose and display many of the toolbars listed above, but many are associated with a specific command and appear only when you choose it (merging, for example). The View Toolbar command lists the toolbars that are always available.

To see what a button on the toolbar does, point to the toolbar button and then read the description in the status bar at the bottom of the window.

To use a toolbar button:

▲ Hold down the mouse button while pointing to the toolbar button, move the pointer away from the toolbar, then release the mouse button. Some exceptions to this are the Insert Table button and the Insert Columns button. If you move the pointer down after clicking and holding on either of these buttons, Word will display a table grid or columns. Exit by clicking the **Insert Table** or **Insert Columns** button again.

To display a toolbar:

▲ Choose **View Toolbar** and select from the list.
▲ Click the right mouse button in the "white space" surrounding the toolbar buttons, and select from the list.

Changing the Toolbar

The Standard toolbar already contains the buttons that you will want to use frequently. However, after you get to know all of Word's features, you may want to add or rearrange buttons on this toolbar or on one of the many others included with the program. Not all toolbars can be changed, however.

Word contains more buttons than you first see when you start the program. You can choose from an array of buttons in the Toolbars tab of the Customize dialog box (shown in Figure 1.9). Word stores the changes you make to the toolbar in the active template, which Word lists at the bottom of the dialog box. You can choose another template in the drop-down list, if necessary.

The number of buttons you can display depends on the kind of display (EGA, VGA, and so forth) you have. You can arrange the toolbar buttons in any order.

Before making any changes, make sure the toolbar you want to change is displayed.

▼ *Figure 1.9. Changing a Toolbar Button in the Customize Dialog Box*

Using Toolbars

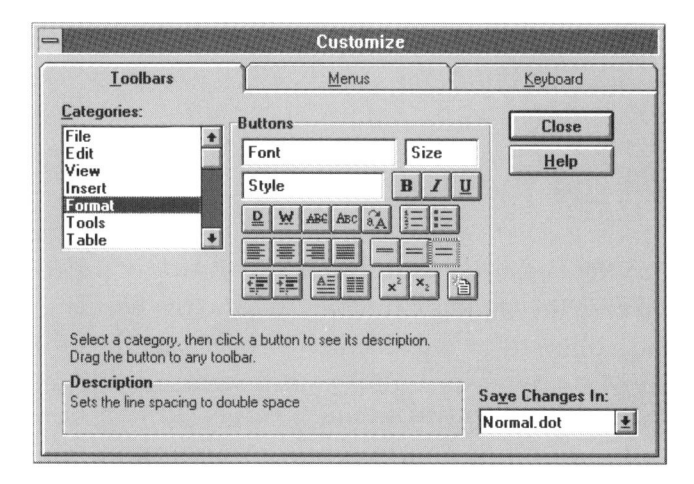

To add or replace a button on the toolbar:

1. Choose **Tools Customize** and click the **Toolbars** tab. Figure 1.9 shows the Customize dialog box.
2. In the Categories list, select the command or area you want to add to a toolbar.
3. From the Buttons array, select a button you want to place on the toolbar.
4. Click the button and drag to the location or blank space on the toolbar that is displayed. Word will insert the button at this location and shift the other buttons to the right. If you want to replace an existing button, drag that button off the toolbar first.
5. Repeat steps 2 through 4 until you've made all the changes you want.
6. Click the **Close** button.

To rearrange buttons on the toolbar:

1. Display the toolbar you want to change.
2. Choose **Tools Customize** and click the **Toolbars** tab.
3. Click on the toolbar button and drag it to a new position.
4. Click the **Close** button.

To delete a button from the toolbar:

1. Choose **Tools Customize** and click the **Toolbars** tab.

2. Click the toolbar button you want to delete and drag it off the toolbar to the Customize dialog box. Word places it in the appropriate area automatically.
3. Repeat step 2 for each button you want to delete.
4. Click the **Close** button.

Moving the Toolbar

For most toolbars, the default position is at the top of the document windows, with the Standard toolbar first and the Formatting toolbar second, followed by the others. However, you can arrange the toolbars any way you want. You can put them in a different order at the top of the document window, or you can drag them to different positions elsewhere on the screen. You can also change their sizes and shapes, and generally treat them as you would any other window.

To move a toolbar to another position:

1. Click in an open space on the toolbar. A dotted line appears around the toolbar.
2. Drag the toolbar to a new position. If it is at the top of the window, the toolbar will remain a long rectangle. However, at any other place on the screen, it will have a border and appear as a smaller window.

If you double-click a toolbar, it will return to its former position.

TIP

Another quick way to access commands is to use Word's "mini-menus." Just click the right mouse button in your document, and Word will display an abbreviated list of commands relating to the task you are doing. You can select from this list just as you would from any other menu in Word. For example, if you are working with a table and you click inside the table, Word's mini-menu will include the Edit Cut, Copy, and Paste commands; Table Insert Rows, Delete Cells, and Table AutoFormat commands; and the Format Font, Paragraph, and Bullets and Numbering commands.

Getting Help

Word has an extensive online help system you can use whenever you need more information about commands, dialog boxes, or procedures. You can get more extensive help by using the techniques shown below:

To	Do This
View the various options available in Help	Select the **Contents** command from the Help menu.
Find all of the topics relating to a specific area	Select the **Search for Help on...** command from the Help menu.
Browse through the help system	Select the **Index** command from the Help menu, then click an item to see a "how to" description, as shown in Figure 1.10.

▼ *Figure 1.10. Topics in the Help Window*

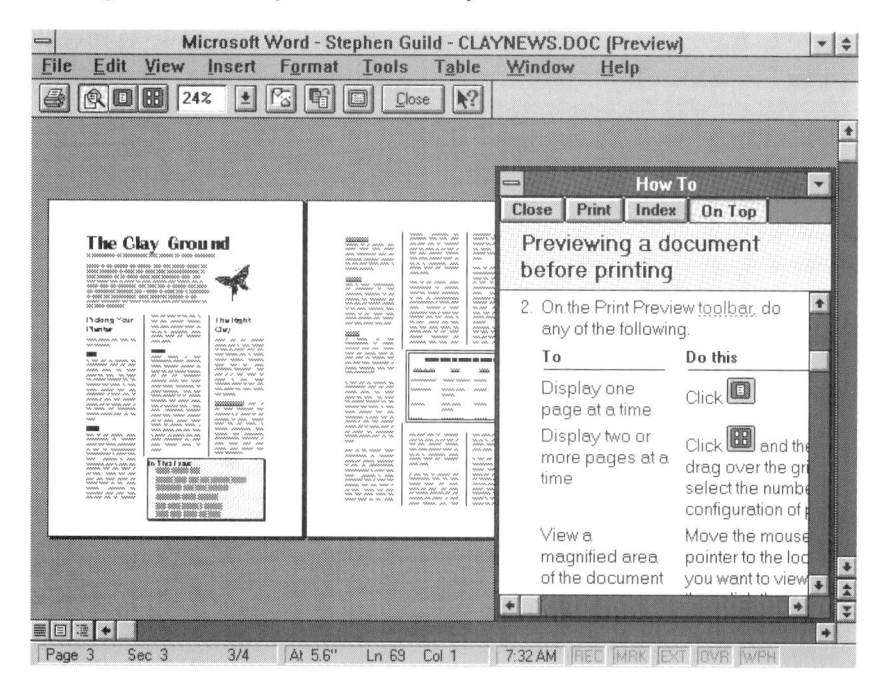

To	Do This
Get information about dialog box options	Display the dialog box, then press **F1**.
Use a mouse pointer to display help about a command or about an area of the window	Press **Shift+F1**, then use the help pointer (a question mark) to click a command or an area of the screen (such as the toolbar, the ruler, or the status bar).

The Help menu also contains commands that provide step-by-step instructions for using Word: Quick Preview, which displays the **Quick Preview** screen; **Examples and Demos**, which show you how features work; and **Tip of the Day**, which provides shortcuts and hints to simplify your work.

Help is a separate application that appears in a separate window—you can move the Help window, change its size, and use the scroll bars to scroll the information in the window, in the same way that you manipulate the Word window. You can browse through all the Help files at your leisure, using the buttons and menus in the Help window. You can also click the Search button and then type a word in the dialog box to find a topic quickly. And you don't have to memorize the instructions in the Help window—you can print them for easy reference by displaying the topic, then choosing Print Topic from the Help window's File menu.

TIP

Here's a quick way for mouse users to find out what a command does: Point to the command name and continue to hold down the mouse button to display a description of the command in the status bar, then move the pointer off the menu (while still holding down the mouse button).

Quitting Word

You can quit Word using either of the following methods:

▲ Double-click the Word Control menu icon.

▲ Press **Alt+F4** (the keyboard shortcut for the File Exit command).

Quitting Word

If you've made any changes that haven't been saved, Word will ask you if you want to save changes before quitting.

QUICK COMMAND SUMMARY

Command	To Do This
Click menu name, then command name	Choose a command with the mouse.
Alt+underlined letter	Drop down a menu or move the focus to a dialog box option.
Press underlined letter in command name	Choose a command with the keyboard.
Drag dialog box by title bar	Move a dialog box with the mouse.
Move on the Control menu	Move a dialog box with the keyboard.
View Normal	Switch to Normal view.
View Page Layout	Switch to Page Layout view.
View Draft	Switch to Draft mode.
View Zoom	Enlarge or shrink the display of the document in the window.
View Master Document	Display all sections of a master document (a book, a long report).
View Full Screen	Display the document without the title bar or other window parts.
File Print Preview	Display miniature versions of your pages.

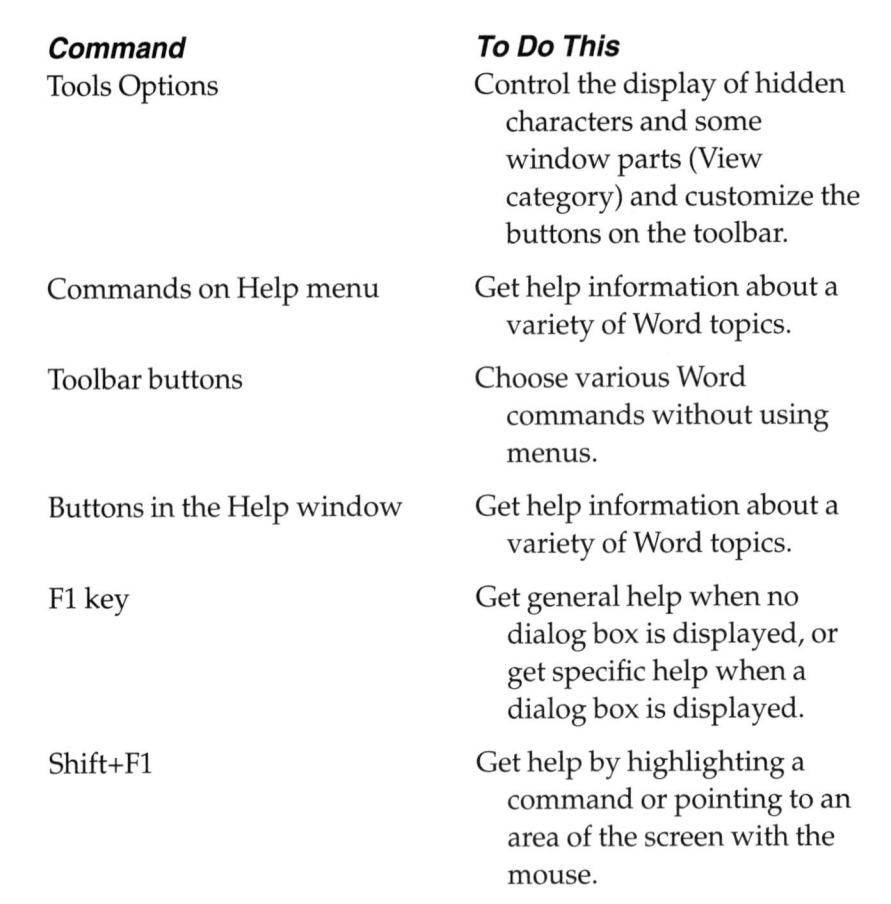

Command	To Do This
Tools Options	Control the display of hidden characters and some window parts (View category) and customize the buttons on the toolbar.
Commands on Help menu	Get help information about a variety of Word topics.
Toolbar buttons	Choose various Word commands without using menus.
Buttons in the Help window	Get help information about a variety of Word topics.
F1 key	Get general help when no dialog box is displayed, or get specific help when a dialog box is displayed.
Shift+F1	Get help by highlighting a command or pointing to an area of the screen with the mouse.

PRACTICE WHAT YOU'VE LEARNED

Open the Tools Options dialog box, and then display help about using the command and dialog box. After reading the information, close the Help window, and then choose an option to display paragraph marks. Type a few sentences, then display your page in miniature so you can see the entire page.

What You Do	What You'll See
1. Choose **Tools Options** with the mouse or by pressing **Alt, T, O**.	1. The Options dialog box with twelve tabs, which control many of Word's settings.

What You Do

2. When the dialog box appears, press **F1** to display the help topic.

3. After reading the Help information, double-click the Help window's Control-menu box, or press **Alt+F4**.

4. In the Tools Options dialog box, click the **View** tab and turn on the **Paragraph Marks** check box, then click **OK** or press **Enter**.

5. Type a few sentences, pressing **Enter** between each one.

6. Choose **File Print Preview** or click the **Print Preview** button. (Click the **Cancel** button or press **Esc** when you're ready to exit from Print Preview.)

What You'll See

2. The Help information relating to the particular tab in the Options dialog box.

3. The Options dialog box again. In most dialog boxes, takes you directly to the relevant Help topic.

4. The View tab with the various options, and then the document screen.

5. The text that you type, with paragraph marks visible.

6. The Print Preview window with your document displayed as a full page.

Creating, Saving, and Managing Files

Because all Word documents are stored in files, it's important for you to understand how to create, save, and manage Word files. In this chapter, you will learn how to:

▲ Name files in Word

▲ Use documents and templates in Word

▲ Enter text

▲ Open and save different files and file formats

▲ Use Word's document management system

DOS Filename Rules

When you name a Word file, you must obey the operating system's rules for filenames. If you try to type an invalid filename in Word or any other program running under DOS, you'll see a message similar to this:

```
Not a valid filename
```

The names of all files you use with DOS must conform to these rules:

▲ A filename must contain no more than eight characters before a period and no more than three characters in the filename extension after the period. No spaces are allowed in filenames. For example, you could use FILE.MY, INVOICE.601, FOSTER.LET, or LETTER, but not MY FILE (which contains a space) or THISIS-MINE.DOC (which has too many characters).

▲ You can't use any of the following characters in a filename:
  * (asterisk)   . (period)
  \ (backslash)   ? (question mark)
  : (colon)   ; (semicolon)
  , (comma)   / (slash)

How Word Names Files

If you don't specify an extension or a period after the basic filename, Word adds a DOC extension to the filename. For example, if you tell Word you want a file named MIKE, it assumes you want the file to be named MIKE.DOC. If you want to name a file with no extension, type a period (.) after the basic filename. For example, if you want a file named simply MIKE, type **MIKE.** when saving or opening the file.

When you want Word to find or place a file in a directory or a disk drive that's different from the one you're working in, type a pathname in front of the filename (or choose directories or drive letters in a dialog box, as explained under "Opening Existing Files" later in this chapter).

For more information about filenames, pathnames, disk drives, and operating system rules, see the operating system manual that came with your computer.

Documents and Templates

When you use Word, you'll create two basic types of files: *documents* and *templates*. A document is a simple word-processing file: it might be a letter, a chapter from a novel, an outline for a newspaper article, or any other text-based file. (Word documents can also contain graphics.)

Every Word document is based on a template, which provides a framework that you can reuse to create documents that are similar in format. Although you may not use the term often, chances are that you're already familiar with the concept of templates. You use a "template" every time you update your company's weekly report, fill out an order form, type a memo using a standard format, and so forth.

In its most basic form, a template is like a sheet of paper with preprinted information. For instance, if you want to create a memo, you might insert your company's standard memo form into your typewriter or printer; if you want to send a letter, you insert letterhead stationery. But in Word, templates are more than just standard forms. A Word template can include:

▲ *Boilerplate* text (text that stays the same from document to document)
▲ Formatting instructions that control the appearance of characters, paragraphs, and documents
▲ *Styles*, which are named sets of formatting instructions that you can apply to text to control how a document looks
▲ *AutoText entries*, which are standard text and graphic items you can paste into a document
▲ *Macros*, which are named sets of instructions that perform sequences of Word commands
▲ *Customized Word command settings*, which can be menus, toolbars, and other items attached to that specific template

The formatting instructions stored in a template control the basic format of all documents based on that template. Once you cre-

Documents and Templates

ate a template (memo, invoice, inventory form, letter, newsletter, and so on), you can then create new documents based on that template, save them as separate documents, and still keep the template in its original form. You could use a document in the same way, but you would have to be careful not to erase the original document while saving the new one. When you base your documents on templates, you don't have to worry about this.

Word comes with a standard template, called NORMAL.DOT, that contains all the default format settings. Word automatically bases new documents on the NORMAL.DOT template, so you don't need to concern yourself with creating templates if you don't want to. If you don't like the NORMAL.DOT settings, you can create your own templates, or you can change the NORMAL.DOT settings. Word also provides several other custom templates that you can use.

If you use standard formats for certain types of documents—such as memos, letters, or invoices—you'll want to create many of your own templates. Templates can even be based on other templates.

TIP

Warning: be careful that you don't change and save NORMAL.DOT with elements that you don't want. Every time Word is loaded, it loads NORMAL.DOT, so you want to make sure NORMAL.DOT is the way you want it for most of your documents. You can always create specialized templates for particular documents.

Creating New Documents or Templates

Word is flexible; it lets you specify exactly what you want when you create new documents and templates and lets you change your mind and specify different options when you save a document or template. Don't worry if you don't know exactly what you want when you start a new file; you can always change settings later.

If you don't load a document when you start Word, the program opens a new empty document so you can start typing right away. Word labels the document "Document1." Later, when you save the Document1 file, you should give it a new, more descriptive name.

If you have already started Word and opened an existing document, you can use the File New command (not the New Document button on the Standard toolbar) to open a new, empty document. You can open several new documents during a work session. By default, Word numbers each new document (Document2, Document3, and so on) to keep track of all new documents that you've opened.

You'll notice that there are various names in the list that don't have file extensions (Brochur1, Directr1, Faxcovr1, and so on). This is Word's way of making it easier for the user to decide which one to use. Each name is attached to a standard template that comes with the program. You'll also see filenames with the word *Wizard* beside them. This indicates that a template has one of Word's built-in, automated sets of instructions to create that type of document. See "Using Word's Wizards" later in this chapter for more information.

Documents and Templates

To create a new document or template:

1. Choose **File New**.
2. Do one of the following:

To	*Do This*
Create a new document based on the NORMAL.DOT template	Click **OK** or press **Enter**.
Create a new template	Choose **Template** in the New area, then click **OK** or press **Enter**.
Create a new document or template based on a template other than NORMAL.DOT	Choose **Document** or **Template** in the New area, choose the template on which you want to base the new document or template in the Template list box, then click **OK** or press **Enter**.

3. Type and format the text.
4. Save the file.

Using Global Templates

There are times when you may want to create a new document using the styles, macros, AutoText entries, and other elements from another template without attaching the new document to the other template. You can designate the template as a global template and use everything in the template without running the risk of having it altered.

For instance, you have a newsletter template, and you want to use the styles and AutoText entries in writing a public relations piece. You can create the public relations document and use the newsletter template as a global template. A global template is open until the end of the current Word session; however, you can always use it again by selecting the template name in the Templates and Add-Ins dialog box.

To load a global template:

1. Choose **File Templates**. Templates that are already available globally will appear in the Global Templates and Add-Ins list box besides a checked box.
2. Click the check box next to the name of the template you want to make available for global use. If the template name is not in the list, then click the Add button, choose the template name (using a different drive or directory, if necessary), and click OK.
3. Press **Enter** or click OK to load the templates available for global use.

If you think you may use global templates frequently, see the *Microsoft Word for Windows User's Guide* for more detailed information.

CHECK YOURSELF

Create a template named GENMEMO.DOT that includes To, From, Date, and Subject headings.

▲ Choose the **File New** commands, then choose **Template** in the New box and press **Enter**. Type and format the text for the template, and then use the **File Save** commands to save the template as GENMEMO.DOT.

Using Word's Wizards

Using Word's Wizards

Word provides a set of predefined templates called "Wizards." Attached to each one is a series of boxes in which you answer questions or make decisions on how you want a document to look, what you want it to include, and so on. As you respond to the questions in the boxes, Word remembers your responses and creates a document based on what you've specified. The Wizards make creating standard documents such as calendars, memos, and legal documents faster and easier.

To create a document based on a Wizard:

1. Choose **File New** (not the New File button on the Standard toolbar).
2. From the template list, choose the Wizard you want to use. The available Wizards include:

To Create	*Choose This Wizard*
A meeting agenda with custom formatting	Agenda
A certificate for an award	Award
A monthly calendar	Calendar
A fax cover sheet	Fax
A letter with custom formatting	Letter
A memo with custom formatting	Memo
A newsletter with custom formatting	Newslttr
Legal pleading papers	Pleading
A resume with custom formatting	Resume
A professional-looking table	Table

3. Click **OK** or press **Enter**.

Word will then prompt you for responses to a series of decisions attached to that Wizard. When you have finished, the new document based on that Wizard template will be created. You can then enter text, format, change, or add to that document as with any other.

Entering Text

Entering text is easy—just type! You don't need to press **Enter** when you come to the end of a line. Word automatically begins a new line when the text reaches the right margin. This feature is commonly called *wordwrap*.

To begin a new paragraph, press **Enter**. To back up and erase errors, press the **Backspace** key. You'll learn more about editing in Chapters 3 and 4.

Opening Existing Files

Word can open not only existing Word files but also many files created by other programs. To convert a file into Word, you need to have a converter file installed in your Word directory. See the Microsoft Word for Windows User's Guide for more information.

To open an exisiting file:

1. Choose **File Open** or the open button on the standard toolbar. Word displays the dialog box shown in Figure 2.1.
2. Select from the list the name of the file you want to open. The list displays the names of DOC files in the active disk drive and directory. To see names of other files, you may need to do one of the following:
   - ▲ To see a list of files on another disk drive, select a drive from the Drives drop-down list, then press **Enter**.
   - ▲ To see the files in another directory on the same disk, double-click the directory name in the Directories drop-down list until you see the files you want; or type the full pathname and directory name in the filename box, then press **Enter**.

▼ *Figure 2.1. The Open Dialog Box*

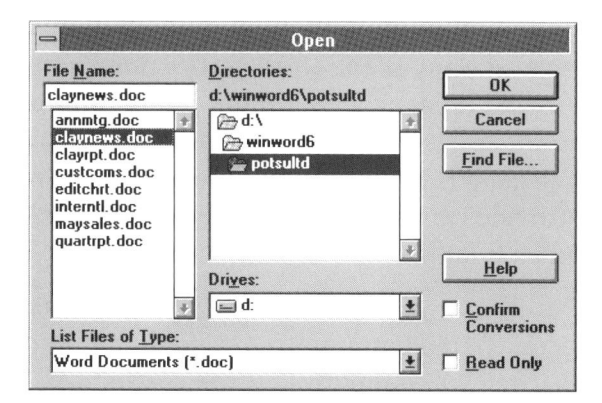

Opening Existing Files

▲ To see files with a different extension, such as TXT, type a different filename extension in the File Name box, or type *.* to see all files, then press **Enter**.

3. If you want to list files of a different type, select the type of file from the List Files of Type drop-down list, then press **Enter**.
4. If you only want to read the contents of the file and not make any changes, turn on the **Read Only** check box.
5. If you want to confirm the converter that Word proposes when you open a file created in a different application, turn on the **Confirm Conversion** check box.
6. If you want to locate a file and get other information, click the **Find File** button. See "Using the Document Management System" later in this chapter for more information on using Find File.
7. Click **OK** or press **Enter** to open the file and close the dialog box.

TIP

To open a file quickly, double-click the name of the file in the File Name box. This selects the file and closes the dialog box at the same time. You can also start Word and open a Word document at the same time by double-clicking the document's name in the Windows File Manager.

Saving Word Files

Word doesn't save any of the work you've done until you choose a **Save** command unless you've turned on the automatic save feature. To minimize the risk of losing your work, you should save frequently. A good rule of thumb is to save every 15 minutes.

Word provides three commands in the File menu to save documents and templates:

To	Choose This
Name a document the first time you save it and subsequently save the document using the same name	Save
Name a document the first time you save it or save a document with a different name or in a different file format	Save As
Save all open documents and templates in one operation	Save All

If you're saving a file for the first time, both the File Save and File Save As commands use the same dialog box, shown in Figure 2.2.

After you've saved your document or template once, File Save saves your file without displaying the dialog box. If at any time you decide to save your file with a different name or in a different format, use File Save As.

▼ *Figure 2.2. The Save As Dialog Box*

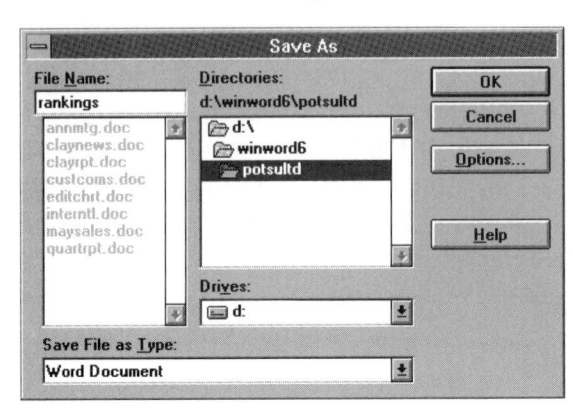

mand's shortcut key combination, **Ctrl+S**.) You won't see a dialog box, but Word displays the "save scale" in the status area as it saves.

Saving Word Files

Saving in a Different File or File Format

Sometimes you'll want to save a version of a document or template with a different name, leaving the original file intact. For example, if you work on billing, you might open a file called APRBILLS.DOC, then update it for May, then save the updated file as MAYBILLS.DOC. Then you would have on disk both files—APRBILLS.DOC and MAYBILLS.DOC—for your billing records.

To save a document or template in a different file:

1. Choose **File Save As**.
2. Type a new name for the file in the File Name box.
3. Select the file format in the Save File As Type box.
4. Click **OK** or press **Enter**. Word saves the file using the new name and leaves the original file intact.

Saving Files Using Save All

When you have several files open and want to save them all at the same time, you can use File Save All.

To save all open files at one time:

▲ Choose **File Save All**.

Before each file is saved, you'll see a prompt asking whether you want to save changes to the file.

Converting Documents into Templates

Perhaps you have written a document that is reused frequently, with only slight modifications made to new versions. You can save your existing document as a template by choosing File Save As. By converting a document into a template, you can then use the template to provide a basic skeleton for similar documents. Then you won't have to worry about mistakenly saving a new document on top of an existing one and losing the information in the existing file.

To convert a document into a template:

1. Choose **File Save As**.
2. Type a template name. Use the DOT extension or type a base filename and let Word add the DOT extension.
3. From the Save File As Type drop-down list, select **Document Template**.
4. Click **OK** or press **Enter**.

You can make changes in the template at any time, just as you would in any other document. You can also base other templates on this template.

Protecting Documents

When you have more than one person working on a Word document, you may want to create some safeguards to limit changes to documents. You can assign a password to restrict others from:

- ▲ Opening a document
- ▲ Saving changes to a document
- ▲ Annotating or revising a document
- ▲ Filling in certain fields in a form

To protect a document with a password:

1. Open the document you want to protect.
2. Chose **File Save As** and click the **Options** button. (Note that this takes you to the same box as the Save tab in Tools Options.)
3. If you want to restrict individuals from opening the document, type a password in the Protection Password box.
4. If you want to restrict individuals from saving changes to the document, type a password in the Write Reservation box.
5. Click **OK** or press **Enter**.

A password can be up to 15 characters long and can include letters, numbers, symbols, and spaces. Word will display asterisks (*)

as you type the password. Make sure you keep the password somewhere else in case you forget it at some point.

If you want to notify a user that the file should be opened as read-only, turn on the **Read-Only Recommended** check box.

To change or delete a password:

1. Open the document you want to protect.
2. Chose **File Save As** and click the **Options** button. (Note that this takes you to the same box as the Save tab in Tools Options.)
3. Select the password in the Protection Password box or the Write Reservation box.
4. Type in a new password or press the **Delete** key.
5. Click **OK** or press **Enter** to return to the Save As dialog box, then click **OK** or press **Enter** to save the document.

To protect documents from changes except revisions and annotations:

1. Choose **Tools Protect Document**.
2. In the Protect Document dialog box, click the **Revisions** and/or **Annotations** button.
3. Type a password in the Password box. The same rules concerning allowable number and types of characters apply.
4. Click **OK** or press **Enter**.

To protect a form field, see "Activating and Protecting a Form Field" in Chapter 12.

Protecting Documents

About the Summary Info Dialog Box

Whenever you save a document or template for the first time in Word, you can choose whether to complete items in the Summary Info dialog box, as shown in Figure 2.3 (unless you have turned off the Prompt for Summary Info check box in the Save category in the Tools Options commands). Summary Info can be used in these three ways:

▲ To help you recall the contents of and details about a document
▲ To help you locate a document
▲ To track a document's history

▼ **Figure 2.3. The Summary Info Dialog Box**

```
┌─────────────────── Summary Info ───────────────────┐
  File Name:  Document4                    ┌────────┐
  Directory:                                │   OK   │
  Title:      │The Korean Ancient Kingdoms│ └────────┘
                                            ┌────────┐
  Subject:    │Shilla and other dynasties │ │ Cancel │
                                            └────────┘
  Author:     │Sue Anne Guild             │ ┌────────────┐
                                            │ Statistics...│
  Keywords:   │Korean, Shilla, kingdom    │ └────────────┘
                                            ┌────────┐
  Comments:   │This report was done as a result of a│ │  Help  │
              │three-month study trip to Korea. It  │ └────────┘
              │encompasses present research on      │
```

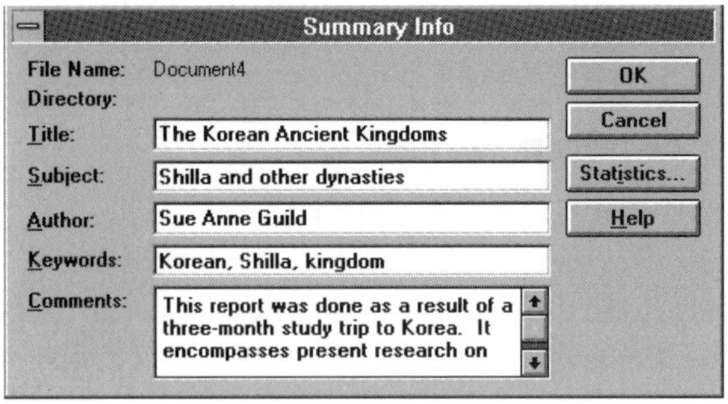

You can type and edit information in the Summary Info dialog box. The File Name box displays the name of the active document. The Directory box indicates where the file is located. (If you want to change either the filename or the directory, use File Save As.) You can enter information in the other text boxes as follows:

Field	*Used to Provide*
Title	A descriptive title for the file. For example, you might type **Letter to Dad asking for more money**.
Subject	A description of the document's contents.
Author	The name of the person who created the document. Word suggests the name of the person who originally used the program, but you can change this if necessary.
Keywords	Words that tell you something about the document and make it easy to locate the document later. For example, you might want to type the name of the company or the person to whom you're sending the document.
Comments	Any further information you want to add to clarify the document. For example, you might type something like **This letter responds to a query from the IRS about our fiscal year**.

Creating, Saving, and Managing Files ▲ 45

You don't *have* to fill in any of these boxes—you can simply press **Enter** to accept the dialog box as is and get on with your work. If you want the Summary Info box to appear each time you save a new document, turn on the **Prompt for Summary Info** check box.

About the Summary Info Dialog Box

Editing Summary Info

When you revise a file, Word doesn't automatically display the Summary Info dialog box. If you want to edit any of the other fields or add new information, use the following procedure.

To edit the Summary Info for a file:

1. Choose **File Summary Info**. Word displays the Summary Info dialog box for the document that currently contains the insertion point.
2. Edit or add new information in the fields of the Summary Info dialog box.
3. Click **OK** or press **Enter**.

Displaying Document Statistics

If you click the Statistics button in the Summary Info dialog box, Word displays the Statistics window, which contains descriptive data about the document. These data are updated each time a document is saved. You cannot edit any information in the Statistics window.

You can check the statistics of an open document at any time by choosing File Summary Info and choosing Statistics. Press **Enter** when you're finished reviewing the statistics.

Using the Document Management System

Word uses a very sophisticated document management system to keep track of all your documents. You can easily locate a specific document or quickly list a series of documents that deal with the same subject, have the same author, were created on the same day, or share almost any common element you can imagine.

For example, say that you produce a number of documents dealing with varied subjects in your advertising business. However, when you need to locate all documents about client presentations, you can't remember all the filenames. Imagine that you also need to find all documents written by a single person in the company, as well as all documents written by an individual before a certain date. Using the searching and sorting features of Word's document management system, you can easily list all the appropriate documents.

You can use the document management system to:

▲ Locate documents by telling Word to look for text, author's name, creation date, last revision date, or other criteria you specify

▲ Print or delete a group of documents with one command

▲ Sort a list of files according to creation or revision date, author's or operator's name, or file size

When you want to locate one or more documents, you use the Find File command on the File menu, which displays the dialog box shown in Figure 2.4.

▼ **Figure 2.4. The Find File Dialog Box**

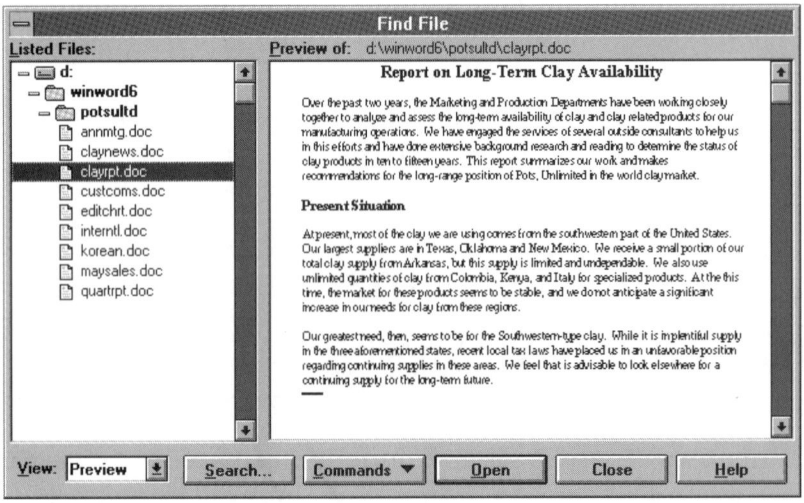

Creating, Saving, and Managing Files ▲ 47

The first time you use Find File on the File menu, Word displays the Search dialog box so that you can narrow down what you are looking for. When you use Find File again, Word quickly lists files from the previous search. You can always access the Search box and specify a different search.

Word initially lists directories and files in alphabetical order, but you can sort the list any way you want. For more information, refer to "Sorting the List of Files" later in this chapter.

Using the Document Management System

Searching for Documents

To search for a single document or a list of documents, you use the Search dialog box, which allows you to enter general search criteria.

To search for documents:

1. Choose **Find File** from the File menu. The first time in a session Word displays the Search dialog box. Thereafter you will see the Find File dialog box, and you can click the **Search** button to open the Search dialog box.
2. If you have performed a search like this previously, you can select it from the Saved Searches drop-down list.
3. Select or type the information you want to search for:

Box	*Type of Information*
File Name	The name of the file you want. The default extension is .doc, but you can change this by choosing a different type of file from the drop-down list. This changes the extension in the File Name box.
Location	One or more drive letters in the Drive drop-down list box. If more than one drive is being searched, separate by commas this way: `c:\Word\Legal,b:\Word\Invoices`. You can also edit the path by clicking on the **Edit Path** button.

4. Click **OK** or press **Enter**.
5. Word displays the Find File dialog box with the list of files you specified in the Listed Files list. To control what appears in the

right side of the Find File dialog box when you select a filename, choose one of the options in the View drop-down list:

To View File Names and	**Select**
The contents of the file	Preview
Information from the Summary Info dialog box	Summary
The size, author, and last date the file was saved	File Info

Refining a Search

You can narrow your search further by specifying other search criteria such as text, creation and saved dates, and keywords.

To do a detailed search:

1. Choose **Find File** from the File menu. The first time in a session Word displays the Search dialog box; thereafter you will see the Find File dialog box. You can click the **Search** button to open the Search dialog box.
2. If you have performed a search like this previously, you can select it from the Saved Searches drop-down list.
3. Click the **Advanced Search** button.
4. In the Advanced Search dialog box, shown in Figure 2.5, do one or more of the following:
    ▲ Click the **Location** tab and select the appropriate information in the filename, Search In, Directories, and Drives list boxes. If you want to include subdirectories in your search, turn on the **Include Subdirectories** check box.
    ▲ Click the **Summary** tab and fill in the boxes as appropriate:

Box	**Type of Information**
Title	Text used in the Title, Subject,
Author	Author, Keywords, or Subject
Keywords	box of the document's
Subject	Summary Info dialog box.
Options	Choose **Create New List** to replace the current list of files in the Find

▼ *Figure 2.5. The Advanced Search Dialog Box*

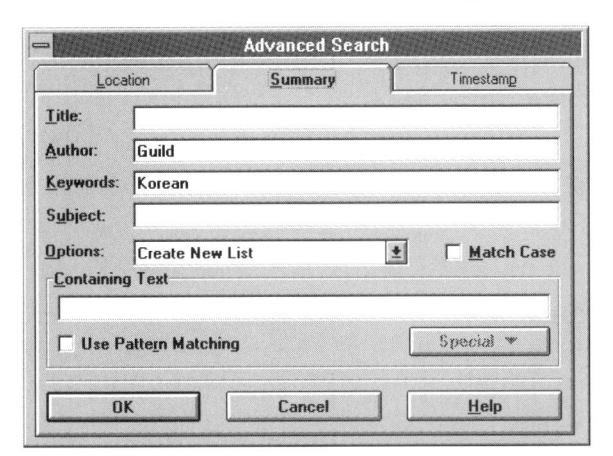

Using the Document Management System

Box	Type of Information
	File dialog box; **Add Matches To List,** to add files that meet the new criteria to the current list in the Find File dialog box; and **Search Only in List** to search only those files in the Find File dialog box.
Containing Text	Any text used in the file. Enclose text you type in quotes if it contains spaces or punctuation.
Match Case	If you filled in the Any Text box and you want Word to search for the exact combination of uppercase and lowercase letters you typed there, turn on the **Match Case** check box. Turn this option off if you want Word to match only the letters, not the cases.
Use Pattern Matching	If you want to match the exact combination of words (such as *apply to*), turn on the **Use Pattern Matching** check box.

▲ Click the **Timestamp** tab and fill in the appropriate boxes:

Box	Type of Information
Last Saved From	The earliest save date to search for; leave blank to list all files saved before the present date.
Last Saved To	The latest save date to search for; leave blank to list all files saved after the last save date.
Created From	The earliest creation date to search for; leave blank to list all files created before the current date.
Created To	The latest creation date to search for; leave blank to list all files created after the creation date.

5. Click **OK** or press **Enter**.
6. Click **OK** or **Search.** Word closes the Advanced Search dialog box and then the Search dialog box and looks for documents that match the criteria you typed in the dialog box. While searching, Word displays a message box that tells you how many documents are being searched and how many match the criteria. Word displays a list of documents that match that criteria in the Find File dialog box.

Word compares text you type in the Title, Subject, Keywords, and other boxes with the corresponding information in a document's Summary Info dialog box. If you didn't fill out these fields in the Summary Info dialog boxes, you shouldn't use them as search criteria. You can select documents from the list and open them, print them, copy them, delete them, or review their Summary Info sheets. See the appropriate section later in this chapter for instructions on how to do each of these tasks.

Opening a File from the Find File Dialog Box

You can open a single file, as well as several files, displayed in the Find File list. If you want to select a range of files, click the first filename, press **Shift**, and then click the last filename you want to select. If you want to select multiple files that are not adjacent, press **Ctrl** and then click each filename you want to select.

Use either of these procedures to open a file (or files) whose name is displayed in the Find File list:

▲ Highlight the filename in the dialog box, then click the **Open** button.
▲ Double-click the filename in the list.

If you want to open the file and read it without making any changes, click the Commands button and select **Open Read Only**.

Sorting the List of Files

You can choose the order for the display of the list of files in the Find File dialog box by sorting the list.

To sort the list of files:

1. In the Find File dialog box, click the **Commands** button and select **Sorting** to display the Options dialog box.
2. Choose an option in the Sort File By box:

Option	Description
Author	Sorts alphabetically by author's name, from A to Z.
Creation Date	Sorts chronologically by creation date, beginning with the file created most recently.
Last Saved By	Sorts alphabetically by person's name, from A to Z.
Last Saved Date	Sorts chronologically by save date, beginning with the file saved most recently.
Name	Sorts alphabetically by filename, from A to Z.
Size	Sorts numerically by file size, beginning with the smallest file.

3. Click either **Filename** or **Title** in the List Files By box.
4. Click **OK** or press **Enter**.

Using the Document Management System

Printing Documents Using the Document Management System

You can print several documents; several Summary Info dialog boxes; documents with field codes, annotations, and hidden characters (if any); or both documents and Summary Info dialog boxes simultaneously— all by using the document management system.

To print documents whose names are displayed in the Find File dialog box:

1. Choose **Find File**.
2. If necessary, use the Search function to display a list of appropriate documents as described in "Searching for Documents" earlier in this chapter.
3. Select the files you want to print.
4. Click the **Commands** button and choose **Print.** Word displays the File Print dialog box. For more information about printing, see Chapter 14.

Deleting Documents Using Find File

If you have a lot of old files to remove from your system, you can use the document management system to select multiple files and delete them with one command.

To delete documents whose names are displayed in the Find File dialog box:

1. Choose **Find File**.
2. If necessary, use the Search function to display a list of appropriate documents, as described in "Searching for Documents" earlier in this chapter.
3. Select the documents you want to delete.
4. Click the **Commands** button and choose **Delete.** To be sure that you mean it, Word displays a message asking whether you want to delete the files.
5. Click **Yes** or type **Y**. Word erases the files and removes the names from the list.

Creating, Saving, and Managing Files ▲ 53

Displaying Summary Info for Files in the Find File Dialog Box

Using the Document Management System

To display summary information about a document whose name is displayed in the Find File dialog box:

1. Choose **Find File**.
2. If necessary, use the Search function to display a list of appropriate documents, as described in "Searching for Documents" earlier in this chapter.
3. Select the document's name in the list.
4. Click the **Commands** button and choose **Summary.** Word displays the Summary Info dialog box on top of the Find File dialog box.
5. When you're finished reading the Summary Info dialog box, click **OK** or press **Enter**.

Copying Files Using Find File

You can copy files from one directory or drive to another by using Find File.

To copy files:

1. Choose **Find File**.
2. Select the file(s) you want to copy or move.
3. Click the **Commands** button and choose **Copy.**
4. In the Path box, specify where you want to copy the file(s), or select a location in the Drives and Directories boxes. You must choose a directory different from the current one. If you want to create a new directory, click the **New** button and type a new directory name.
5. Click **OK** or press **Enter**.

Changing Startup Options and Paths

At times, you may want to change the location for storing documents and other files—such as the speller, the thesaurus, and so on. You can do this by using the Options dialog box available from the Tools menu.

To change any of the default path settings:

1. Choose **Tools Options** and click the **File Locations** tab.
2. Using the File Types list, select the file type you want to change.
3. If you want to modify the location of the file type, choose **Modify** and make your changes. If you want to create a new directory, choose **New**. When you have finished, click **OK** or press **Enter**.
4. Click **Close** when you have finished making all of the modifications.

Changing the User Info Options

You can change the name, address, and other information in the Tools Options User Info dialog box. This will affect some of the information in the Summary Info dialog box. For more details, see "About the Summary Info Dialog Box" earlier in this chapter.

To change User Info options:

1. Choose **Tools Options** and choose **User Info**.
2. Fill in the Name and Initials boxes. The name will appear in the Author box within the Summary Info dialog box. If you don't fill in the Initials box, Word will automatically use the first letters of the first and last name in the Name box when you click OK.
3. Fill in the Address box.
4. Click **OK** or press **Enter**.

QUICK COMMAND SUMMARY

Command	*To Do This*
File New	Open a new file.
Enter	Begin a new paragraph.
Backspace	Erase any errors.

Command	To Do This
File Save	Name a document the first time you save it and subsequently save the document using the same name.
File Save As	Name a document the first time you save it; save a document with a different name or in a different file format.
File Save All	Save all documents and templates in one operation.
Save category in Tools Option	Display the available Save options.
File Summary Info	Display the Summary Info dialog box.
Find File	Display the Find File dialog box.
Ctrl+S	Save a file.
Hold down Shift and click	Select a range of files in a drop-down list.
Hold down Ctrl and click	Select multiple files that are not adjacent.

PRACTICE WHAT YOU'VE LEARNED

Start a new file and save it as MYFILE.DOC, filling out the summary info. Using the File Find File command, view the statistics on the file and then copy the file to a different directory.

What You Do	What You'll See
1. Choose **File New** and click **OK**.	1. The New dialog box with the names of the available templates in the Template list and the suggested template—Normal—in the list box. The Document button should be selected by default. After clicking OK, a blank document window appears.
2. Enter several lines of text.	2. The text you type in the document window.
3. Choose **File Summary Info**.	3. Word will display the Summary Info box with the Author box already completed. This information comes from the User Info tab in Tools Options.
4. Type a title in the Title box and some identifying words in the Keyword box.	4. The text you type in both of these boxes. This text should provide enough information so that you, or someone else, can identify the file easily.
5. Choose **File Save**.	5. The Save As dialog box, since this is the first time the file is being saved.

What You Do	*What You'll See*
6. Type **MYFILE** in the File Name box and then click OK.	6. A distinctive filename in the box, and the drive and directory you want the file to be in is also necessary. The document, and while it is being saved, the "save scale" at the bottom with the amount of the file that's been saved. Once the Save process has ended, Word will display the filename in the title bar at the top of the document window appears.
7. Choose **Find File** on the File Menu.	7. The Search dialog box, if this is the first time you've usedFind File this session; otherwise the Find File dialog box.
8. Select Summary in the View drop-down list.	8. The information you entered in the Summary Info dialog box and statistics relating to the file. You can see additional statistics if you choose Tools Word Count.
9. Click the **Commands** button and select Copy.	9. A menu of other actions you can take then the copy dialog box.
10. Type a new drive and directory in the Path box and click **OK.**	10. A message that the file is copied and then the Find File dialog box again. You can perform other actions or return to the document.
11. Click **Close.**	11. The document window.

3

Basic Editing

A document or template is rarely perfect the first time you create text. You'll usually want to go back and delete, add, or reorder text in your file. You might also want to copy text from another file or work with multiple windows. All of these tasks can be accomplished with easy-to-use editing features. In this chapter, you will learn how to:

- ▲ Select text
- ▲ Move through a document
- ▲ Cut, copy, and paste text
- ▲ Work with multiple document windows

Scrolling Through a Word File

If your Word file has more text than will fit in the document window, you need to scroll to see the complete file. If you're a mouse user, you're probably already familiar with using scroll boxes and scroll arrows. If you like to keep your hands on the keys, you can use the scroll bars as visual guides to tell you where you are in your file, or you can choose to hide one or both scroll bars.

You can control the display of the scroll bars in the Word window. By hiding the scroll bars, you can enlarge the text area of the window to see more of your file.

To control the display of the scroll bars:

1. Choose **Tools Options** and choose the View tab.
2. Turn on or turn off the **Horizontal Scroll Bar** and/or the **Vertical Scroll Bar** check boxes.
3. Click **OK** or press **Enter**.

Figure 3.1 shows how to use the scroll bars. You click the vertical scroll bar to scroll up or down; you click the horizontal scroll bar to scroll right or left (if your document text is wider than the window).

If you use the keyboard to scroll when the scroll bars are displayed, the scroll boxes move to reflect the position of the text in the window relative to the entire file. For example, if the scroll box is near the bottom of the vertical scroll bar, the text you see in the window is near the end of your file. If the scroll box is near the center of the vertical scroll bar, the text you see in the window is near the middle of your file. As you move the scroll box up and down the scroll bar, the page number on the left-hand side of the status bar will change to indicate the page you are in.

Scrolling with keys is the same as moving the insertion point with keys. The next section provides more information on using the keyboard to navigate through files.

Basic Editing ▲ 61

▼ **Figure 3.1. Using Scroll Bars With the Mouse**

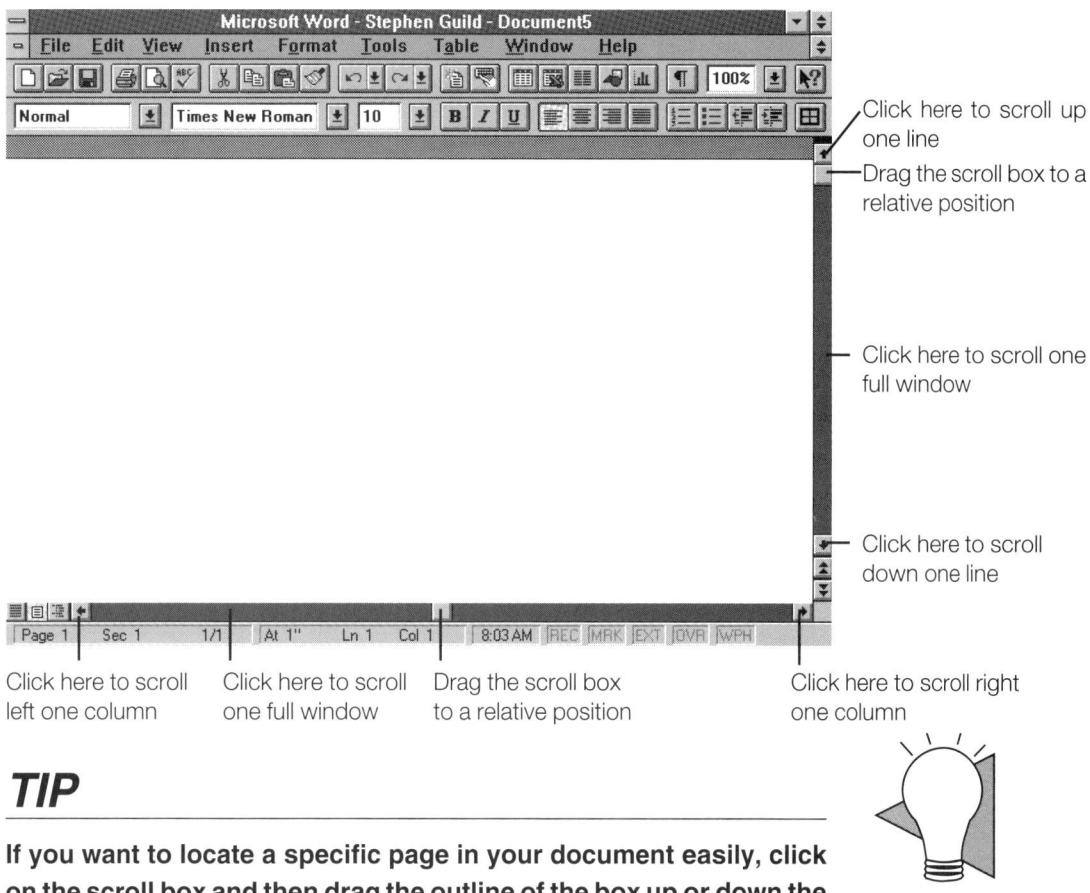

Click here to scroll up one line

Drag the scroll box to a relative position

Click here to scroll one full window

Click here to scroll down one line

Click here to scroll left one column

Click here to scroll one full window

Drag the scroll box to a relative position

Click here to scroll right one column

TIP

If you want to locate a specific page in your document easily, click on the scroll box and then drag the outline of the box up or down the vertical scroll bar. The page number in the status bar will change to reflect the page you're on.

Moving the Insertion Point

The first editing step is to move the insertion point (the blinking cursor) around in a file. The insertion point moves only within text—you can't just position the insertion point anywhere in a blank screen.

To move the insertion point with the mouse:

▲ Click where you want to place the insertion point in your text. (You may need to move the I-beam mouse pointer to see the blinking insertion point underneath it.)

Note that the insertion point and the I-beam mouse pointer are two different objects—you can move the I-beam pointer by rolling the mouse, but the insertion point stays in the same place until you click a new location.

To move the insertion point with keys:

▲ Use the arrow keys to move short distances, or use the keys on the numeric keypad (with NumLock off), as shown in Figure 3.2. If you have an extended keyboard, you can also use the other set of arrow keys to the left of the numeric keypad.

▼ *Figure 3.2. Using the Numeric Keypad to Move the Insertion Point*

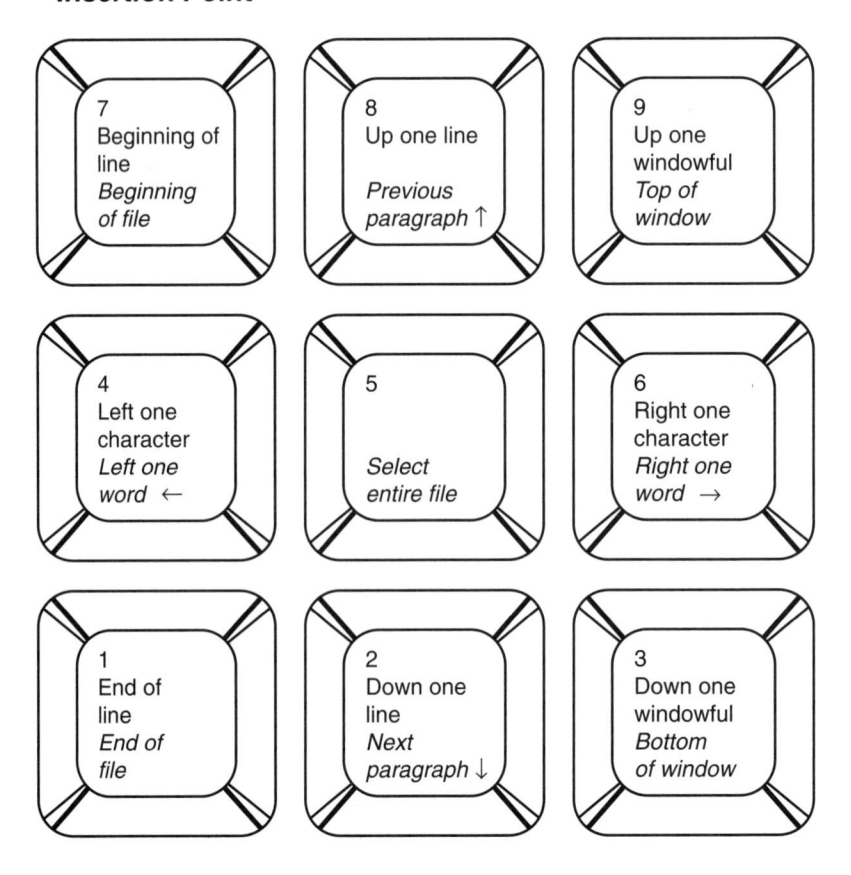

7 Beginning of line *Beginning of file*	8 Up one line *Previous paragraph* ↑	9 Up one windowful *Top of window*
4 Left one character *Left one word* ←	5 *Select entire file*	6 Right one character *Right one word* →
1 End of line *End of file*	2 Down one line *Next paragraph* ↓	3 Down one windowful *Bottom of window*

▲ Hold down the **Ctrl** key while you press the number key to get the action described in italics in Figure 3.2.

Selecting: Telling Word Where to Make Changes

Selecting: Telling Word Where to Make Changes

To edit or format text in Word, you first *select* the text, and then you choose a command or use a key combination to change the selected text.

Selecting highlights the text so you can easily see what you've selected, as shown in Figure 3.3. The commands you choose affect that text as long as the text is highlighted.

One word of caution about selecting: if you've turned on the Typing Replaces Selection check box (in the Edit tab of the Tools Options command), Word *replaces* selected text with any character you type. If you press a key after you've selected text, Word replaces the selected text with the character you typed. If you do this by accident, choose **Edit Undo** to undo the replacement.

▼ *Figure 3.3. Selecting Text*

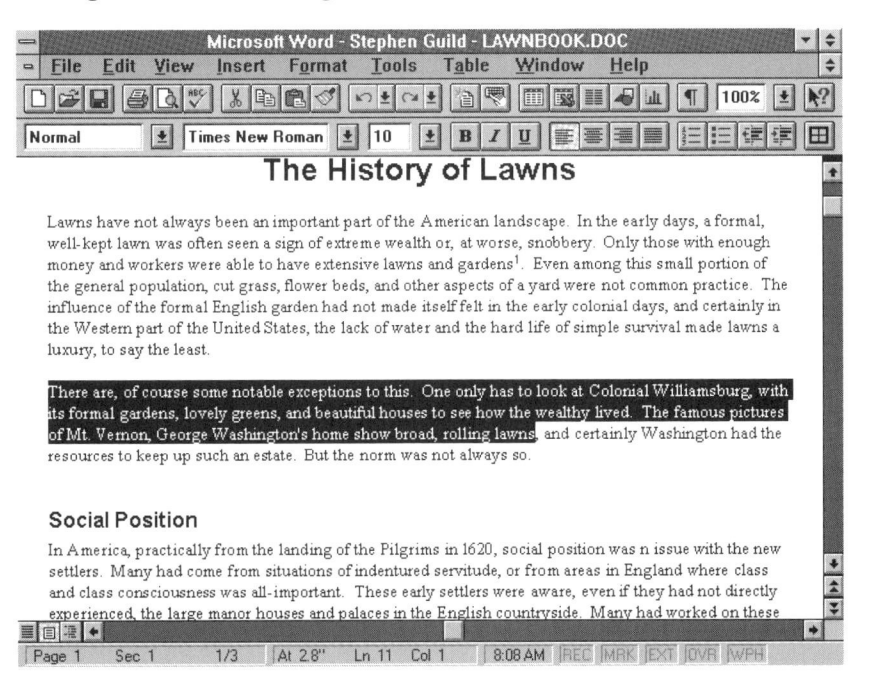

Selecting Text Using the Mouse

Here's the basic procedure to select text with the mouse:

1. Click to set the insertion point at the beginning of the text you want to select.
2. Hold down the mouse button while you move the insertion point to the end of the text you want to select.
3. When all the text you want is highlighted, release the mouse button.

If you change your mind while you are selecting and want to start over, just release the mouse button, then click to remove the highlight and set the insertion point in a new location.

Word has many variations for selecting text with the mouse. Here are a few of the most useful options:

To Select	*Do This*
One word	Double-click anywhere in the word. This selects the word and the following space (if any).
One line of text	Move the mouse pointer into the selection bar (an invisible area at the left edge of the document window) to the left of the line you want to select (the pointer becomes an arrow in the selection bar), then click.
Multiple lines	Move the mouse pointer into the selection bar to the left of the line you want to select (the pointer becomes an arrow in the selection bar), then hold down the mouse button and drag the mouse pointer down the selection bar until you've selected all the lines you want.
A large amount of text	Set the insertion point at the beginning of the text, move the mouse pointer to the end of the text (using the scroll bars if necessary),

> **Selecting: Telling Word Where to Make Changes**

To Select	Do This
	then hold down the **Shift** key while you click to set the endpoint. Word highlights the text between your mouse clicks. It's important that you first hold down the **Shift** key, then click—if you don't press **Shift** first, clicking moves the insertion point instead of selecting the text.
A block of text, such as a column	Point to one corner of the block, click and hold down the mouse button, and then drag.
The entire file	Move the mouse pointer into the selection bar, hold down the **Ctrl** key, and click the left mouse button.

For information about selecting text in tables, see Chapter 12.

CHECK YOURSELF

Scroll to the middle of the document, and then select a word.
- ▲ To scroll to the middle of the document, drag the scroll box in the vertical scroll bar to the middle, or press the **Page Down** key until you reach the approximate midpoint of the text.
- ▲ To select a word, double-click the word, or press **Ctrl+Shift+** right arrow key.

Selecting Text Using the Keyboard

Word has several basic methods you can use to select text with keys. You should choose a command or press a key combination immediately after selecting the text. If you move the insertion point instead, Word removes the highlighting and the text is no longer selected. For information about selecting text in tables, see Chapter 12.

To Select	Do This
Short pieces of text	Hold down the **Shift** key while you use the keys indicated in Figure 3.2 to move the insertion point.
Long pieces of text	Press **F8** to turn on Extend mode, and then move the insertion point until all the text you want to select is highlighted. Word displays EXT in the status bar to remind you that you're using Extend mode. If you make a mistake and want to start over, press **Esc** to turn off Extend mode, then press an arrow key to remove the highlight.
A block of text, such as a column (outside of a table)	Press **Ctrl+Shift+F8**, then use the arrow keys to highlight the block.
The entire file	Press **Ctrl+5** on the numeric keypad.

CHECK YOURSELF

Select all text in a document.
▲ Move the mouse pointer into the selection bar, then hold down **Ctrl** and click; or press **Ctrl+5**. (Make sure you use the number 5 on the numeric keypad.)

Making Inserted Text Replace Selected Text

By default, Word for Windows replaces selected text with new text. However, if you've used other word-processing programs, you may be accustomed to having inserted text appear in front of selected text. You can set an option to make Word for Windows behave in this way.

Making Inserted Text Replace Selected Text

To make inserted text appear in front of selected text:

1. Choose **Tools Options** and choose the **Edit** tab.
2. Turn off the **Typing Replaces Selection** check box.
3. Click **OK** or press **Enter**.

This option stays set from session to session, so you'll need to use the Tools Options commands again if you want to turn on the **Typing Replaces Selection** check box in later sessions.

Typing over Text

You can use Word's Overtype mode to type new text on top of existing text, just as you would on a typewriter. You can turn on Overtype mode in three ways, depending on whether you want to use the Insert key to paste in text, an option you can set in the General tab of Tools Options.

To use Overtype mode when you're not using the Insert key as the paste key:

1. Press the **Insert** key. Word displays OVR in the status bar to remind you that you're using Overtype mode.
2. Type over the text.
3. Press the **Insert** key again to turn off Overtype mode.

or

▲ Double-click OVR in the right-hand portion of the status bar.

To use Overtype mode when you have chosen to use the Insert key as the paste key:

1. Choose **Tools Options** and click the **Edit** tab.
2. Turn on the **Overtype Mode** check box. Word displays OVR in the status bar to remind you that you're using Overtype mode.
3. Type over the text.
4. Repeat Steps 1 through 3 to turn off the **Overtype Mode** check box when you're done.

Deleting Text

To delete text in Word:

1. Select the text.
2. Press the **Delete** key.

You can reverse a deletion if you choose **Edit Undo** immediately after pressing the **Delete** key.

If you want to delete text and paste it somewhere else, you should use the Edit Cut commands, as described in the following section.

Moving or Copying Text

When you move text, you'll use the Edit Cut and Edit Paste commands or the Cut and Paste buttons on the Standard toolbar. When you copy text, you'll use the Edit Copy and Edit Paste commands or the Copy and Paste buttons on the Standard toolbar. When you use Edit Cut to remove text, Word moves the text to the Clipboard; when you use Edit Copy, Word places a copy of the text in the Clipboard. Text stays on the Clipboard until the next time you cut or copy text. The Clipboard always contains the last piece of text or the last graphic you cut or copied. Use of the Clipboard is illustrated in Figure 3.4.

To move or copy text using the Clipboard:

1. Select the text you want to move or copy.
2. To move the text, choose **Edit Cut** and click the **Cut** button on the toolbar, or press **Shift+Delete** or **Ctrl+X**. To copy the text, choose **Edit Copy** and click the **Copy** button on the toolbar, or press **Ctrl+Insert** or **Ctrl+C**.
3. Place the insertion point where you want to insert the text. If the Typing Replaces Selection option is turned on (the default state) and you want the inserted text to replace existing text, select the text you want to replace. Otherwise, make sure no text is selected.
4. Choose **Edit Paste** and click the **Paste** button on the toolbar, or press **Shift+Insert** or **Ctrl+V**. (You could also press **Insert** if

Basic Editing ▲ 69

▼ **Figure 3.4. The Edit Cut, Edit Copy, and Edit Paste Commands Using the Clipboard**

Moving or Copying Text

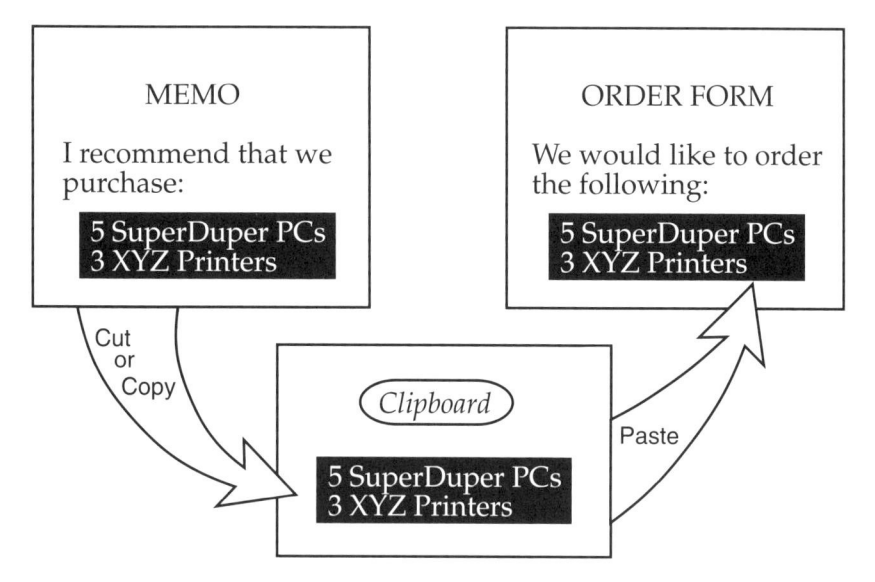

MEMO

I recommend that we purchase:

5 SuperDuper PCs
3 XYZ Printers

ORDER FORM

We would like to order the following:

5 SuperDuper PCs
3 XYZ Printers

Cut or Copy

Clipboard

5 SuperDuper PCs
3 XYZ Printers

Paste

you've turned on the Use INS for Paste check box in the Tools Options Edit tab.) Word inserts a copy of the text from the Clipboard.

You can also use the following methods to move or copy text or graphics quickly without using the Clipboard.

To move or copy text or graphics using the mouse:

1. Select the text or graphic.
2. Drag the selected text to a new location. A dotted vertical line moves with the mouse pointer.
3. When the vertical line is where you want to place the text, release the mouse button. This technique is called "drag and drop."

TIP

You can turn off the drag-and-drop capability by choosing Tools Options, **clicking the** Edit **tab, then turning off the** Drag and Drop Text Editing **check box.**

You can also use this technique to move or copy text or graphics:

1. Select the text or graphic.
2. Point to where you want to insert the selected text or graphic.
3. If you're moving the text, hold down **Ctrl** and click the right mouse button. If you're copying the text, hold down **Ctrl+Shift** and click the right mouse button.

To move or copy text or graphics using the keyboard:

1. Select the text or graphic you want to move or copy.
2. To move the text, press **F2**. "Move to where?" appears in the status bar. To copy the text, press **Shift+F2**. "Copy to where?" appears in the status bar.
3. Place the insertion point where you want to insert the text. The insertion point becomes a dotted vertical line. If you've turned on the Typing Replaces Selection option and you want the inserted text or graphic to replace existing information, select the information you want to replace. Selected text is marked with a dotted underline. If you don't want to replace information, make sure nothing is selected.
4. Press **Enter** to insert the text or graphic.

Cutting and Pasting Several Items at Once: Using the Spike

Word has a special place to save text and graphics called the "Spike." The Spike is somewhat like the Clipboard in that you can cut parts of Word files and send those selections to the Spike. However, unlike with the Clipboard, each item you put in the Spike is added to items already there, so you can use the Spike to collect a lot of items, then insert them all at once.

For example, you might want to open all your monthly financial reports in sequence, cut the summary paragraph from each monthly report to the Spike, then insert all of the paragraphs at once into your annual report.

To send an item to the Spike:

1. Select the text or graphics you want to send to the Spike.

> **Cutting and Pasting Several Items at Once: Using the Spike**

2. Press **Ctrl+F3** to add the selected text or graphics to the Spike. Each item is added to the previous contents of the Spike.

To insert the contents of the Spike:

1. Move the insertion point to where you want to insert the contents of the Spike.
2. Do one of the following:
   ▲ To insert the contents of the Spike and empty the Spike press **Ctrl+Shift+F3**.
   ▲ To insert the contents of the Spike, but leave the information in the Spike unchanged, type **spike**, then press **F3**.

CHECK YOURSELF

What is the difference between using the Spike and using the Clipboard?
   ▲ The Spike can hold multiple items, while the Clipboard can hold only one cut or copied section at a time. When you copy an item to the Spike, the item is appended to the Spike's existing contents. When you copy an item to the Clipboard, the item replaces the Clipboard's existing contents.

Undoing a Change

You probably know the desperate feeling that occurs when you've made a mistake you don't think can be fixed. For instance, suppose you've just deleted text you should have kept, moved a phrase to the wrong place, or chosen the wrong command. When this happens, don't panic. Word has made allowances for mistakes, and there is practically nothing you can do in Word that can't be undone.

If you realize your mistake immediately after you've made it, you can choose Edit Undo. Edit Undo can, in most cases, reverse the last action you took. The wording of the Undo command changes to reflect what you've been doing most recently. If you've just done something that Word can't undo, the Undo command says "Can't Undo." In that case, you can probably choose a different command to correct the problem.

Because you'll use Edit Undo frequently, you may want to get in the habit of clicking the Undo button on the toolbar (a counterclockwise arrow). You can also use one of the shortcut key combinations, **Alt+Backspace** or **Ctrl+Z**, to undo the last action without using the Edit menu or the toolbar. If Word can't undo something (like removing the highlight from selected text), it beeps when you click the Undo button or press the shortcut keys.

If you've made a disastrous mistake and Word tells you it "Can't Undo," consider closing your file without saving it. You'll lose all the changes you've made since the last time you saved the file, but that may be more desirable than keeping the file in its altered state.

Working with Multiple Document Windows

There are many instances when you'll want to have more than one Word file open at a time. You might just want to refer to another document to see what you've written, or you might want to copy or move text between Word files. As many Windows applications, Word lets you create multiple windows within the Word window. Each of these windows is called a *document window*, and each can contain a different file.

Only one document window—the *active* document window—can contain the insertion point. Each open window displays its own Document Control menu (not to be confused with the Word Control menu, which controls the entire Word window), as well as its own ruler and scroll bars.

Opening Another Document

You always use the same procedure to open a file, whether it's the first or the fourth file you've opened. You can use either of these methods:

▲ Choose **File New** or click the **New** button (it looks like a page) on the toolbar to open a new, empty file.

▲ Choose **File Open** or click the **Open** button (it looks like a folder) on the toolbar to open an existing file. (For more information on opening files, see Chapter 2.)

The following sections will tell you how to move from window to window and how to rearrange windows so you can see more than one window at a time on the screen.

Working with Multiple Document Windows

TIP

Word lists several of the most recently opened files at the bottom of the File menu. To open one of these files quickly, click the filename in the File menu or type the number listed beside the filename. Word opens a file in a new window, on top of any previously opened files.

Moving from Window to Window

The Window menu lists all the files you have opened. A check mark appears to the left of the file in the active window—the one that contains the insertion point.

With the mouse, do one of the following:

▲ If the window is hidden, click the Window menu, then click the name of the file you want.

▲ If you can see any part of the window you want, click it to activate that window.

Word places the file you choose on top of other open files.

With keys, do one of the following:

▲ Press **Ctrl+F6** until the window you want is activated.

▲ Press **Alt, W** to display the Window menu, then press the number shown beside the filename.

Changing the Sizes of Windows

When you have multiple document windows open, you can change their sizes and positions to display more than one window on the screen at once. It's usually not practical to try to display more than two or three windows at once: the screen just gets too cluttered. However, you can experiment until you find an arrangement you like.

To divide the space in the Word window among all open document windows, as shown in Figure 3.5:

▲ Choose **Window Arrange All**.

You can also change the sizes of individual windows and then move them to new positions to see more than one document window within the Word window. (Before you can change the size of a window, you may need to choose the Window Arrange All command so that you can see window borders on the screen.)

To change the size of a document window with the mouse:

1. Move the mouse pointer to the border you want to move. If you position the pointer over a corner, you can change both the height and width of the window at once. The pointer becomes a two-headed arrow.
2. Drag the border to the new position.

▼ *Figure 3.5. Documents Arranged with Window Arrange All*

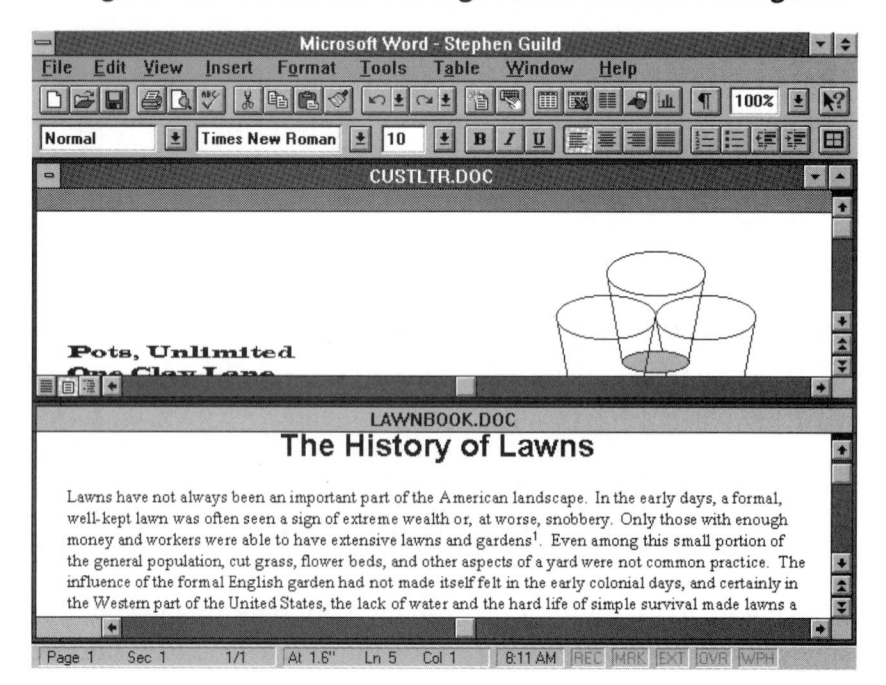

3. Repeat Steps 1 and 2 to move other borders.

To change the size of a document window with keys:

1. Press **Ctrl+F8**. Word displays a four-headed arrow in the window.
2. Press the arrow key that points toward the window border you want to move. For example, to move the bottom border, press the down arrow key. The arrow moves to that border.
3. Press the arrow key that points in the direction you want to move the border. For example, to move the border left, press the left arrow key until the border is in the position you want.
4. Press **Enter** to set the new position.
5. Repeat Steps 1 through 4 to move other borders as necessary.

You might want to resize and move windows to arrange them side by side, as shown in Figure 3.6.

To make a document window full size:

▲ Click the maximize button (the "up triangle") in the document window's upper right corner, or press **Ctrl+F10**.

Working with Multiple Document Windows

▼ *Figure 3.6. Side-by-Side Windows*

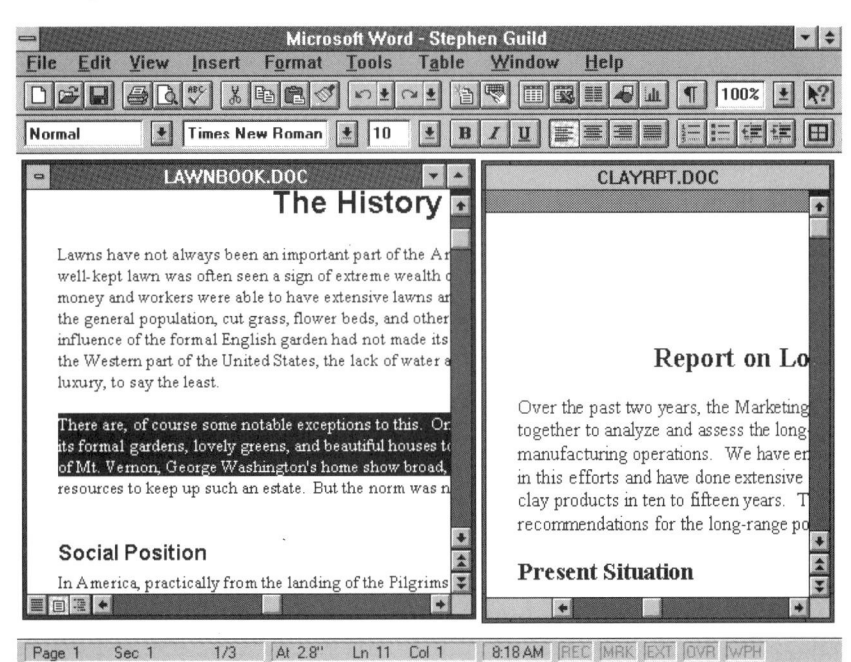

After you've maximized a document window, you can return the window to its previous size:

▲ Click the restore button (two triangles) in the document window's upper right corner, or press **Ctrl+F5**.

Moving Document Windows

Use either of these techniques to move a window to a new location:

▲ Point to the window's title bar, and then drag the window to a new location.

▲ Press **Ctrl+F7** to display a four-headed arrow in the window, use the arrow keys to move an outline of the window, and then press **Enter** to set the new position.

Closing Document Windows

When you're finished with a file, you can close that file and remove its document window from the screen:

▲ Double-click the Control-menu box in the document window's upper left corner, or make sure the window is active, then press **Ctrl+W**.

If you've made any changes since you last saved the file, Word asks whether you want to save the changes before closing the file.

If you close all of the open files, you'll see a nearly blank screen on which menus are missing and File menu commands have been rearranged. Don't panic—you can still use File Open to open a file, File New to create a new file, or File Exit to quit Word.

CHECK YOURSELF

How can you rearrange two document windows so that they occupy equal screen space?

▲ Choose the Window Arrange All command.

Working with Two or More Views of the Same Document

Working with Multiple Document Windows

At times, you may wish you could view more than one part of your document at once. For example, you might want to view both the beginning and the end of your document to see if you've used the same phrasing, or view both the place where you want to delete text and the location to which you want to move that text.

With Word you can use either of two methods to see more than one view of your document. You can split a document window into two *panes*, or you can open another window containing the same document. In either case, you'll find that it's easier to have different views of your document than to scroll through a long document. You should also keep in mind that you're working on a single document, even though you may see different sections in different windows or panes.

Splitting the Document Window into Panes

You can split the document window into two panes, one above the other. Each pane has its own scroll bars that you can use to view different parts of one document at the same time. You can't move panes to new locations or hide one behind another as you can document windows—panes divide one document window into two parts.

To use the mouse to split a window into panes:

1. Point to the split bar (the black rectangle) above the vertical scroll bar. The mouse pointer becomes a split symbol (two lines with arrows pointing up and down).
2. Drag the dotted line representing the split bar to the place where you would like the split to appear, and then release the mouse button.

To use the keyboard to split a window into panes:

1. Choose the **Split** command from the Window menu (**Alt, W, P**). Word displays a dotted split line across the window with a split symbol positioned on the line.

2. If you want to move the split line, press the arrow key that points in the direction you want to move it. For example, to move the split line down, press the down arrow key. Otherwise, press **Enter** to set the split line's position.

TIP

To use the mouse to split a window in half, quickly double-click the black split bar icon above the vertical scroll bar.

Moving the Insertion Point from Pane to Pane

Just as with multiple windows, only one pane can be active (contain the insertion point) at a time.

To move the insertion point back and forth between panes:

▲ Click the pane or press **F6**.

You can scroll the text in each pane separately to see different parts of the same document.

To remove a window split:

▲ Double-click the split bar icon (the black bar between the vertical scroll bars), or choose the **Split** command from the document control menu, press **Page Up** or **Page Dn** to move the split line to the window border, and then press **Enter** to make the line disappear.

Viewing the Same Document in Two or More Windows

To look at two horizontal views of the same document, you can split a window, as described in the previous section. You can also open a new window containing the same document, then rearrange the windows side by side or any way you like.

To open a new window containing the same document:

▲ Choose the **New Window** command from the Window menu. Word opens a new window on top of the previous one.

You can move the windows and change their sizes so that you can see several different views of your document at once, and you can move the insertion point between the different windows. See "Moving from Window to Window" and "Changing the Sizes of Windows" earlier in this chapter.

Working with Multiple Document Windows

CHECK YOURSELF

Why would you want to look at the same document in two or more windows or panes?

▲ So that you can view different parts of the same document at one time.

QUICK COMMAND SUMMARY

Command	To Do This
Scroll bars	Scroll through a file with the mouse.
Keys on numeric keypad	Scroll though a file with keys.
Drag over text	Select text with the mouse.
Shift+arrow keys	Select text with keys.
Tools Options	Control whether what you type replaces selected text or is inserted in front of the selection, or switch between overtype and insert modes.
Insert key	Toggle between overtype and insert modes (when not used as the paste key).
Delete key	Delete selected text.
Edit Cut, Cut toolbar button, Shift+Delete, or Ctrl+X	Remove selected text and place it in the Clipboard.

Command	To Do This
Edit Copy or Copy toolbar button, Ctrl+Insert, or Ctrl+C	Copy selected text and place the copy in the Clipboard.
Edit Paste or Paste toolbar button, Shift+Insert, or Ctrl+V	Insert the contents of the Clipboard, replacing selected text (if any).
"Drag and drop" mouse shortcuts	Move or copy selected text.
F2 and Shift+F2 keyboard shortcuts	Move or copy selected text.
Ctrl+F3	Add selected items to the Spike.
Ctrl+Shift+F3	Insert the Spike's contents and empty the Spike.
Edit Undo, Undo toolbar button, Alt+Backspace or Ctrl+Z	Undo the last change.
File New or New toolbar button	Open a new document in another window.
File Open, Ctrl+O, or Open toolbar button	Open an existing document in another window.
Click window, click filename on Window menu, press Ctrl+F6, or press Alt, W, then press window number	Place the insertion point in another window.
Window Arrange All	Divide screen space equally among all open windows.
Drag window border with mouse or use Ctrl+F8, arrow keys	Change the size of a window.
Click maximize button or press Ctrl+F10	Make a window full size (maximize the window).
Click restore button or press Ctrl+F5	Restore a window to previous size after maximizing.

Command	To Do This
Double-click document control menu box or press Ctrl+W	Close a document window.
Double-click split bar or choose Split on Window menu	Split a window into two panes.
Double-click split bar or choose Split on Window menu, then move split line off window	Remove a window split.
Window New Window command	Open a second window containing the active document.

PRACTICE WHAT YOU'VE LEARNED

Create a file named GROCERY1.DOC and type the following list:

    apples
    milk
    cereal
    bacon
    bread

Create another file named GROCERY2.DOC that contains this list:

    cat food
    lettuce
    carrots
    shampoo
    shaving cream
    film

Arrange the two files so that you can see both at once, and then copy the list in GROCERY2.DOC and add it to the end of GROCERY1.DOC.

What You Do

1. Use File New to create an empty document if necessary, then type the list, and use File Save to save the file with the name GROCERY1.DOC.

2. Choose **File New**, type **GROCERY2.DOC** in the dialog box, and click **OK** to create another file.

3. Type the list in GROCERY2.DOC.

4. Choose **Window Arrange All** to display both windows.

5. Select the list in GROCERY2.DOC.

6. Choose **Edit Copy**.

7. Move the insertion point to GROCERY1.DOC, then choose **Edit Paste** to add the copied list.

What You'll See

1. The New dialog box with the names of the available templates in the Templates list and the suggested template—Normal— in the list box. After you click **OK** and type the text, the grocery list will be displayed. When you choose **File Save**, the Save As dialog box appears with the file you enter: GROCERY1

2. The New dialog box and the name of the filename GROCERY2. After you click **OK,** a blank document will be displayed.

3. The text of the second grocery list.

4. Both documents on the screen stacked one on top of the other. You can move between the two by pressing **Ctrl+F6**.

5. The black selection bars over the selected text.

6. The Edit menu that drops down from the menu bar with Copy selected.

7. The insertion point at the end of the first grocery list, the Edit menu that drops down from the menu bar with Paste selected, and then the combined lists.

4

Power Editing

This chapter shows you how to use Word's change-control features to make document management easier. You'll also find out how to tag selected text so you can easily locate it later. In this chapter, you will learn how to:

- ▲ Search for and replace text and formatting
- ▲ Use AutoText entries
- ▲ Use revision marks
- ▲ Compare two different versions of a document
- ▲ Add and review annotations in a document
- ▲ Tag selected text with a bookmark

Searching for and Replacing Text and Formatting

You can quickly find a word, a phrase, or even a hidden formatting character with the Edit Find and Edit Replace commands, and you can replace occurrences of text individually or replace all occurrences at once.

Word can search the entire file or from the insertion point to the beginning or end of the file. Before you choose a command, be sure the insertion point is positioned where you want to start. If you begin a search in the middle of a file, when Word reaches the file's beginning or end it displays a message asking you if you want to continue the search from the other end of the file.

Word's Edit Find and Edit Replace commands allow you to find and replace almost anything, so the dialog boxes can seem complex. The important thing to remember is that all options in the dialog box work together to specify the search criteria. In other words, if you type **dog** and specify bold formatting and the Normal style, Word will find the word dog only if it has bold formatting and uses the Normal style.

TIP

When you want to search for or replace a long string of text or special characters in your document, you can just copy that string of text or characters to the Find or Replace dialog box in this way: select the text in your document, press Ctrl+C **to copy it to the Clipboard, choose** Edit Find **or** Edit Replace, **position the insertion point in the dialog box, and then press** Ctrl+V **to paste the Clipboard contents.**

Searching for Text or Formatting

To search for text or formatting:

1. Choose **Edit Find**. Word displays the dialog box shown in Figure 4.1.

▼ *Figure 4.1. Using the Find Dialog Box to Search for a Page Break*

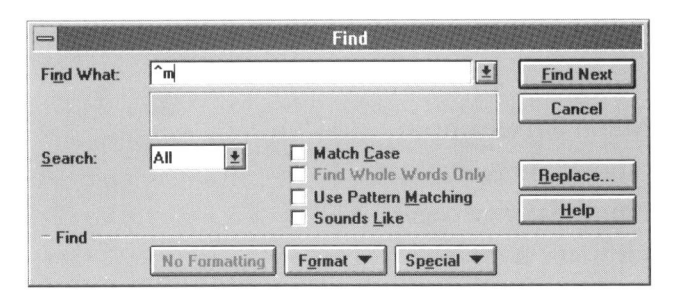

Searching for and Replacing Text and Formatting

2. In the Find What box, do one of the following:
   ▲ If you want to find or replace regular text, type exactly the text you want to search for. If you type two spaces between words in a phrase, for example, Word won't find the phrase with just one space between words in your file.
   ▲ To find variations of similar spellings, use a caret (^) and a question mark (?) as a wildcard character to take the place of any character (for example, type **n^?w** to find *new* and *now*).
   ▲ To find any text with specific formatting (such as any bold word or any text with a certain style), make sure the box is blank. If necessary, select any text in the box and then press **Delete**.
   ▲ To search for special characters, you can choose the **Special** button and select from the list or type the following codes:

To Search for	Type
Paragraph mark	^p
Tab character	^t
Annotation mark	^a
Any character	^?
Any digit	^#
Any letter	^$
Caret	^^
Column break	^n
Em dash	^+
En dash	^=
Endnote mark	^e

To Search for	Type
Field	^d
Footnote mark	^f
Graphic	^g
Line break	^l
Manual page break	^m
Nonbreaking hyphen	^~
Nonbreaking space	^s
Optional hyphen	^-
Section break	^b
White space	^w

The Find What box is also a drop-down list that contains the four most recent searches you've done in that editing session.

3. Select the following options if desired:
    - ▲ Turn on the **Match Case** check box if you want Word to pay attention to uppercase and lowercase letters in its search. If you don't turn on the Match Case check box, Word searches for all occurrences of the letters you type, regardless of whether they're uppercase or lowercase.
    - ▲ Turn on the **Find Whole Words Only** check box if you want to find the text only when it appears as a separate word rather than as part of a word.
    - ▲ Turn on the **Use Pattern Matching** check box if you want to match the exact combination of words (such as *apply to*).
    - ▲ Turn on the **Sounds Like** check box if you want to find words that sound alike but are spelled differently. For example, Suzy and Susie.
4. In the Search drop-down list, select **Up** to search from the insertion point to the beginning of the file; select **Down** to search from the insertion point to the end of the file; select **All** if you want to search the entire document.
5. To specify formatting or styles, choose the **Format** button and choose one of the options (Font, Paragraph, Language, or Style), then select options in these dialog boxes to specify the formatting to search for. For example, to search for italic text, click **Format**, then choose **Font**, and select **Italic** in the list, then click **OK**; to specify the Heading 1 style, click **Format**, then

Searching for and Replacing Text and Formatting

choose **Style**, select **Heading 1** from the styles list, then click **OK**. Word displays a description of the formatting you've selected beneath the Find What box.

6. Click **Find Next** or press **Enter** to begin the search. Word highlights the first occurrence of the text and/or formatting you specified. If Word reaches the end of the file before finding an occurrence, it displays a message asking whether you want to search from the other end of the file.

To search again for the same text or formatting when the Find dialog box is still open:

▲ Click **Find Next** or press **Enter**.

To search again for the same text after closing the Find dialog box, press **Shift+F4**. You can use this shortcut even after moving the insertion point to a different window.

TIP

When using the Edit Find or Edit Replace command, you can search for formatting by pressing shortcut keys to specify the format you want. For example, to replace bold text with italic text, you could place the insertion point in the Find What box, then press Ctrl+B; place the insertion point in the Replace With box, then press Ctrl+I. To specify removal of all formatting, press Ctrl+Spacebar. For lists of shortcut keys used in character and paragraph formatting, see Chapters 6 and 7.

Replacing Text and Formatting

You can replace existing text with new text in one easy step. You can ask Word to make all changes automatically, or you can approve each change before it's made.

To replace text or formatting:

1. To replace text or formatting only in part of your file, select the desired text or formatting to be changed. To replace text or formatting in all of your file, make sure nothing is selected.
2. Choose **Edit Replace**.

3. Fill in the Find What and Replace With boxes, using one of the following techniques:
   ▲ If you want to find or replace regular text, type exactly the text you want to search for. If you type two spaces between words in a phrase, for example, Word won't find the phrase with just one space between words in your file.
   ▲ To find variations of similar spellings, use a caret (^) and a question mark (?) as a wildcard character to take the place of any character (for example, type **n^?w** to find *new* and *now*).
   ▲ To find any text with formatting you specify (such as any bold word or any text with a certain style), make sure the box is blank. If necessary, select any text in the box and then press **Delete** (see Figure 4.2).
   ▲ To search for special characters, you can choose the **Special** button and select from the list or type the codes. (For a complete list see "Searching for Text or Formatting," earlier in this chapter.)
4. To specify formatting or styles, choose the **Format** button and choose one of the options (Font, Paragraph, Language, or Style), then select options in these dialog boxes to specify the formatting to search for or replace. For example, to search for italic text, click **Format**, then choose **Font**, and select **Italic** in the list, then click **OK**; to specify the Heading 1 style, click **Format**, then choose **Style**, select **Heading 1** from the styles list, then click **OK**. Word displays a description of the format-

▼ *Figure 4.2. Replacing Bold Text with Italic Text*

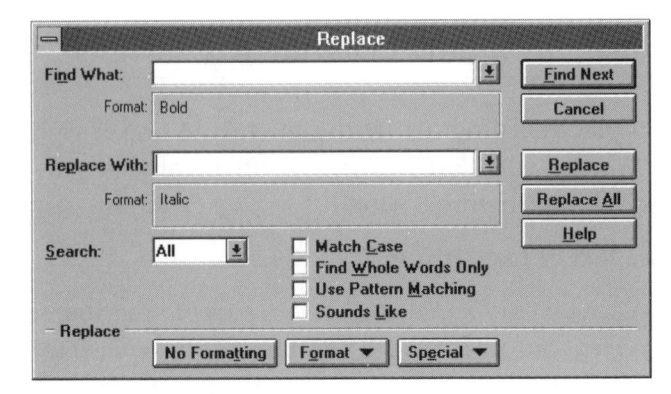

ting you've selected beneath the Find What box. You can also click on the style name in the Style drop-down list on the Formatting toolbar.

5. Select the following options if desired:
   ▲ Turn on the **Match Case** check box if you want Word to pay attention to uppercase and lowercase letters in its search. If you don't turn on the Match Case check box, Word searches for all occurrences of the letters you type, whether they're uppercase or lowercase.
   ▲ Turn on the **Find Whole Words Only** check box if you want to find the text only when it appears as a separate word rather than as part of a word.
   ▲ Turn on the **Use Pattern Matching** check box if you want to match the exact combination of words (such as *apply to*).
   ▲ Turn on the **Sounds Like** check box if you want to find words that sound alike but are spelled differently. For example, Suzy and Susie.
6. Do one of the following:
   ▲ To make replacements one at a time, click **Find Next** or press **Enter**. When Word displays the first match, click **Replace** to make the replacement or click **Find Next** to skip to the next match.
   ▲ To make all replacements at once, click **Replace All**. Word makes all the replacements automatically and lists the number of replacements in the status bar. If this number looks suspiciously high, you can choose **Edit Undo** immediately or check your replacements, then use the **Edit Replace** command again (reversing the entries in the Find What and Replace With boxes) to correct any mistakes.

Searching for and Replacing Text and Formatting

TIP

You can use Edit Replace to help you enter lengthy text faster and with fewer mistakes. Just substitute a two- or three-character code for long words or phrases that you type often. For example, instead of typing Hi-Tech Services, Inc. **several times in a memo, just type** hhh, **then use Edit Replace later to replace all instances of** hhh **with** Hi-Tech Services, Inc.

CHECK YOURSELF

Press the **Enter** key twice at the end of each paragraph in your file: once to end the paragraph, and once to insert a blank line before beginning the next paragraph. Next, eliminate the blank lines between paragraphs. Use Edit Replace to do this.

▲ Choose **Edit Replace**, type **^p^p** in the Find What box to find two sequential paragraph marks, type **^p** in the Replace With box to replace the two paragraph marks with one paragraph mark, and then click **Replace All**.

Using AutoText Entries

Do you have an address, a letterhead, or a picture that you would like to use repeatedly in different documents? With Word you can save text and graphics as AutoText entries (in former versions of Word, these were called glossaries). Using an AutoText entry is like renting a safety deposit box—you can put in the AutoText entries you want to keep, then you can take out the entries anytime you like.

Almost anything can be kept in an AutoText entry, from one character to an entire file. You can even store formatting by creating paragraph marks and section marks.

AutoText entries are stored in a template, either in the default template, NORMAL.DOT, or in a special template you've created and attached to a document. AutoText entries in the NORMAL.DOT template are automatically available to all Word documents. If you want to use other AutoText entries, base your document on the template that contains the AutoText entries.

Specifying Where to Save AutoText Entries

To tell Word where to save the AutoText entries you create:

1. Choose File Templates.
2. Click the **Organizer** button and then the **AutoText** tab.

Using AutoText Entries

3. The AutoText entries in the current document are displayed in the In (document name) drop-down list. If you want to use AutoText entries in a different file, click the **Close File** button and click the **Open File** button. Select a directory and a filename to specify the document the styles you want to use. Word displays the names of all the files in that directory that have the .DOC extension. If you want to see all files or just template files (those with the extension .DOT), you'll need to select **All Files or Templates** from the List Files of Type drop-down list.
4. Select the name of the document in which you want to save the AutoText entries in the To (document name) drop-down list. If the name of the document you want to use is not displayed, then close the present file and open the document using the procedure described above.
5. Select the names of the AutoText entries you want to copy and then click the Copy button. You can also choose to Delete or Rename an entry at this point.
6. When you have finished, click **Close**.

Defining AutoText Entries

Figure 4.3 illustrates how to define an AutoText entry.

To save text or graphics as an AutoText entry:

1. Select the text and/or graphics you want to save. You can select any reasonable amount of text and/or graphics, from one character to several pages.
2. Choose **Edit AutoText**.
3. Type a name for your AutoText entry in the AutoText Name box. For example, if you are saving your company logo, you may type **logo**. An AutoText entry name can contain up to 31 characters and can include spaces.
4. Click the **Add** button or press **Enter**.

AutoText entries are saved in the template. Word will prompt you with a message about saving AutoText and command changes when you quit.

▼ *Figure 4.3. Defining an AutoText Entry*

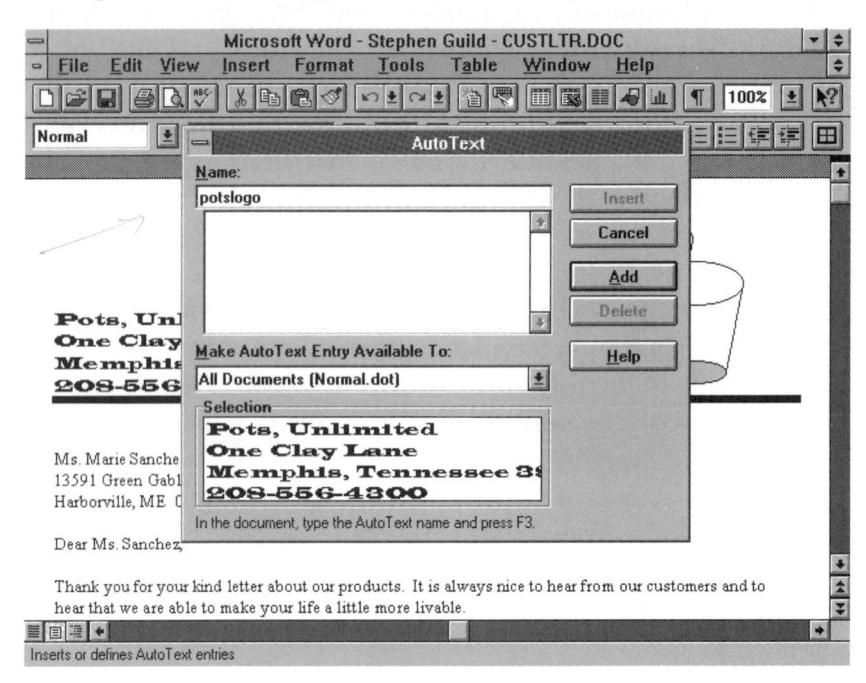

Inserting AutoText Entries

When you've saved an AutoText entry attached to a template, you can insert that entry into your documents any time you like.

To insert an AutoText entry:

1. If the AutoText entry you want to use is in a special template, base your document on that template.
2. Position the insertion point where you want to insert the entry.
3. Choose **Edit AutoText**.
4. Double-click the AutoText entry in the AutoText Name list, or select the entry and then click **Insert** or press **Enter**.

TIP

If you know the name of the AutoText entry you want, you can insert it this way: position the insertion point, type the name of the AutoText entry, then press F3. Word replaces the AutoText name with the contents of the entry. If you want to insert the AutoText entry at the end of other text, make sure you add a space, tab, or paragraph mark before typing the entry name so that the program can recognize the name as a separate word.

Using AutoText Entries

CHECK YOURSELF

How would you save your name and address as an AutoText entry?
▲ First, type and format your name and address, then select all the lines. Next, choose **Edit AutoText**, type **address** (or another name) in the Name box, and click **Add**. When you want to insert the AutoText entry, you can just type **address** and press **F3**, as described in the preceding Tip.

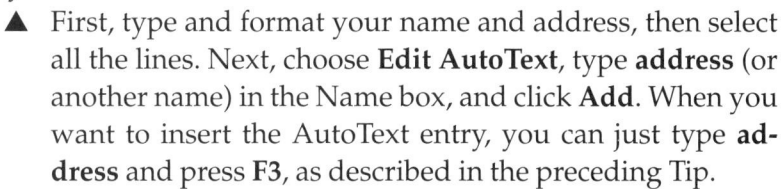

Changing an AutoText Entry

To change an AutoText entry:

1. Select the information you want an existing AutoText entry to contain.
2. Choose **Edit AutoText**.
3. Select the name of the entry that you want to contain the selected information.
4. Click the **Add** button. Word displays this message: "Do you want to redefine the AutoText entry?"
5. Click **Yes** or press **Y**. Word replaces the entry's contents with the information you selected in your file.

Deleting an AutoText Entry

You can delete AutoText entries that you no longer use.

To delete an AutoText entry:

1. Choose **Edit AutoText**.
2. Select the name of the entry you want to delete from the AutoText Name list.

3. Click **Delete.** Word changes the Cancel button to "Close."
4. Repeat Steps 2 and 3 to delete as many entries as you like.
5. Click **Close** or press **Enter** to save your changes and close the dialog box.

Printing AutoText Entries

If you want to print a copy of the AutoText entries attached to a file, use the following procedure.

To print AutoText entries:

1. If necessary, open the template (DOT file) containing the AutoText entries you want to print.
2. Choose **File Print**.
3. Select **AutoText Entries** from the drop-down Print What list, then click **OK** or press **Enter** to print the AutoText entries.

Word prints AutoText entries in alphabetic order. The printed page includes not only the entry names but also their contents.

Using Revision Marks

When you need to keep track of several versions of a document, you can use revision marks to mark changes in a document before the actual corrections are made. When you turn on revision marking, Word will:

▲ Mark any new text you insert with a format you specify (such as an underline).
▲ Mark text you delete with the strikethrough format, without deleting the text from the document.
▲ Insert revision bars in the margin next to each line you change (if you request this).

Revision marks indicate only changes to words, not any changes in formatting—such as bold, italic, indents, and so forth. Figure 4.4 shows an example of revision marks in a Word document.

Using Revision Marks

▼ **Figure 4.4. Revision Marks Added by Word**

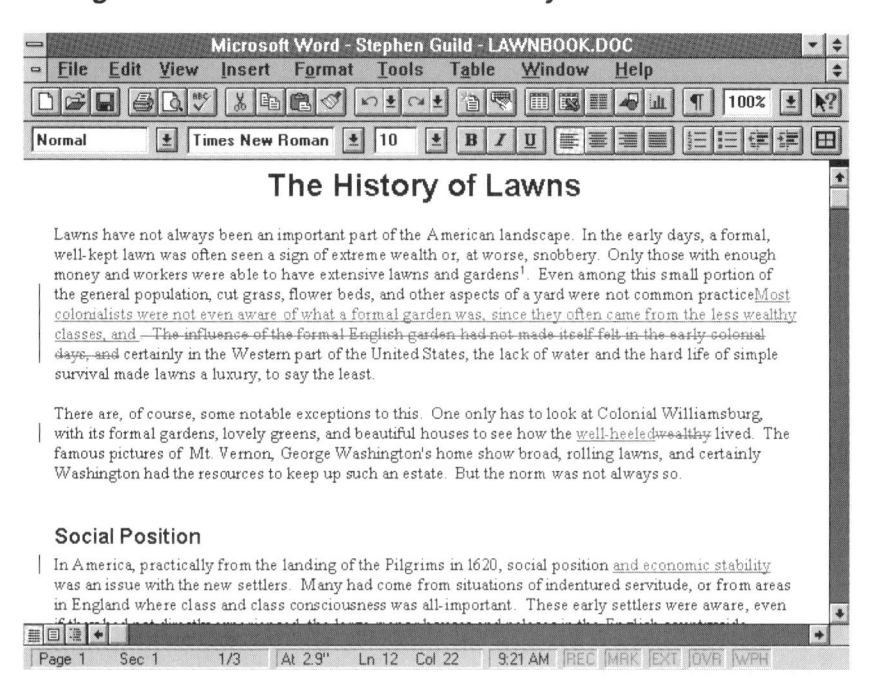

Activating Revision Marking

To begin revision marking:

1. Choose **Tools Revisions**.
2. Turn on the **Mark Revisions While Editing** check box.
   - ▲ If you want the revisions to appear on your screen, turn on the **Show Revisions on Screen** check box.
   - ▲ If you want the revisions to be printed, turn on the **Show Revisions in Printed Document** check box.
3. To determine the display of the inserted text, the revised text, and the revision bars, choose **Options** and make your choices in the Revisions tab:
   - ▲ In the Inserted Text box, choose the mark (Nothing, Bold, Italic, Underline, Double Underline) from the drop-down list you want Word to use for any text you add to the document. For example, if you select Italic, Word formats all inserted text as italic. Choose the color of the revision marks from the drop-down list. (You can have a different color revision mark for each new person entering his or her name in the Tools Option User Info tab.)

▲ In the Deleted Text box, choose the mark (Strikethrough or Hidden) from the drop-down list you want Word to use for any text you remove from the document. For example, if you select Strikethrough, Word marks all deleted text with a strikethrough. Choose the color of the deleted text mark from the drop-down list. (You can have a different color revision mark for each new person entering his or her name in the Tools Option User Info tab.)

▲ In the Revised Lines box, select one of the following options from the Mark drop-down list:

Option	Action
None	Does not add revision bars.
Left Border	Inserts revision bars in the left margin, next to every line you change.
Right Border	Inserts revision bars in the right margin, next to every line you change.
Outside Border	Inserts revision bars in the right margin on odd-numbered pages and in the left margin on even-numbered pages, next to every line you change.

You can also choose the color of the revision line. If your document has multiple columns, Word inserts revision lines beside the column containing the edited line.

4. Click **OK** or press **Enter**. Word displays MRK in the status bar to remind you that revision marking is turned on.

You can hide the revision marks by turning on the Hide Marks check box. After you have activated revision marking, edit the document. Word marks the revisions according to your instructions. When you're finished editing, you (or someone else) will want to review the changes; then approve the changes and make them individually or all at once, or reject the changes and delete all the revision marks. If you want to accept some changes and reject others, search for the portions of text that have been revised, as described in the following section.

Searching for Revised Text

Using Revision Marks

To review revisions made while revision marking is active, you can use the following procedure. You can choose to make the revision as marked; reject the revision and remove the marks; skip over the revision but leave it marked for later action; or make a different correction of your own.

To find text marked with revision marking:

1. Choose **Tools Revisions**.
2. Choose **Review**. Choose **Find** in the direction you want Word to select the first revised line. If necessary, drag the dialog box out of the way so you can see the revision.
3. Do one of the following:
   ▲ To make the change as marked, click **Accept**.
   ▲ To reject the change and remove the revision marks from the selected text, click **Reject**.
   ▲ To leave the selected text alone and move to the next revision, click **Find** in the direction you want Word to select again.
4. If you make a mistake and want to undo the previous change you made, click the **Undo Last** button
5. If you want Word to find the next revision automatically, turn on the **Find Next After Accept/Reject** check box.
6. If you want to hide the revision marks, choose **Hide Marks**.
7. To close the dialog box, click **Close** or press **Esc**.

Making All Marked Changes

When you have reviewed the changes and accepted them, you can make the changes all at once—in part or all of the document.

To make the marked changes:

1. Select the part of your document where you want to make the changes and remove the marks. To select the entire document, hold down **Ctrl** and click the left mouse button while the pointer is in the selection bar, or press **Ctrl+5** on the numeric keypad.

2. Choose **Tools Revisions**.
3. Click **Accept All**. Word deletes any text marked with strikethrough lines or hidden text, removes the special format (italic, for example) you specified for revised text, and removes revision bars from the margins.
4. Click **OK** or press **Enter** to close the dialog box.

Rejecting All Marked Changes and Removing Revision Marks

To reject the marked changes and remove the revision marks:

1. Select the part of your document where you want to remove the marks. If you want to select the entire document, hold down **Ctrl** and click the left mouse button while the pointer is in the selection bar, or press **Ctrl+5** on the numeric keypad.
2. Choose **Tools Revisions**.
3. Click **Reject All**. Word deletes any text inserted while revision marking was turned on, removes the strikethrough or hidden text format from all text, and removes revision bars from the margins.
4. Click **OK** or press **Enter** to close the dialog box.

Turning Off Revision Marking

Word continues to mark revisions as long as the Mark Revisions While Editing check box is turned on.

When you want to quit marking revisions and return to normal editing:

1. Choose **Tools Revisions**.
2. Turn off the **Mark Revisions While Editing** check box.
3. Click **OK** or press **Enter**.

Comparing Versions

If you work on a document over a long period, you may want to save several different versions of that document. You may also end up with several versions of a document if different people work on the same document. Word can quickly compare two versions of a document and add change bars beside the lines that don't match.

Comparing Versions

To compare two versions of a document:

1. Open the file to which you want Word to add change bars.
2. Choose **Tools Revision** and choose **Compare Versions**.
3. Type the name of the second file you want to compare in the Original File Name box, including any drive letters or pathnames that Word needs to find the file. (Or select the directory containing the file you want to compare from the Directories list, then select the file you want from the Original File Name list.)
4. Click **OK** or press **Enter**. Word compares the two files and adds underlining and change bars to the lines that are different in the open file. (You can remove the marks by using the Tools Revision Marks commands.)

You can also merge revisions from two different documents.

To merge revisions of two different documents:

1. Open the file to which you want Word to merge the revisions.
2. Choose **Tools Revisions** and choose **Merge Revisions**.
3. Type the name of the second file you want to compare in the Original File Name box, including any drive letters or pathnames that Word needs to find the file. (Or select the directory containing the file you want to compare from the Directories list, then select the file you want from the Original File Name list.)
4. Click **OK** or press **Enter**. Word compares the two files and adds underlining and change bars to the lines that are different in the open file. (You can remove the marks by using the Tools Revision Marks commands. See the previous section in this chapter.)

Using Annotations

If you want to add comments to a Word document created by another person, you can use a special form of footnotes called annotations.

Like footnotes, annotations are indicated by reference marks—in this case, the commentator's initials and a number—at specific locations in the document text, as shown in Figure 4.5. These reference marks tell the reader to look for comments at the bottom of the printed page or (when viewing it on the screen) at the end of the document.

As a reference mark, Word uses the initials given to Word on that computer during the setup process. You can use different initials during the annotating process by choosing Tools Options, clicking the User Info tab, and then changing the initials.

To add annotations:

1. Move the insertion point to where you want to enter an annotation.
2. Choose **Insert Annotation**. Word inserts a reference mark and moves the insertion point to an annotation pane at the bottom of the screen, as shown in Figure 4.5.
3. Type the annotation text.
4. To insert more annotations, move the insertion point (press **F6**, then use the arrow keys; or point and click with the mouse) to

▼ *Figure 4.5. Adding Annotations to a Document*

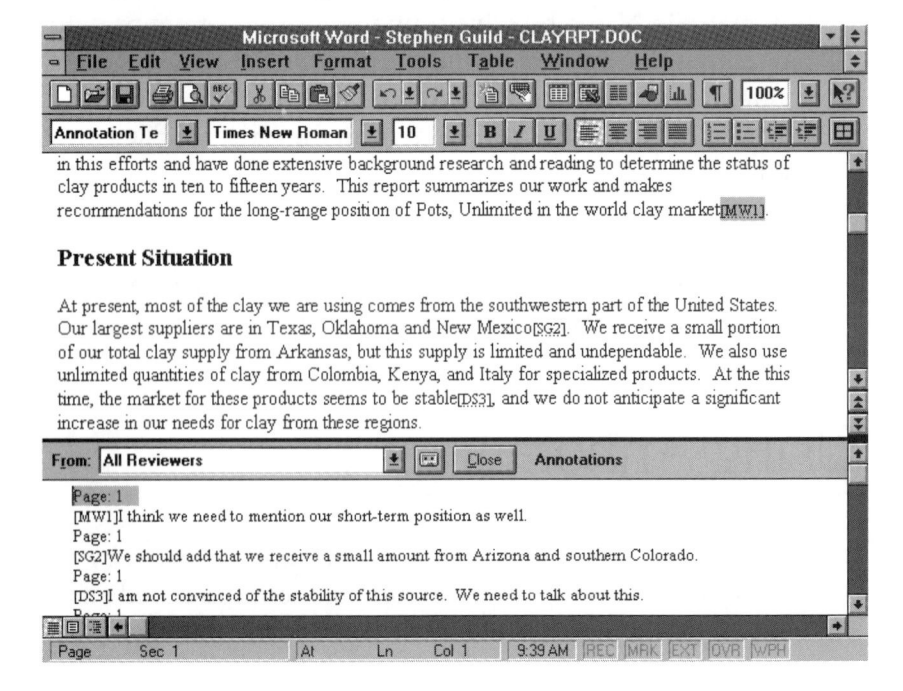

the next place in the document where you want to insert a comment, then repeat Steps 1 through 3.
5. When you're through entering annotations, click the **Close** button in the annotations pane.

Using Annotations

Viewing Annotations

Annotation marks are formatted as hidden text.

To view annotations:

Do one of the following:
▲ Choose **Tools Options**, click the **View** tab, and turn on the **Hidden Text** or **All** check box.
▲ Choose the **View Annotations** command.

Word displays annotation marks and opens the annotations pane at the bottom of the Word window.

You can edit and format annotations just as you would any other text.

TIP

You can double-click an annotation mark (the initials) to display the annotations pane.

Moving Between Annotation Marks and Annotation Text

You can use the mouse, Edit Go To, or the F5 key to move the insertion point quickly to the next annotation mark or back and forth between annotation marks and their associated text:

To Jump to	*Do This*
An annotation mark	Choose **Edit Go To** or press **F5**, then type **a** followed by the number of the annotation mark to which you want to jump (**a5** to jump to the fifth

To Jump to	Do This
	annotation mark, for example), then press **Enter**.
The text associated	Double-click the annotation mark, or with an annotation mark select the mark and choose **View Annotations**.
The annotation mark associated with annotation text	Double-click the annotation mark (the initials) in the annotation pane; or move the insertion point into the annotation text in the annotations pane, then press **F5**.

Deleting Annotations

To delete annotations:

1. Select the annotation mark.
2. Press the **Delete** key. Word automatically deletes both the reference mark and the annotation text.

Locking a File to Add Only Annotations

The author of a document or template can lock that file so that others can add only annotations. This prevents others from making changes to the file. To determine the author of a file, Word compares the initials associated with the file and the initials given to Word during the setup process. You can check the author of a file by choosing File Summary Info. You can change the author's name in the Tools Options User Info tab.

To lock a file so that others can add only annotations:

1. Choose **Tools Protect Document**.
2. Click the **Annotations** button.
3. Click **OK** or press **Enter**.
4. Choose **File Save** to save the file or click the **Save** button on the Standard toolbar.

Power Editing ▲ 103

To unlock the file, follow the same procedure, but turn off the Annotations button.

Using Annotations

Printing Annotations

To print annotations:

1. Choose **File Print**.
2. To print the annotations in the document, click the **Options** button, and then turn on the **Annotations** check box in the Include with Document box. (Or, to print only Annotations, select annotations from the drop-down Print What list in the Print dialog box.)
3. Click **OK** or press **Enter**.

Adding Bookmarks

An easy way to mark a specific item or section so that you can easily return to it is to add a *bookmark*. In Word, a bookmark is an invisible name tag that you add to selected text. Bookmarks can mark selected text, graphics, and tables or rows within a table.

When you define a bookmark, you give a specific name to a specific location. For example, you might want to assign the name STATS to a table of statistics so that you could easily find the table again. You can also use bookmarks to set up fields that will automatically keep track of page numbers. You will learn more about fields in Chapter 18.

To add a bookmark:

1. Select the text that you want to include in the bookmark.
2. Choose **Edit Bookmark**.
3. Type the name for the bookmark in the dialog box. The name must start with a letter. It can contain only letters, numbers, and underlines (no spaces) and not more than 40 characters.
4. Click **Add**. Figure 4.6 illustrates how to add a bookmark.

Don't expect to see anything new on the screen. Bookmarks are invisible.

▼ **Figure 4.6. Tagging Text with a Bookmark**

When you want to find text that you've bookmarked, use the following procedure:

1. Choose **Edit Bookmark**. Word displays a list of bookmarks in the document.
2. Double-click the name of the bookmarked text you want to jump to, or choose **Edit Go To**.

To delete a bookmark when the Bookmark dialog box is open:

1. Select the name of the bookmark in the list.
2. Click the **Delete** button. Word removes the invisible bookmark tags from the text but leaves the text intact.

QUICK COMMAND SUMMARY

Command	To Do This
Edit Find	Search for text, formatting, special characters, or styles.
Shift+F4	Repeat a search after the Find dialog box has been closed.

Command	To Do This
Edit Replace	Replace text, formatting, special characters, or styles.
Edit AutoText	Add entries to an AutoText or insert AutoText entries.
F3	Insert the AutoText entry whose name you just typed.
Tools Revisions	Add, review, or delete revision marks.
Insert Annotation	Add an annotation.
View Annotations	Display annotation text.
Edit Go To, or F5	Jump to annotations.
Edit Bookmark	Tag selected text with a book mark, jump to bookmarked text, or delete a bookmark.

PRACTICE WHAT YOU'VE LEARNED

Open the memo you created earlier in this chapter and add the following paragraph:

Please reserve all day Friday for the big meeting. If you need directions on how to get to the meeting, call 999-0077.

Turn on revision marking and set new text to italic. Next, use Edit Replace to change *meeting* to *conference*. Observe the differences, then accept all the changes to make the revisions final.

What You Do

1. Use **File Open** or the **Open** button to open the memo, then type the text shown above.

2. Choose **Tools Revision Marks**, and turn on the **Mark Revisions While Editing** check box.

What You'll See

1. The Open dialog box, if you used the command, and then the memo text in the document window.

2. The Revisions dialog box with the various options to use while marking revisions.

What You Do

3. Turn on **Italic** for new text, then click **OK** to return to your document.

4. Choose **Edit Replace**, type **meeting** in the Find What box, type **conference** in the Replace With box, and then click **Replace All** to make the changes.

5. Choose **Tools Revision Marks**, and then click the **Accept All** button.

What You'll See

3. The Revision tab in Tools Options and the Inserted Text drop-down list with Italic selected.

4. The Replace dialog box, which is an extension of the Find dialog box, and the text you enter in the two boxes.

5. The Revisions dialog box again and then the text marked with italic changes to regular text when you click Accept All.

5

Checking Spelling and Word Usage

After you've finished revising your document, you'll probably want to check the spelling. If you use one word too frequently, you might want to substitute some synonyms. And if you're submitting your masterpiece for publication, you'll need a word count. In this chapter, you will learn how to:

- ▲ Use Word's spelling checker
- ▲ Use the thesaurus
- ▲ Count words and characters automatically
- ▲ Use the grammar checker

Checking Spelling

You can use Word's built-in spelling checker to detect typing errors and spelling mistakes. The spelling checker compares words in your document with those in its main dictionary or in a dictionary you create. It also checks for repeated words (like *an an*) and for mistakes in capitalization (like *hEre* or *washington*).

Word's spelling checker is relatively sophisticated, but it can't do all your work for you. To test whether a word is spelled correctly, the spelling checker compares each word in your document with words in its dictionaries. If there's a match, it assumes that the word is correct. So if you type *too* when you mean *two*, the spelling checker won't catch that error. Word also won't tell you whether numbers or single letters surrounded by spaces are wrong, because its main dictionary contains all the letters of the alphabet and all numbers.

You can check the spelling of:

▲ An entire document. Word checks the spelling in a document from the insertion point to the end of the document, so you probably want to move the insertion point to the beginning of the document before you start the checking process.

▲ Selected text. You can select a single word or a block of text for Word to check. This is especially handy if you've just added a small portion of text to a document that you've already checked for spelling mistakes.

When you check grammar, as described under "Checking the Grammar in Your Document" later in this chapter, Word checks the spelling in your document as well as grammatical and style problems.

Beginning the Spelling Check

To begin a spelling check in a document:

1. Move the insertion point to the place where you want to begin checking, or select text if necessary.
2. Choose **Tools Spelling**.

Checking Spelling

3. When the spelling checker encounters a word that is not in its main dictionary, it displays the dialog box shown in Figure 5.1. (If all words in the text match words in the dictionary, Word displays a message telling you that the spelling check is complete.)
4. Click an appropriate button to deal with the word and continue checking spelling. See the next section, "What to Do When Word Finds a Term Not in Its Dictionary," for more information about the various options.
5. If you want to specify more options, choose **Options** to display the Options dialog box, then do the following:
   ▲ If you want Word always to suggest alternatives, turn on **Always Suggest**.
   ▲ If you want Word to suggest words that are found only in Word's main dictionary, turn on **From Main Dictionary Only**.
   ▲ If you don't want Word to check words typed in all capital letters, turn on the **Ignore Words in UPPERCASE** check box. Turning on this feature can save a lot of time if your

▼ *Figure 5.1. The Spelling Dialog Box*

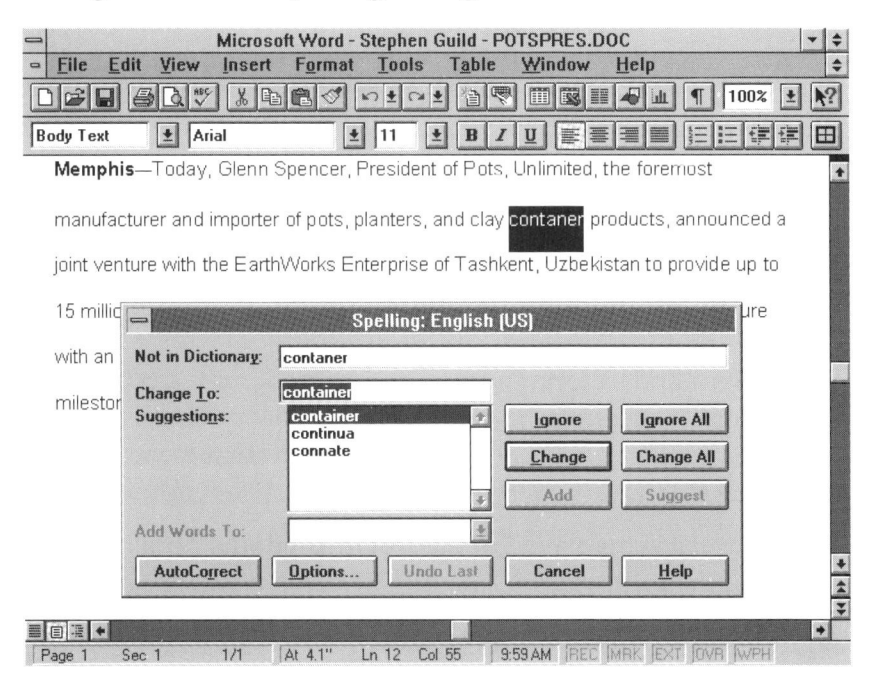

text is filled with acronyms (such as NASA, NYC, EPA, and so on).
- ▲ If you want to ignore words that include numbers, such as 20mg, 1040X, or 4F, turn on the **Ignore Words with Numbers** check box.
- ▲ To open a custom dictionary, select a new dictionary from the Custom Dictionaries drop-down list. You can find out more about using different dictionaries later in this chapter.

When the spelling check is finished, Word displays a message telling you that the spelling check is complete.

TIP

To use the default settings in the Spelling dialog box, select the text you want to check, then press F7. Word immediately begins checking the spelling.

CHECK YOURSELF

Correct a sentence with a misspelled word.
- ▲ Choose **Tools Spelling**, then choose the correct word and click **Change** or **Change All**.

What to Do When Word Finds a Term Not in Its Dictionary

When Word finds a term that is not in its dictionary, the unrecognized word is displayed in the Not in Dictionary box. The word may not actually be misspelled; this just means that the word does not match anything in Word's dictionary.

When a word is displayed in the Not in Dictionary box, you can do any of the following:

- ▲ Ignore the word and continue checking by clicking **Ignore**. You'll want to do this when Word displays names of people or

Checking Spelling

places, or specialized terminology that you don't want to save in a dictionary. If you want to ignore all occurrences of the word, choose **Ignore All**.

▲ Type the correct spelling in the Change To box and click the **Change** button. If you want to change all occurrences of the word, click **Change All**.

▲ Ask Word to suggest alternative spellings by clicking the **Suggest** button if necessary, then select a spelling from the Suggestions list and click the **Change** or **Change All** button. Word displays a list of alternatives in the Suggestions list. If Word can't find any alternatives, it displays a message telling you so. If this happens, or if none of the alternatives is correct, type the correct spelling in the Change To box, then click the **Change** or **Change All** button.

▲ Add the word to a personal dictionary that appears in the Add Words To drop-down list. For example, if your business uses certain terms not normally found in Word's dictionary, you may want to create your own dictionary containing these terms; then you can use that dictionary to check selected documents. See "Using Your Own Dictionaries" later in this chapter for more information about creating and using your own dictionaries.

▲ If you make a mistake and want to undo the previous change you made, click the **Undo Last** button.

▲ Click **Cancel** or press **Esc** to return to the document.

Using AutoCorrect

If you regularly misspell certain words, such as *adn* for *and* and *teh* for *the*, you can speed up the spell-checking process by adding these words to the AutoCorrect list. When you encounter one of these words during the spelling check, type the correct spelling in the Change To box and then click the **AutoCorrect** button and choose **Yes**. The next time the spelling checker encounters one of the words on the AutoCorrect list, it will automatically correct the word while you are typing.

You can also add words to the AutoCorrect and specify other AutoCorrect options by using the Tools AutoCorrect command. You can change straight quotes (") to "Smart Quotes" (" "); change the two initial capital letters in a word, such as TRouble in TAhiti; and make sure the first letters of sentences and the names of days are always capitalized.

Checking Foreign Words

If your document contains foreign words as well as English words, you can check spelling in both languages by marking the foreign language words. When you do a spelling check, these words will be checked against the proper language dictionary. For this to occur, however, the dictionary for that language must be in the Winword directory, and the correct information must be in the WIN.INI.

To mark foreign words:

1. Select the words.
2. Choose **Tools Language** and select the appropriate language from the list in the dialog box.
3. Click **OK**.

Using Your Own Dictionaries

You can't alter Word's main dictionary, but you can create your own specialized dictionaries and use them as well as the main dictionary to check your documents. When you choose Tools Spelling, Word opens the main dictionary. If you want to use a dictionary with your own special terms or words, you can create one as explained below.

To create a new personal dictionary:

1. Choose **Tools Options**, then click the **Spelling** tab.
2. In the Custom Dictionaries area, click **New** and then type the name for your dictionary in the File Name box, using a DIC extension. For example, you might type **MATH.DIC** or **LEGAL.DIC**.
3. Click **OK** or press **Enter**. Word adds the filename to the Custom Dictionaries list.

When you choose Tools Spelling, the name of the new dictionary appears in the Custom Dictionaries list with a check box beside it. When you want to use one or more custom dictionaries, just click the check boxes. If a dictionary has been created but does not appear on the Custom Dictionaries list, choose **Add** and select that dictionary.

You can also open the DIC file and add, correct, or delete words within the file itself by clicking the **Edit** button. Word automatically saves any changes you make to dictionaries.

If you are not currently spell-checking, you can also add, edit, or remove dictionaries by choosing **Tools Options** and clicking the **Spelling** tab.

Checking Spelling

Using the Thesaurus

If you use the same word repeatedly in a document, your writing can become monotonous. To introduce some variety, use the thesaurus to look up synonyms for frequently used words.

Looking Up Synonyms for a Word

You can select a word in your document and then look up synonyms for the word. The Thesaurus dialog box shows a definition for each synonym, so you can choose the word that has the most appropriate shade of meaning.

To look up synonyms for a word:

1. Select the word.
2. Choose **Tools Thesaurus** or press **Shift+F7**. The Thesaurus dialog box appears with a list of synonyms for the selected word, as shown in Figure 5.2. If the word is not in the thesaurus, Word displays an approximate word and the grayed-text message "No synonyms" in the Replace with Synonym box. Make sure you've spelled the selected word correctly.
3. Do one of the following:
    ▲ To replace the selected word with a synonym, select a word from the Replace with Synonyms list, then click **Replace**.

▼ **Figure 5.2. The Thesaurus Dialog Box Listing Synonyms for a Word**

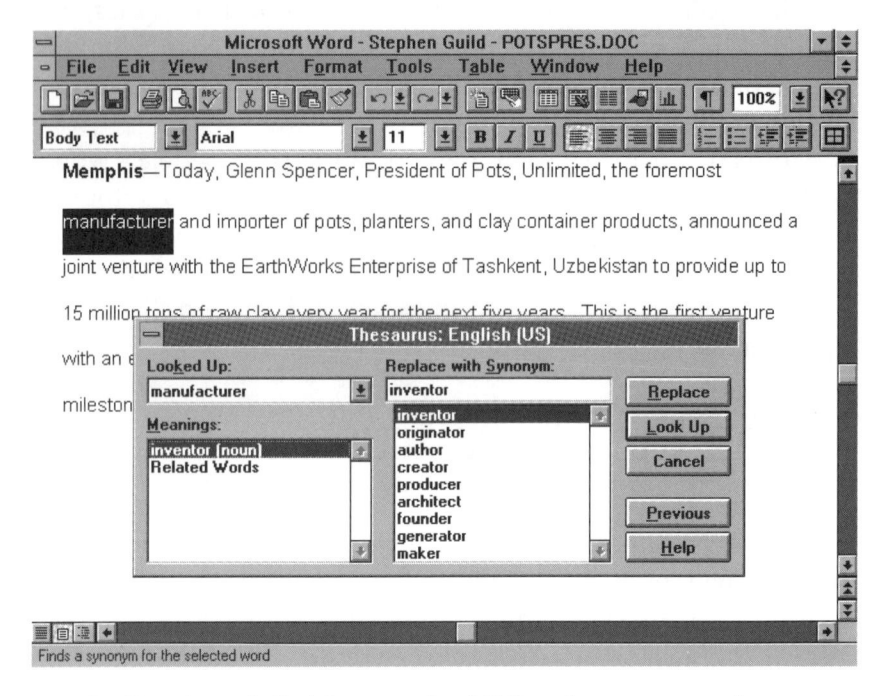

▲ To view definitions and additional synonyms for a synonym, select a word from the Replace with Synonyms list, then click **Look Up** to display definitions in the Meanings list. You can also display Antonyms and Related Words by selecting these terms in the Meanings box.
▲ To see the previous meaning or synonym, click **Previous**.
▲ To close the Thesaurus dialog box, choose **Cancel** or press **Esc**.

Counting Characters or Words in Your Document

You may sometimes want to know how many characters or words your document contains.

To find out how many characters or words your document contains:

▲ Choose **File Summary Info** and click **Statistics**.
▲ Choose **Tools Word Count**.

CHECK YOURSELF

Replace a word in a paragraph with a word with a similar meaning.
   ▲ Select a word and choose **Tools Thesaurus**. Choose a different word and click **Replace**.

Checking the Grammar in Your Document

Word has a built-in grammar checker that will examine your document and detect errors in grammar in sentences or in phrases. Word will also check spelling as it is checking the grammar. At the end of the check, a Readability Statistics box appears, showing the number of passive sentences used, reading ease and grade level, and an index of sentence length and clarity.

To check the grammar in a document:

1. Place the insertion point where you want to begin, or select the portion you want to check.
2. Choose **Tools Grammar**.
3. When there is a suspected error, the sentence appears in the Grammar dialog box, as shown in Figure 5.3. You can indicate your preference by doing one of the following:

To	*Do This*
Make a suggested correction	Select a correction in the Suggestions box and click the **Change** button.
Type a correction in the document	Click in the document window, edit the sentence, and then click the **Start**

▼ ***Figure 5.3. The Grammar Dialog Box***

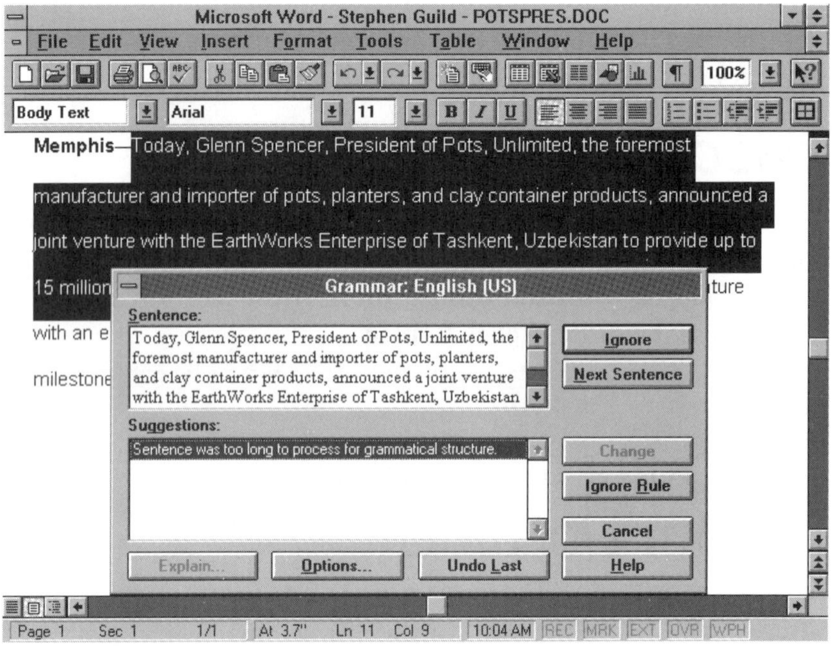

To	***Do This***
	button in the Grammar dialog box.
Skip a suggestion	Click the **Ignore** button for that occurrence only, or click **Ignore Rule** to bypass all occurrences of the possible error.
Leave the present sentence unchanged	Click the **Next Sentence** button.
Get more information about the error	Click the **Explain** button and read the description in the Explain dialog box.
Change the rules of style and grammar	Click the **Options** button.
Change the last action	Click the **Undo Last** button.

4. When you click the **Options** button, Word displays the Tools Options Grammar tab.

Checking the Grammar in Your Document

- ▲ You can choose Strictly (All Rules); For Business Writing; For Casual Writing; or Custom 1, Custom 2, or Custom 3 rules in the Use Grammar and Style Rules box.
- ▲ Click **Customize Settings** if you want to make specific changes to grammar rules. The Customize Grammar Settings dialog box, with a variety of options, will appear. Click on the **Grammar** and **Style** buttons and turn the corresponding check boxes on or off as desired, and then click **OK** or press **Enter**. If you click the Explain button, Word will display a separate window that contains an explanation of the grammar or style rule you have selected. Select another and the Explain list will switch to that rule. If you want to revert to the default settings, click **Reset**.
- ▲ In the Catch area you can specify rules for split infinitives, consecutive nouns, prepositional phrases, and sentences containing more than the number of words you specify. If you click the Explain button, Word will display a separate window that contains an explanation of the catch rule you have selected. Select another and the Explain list will switch to that rule. If you want to revert to the default settings, click **Reset**.

5. If you want to check spelling before checking the grammar, turn on the **Check Spelling** check box. If you want to know more about word and sentence count, number of passive sentences, and so forth, turn on the **Show Readability Statistics** box.
6. Click **OK** or press **Enter** and then click **OK** or press **Enter** again to return to the Grammar dialog box.
7. When the check is finished, click **OK** or press **Enter**. The Readability Statistics box will appear if you have checked this option in the Grammar category of the Options dialog box.

QUICK COMMAND SUMMARY

Command	To Do This
Tools Spelling, or Spelling Toolbar button	Display the Spelling dialog box, which controls the various spelling options.
F7 (with selected text)	Begin a spelling check of the selected text.

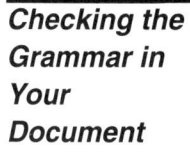

Command	To Do This
Format Language	Mark text as foreign language text.
Tools Thesaurus, or Shift+F7	Display the Thesaurus dialog box, which controls the various thesaurus options.
File Summary Info	Display the Summary Info dialog box, from which you can choose Statistics to get a word and character count in a document.
Tools Grammar	Display the Grammar dialog box, which controls the various grammar options.

PRACTICE WHAT YOU'VE LEARNED

Create a paragraph with some misspelled words, correct the misspellings, replace one of the words with a synonym, and then check the grammar.

What You Do	What You'll See
1. Type the text.	1. The text in the document window.
2. Select a word.	2. The highlighted text.
3. Choose **Tools Thesaurus**.	3. The Thesaurus dialog box with the various boxes displaying suggestions and word definitions.
4. Choose a different word.	4. The word you've selected highlighted in one of the lists.
5. Click **Replace**.	5. The selected word changed to the new word.

What You Do

6. Choose **Tools Grammar**.

7. Correct spelling and make any other desired corrections.

What You'll See

6. The Grammar box displayed with suggestion revisions, after a check of the entire document, including spelling.

7. The corrected text.

6

Character Formatting

Formatting that affects the individual letters, numbers, and symbols that you type is called *character formatting*. You can format one character, or all characters in your document at one time. In this chapter, you will learn how to:

- ▲ Change fonts and point sizes
- ▲ Use the Formatting toolbar to format characters
- ▲ Display hidden characters such as tabs and paragraph marks
- ▲ Use the Font dialog box
- ▲ Create subscripts and superscripts
- ▲ Insert symbols
- ▲ Copy character formatting

What Is Character Formatting?

Figure 6.1 shows all the formats you can add to characters. You can:

▲ Give characters the following formats: bold, italic, single (continuous) underline, word only (not spaces) underline, double underline, dotted underline, strikethrough, small capitals, all capitals, or "hidden."

▲ Make characters superscript and subscript. When you specify superscript or subscript characters, you can also set the amount of space between the baseline and the raised (superscript) or lowered (subscript) characters. The baseline is the invisible line the letters in a sentence "sit on." For example, the letters *w* and *c* sit on the baseline, whereas *p* and *g* have parts that descend beneath the baseline.

▲ Change fonts and sizes.

▲ Condense or expand spacing between letters and control the amount of space between letters.

▼ Figure 6.1. Font Formatting Examples

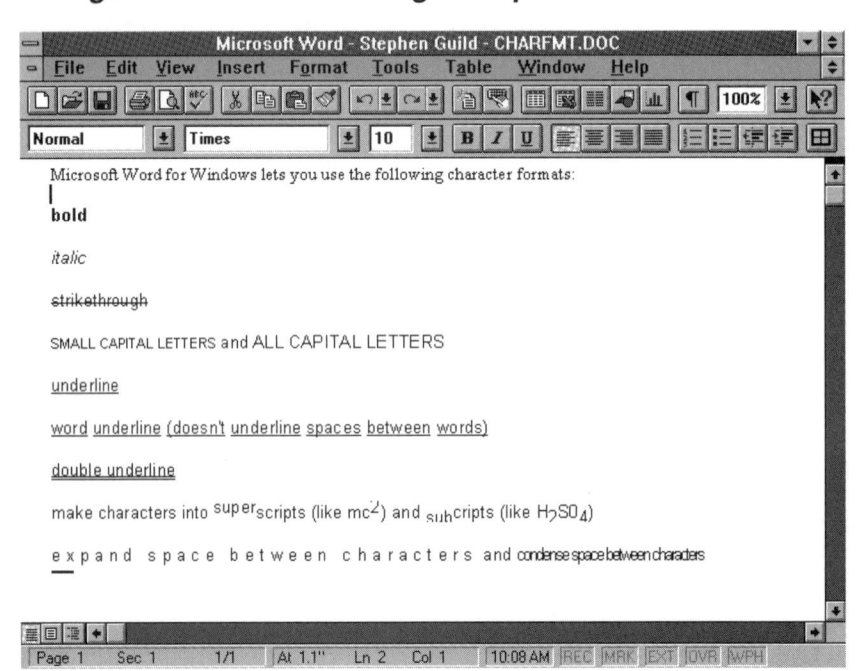

▲ Change letter cases. You can make all text lowercase, all text uppercase, or each word upper- and lowercase (title case). You can create the reverse of title case (which Word calls "toggle case").

What Is Character Formatting?

If you have a color monitor, you can also change the color of your text. Note that this changes the color of text only on your screen; the color won't print unless your printer is capable of producing multiple colors.

About Fonts and Font Sizes

A font is a family of characters that share a style—for example, very straight and simple (as in a Helvetica font) or very curvy and ornate (as in an Old English font). Figure 6.2 shows a variety of fonts.

Word uses three classes of fonts: scalable fonts, such as those available with TrueType and Adobe Type Manager; printer fonts,

▼ *Figure 6.2. A Variety of Fonts and Sizes*

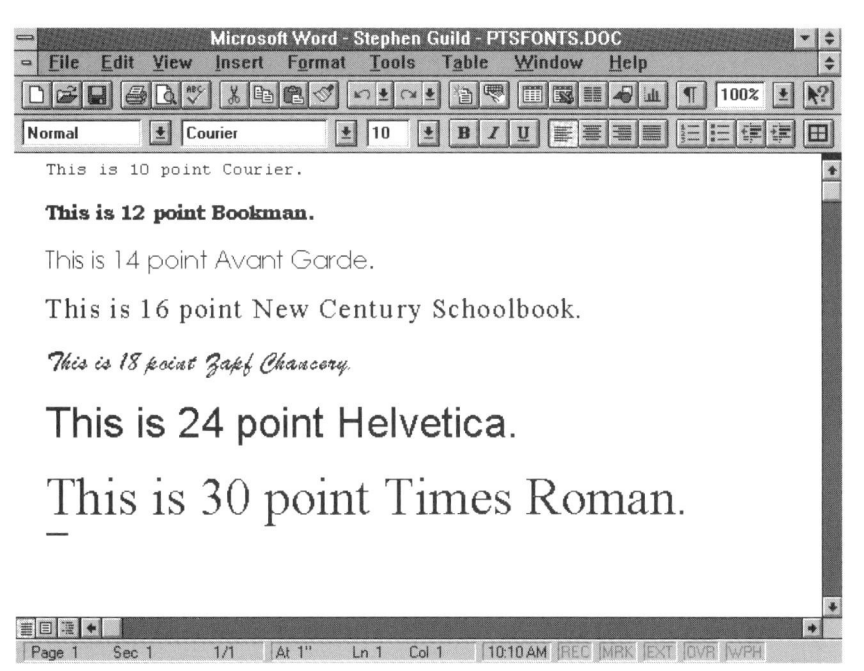

which come from the printer driver file that Word uses to control your particular printer; and screen fonts, which come from Windows.

Most fonts for Word are proportional fonts—that is, fonts in which the letters are of varying widths. For example, in a proportional font, an *M* takes up more space than an *I*. There are also a few fixed-width, or monospace, fonts. In these fonts, each character occupies exactly the same amount of space both on the screen and on paper. Generally speaking, you'll want to use proportional fonts for most documents and use fixed-width fonts only when you create text in which characters must align precisely within rows and columns (as in a computer program listing, for example).

Fonts come in different sizes, which are measured in *points*. A point is 1/72 inch. Because different fonts may have different sizes, you should always choose a font before you choose the point size for that font.

Word offers three methods to control the way characters look in your document: you can use the Formatting toolbar, the Font dialog box, or key combinations. All formatting is applied to the selected text. If nothing is selected, the formatting is applied beginning at the insertion point. Anything you type after that point will have the specified formatting.

Using the Formatting Toolbar

The Formatting toolbar (shown beneath the Standard toolbar in Figure 6.3) is a graphic device that helps you format characters with the mouse. You can display or remove the Formatting toolbar anytime you like. Using the Formatting toolbar, you can:

- ▲ Change styles.
- ▲ Change fonts and point sizes.
- ▲ Make characters bold, italic, or underlined.
- ▲ Align text and set tabs.
- ▲ Create numbered and bulleted lists.
- ▲ Decrease or increase the indentation of a paragraph.

To display the Formatting toolbar:

▲ Choose **View Toolbars** and turn on the **Formatting** check box.

Character Formatting ▲ 125

▼ *Figure 6.3. The Formatting Toolbar*

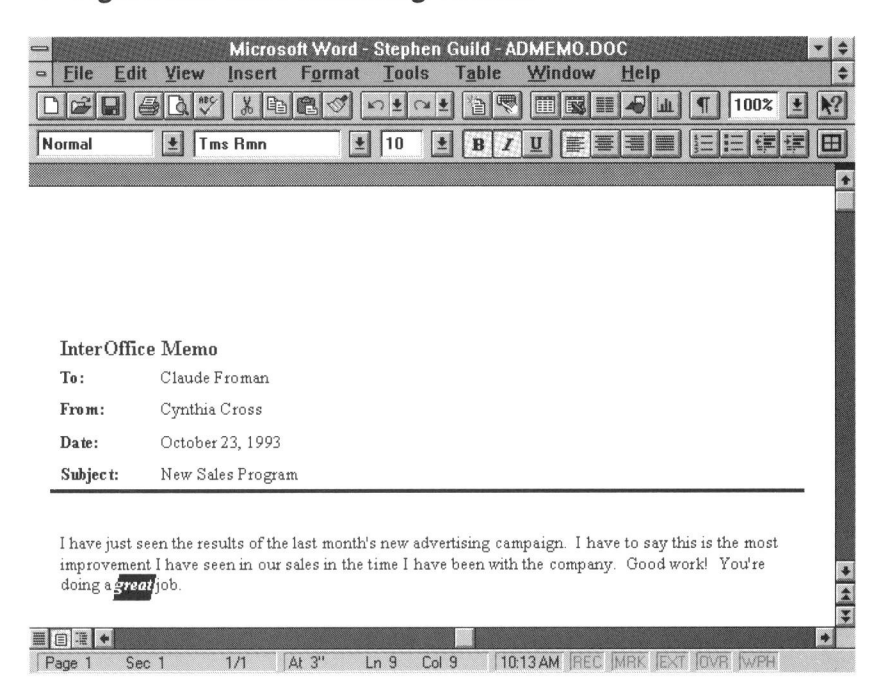

Using the Formatting Toolbar

The Formatting toolbar will also indicate the existing format of text you select. For example, if you select a word that has been formatted for bold, 14-point Helvetica type, the Font box displays Helv, the Font Size box displays 14, the bold icon is highlighted, and the Style box displays the paragraph style.

Choosing a New Font or Font Size

To choose a new font or point size with the Formatting toolbar:

1. Select the characters you want to change.
2. Click the arrow beside the Font box or Font Size box to drop down the list, then click the font or size you want. You can also type the font or point size you want in the Font or Font Size box.

Choosing Bold, Italic, or Underlined Format

To choose a format option from the Formatting toolbar:

1. Select the characters you want to change.

2. Click one of the buttons to choose bold, italic, or underline.

When you apply a format from the Formatting toolbar, Word "pushes" the button. To remove a format (such as bold), just click the button again.

CHECK YOURSELF

Make a word bold and change another word to 18-point Helvetica type.

▲ Select a word and click the **Bold** button. Select a second word and select **Helvetica** in the Font box and **18** in the Font Size box.

Displaying Hidden Formatting Characters with the Standard Toolbar

To display space marks (·), paragraph marks (¶), tab characters (→), and other hidden formatting characters with the Standard toolbar:

▲ Click the paragraph mark button (¶) at the right side of the Standard toolbar.

Figure 6.4 shows text with paragraph marks and tab characters displayed.

Using the Font Dialog Box

The Font dialog box is shown in Figure 6.5. This dialog box, which you display by choosing Format Font, allows you to select most of the formatting options you can apply with the Formatting toolbar—such as font, point size, bold, italic, and underline. The Font dialog box also enables you to control other formats that you can't apply with the Formatting toolbar. You can use the Font dialog box to:

▲ Specify the number of points by which to raise or lower text to create superscript or subscript text.

Character Formatting ▲ 127

▼ *Figure 6.4. Formatting Marks Displayed*

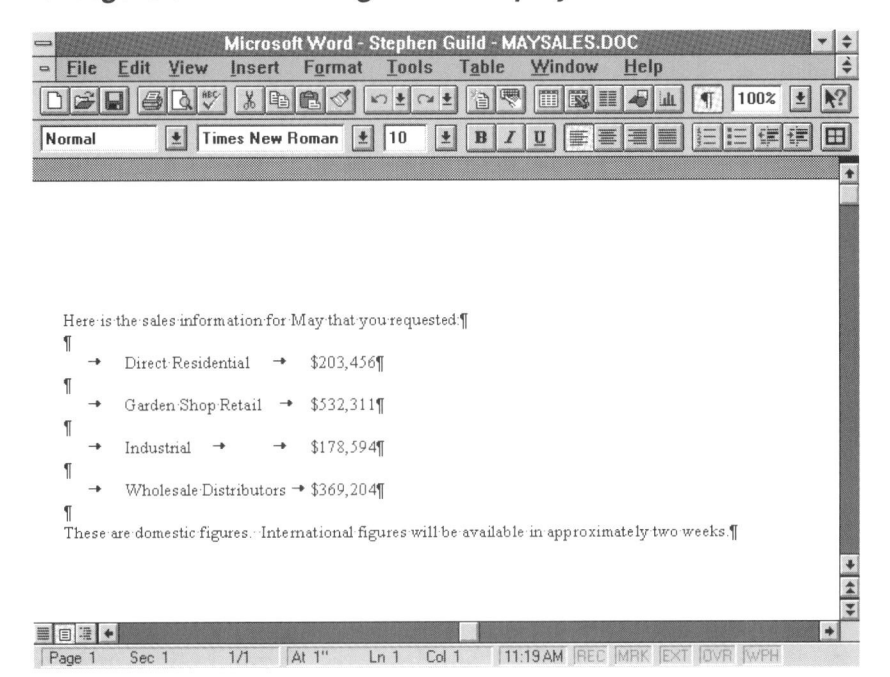

Using the Font Dialog Box

▼ *Figure 6.5. The Font Dialog Box*

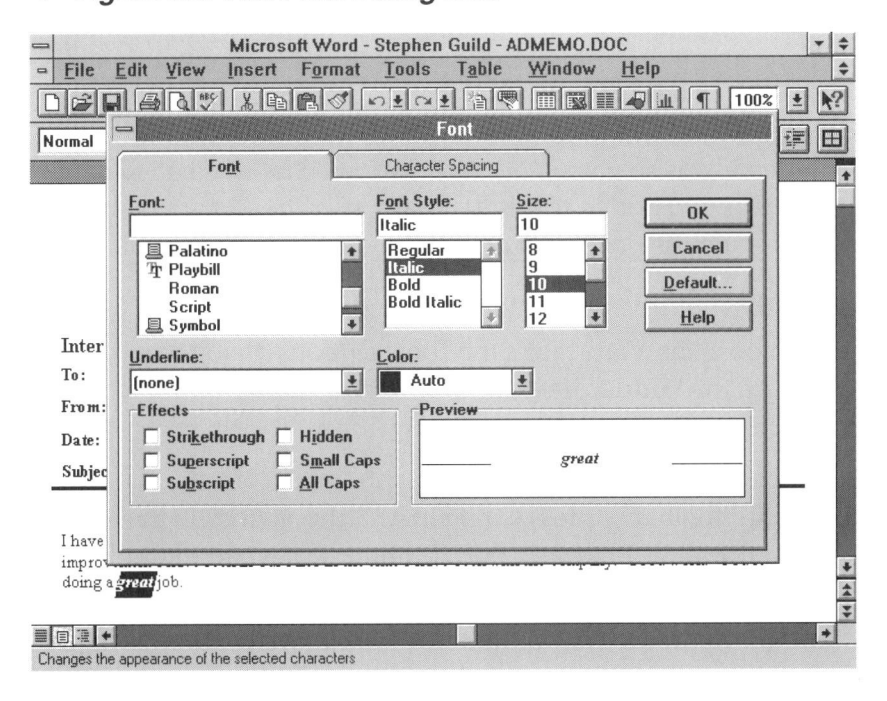

- ▲ Expand or compress text by controlling the amount of space between characters.
- ▲ Specify the color of the text.
- ▲ Format text as strikethrough, small capital letters, all capital letters, or hidden text.
- ▲ Choose four types of underlines: single, word only, double, and dotted.

To format characters with the Font dialog box:

1. Select the characters you want to format.
2. Choose **Format Font**.
3. Choose options in the dialog box.
4. Click **OK** or press **Enter**.

Changing the Color of Text

You can change the color of text on your monitor in two ways:

- ▲ By changing the color of "window text" through the Windows Control Panel, which changes all text.
- ▲ By formatting selected text in color with the Font dialog box.

Using Hidden Text

Hidden text is so named because you can choose when to hide or to display it. Hidden text is generally used to add annotations or codes—such as PostScript or index codes—to a document.

To display or hide hidden text:

1. Choose the **View** tab in the Tools Options dialog box.
2. Turn the **Hidden Text** check box on or off.
3. Click **OK** or press **Enter**.

You can also use the paragraph mark button (¶) on the Standard toolbar or press **Ctrl+Shift+*** (the asterisk in the number row of the main keyboard, not the numeric keypad multiplication key) to hide or display hidden text.

Word displays hidden text with a dotted underline in Page Layout and Normal views and with a solid underline when you are using draft font. Whether or not it's displayed, hidden text won't print unless you turn on the Hidden Text check box in the in the Tools Options Print tab. However, when hidden text is displayed, Word counts it to calculate page breaks. Therefore, if you don't want to include any text formatted as hidden when calculating page breaks, be sure to hide hidden text before choosing any command that causes Word to repaginate (such as the File Print, View Page Layout, or File Print Preview command).

Using the Font Dialog Box

Creating Superscript and Subscript Text

Word easily creates superscript text (text raised above the baseline) and subscript text (text lowered beneath the baseline). Superscript characters are commonly used in mathematical formulas, in trademark and copyright symbols, and as footnote reference marks:

```
The statue appeared to be an undiscovered
Michelangelo.1
```

Subscripts are frequently used in chemical equations such as H_2O and CO_2.

You can raise a superscript or lower a subscript from the baseline. Before you create super- or subscripts, you should be aware that using a large point size for those features may create uneven line spacing in paragraphs that contain superscript or subscript characters. Word bases line spacing on the character that extends farthest above or below the baseline in any line. Thus, when formatting superscripts or subscripts, you might want to choose a point size smaller than the surrounding text.

CHECK YOURSELF

Create a formula, such as $E=mc^2$, that has an 8-point superscript.
- ▲ Type **E=mc2** and select the number 2. Then choose **Format Font**, select **Superscript** in the Super/subscript list, and select **8** in the Font Size box.

Expanding or Condensing Text

You can expand or condense text by choosing Format Font, clicking the Character Spacing tab, selecting either Expanded or Condensed in the Spacing drop-down list, and typing or selecting a measurement (in points) in the By box to change the spacing between characters. You can type measurements in point increments, such as 4.75. You might want to expand or condense a few characters, a word, or a sentence to create a special effect in a headline or just to make the text fit better on a line. The sample in the dialog box shows you how your text will look.

Keyboard Shortcuts for Character Formatting

You can quickly apply character formats to selected text, without using the Formatting toolbar or choosing commands, by using the following key combinations:

To Apply This Format	Press
Bold	Ctrl+B
Italic	Ctrl+I
Underline	Ctrl+U
Word underline	Ctrl+Shift+W
Double underline	Ctrl+Shift+D
Small capitals	Ctrl+Shift+K
All capitals	Ctrl+Shift+A
Change letters to uppercase or lowercase	Shift+F3
Hidden text	Ctrl+Shift+H
Change font	Ctrl+Shift+F, type font name; or press Alt+Down arrow key to select font, then press Enter

To Apply This Format	Press
Change point size	Ctrl+Shift+P, type point size; or press Alt+Down arrow key to select size, then press Enter
Change to next larger point size	Ctrl+F2
Change to next smaller point size	Ctrl+Shift+F2
Superscript	Ctrl++ (plus sign)
Subscript	Ctrl+= (equal sign)
Display all characters	Ctrl+Shift+* (asterisk in the number row, not the numeric keypad)
Revert to plain text	Ctrl+Spacebar

Keyboard Shortcuts for Character Formatting

TIP

You can specify character formats before you type by choosing the format options with no text selected. Any text typed afterward will have the specified formats. For example, a speed typist might enter "keys can be faster" by pressing Ctrl+B **(for bold), typing** keys, **pressing** Ctrl+Spacebar **(for plain text), typing** can be, **pressing** Ctrl+I **(for italic), then typing** faster.

Changing the Case of Text

You can change the case of an individual word, or a whole sentence or paragraph, without having to retype the text. If you typed **notice** (all in lowercase) and then decided that you wanted it all uppercase, you could use Format Change Case to make the word all uppercase.

To change case of text:

1. Select the text.
2. Choose **Format Change Case**.

3. Click one of the options. The dialog box labels are examples of the options.
4. Click **OK** or press **Enter**.

Inserting Symbols

You can include symbols or special characters in your document if you want. Perhaps you need to refer to several Greek letters—Θ, Π, and Ω—in your text. Or say you want to include some special symbols—such as ✆, ✍, or ✂. You can insert a variety of symbols and special characters easily by using Insert Symbol.

To insert symbols or special characters:

1. Place the insertion point where you want to insert the symbol or special character.
2. Choose **Insert Symbol** click the **Symbols** tab. In the Font box, choose the name of the font that contains the symbols you want to use. The number of available fonts will depend upon the printer fonts you have installed on your computer.
3. If you want to insert a special character, choose the **Special Characters** tab. In the Character list box, click the special character you want to insert.
4. Click **Insert** or press **Enter**.

If you want to change the size of the symbol, you can do this by selecting the symbol and using the Font Size box in the Font dialog box or on the Formatting toolbar.

Copying Character Formatting

If you have a certain combination of character formats that you like (such as Bold Italic Helvetica 14), you can use that combination repeatedly without choosing all the character formatting commands each time. Once you have formatted some text the way you want it, you can use the mouse to copy the format to new text.

To copy character formatting with the mouse:

1. Select or format some text the way you want it.

2. Click the **Format Painter** button (the one that looks like a paintbrush) on the Standard toolbar. If you want to copy the format to several locations, double-click the button.
3. Select the next text you want to format and click the text. If you have double-clicked on the button, then click the rest of the text you want to format.
4. When you have finished, click the **Format Paintbrush** button or press **Esc**.

Copying Character Formatting

Removing Character Formatting

To remove character formatting:

▲ Press **Ctrl+Spacebar**

TIP

You can press the F4 **key or choose** Edit Repeat Formatting **to repeat the previous character format you used. For example, if you add italic, then add bold to a word, you can press** F4 **to add bold to another selected word.**

QUICK COMMAND SUMMARY

Command	To Do This
View Formatting toolbar	Display the Formatting toolbar at the top of the screen.
Paragraph mark button (¶)	Display space marks, paragraph marks, tab characters, and other hidden formatting characters.
Format Font	Display the Font dialog box, which controls the various character formatting options
Ctrl+B	Turn bold on or off.
Ctrl+I	Turn italic on or off.

Command	To Do This
Ctrl+U	Turn underline on or off.
Ctrl+Shift+W	Obtain word underline.
Ctrl+Shift+D	Obtain double underline.
Ctrl+Shift+K	Change to small capitals.
Ctrl+Shift+A	Change to all capitals.
Shift+F3	Change letters to uppercase or lowercase.
Ctrl+ Shift+H	Add or remove hidden text formatting.
Press Ctrl+Shift+F, type font name; or press Alt+Down arrow key to select font, then press Enter	Change font.
Press Ctrl+Shift+P, type point size; or press Alt+Down arrow key to select size, then press Enter	Change point size.
Ctrl+F2	Obtain next larger point size.
Ctrl+Shift+F2	Obtain next smaller point size.
Ctrl++ (plus sign)	Obtain 3-point superscript.
Ctrl+= (equal sign)	Obtain 3-point subscript.
Ctrl+Shift+* (asterisk)	Display all formatting characters.
Ctrl+Spacebar	Return to plain text.
Insert Symbol	Display the Symbol dialog box, which controls the various symbol options.
Ctrl+Shift+point and click character format.	Format the selected text with the same a character
Edit Repeat Formatting, or F4	Repeat the previous character format used.

PRACTICE WHAT YOU'VE LEARNED

Duplicate the following (using the Helvetica font):

Translators Wanted
40 hours per week.
Must be *fluent* in **Spanish**.
Call 999-6207.

What You Do	*What You'll See*
1. Type the text, then select all four lines of text.	1. The unformatted text in the document window.
2. Select the Helvetica font from the Formatting toolbar's Font box. (If this font isn't available on your printer, choose another.)	2. The Font drop-down list with "Helvetica" highlighted.
3. Select **Translators Wanted**.	3. The highlighted text.
4. Select **14** from the Formatting toolbar's Font Size box.	4. The Font Size drop-down list with "14" highlighted.
5. Click the **Underline** button and click the **Bold** button.	5. The Underline and Bold buttons on the Formatting toolbar changed to a light shade of gray to indicate it is in use, and the text underlined.
6. Select **fluent**.	6. The highlighted word *fluent*.
7. Click the **Italic** button.	7. The Italic button on the Formatting toolbar changed to a light shade of gray to indicate it is in use, and the selected text in italic.
8. Select **Spanish**.	8. The word *Spanish* is highlighted.
9. Click the **Bold** button.	9. The Bold button on the Formatting toolbar changed to a light gray to indicate it is in use, and the selected text in bold.

Paragraph Formatting

Paragraph formatting includes indenting, setting tabs, changing line spacing within and between paragraphs, and controlling how page breaks affect paragraphs. In this chapter, you will learn how to:

- ▲ Use the Formatting toolbar and the ruler for speedy formatting
- ▲ Format tabs
- ▲ Align paragraphs
- ▲ Change line spacing within and between paragraphs
- ▲ Add boxes, lines, and bars
- ▲ Control the locations of page breaks
- ▲ Control line numbers in paragraphs
- ▲ Copy paragraph formatting

What Is a Paragraph in Word?

In Word, a paragraph is anything (even a blank line) that ends with a paragraph mark. You insert a paragraph mark into your document every time you press the **Enter** key. Paragraph marks are always present, though they may be hidden. You can see them by choosing the View tab in Tools Options or the paragraph mark (¶) on the Standard toolbar.

TIP

Word stores a paragraph's format in the paragraph mark (¶). So, if you delete a paragraph mark, you'll lose the formatting attached to the paragraph, and the text will become part of the next paragraph.

Selecting Paragraphs

Before you can format paragraphs, you must select them. Selecting text is explained in Chapter 3, but here are a few reminders:

- ▲ If you want to format only one paragraph, you don't have to highlight it; just move the insertion point into the paragraph.
- ▲ Drag the mouse pointer in the selection bar to select several paragraphs.
- ▲ To select a paragraph, quickly double-click in the selection bar to the left of any line in the paragraph.
- ▲ To select every paragraph in the document, press **Ctrl+5** on the numeric keypad, or hold down the **Ctrl** key and click the left mouse button in the selection bar.

Using the Formatting Toolbar and the Ruler

The Formatting toolbar and the ruler are graphic devices you use to format paragraphs and see the results immediately. You can display and use the ruler any time you like. The Formatting toolbar and the ruler are shown in Figure 7.1.

To display the Formatting toolbar:

▲ Choose **View Toolbars** and turn on the **Formatting** check box.

To display the ruler:

▲ Choose **View Ruler**.

To hide the Formatting toolbar:

▲ Choose **View Toolbars** again and turn off the Formatting check box.

To hide the ruler:

▲ Choose **View Ruler** again.

The Formatting toolbar lets you format paragraphs in several ways. You can choose a style from the drop-down list or click a button to choose an alignment option. Styles, which can contain every element available for paragraph formatting, are covered in Chapter 8.

Using the Formatting Toolbar and the Ruler

▼ *Figure 7.1. The Formatting Toolbar and the Ruler*

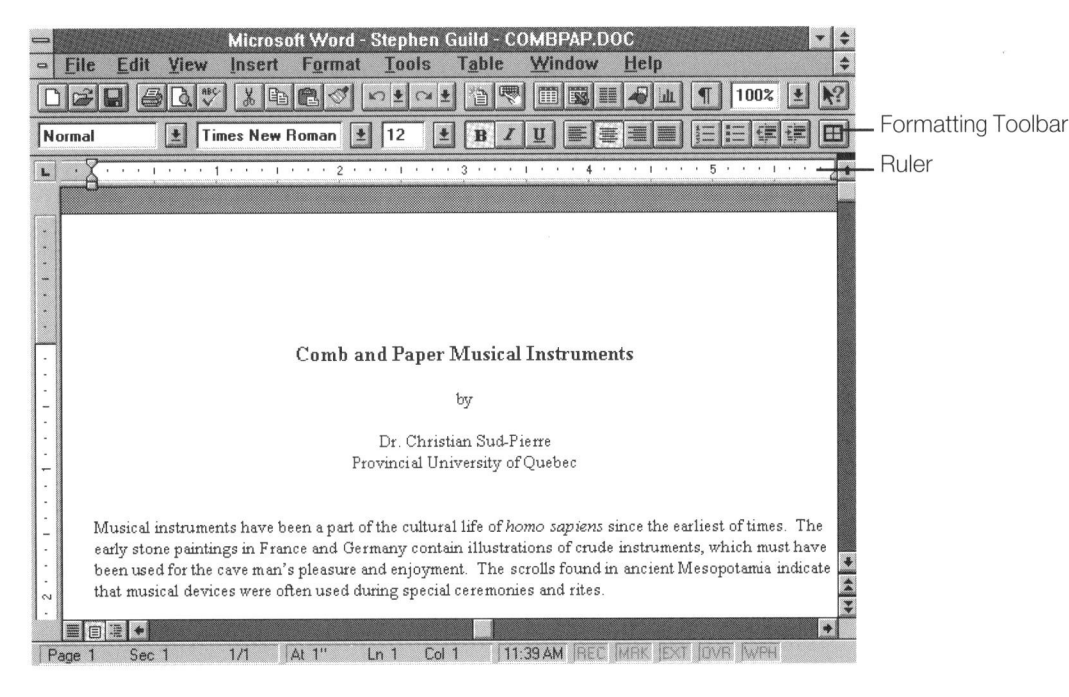

The Formatting toolbar reflects the settings of any paragraph or paragraphs you have selected. If you've selected multiple paragraphs that have a variety of settings, buttons in the Formatting toolbar are dimmed to indicate that multiple settings are in use.

The ruler can display margins, indents, and tabs. In addition, you can set tabs and change margins, indents, and column widths.

If you click in various spots on the ruler, different dialog boxes will be displayed:

To Display	Double-Click
File Page Setup with the Margins and Layout tabs	Top half of ruler
Format Tabs dialog box	Tab indicators
Format Paragraph dialog box	One of the indent markers

Using the Paragraph Dialog Box

With the Paragraph dialog box, you can perform the same operations as those available with the buttons on the Formatting toolbar and the ruler. In addition, you can perform these tasks:

▲ Type exact measurements for indents, line spacing, and spacing before and after paragraphs.
▲ Choose options that prevent page breaks within and between paragraphs.
▲ Control line spacing.
▲ Suppress line numbers and hyphenation for selected paragraphs. For more information about line numbers and hyphenation, see Chapter 16.

You'll learn how to use the Paragraph dialog box in the following sections.

TIP

To keep text aligned in straight columns, always use indent settings or tab settings. If you use spaces and later change fonts or point sizes, you may find that your text is no longer aligned.

Indenting Paragraphs

Indenting Paragraphs

When you indent a paragraph, you set the spacing between the paragraph and the margin. You can specify a left indent, a right indent, or a first-line indent.

To indent paragraphs using the ruler and the mouse:

1. Select the paragraphs.
2. If the ruler is not displayed, choose **View Ruler**. Figure 7.2 shows the different parts of the ruler.
3. Set the indents you want:

    Left indent   Click the left indent marker (the bottom triangle on the ruler) and drag the marker to the position you want. If you want to move the left indent and the first-line indent together, click and drag the small box underneath the triangle.

▼ **Figure 7.2. The Different Parts of the Ruler**

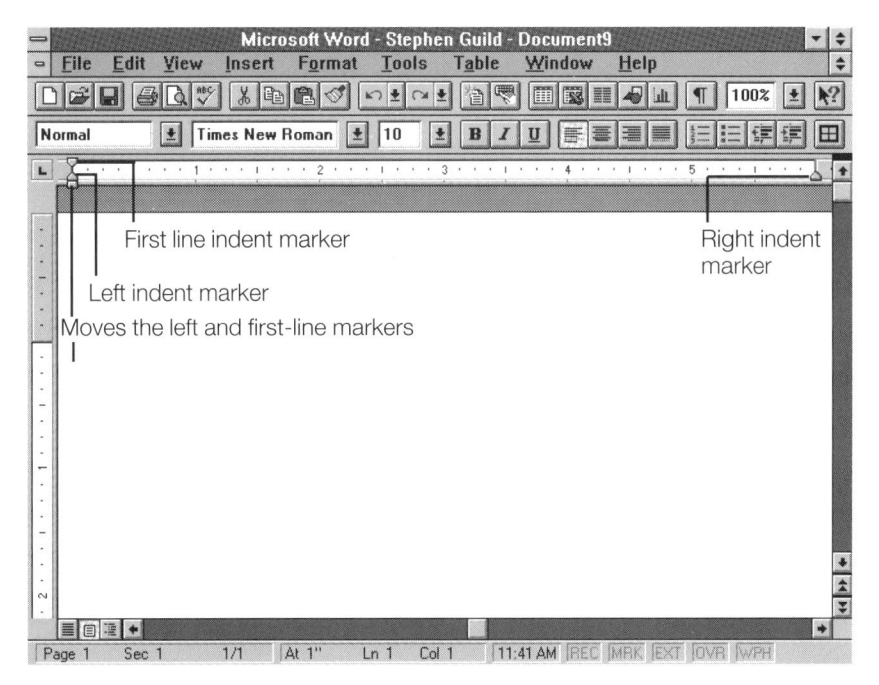

- First line indent marker
- Left indent marker
- Moves the left and first-line markers
- Right indent marker

▼ Figure 7.3. Setting a First Line Indent with the Ruler

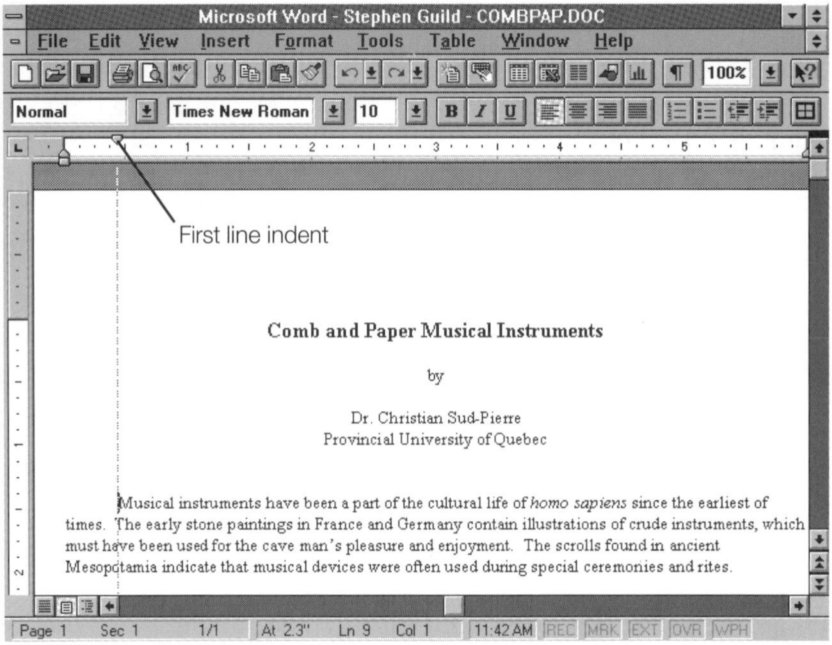
Microsoft Word - Stephen Guild - COMBPAP.DOC
File Edit View Insert Format Tools Table Window Help
Normal
Times New Roman
10
100%
First line indent
Comb and Paper Musical Instruments
by
Dr. Christian Sud-Pierre
Provincial University of Quebec
Musical instruments have been a part of the cultural life of homo sapiens since the earliest of times. The early stone paintings in France and Germany contain illustrations of crude instruments, which must have been used for the cave man's pleasure and enjoyment. The scrolls found in ancient Mesopotamia indicate that musical devices were often used during special ceremonies and rites.
Page 1 Sec 1 1/1 At 2.3" Ln 9 Col 1 11:42 AM REC MRK EXT OVR WPH

First-line indent	Drag the first-line indent marker (the top triangle on the ruler) to the position you want. Drag it right to create a normal first-line indent, or drag it left to create a hanging indent. Figure 7.3 illustrates how to set a first-line indent.
Right indent	Drag the right indent marker to the position you want.

If you want to do indentations at set intervals or format the paragraphs with bullets or numbers quickly, you can click the appropriate buttons on the toolbar, as shown in Figure 7.4.

To set indents with the Paragraph dialog box, you type measurements in the indent boxes. These measurements are distances from the margins. For example, if you type **1** in both the Left and Right boxes, Word sets a left indent one inch from the left margin and a right indent one inch from the right margin.

Indenting Paragraphs

▼ ***Figure 7.4. The Number, Bullet, and Paragraph Indent Buttons***

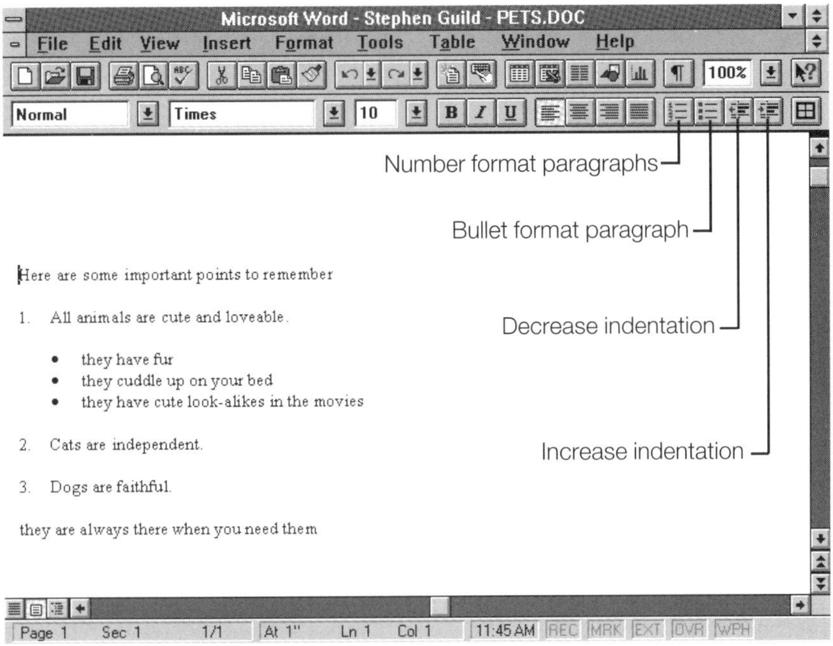

Microsoft Word - Stephen Guild - PETS.DOC
File Edit View Insert Format Tools Table Window Help
Normal
Times
10
Number format paragraphs
Bullet format paragraph
Decrease indentation
Increase indentation
Here are some important points to remember
1. All animals are cute and loveable.
they have fur
they cuddle up on your bed
they have cute look-alikes in the movies
2. Cats are independent.
3. Dogs are faithful.
they are always there when you need them
Page 1 Sec 1 1/1 At 1" Ln 1 Col 1 11:45 AM REC MRK EXT OVR WPH

To set indents with the Paragraph dialog box:

1. Select the paragraphs you want to indent.
2. Choose **Format Paragraph**.
3. Type measurements in the Indentation boxes.
4. Click **OK** or press **Enter**.

Hanging indents (where the first line is farther to the left than the rest of the paragraph) are an exception to the measure-from-the-margin rule. To set a hanging indent, choose Hanging from the drop-down list and type a measurement in the By box. To set a first-line indent, choose First Line from the drop-down list and type a measurement in the By box. Figure 7.5 illustrates how to set hanging indents using the Paragraph dialog box.

Word assumes that the measurements you type are in inches, unless you've changed the unit of measurement in the Tools Options General tab.

You can use the following key combinations to indent selected paragraphs without using the ruler or a command. When you use one of these shortcuts, Word sets the indent at the closest tab setting (.5 inch if you haven't changed the default settings).

▼ *Figure 7.5. Setting Hanging Indents with the Paragraph Dialog Box*

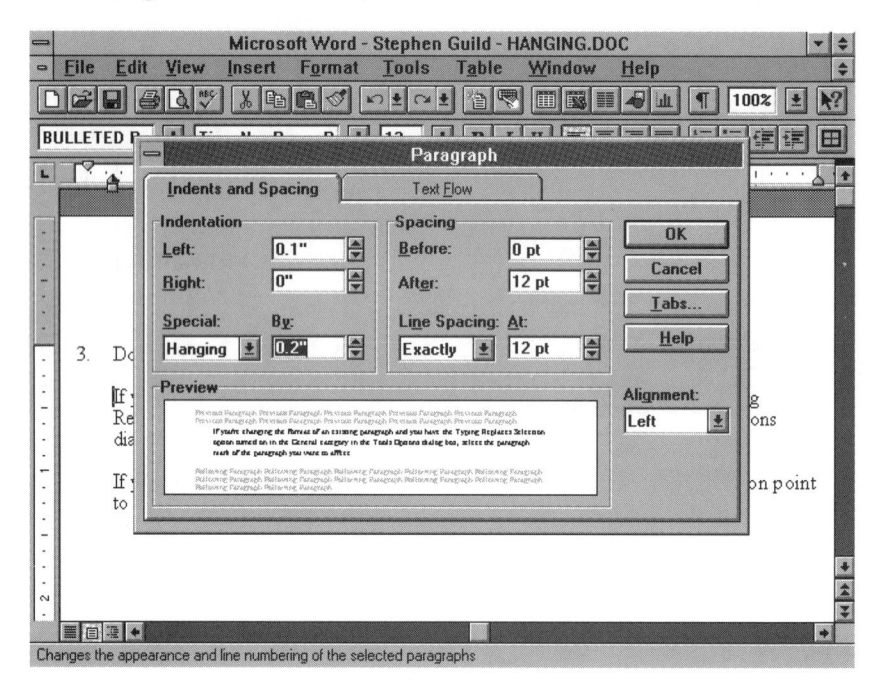

To Do This	Press
Shift the entire paragraph left	Ctrl+M
Shift the entire paragraph right	Ctrl+Shift+M
Shift all lines to the right except the first line, creating a hanging indent	Ctrl+T
Shift all lines to the left except the first line	Ctrl+Shift+T

You can use these key combinations repeatedly to get the indents you want. The paragraph indent buttons on the Formatting toolbar also provide a way to indent paragraphs at set intervals quickly.

CHECK YOURSELF

Indent the first line of a paragraph at 1.3 inches.

▲ Choose **Format Paragraph**, choose **First Line** from the Special drop-down list, and type **1.3** in the By box. Then click **OK**, or drag the top indent marker on the ruler to 1.3.

Setting Tabs

You can set tabs for a paragraph before you type the text by placing the insertion point before the paragraph mark on a blank line, then setting the tabs for that paragraph. However, it's usually easier to type your text first, pressing the Tab key wherever you want a tab. Don't be alarmed if your text doesn't line up—that will be taken care of when you set tabs using one of the procedures described next.

Setting Tabs with the Ruler

To set tabs with the ruler and the mouse:

1. Type the text, pressing the **Tab** key where you want tabs.
2. Select the paragraphs containing the tab characters. (Remember, tabs are part of paragraph formatting.)
3. If necessary, choose **View Ruler**.
4. Choose a tab type by clicking on the tab button at the far left-hand side of the ruler. For example, if you want the text at the tab to line up on a decimal point, click until you see the decimal tab button (it looks like an upside-down T with a period on it).
5. Point to the position on the ruler where you want the tab, then click the mouse button. A marker for that tab type appears, and the paragraphs adjust to show the new setting.
6. Repeat Steps 4 and 5 for each tab you want to set in the paragraphs.

The first tab marker you set in the ruler controls the location and type of the first tab character in your paragraph, the second tab marker marks the setting for the second tab character, and so on. You'll need to position one marker in the ruler for each tab character in a selected paragraph. If you're not concerned about exact tab measurements, using the ruler is easier, but if you need specific tab measurements, then you should use the Tabs dialog box.

Setting Tabs with the Tabs Dialog Box

Figure 7.6 shows different types of Tab alignments. You can also use the Tabs dialog box to set tabs or see the positions of tabs. You can get to the Tabs dialog box by choosing Format Tabs or by displaying the Paragraph dialog box (choose Format Paragraph), and then clicking the Tabs button.

To set tabs with the Tabs dialog box:

1. Type the text, pressing the **Tab** key where you want tabs.
2. Select the paragraphs containing the text and tab characters.
3. Choose **Format Tabs**.
4. Type a position in the Tab Stop Position box.
5. Choose a tab type in the Alignment area.
6. Click the **Set** button to set the tab in the paragraphs.
7. If necessary, repeat Steps 4 through 6 to set more tabs in the paragraphs. All of your settings will appear in the Tab Stop Position list.
8. Click **OK** or press **Enter**.

▼ *Figure 7.6. Text Aligned at Different Types of Tabs*

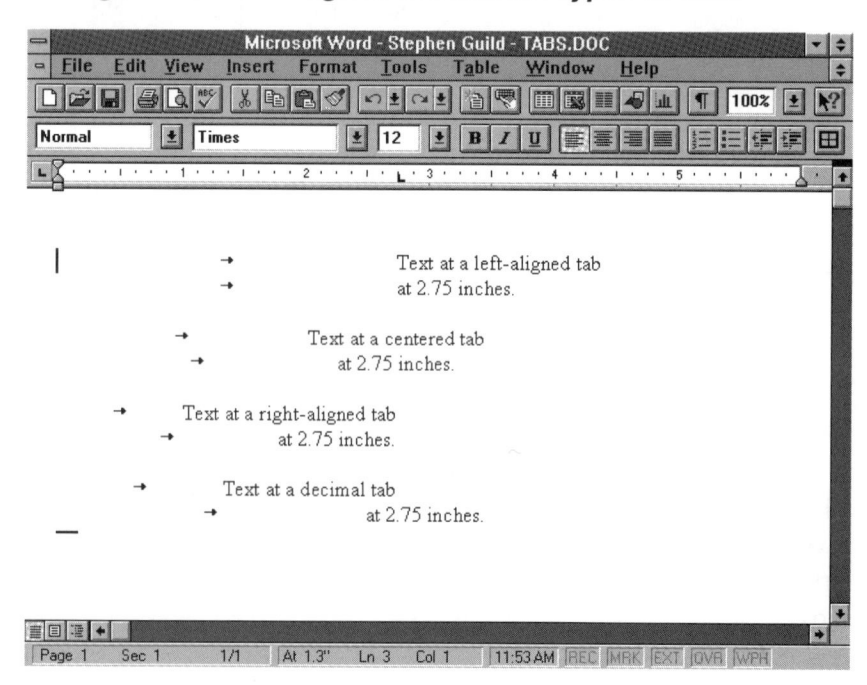

Changing the Default Tab Spacing

Setting Tabs

Word sets default tabs every half inch; that's why the insertion point jumps to the next inch or half-inch position when you press the **Tab** key. As you saw in the previous section, you can set individual tabs wherever you like. You can also change the default tab spacing to a new measurement.

To change the default tab spacing:

1. Choose **Format Tabs**.
2. Type a measurement in the Default Tab Stops box. For example, type **.75** if you want to set default tabs every 3/4 inch—at .75", 1.5", 2.25", and so forth.
3. Click **OK** or press **Enter**.

CHECK YOURSELF

Using the ruler, set three left-aligned tabs at 2.2", 4.6", and 6.1".
- ▲ Type the paragraph, then select it. If the ruler is not displayed, choose **View Ruler**. Finally, set the three tabs by clicking at the specified measurements on the ruler.

Deleting or Changing Tabs with the Ruler

To delete a tab using the ruler and the mouse:

1. Select the paragraphs you want to affect.
2. Drag the tab marker off the ruler and release the mouse button. The tab marker will disappear, and the paragraphs will adjust accordingly.

To change a tab's position using the ruler and the mouse:

1. Drag the tab marker to a new position on the ruler.
2. The paragraphs will change to reflect the new setting.

To use the ruler and mouse to change the type of tab at a specific position:

1. Drag the tab marker you no longer want off the ruler.
2. Choose a new type of tab and set it at the same position.

Deleting or Changing Tabs with the Tabs Dialog Box

To delete a tab or change the type of tab:

1. Select the paragraphs you want to affect.
2. Choose **Format Tabs**.
3. Type the position of the tab you want to affect in the Tab Stop Position box, or select the position from the list.
4. Choose **Clear** to delete the tab or to choose a new tab type in the Alignment area.
5. Click **OK** or press **Enter**.

To move a tab with the Tabs dialog box:

▲ Clear the tab at the old position, then set a new tab at the new position.

Filling Tab Spaces with Leader Characters

If you don't want spaces to appear before a tab, you can fill in the tab space with leader characters. For example, you might want to use periods for leader characters in an index, like this:

```
The Beginning..............................1
The Middle..................................99
The End......................................250
```

Word has three types of leader characters you can use: periods, hyphens, and underlines.

To fill a tab space with leader characters:

1. Select the paragraphs to be affected.
2. Choose **Format Tabs**.
3. Type the tab's position in the Tab Stop Position box.
4. Choose the option you want in the Leader area. Choose **None** if you want to remove an existing tab leader.
5. Choose **Set**.
6. Click **OK** or press **Enter**.

The leader character will appear after you press the **Tab** key.

CHECK YOURSELF

Set a decimal tab at 5.9", with dash leaders.

▲ Select the paragraph, and choose **Format Tabs**. Type **5.9** in the Tab Stop Position measurement box; click the **Decimal** button in the Alignment area and the **3** button (for dash leaders) in the Leader area. Click the **Set** button and then click **OK** or press **Enter**.

Displaying Tab Characters

You insert a tab character every time you press the **Tab** key. (Tab characters are bold arrows that point right.) Tab characters are invisible unless you tell Word to display them.

To display tab characters:

▲ Click the paragraph mark (¶) button on the Standard toolbar, or press **Ctrl+Shift+*** (asterisk). (Use the asterisk key in the top row of the main keyboard, not the multiplication key on the keypad.) This displays not only tab characters but also paragraph marks, space marks, and newline characters.

TIP

To select one tab in the text quickly, double-click the tab character (→).

Aligning Paragraphs

Word has four alignment options to determine the placement of text in paragraphs between indents (or between margins, if you haven't set indents). Figure 7.7 shows how these different paragraph alignments appear.

Aligning Paragraphs with the Formatting Toolbar

You can choose from four Formatting toolbar buttons that align paragraphs horizontally between indents (or between margins if you haven't set indents). Figure 7.7 shows the alignment buttons.

To align paragraphs with the Formatting toolbar:

1. Select the paragraphs.
2. Click the Formatting toolbar button that represents the alignment you want.

Aligning Paragraphs with the Paragraph Dialog Box

To align paragraphs with the Paragraph dialog box:

1. Select the paragraphs.

▼ *Figure 7.7. Four Types of Paragraph Alignments*

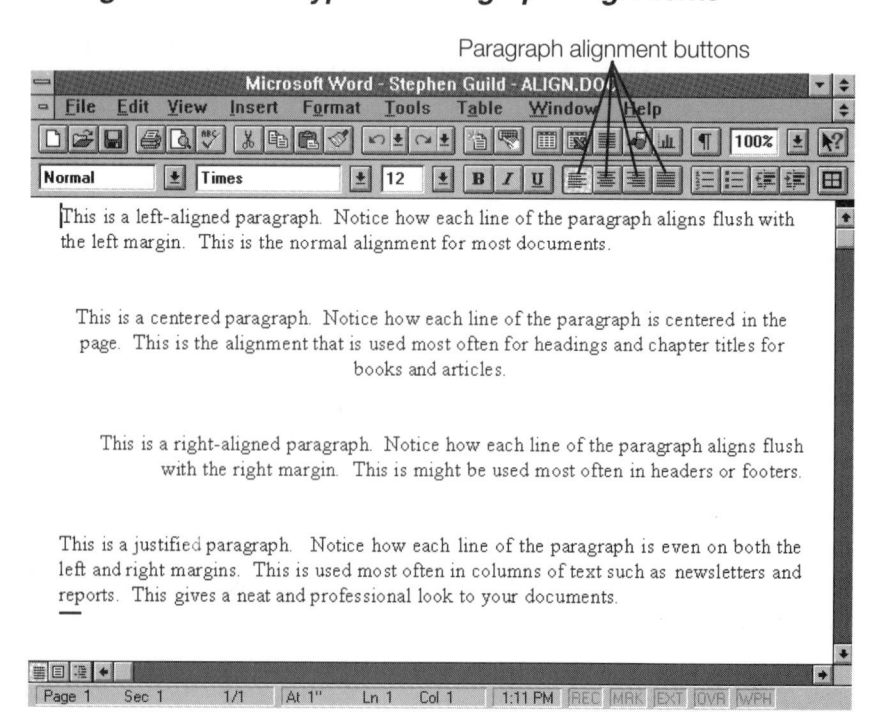

> *Aligning Paragraphs*

2. Choose **Format Paragraph**.
3. Select an option in the Alignment area.
4. Click **OK** or press **Enter**.

You can use the following key combinations to align paragraphs without using the ruler or choosing commands:

To Do This	Press
Align text with left indent	Ctrl+L
Center text between indents	Ctrl+E
Align text with right indent	Ctrl+R
Justify text	Ctrl+J

CHECK YOURSELF

Center a single paragraph.
- ▲ Select the text. Press **Ctrl+E** or click the **Centered** button on the Formatting toolbar.

Changing Line Spacing Within and Between Paragraphs

You may want to change the line spacing in all or part of your document. You can choose among single, double, and 1½-line spacing using the Paragraph dialog box. You can also set spacing between paragraphs by typing measurements in the Before and After boxes of the Paragraph dialog box.

Changing Line Spacing with the Paragraph Dialog Box

If you want to control the spacing more precisely, you can type measurements in the Before, After, and Line Spacing boxes of the Paragraph dialog box. To determine the spacing between paragraphs, Word adds the Before measurement of a paragraph to the After measurement of the preceding paragraph. By default, Word measures line spacing in points.

To change line spacing in paragraphs:

1. Select the paragraphs.
2. Choose **Format Paragraph**.
3. To set the spacing within the paragraphs, select one of the options in the Line Spacing drop-down list:

Choose	To Do This
Single	Make paragraphs single-space
1.5	Make paragraphs space-and-a-half
Double	Make paragraphs double-space
At Least	Indicate the minimum space necessary for Word to accommodate larger font or graphic sizes
Exactly	Make paragraph spacing at exactly the measurement indicated in the At box
Multiple	Make paragraph spacing multiples of the number in the At box

4. Type a measurement in the At box. If you want a special measurement, type a measurement or select one from the list in the At box.
5. To set the spacing before each paragraph, if you want a special measurement, type a measurement or select one from the list in the Before box.
6. To set the spacing after each paragraph, if you want a special measurement, type a measurement or select one from the list in the After box.
7. Click **OK** or press **Enter**.

You can use the following key combinations to change line spacing in paragraphs without choosing commands or using the ruler. Don't use the number keys on the numeric keypad in these combinations.

To Do This	Press
Single-space text	Ctrl+1
Double-space text	Ctrl+2
1½-space text	Ctrl+5

To Do This	Press	Changing Line Spacing Within and Between Paragraphs
Set or eliminate spacing before paragraphs (adds or removes one line of blank space before the paragraph	Ctrl+0 (zero) (Make sure to press the zero, not the letter O. Use the zero on the top row, not the zero on the keypad.)	

CHECK YOURSELF

Change a paragraph so that .9" spaces are placed between lines.

▲ Select the paragraph and choose **Format Paragraph**. Choose **Exactly** in the Line Spacing drop-down list, type **.9** in the At box, and then click **OK** or press **Enter**.

Adding Boxes, Lines, or Shading to Paragraphs

You can draw lines above, below, or beside a paragraph, or you can enclose a paragraph in a box to make it stand out from the rest of your text. You can also add background shading to paragraphs. Figure 7.8 shows some sample uses for the border options.

The lines, boxes, and shading you add to paragraphs extend from the indents, no matter how much text is in the paragraph. Therefore, if the lines seem too long, increase the paragraph indents until you get the effect you want (see "Indenting Paragraphs" earlier in this chapter). You can align text within the borders by choosing alignment options from the ruler (see "Aligning Paragraphs" earlier in this chapter).

Using the Borders toolbar will make the job of adding borders and shading much easier.

To display the Borders toolbar:

▲ Choose **View Toolbars** and turn on the Borders check box.
▲ Click the **Borders** toolbar button on the Standard toolbar.

To add boxes, lines, or shading to paragraphs:

1. Select the paragraphs.

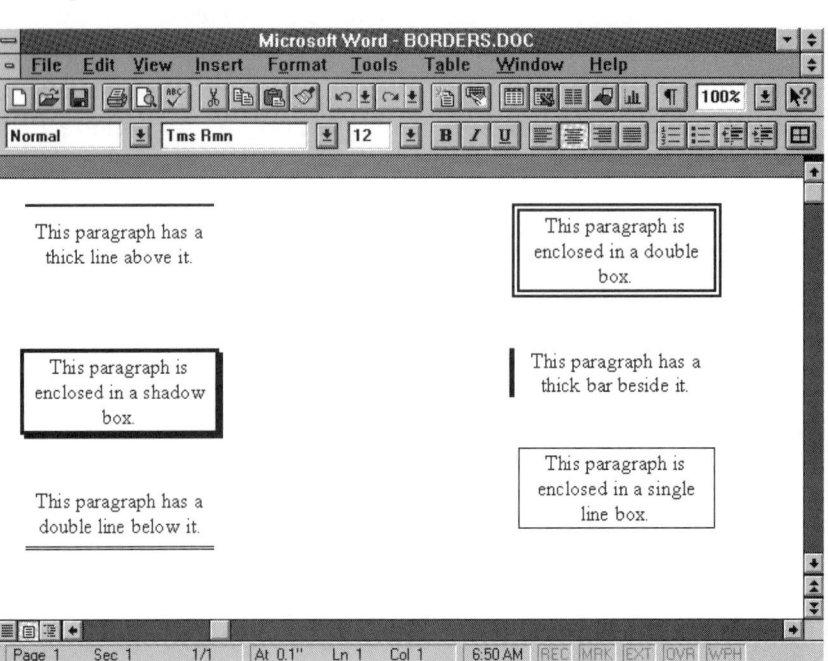

▼ *Figure 7.8. Paragraphs with a Variety of Borders*

2. Choose **Format Borders** and **Shading**.
3. To add a box, choose one of the options in the Presets area: **None** for no border, **Box** for a box around the paragraph, or **Shadow** to create a paragraph with a shadow effect.
4. If you don't want a border on all four sides or if you want a different border for one or more sides of the paragraph, click the side on which you want a particular border to appear, and then click the border style in the Line area. If you want a colored border, choose the color from the Color drop-down list. Continue with this approach until you have set all borders.
5. In the From Text box, type or select a measurement for the spacing between the border and the enclosed text.
6. If you want to include shading, click the **Shading** tab and choose options for Shading, Foreground, and Background in the Fill area. The default is None.
7. Click **OK** or press **Enter**.

You can also display the Borders toolbar by clicking the Show Toolbar button.

Creating a Dropped Capital Letter

If you want a large initial capital letter (or the first word) called a *dropped cap* to start a paragraph, you can format a paragraph to contain the dropped cap letter. When you create a dropped cap, Word places the first letter (or the initial text you have selected) in a frame, and the rest of the text in the paragraph wraps around the frame.

Dropped caps can be formatted in any font, but scalable fonts—such as TrueType and Adobe Type Manager—or Postscript printer fonts work best.

To create a dropped capital letter:

1. Place the insertion point at the beginning of the paragraph that you want to contain the dropped cap.
2. Choose **Format Drop Cap**.
3. In the Position area, click **Dropped** if you want the letter or word to be part of the paragraph; click **In Margin** if you want the letter to appear in the margin beside the paragraph.
4. In the Font box, select the font you want to apply to the dropped cap, if different from the present style.
5. To specify the height of the letter, type or select the number of lines in the Lines to Drop box.
6. To specify the amount of space between the dropped cap and the rest of the paragraph, type or select a number in the Distance for Text box.
7. Click **OK** or press **Enter**.

After you have created the dropped cap, you can apply borders and shading patterns and put them in newspaper-style columns. If you want to use a graphic as a dropped cap, Word will automatically size the graphic to fit the number of lines by which you want it dropped.

To remove a dropped cap:

1. Place the insertion point in the paragraph with the dropped cap.
2. Chose **Format Drop Cap**.
3. Click on **None**, then click **OK** or press **Enter**.

Controlling Page Breaks in Paragraphs

Sometimes you have a paragraph that must be kept all on one page or kept with the next paragraph in order to make sense. You can control page breaks in paragraphs by using the Paragraph dialog box and choosing the Text Flow tab.

To use the Paragraph dialog box to set page breaks:

1. Select the paragraph(s) you want to affect.
2. Choose **Format Paragraph**.
3. Turn on the options you want in the Pagination box:

Option	*Action*
Widow/Orphan Control	Prevents a single line of a paragraph at the top or bottom of the page.
Keep Lines Together	Keeps all lines in the paragraph on the same page. (If a page break would naturally occur within the paragraph, Word forces the page to break before the paragraph.)
Page Break Before	Places the paragraph at the top of a new page.
Keep With Next	Keeps the paragraph on the same page with the following paragraph. (If a page break would naturally occur within the first paragraph or between the paragraphs, Word forces the page to break before the first paragraph.)

4. Click **OK** or press **Enter**.

For more information about controlling page breaks, see "Controlling Pagination" in Chapter 14.

Controlling Line Numbers in Paragraphs

If you've added line numbers to your document, you can turn on the Suppress Line Numbers check box in the Format Paragraph dialog box to remove line numbers from selected paragraphs; you can turn it off to restore line numbers to selected paragraphs. You can't choose this option unless you've added line numbers.

For more information about using line numbers in documents, see "Numbering Lines" in Chapter 16.

Copying Paragraph Formatting

You can copy paragraph formatting in four different ways: by using the mouse, by repeating a previous formatting action, by using the clipboard, and by using a saved paragraph. The first and second methods work during one editing session with Word. The third and fourth methods save paragraph formatting for later use.

Using the Mouse to Copy Paragraph Formatting

To use the mouse to copy a paragraph format from one place to another quickly:

1. Format and select a paragraph the way you want it. Make sure you select the entire paragraph, including the paragraph mark.
2. Click the **Format Painter** button (the one that looks like a paintbrush) on the Standard toolbar. If you want to copy the format to several locations, double-click the button.
3. Select the next text you want to format, and click the text. If you have double-clicked on the button, then click the rest of the text you want to format.
4. When you have finished, click the **Format Painter** button or press **Esc**.

Repeating the Last Paragraph Formatting Action

You can press **F4** or choose Edit Repeat to repeat the previous formatting action you performed on a paragraph. For example, you could double-space a paragraph, then select another paragraph and repeat the double spacing.

To repeat the previous paragraph formatting that you made:

1. Format a paragraph the way you want it.
2. Select the next paragraph you want to format the same way.
3. Press **F4** or choose **Edit Repeat Formatting**.

Using the Clipboard to Copy Paragraph Formatting

You can choose Edit Copy and Edit Paste to copy paragraph formatting quickly.

To copy paragraph formatting, copy a paragraph mark that contains all the formatting:

1. Select the paragraph mark (¶) of the paragraph whose format you want to copy. (Click the Standard toolbar's paragraph mark button to see paragraph marks, if necessary.)
2. Choose **Edit Copy** to copy the paragraph mark to the Clipboard.
3. Do one of the following:
    - ▲ If you're changing the format of an existing paragraph and the Typing Replaces Selection option is turned on in the Tools Options Edit tab, select the paragraph mark of the paragraph you want to affect.
    - ▲ If you want to insert the paragraph mark and then type new text, move the insertion point to the new location.
4. Choose **Edit Paste** to paste the copied paragraph mark and its associated formatting. If you selected an existing paragraph mark and you have activated the Typing Replaces Selection option, the copied formatting replaces the old formatting. To type new text, move the insertion point in front of the copied paragraph mark, then type.

Saving a Paragraph Format as an AutoText Entry

If you want to use a certain paragraph format repeatedly, you can save the paragraph mark (¶) as an AutoText entry. Then you can insert the paragraph mark any time you want to replace the format of an existing paragraph or type new text in front of it. (See "Using AutoText Entries" in Chapter 4 for more information about defining and using glossary entries.)

Saving Paragraph Formatting as a Style

You can save both paragraph formatting and character formatting as a style in Word, then you can use that style repeatedly to format new paragraphs. Chapter 8, *Using Styles*, tells you more about creating and using styles.

Copying Paragraph Formatting

QUICK COMMAND SUMMARY

Command	To Do This
Ctrl+5 on numeric keypad	Select every paragraph in a document.
View Ruler	Display the ruler.
Double-click the top half of the ruler	Display the Page Setup dialog box.
Double-click one of the indent markers	Display the Paragraph dialog box.
Double-click a tab button	Display the Tabs dialog box.
Format Paragraph	Display the Paragraph dialog box.
Paragraph marker	Display paragraph indentations on the ruler.
Ruler scale icon	Display page margin markers, table column markers, or indent markers.

Command	**To Do This**
Ctrl+M	Shift whole paragraph left.
Ctrl+Shift+M	Shift whole paragraph right.
Ctrl+T	Shift all lines except the first line to the right, creating a hanging indent.
Ctrl+Shift+T	Shift all lines except the first line to the left.
Format Tabs	Display the Tabs dialog box.
Paragraph mark (¶) button on the Standard toolbar, or Ctrl+Shift+* (asterisk)	Display paragraph marks, tab characters, spaces, and other hidden characters.
Ctrl+L	Align text with left indent.
Ctrl+E	Center text.
Ctrl+R	Align text with right indent.
Ctrl+J	Justify text.
Ctrl+1	Single-space text.
Ctrl+2	Double-space text.
Ctrl+5	1½-space text.
Ctrl+0 (zero)	Set or eliminate space between paragraphs (delete any blank space not controlled by paragraph marks in front of the paragraph).
Format Border	Display the Border dialog box.
F4 or Edit Repeat	Repeat the last formatting action you performed on a paragraph.

PRACTICE WHAT YOU'VE LEARNED

The Clearance Items list has these formats:

▲ Title is in 14-point type and centered, with bars 3 points above and below.

▲ Tabs are set at .4" and .75" for the left tabs and 4.5" for the decimal tab.

Duplicate the text (shown below reduced to 75 percent).

	Clearance Items	
4	Remote-Controlled Answering Machines	$59.95
2	Fax Machines	$598.00
7	Computer Desks	$79.95
10	Secretarial Chairs	$45.95

What You Do	*What You'll See*
1. Press **Enter** twice and then place the insertion point in the first paragraph.	1. The insertion point in the first paragraph mark on the page (click the Hidden Text button on the toolbar to see the paragraph marks).
2. Type **Clearance Items**, select the text, and use the Formatting toolbar to change the point size to 14.	2. The text "Clearance Items" highlighted, and then "14" selected in the Font Size drop-down list. The text changes to 14 point.
3. Click the **Centered** button on the Formatting toolbar.	3. The Centered button on the Formatting toolbar changed to light gray to indicate it is in use, and the text centered in the document window.
4. Choose **Format Borders** and **Shading**. Make sure the Presets box indicates None.	4. The Borders and shading dialog box, with a blue line around the Presets figure labeled "None" to indicate it is turned on.

What You Do	*What You'll See*
5. Click the top of the sample page in the Border box.	5. A line at the top of the sample page where you clicked.
6. Click the second border type in the left column of the Line box.	6. The line with this thickness replacing the line at the top of the sample page.
7. Click the bottom of the sample page.	7. A line at the bottom of the sample page where you clicked.
8. Set the From Text box at 10.	8. The number 10 displayed in the From Text box, and the sample page changed slightly to illustrate the measurement change.
9. Click **OK** to close the dialog box.	9. The Borders and Shading dialog box closed. The full document is now visible on the screen.
10. Place the insertion point where you want the tabs to begin.	10. The insertion visible where you clicked.
11. Choose **Format** Tabs and type **.4** and **.75**, clicking the **Set** button each time.	11. The Tabs dialog box displayed, with the numbers .4 and .75 in the Tab Stop Position list.
12. Type **4.75**, click the **Decimal** button, then the **Set** button, and then click **OK** to close the dialog box.	12. The number 4.75 in the Tabs Stop Position list box, the Center Alignment button black, and the dialog box closed.
13. Type the rest of the text.	13. The rest of the text with the tab formatting you've indicated.

8

Using Styles

Word offers you a quick, powerful way to apply both character and paragraph formats to paragraphs by defining and saving these formats as styles. In this chapter, you will learn how to:

- ▲ **Define, apply, and change styles**
- ▲ **Automatically format a document with styles**
- ▲ **Use shortcut keys to apply styles**
- ▲ **Set up a chain of styles**
- ▲ **Use styles from another document**
- ▲ **Add styles to documents and templates**

What Are Styles?

Styles are named sets of formatting instructions that you can apply repeatedly to different paragraphs. Using a style is simple. Say you've formatted a paragraph to look like this:

> **Chapter 2**

The text is bold, the font is New Century Schoolbook, the size is 14 points, the paragraph is indented 1.5" from the left and right margins, and the text is centered and enclosed in a 2 1/4-point shadow box. To use this format for all chapter headings, you could define all of the formats as a single style named *Chapter*, then apply the *Chapter* style to all your chapter heading paragraphs.

There are two types of styles: paragraph and character. Paragraph styles can contain tab settings, borders, positions that are fixed with the Frame dialog box settings (explained in Chapter 9), and any paragraph and character formats, such as indents, line spacing, fonts, bold, italic, and so forth. Character styles apply only character formatting to the selected paragraph.

There are three advantages to using styles:

▲ When you apply a style, you can apply both character and paragraph formatting in one step to save time.
▲ You can use the same styles repeatedly to give your documents a consistent format.
▲ If you change a style, Word automatically reformats all paragraphs that have been formatted with the style.

Every paragraph in Word has a style attached to it. If you haven't applied any styles of your own, all paragraphs have Word's default style, Normal.

Word controls styles through the Style dialog box and the Styles list on the Formatting toolbar. You display the Style dialog box by choosing Format Style. Word automatically stores styles in the same file as the active document. You can also store styles in template files, as described in "Styles and Templates" later in this chapter.

Styles Provided with Word

If you choose Format Style, you'll see a list of styles (shown in the Style Name list displayed on the Formatting toolbar), even if you haven't defined any of your own. These are called automatic styles and are provided by Microsoft for you to use.

Normal style, as already mentioned, is Word's default style. All paragraphs have this style until you apply a different one. You can use the Heading styles to format headings—from which you can easily create outlines and tables of contents. (For more information, see "Working with Outlines" in Chapter 16 and "Creating a Table of Contents" in Chapter 17.) Word's automatic styles are stored in the default template file, NORMAL.DOT.

You can change the automatic styles to change the formats that Word automatically applies to paragraphs and to headings. You can find out more about style editing in "Changing a Style" later in this chapter.

Using the Style Gallery

Word provides a collection of already-designed templates containing styles sheets that you can use to make formatting a document just that much easier. These templates fall into four "families": Classic, Contemporary, Typewriter, and Elegant. Numbers have been assigned to these families, so that you can choose different kinds of documents within the same family.

Within these families there are templates for many of the following:

- ▲ Brochures
- ▲ Directories
- ▲ Faxes
- ▲ Cover sheets
- ▲ Letters
- ▲ Manuals
- ▲ Manuscripts
- ▲ Memos
- ▲ Presentations
- ▲ Press releases
- ▲ Reports
- ▲ Resumes
- ▲ Theses

To use the styles from another template:

1. Choose **Format Style Gallery.**
2. Select the template you want to use in the Template list box. Click on the **Browse** button if you want to use a different template.
3. Select one of the following to preview the styles:

Select	To Display
Document	The active document as it will look when formatted with the selected template
Example	A sample document formatted with the selected template
Style Samples	A list of all styles in the template formatted with the available styles

4. Press **Enter** or click **OK.**

Defining a Style

The first step in using a style is to define the format you want to save. You can define a style in two ways:

▲ By recording the formatting of a selected paragraph.
▲ By choosing commands to specify a format.

Because recording the formatting of a paragraph is the easiest way to define a style, we'll concentrate on this method first, then move on to defining a style with commands.

Defining a Style by Recording the Formatting of a Paragraph

The easiest way to define a style is to use a formatted paragraph as a model, then assign a name to the style and save it. You can do this with the Formatting toolbar or by using the Style dialog box.

When you format a paragraph to define a style, you can use any combination of character and paragraph format options from the ruler; the Formatting toolbar; and the Character, Paragraph, Tabs, Border, Language, and Frame dialog boxes. However, all characters in the paragraph must have the same character format. You can't format part of the text one way and part another: you can't use half bold and half italic, for example, or different fonts in different words.

Defining a Style

Defining a Style with the Formatting Toolbar and a Formatted Paragraph

To use the Formatting toolbar to define a style by saving the format of a paragraph:

1. Format a paragraph the way you want it to appear.
2. Place the insertion point in the paragraph.
3. If necessary, choose **View Toolbars** and check the Formatting box to display the Formatting toolbar.
4. Use the mouse to activate the Style box, as shown in Figure 8.1, then type a name for the style. For example, if you want to save

▼ **Figure 8.1. The Styles List on the Formatting Toolbar**

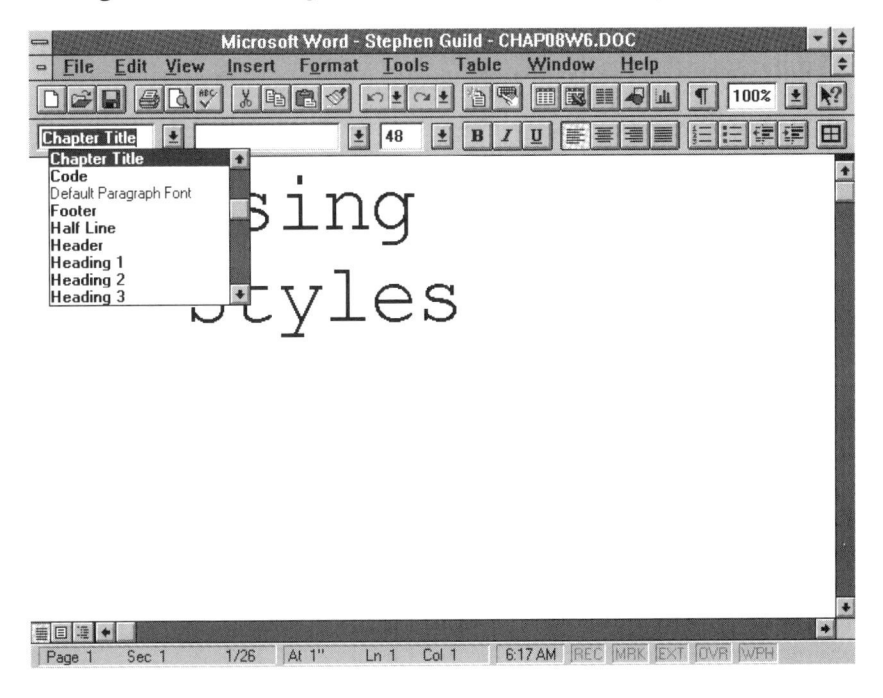

a style for quotations, you can type: **quote**. A style name can contain up to 253 characters and may include spaces but not backslashes (\), braces ({}), or semicolons.

Word saves the paragraph's format with the style name that you specify.

CHECK YOURSELF

Create a new style by copying the current formatting of a paragraph.

▲ Format the text with any formatting you choose, then select the paragraph. Choose **View Toolbars** and turn on the **Formatting** check box to display the Formatting toolbar. Use the mouse to activate the Style box, then type a name for the style.

Defining a Style with the Style Dialog Box and a Formatted Paragraph

To use the Style dialog box to define a style by saving the format of a paragraph:

1. Format a paragraph the way you want it to appear.
2. Place the insertion point in the paragraph.
3. Choose **Format Style** and click the **New** button. Word displays the New Style dialog box, as shown in Figure 8.2. (Note the description of the selected paragraph in the Description box.)
4. Type a name for the new style in the Name box. For example, you might type: **chapter heading**. A style name can contain up to 20 characters and may include spaces.
5. Click **OK** or press **Enter** to return to the Style dialog box, and then click **Close** or **Apply.**

Word saves the paragraph's format as a style that you can apply to other paragraphs.

▼ **Figure 8.2. The Styles List in the Style Dialog Box**

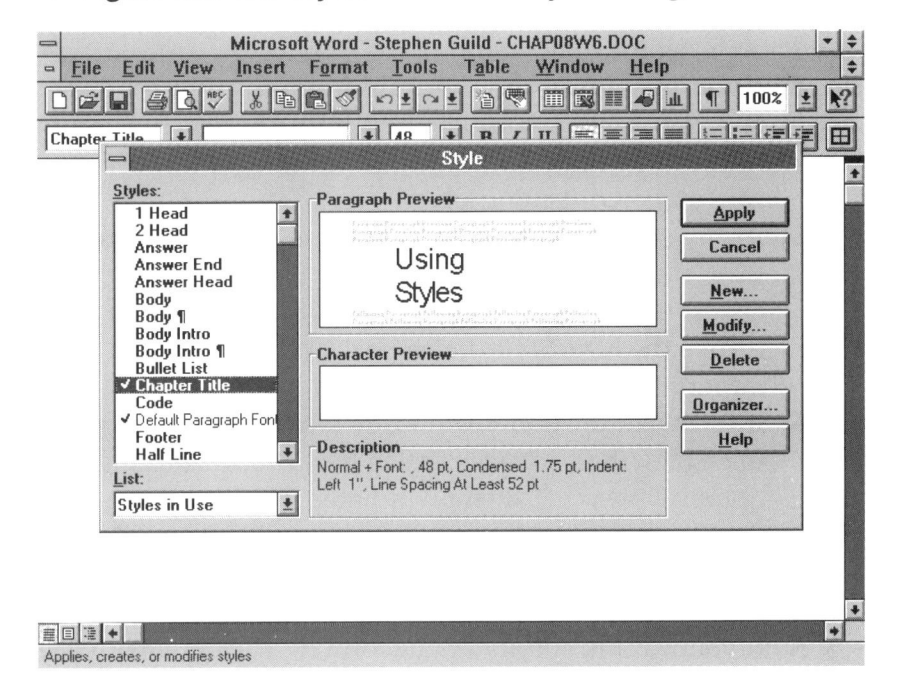

Defining a Style

Creating a Paragraph Style

You can use options in the New Style dialog box to define a new paragraph style without formatting any text first.

To use dialog box options to define a new style:

1. Choose **Format Style** and click the **New** button.
2. Type a name for the new style in the Name box.
3. Click the **Format** button and choose from the following options to develop the style's formatting:
   - ▲ If you want to specify character formats, click **Font** to display the Font dialog box, choose the character format options you want, then press **Enter** to return to the New Style dialog box. All characters in that style will assume the formatting you have chosen. (See Chapter 6 for more information on formatting characters.)
   - ▲ If you want to specify paragraph formats, click **Paragraph** to display the Paragraph dialog box, choose the paragraph

format options you want, then press **Enter** to return to the New Style dialog box. (See Chapter 7 for more information on formatting paragraphs.)
- ▲ If you want to set tabs, click **Tabs** to display the Tabs dialog box, choose the tab options you want, then press **Enter** to return to the New Style dialog box. (See Chapter 7 for more information on setting tabs.)
- ▲ If you want to specify Border formats, click **Border** to display the Paragraph Borders and Shading dialog box, choose the border options you want, then press **Enter** to return to the New Style dialog box. (See Chapter 7 for more information on formatting borders.)
- ▲ If you want to specify Language formats, click **Language** to display the Language dialog box, choose the language options you want, then press **Enter** to return to the New Style dialog box. All text in that style will assume the language format you have chosen. (See Chapter 5 for more information on language formats.)
- ▲ If you want to specify Frame formats, click **Frame** to display the Frame dialog box, choose the frame options you want, then press **Enter** to return to the New Style dialog box. (See Chapter 9 for more information on formatting frames.)
- ▲ If you want to specify Number and Bullet formats, click **Numbering** to display the Bullets and Numbering dialog box, choose the options you want, then press **Enter** to return to the New Style dialog box. (See Chapter 16 for more information on formatting bullets and numbers.) The description of the style (beneath the list box) changes as you add formats for the style.
4. When the description reflects the formats you want in the style, click the **OK** button or press **Enter** to return to the Style dialog box.
5. If you want to define another style, repeat Steps 2 through 4.
6. Click the **Close** button.

CHECK YOURSELF

Create a paragraph style for a course catalog, like the example, with 14-point type and bold and centered text:

Creating a Paragraph Style

Introduction to the Swahili Language
MWF 9-10 AM

▲ Type the sample paragraph, and then select it. Choose **View Toolbars** and turn on the **Formatting** check box to display the Formatting toolbar. Then click the down arrow in the Points box. Select 14 from the list and press **Enter**. Click the centered and bold buttons on the Formatting toolbar, then choose **Format Style** and click **New.** Type **course catalog** in the Name box, click the **OK** button, then click the **Close** button.

Creating a Character Style

You can use options in the New Style dialog box to define a new style with only character formatting.

To use dialog box options to define a new character-only style:

1. Choose **Format Style** and click the **New** button.
2. Type a name for the new style in the Name box.
3. Click the **Format** button and click **Font** to display the Font dialog box, choose the character format options you want, then press **Enter** to return to the New Style dialog box. All characters in that style will assume the formatting you have chosen. (See Chapter 6 for more information on formatting characters.)
4. When the description reflects the formats you want in the style, click the **OK** button or press **Enter** to return to the Style dialog box.
5. If you want to define another style, repeat Steps 2 through 4.
6. Click the **Close** button.

Basing a New Style on an Existing Style

If you want to use the basic format of one style but not modify the original style, you can base a new style on an existing style.

If you change a style on which other styles are based, all the styles will change to reflect the changes in the base style. For example, if you base a style called *Quotation* on a style called *Sayings*, then make the *Sayings* style bold, the *Quotation* style will also become bold to reflect the change in its base style.

To base a new style on an existing style:

1. Choose **Format Style** and click the **Modify** button to display the Modify Style dialog box as shown in Figure 8.3.
2. Type a name for the new style in the Name box.
3. In the Based On box, type the name of the style on which you want to base your new style, or select the style's name from the drop-down list.
4. Click the **Format** button and choose the Character, Paragraph, Tabs, Border, Language, Frame, or Numbering button to open dialog boxes and make any changes you want. The description beneath the list changes as you modify the style.
5. Click the **OK** button or press **Enter**. (If you want to define another style, you can type a new name in the Name box and repeat Steps 3 and 4.)
6. When you have finished modifying all of the styles you want to change, click **Close** in the Style dialog box.

▼ *Figure 8.3. Basing One Style on Another*

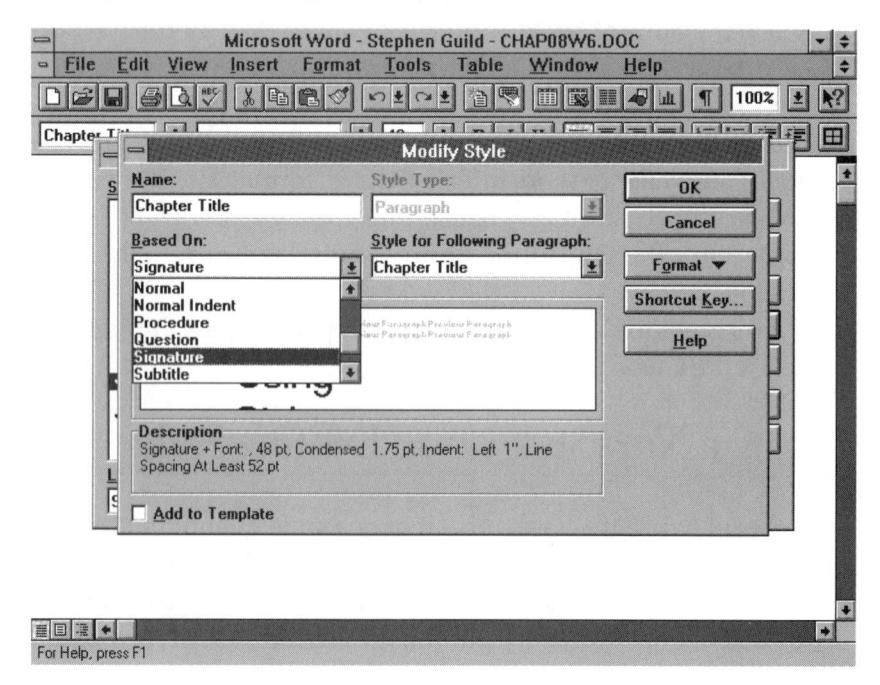

Applying Styles

Once you've saved a style, you can apply it to a paragraph you've already typed, or you can apply it to a paragraph mark before you type the text. You can apply a style with a command or with the Formatting toolbar.

Applying Styles with the Formatting Toolbar

To apply a style using the style list on the Formatting toolbar:

1. Select the paragraphs you want to format.
2. If necessary, choose **View Toolbar** and turn on the **Formatting toolbar** check box to display the Formatting toolbar.
3. Select a style from the drop-down Styles list at the left side of the Formatting toolbar.

TIP

If you want to apply an existing style that is not on the list in the Formatting toolbar, hold down the Shift **key and click the arrow beside the Style box. A list of all the styles currently in the Word templates will be displayed. You can then select the style you want from this list.**

Applying Styles by Using the Style Dialog Box

To apply a style using the Style dialog box:

1. Select the paragraphs you want to format.
2. Choose **Format Style.**
3. Use the arrow keys to select the style name from the list.
4. Click **Apply** or press **Enter** to apply the style. To quickly apply a style and close the dialog box at the same time, double-click the style name in the Style Name list box.

Using Shortcut Keys to Apply Styles

You can make applying styles even easier by assigning key combinations to frequently used styles. Then, when you press a key combination, the selected paragraph will automatically assume the formatting of the assigned style.

To assign a shortcut key to a style:

1. Choose **Format Style.**
2. Select a style in the Style Name box.
3. Click either **New** or **Modify,** depending on whether or not you have created the style previously. Click the **Shortcut Key** box and press a combination of **Ctrl, Alt**, and a letter, number, function key, or the **Insert** or **Delete** key. If the combination is already assigned to some other operation in Word, the Currently Assigned To area will indicate what the key combination is being used for, and the Current Key box will show what other keys are assigned to that style. (You can assign more than one shortcut key combination to the same style.) You can choose to remove the current use by clicking on the Remove button or try another combination.
4. Click **Assign** and then click **Close** to close the dialog box.

Applying Styles Repeatedly

If you want to apply the same style in several different places in your document, you can use this quick technique:

1. Apply the style to the first selection.
2. Select the next paragraphs to apply the style to.
3. Press **F4** or choose **Edit Repeat Style.** Word repeats the previous formatting action, applying the same style to the selected paragraphs.
4. Repeat Steps 2 and 3 to format more text with the same style.

Displaying Style Names in the Document Window

Displaying Style Names in the Document Window

You can see at a glance which styles are attached to your text by displaying style names in the *style area pane*. This is a vertical pane you can add to the left of the text area, as shown in Figure 8.4. This option is not available when you are in Page Layout view.

Opening the Style Area Pane

To display style names in the style area pane:

1. Choose **Tools Options** and click the **View** tab.
2. In the Style Area Width box, type a measurement to indicate the width of the style area. (One inch is a good width to start with; you can always adjust this later.)
3. Click **OK** or press **Enter**. Word opens the style area pane.

▼ **Figure 8.4. Displaying the Names of Attached Styles**

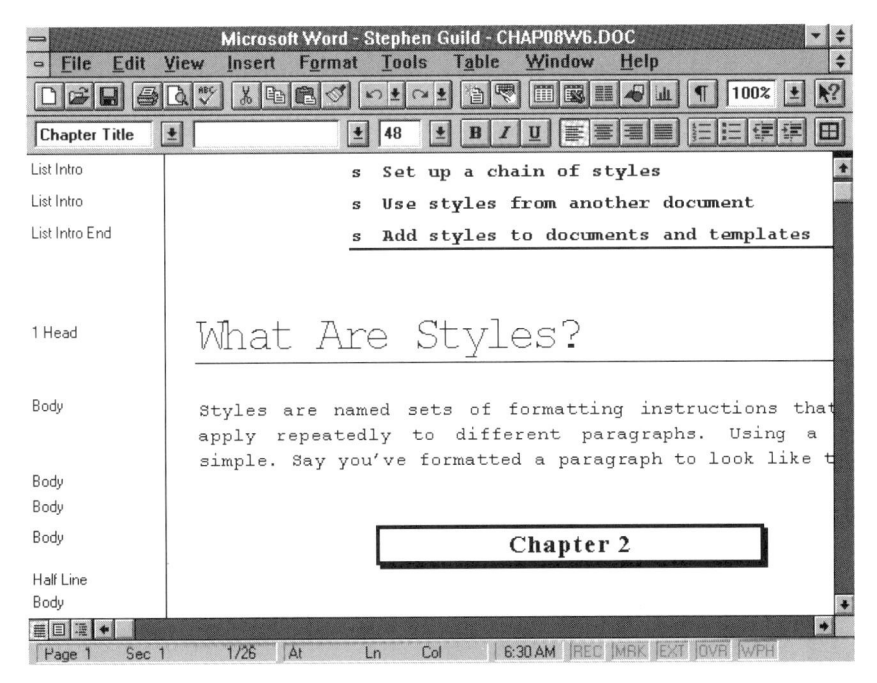

Resizing or Closing the Style Area Pane

You can change the size of the style area pane with the keys or with the mouse (as shown in Figure 8.5), or you can close the style area pane, removing style names from the document window.

To change the size of the style area pane with keys:

1. Choose **Tools Options,** then click the **View** tab.
2. In the Style Area Width box, type a new measurement to change the size of the style area. Type **0** (zero) to close the style area.

To change the size of the style area pane with the mouse:

1. Move the mouse pointer to the style area split line. The pointer becomes two vertical lines with opposing arrows.
2. Drag the split line to the new location. If you want to close the style area pane, drag the split line to the left edge of the document window.

▼ **Figure 8.5. Changing the Size of the Style Area with the Mouse**

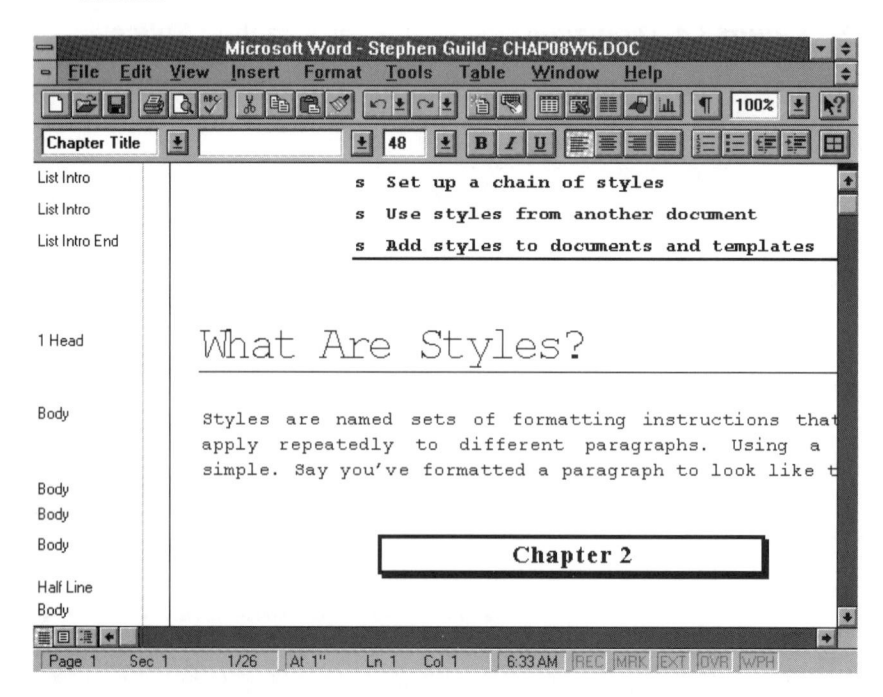

Using AutoFormat to Apply Styles

With automatic formatting, you can easily give your document a certain look without applying a style to each individual paragraph manually. The automatic formatting feature, called AutoFormat, lets you apply a whole set of styles to a document with just a few steps. Word looks at your document and then formats certain text elements with a predetermined style. You can always choose another style if you're not happy with what Word has done.

The AutoFormat styles include such common elements as topic headings, body text, bulleted lists, quotations, and inside addresses in business letters. AutoFormat also can remove extra returns or paragraph marks; replace straight quotation marks with curved ones; insert registration, copyright, and trademark symbols; and replace asterisks and other characters with bullets.

You can ask Word to AutoFormat your document without your reviewing each change, or you can look at each suggested change and accept or reject it.

To format text automatically:

1. If you want to format the entire document, place the insertion point anywhere in the document. If you want to format a part of the document, select only that portion.
2. Choose **Format AutoFormat**, and then in the AutoFormat dialog box click **OK** to begin the formatting.
3. If you want to change the AutoFormat options, click the **Options** button and make changes by turning the check boxes on or off in the AutoFormat tab. When you have finished, click **OK** or press **Enter**.
4. Word analyzes the document and makes suggested style changes, then displays the AutoFormat dialog box. In the dialog box, do one of the following:

To	Do This
Accept all of the formatting changes	Click **Accept**
Cancel all of the formatting changes	Click **Reject All**

To	Do This
Review and reject particular formatting changes	Click **Review Changes**
Use styles from a different template	Click **Style Gallery**

You can undo any changes made immediately after you've used AutoFormat by choose Edit Undo or pressing **Ctrl+Z** or **Alt+Backspace**.

Reviewing AutoFormat Changes

If you click the Review Changes button, Word displays the Review AutoFormat Changes dialog box. You can review changes sequentially, or you can scroll through the document and select the specific changes you want to look at.

The changes that Word suggests are indicated by temporary revision marks, which will appear in colors if you have a color monitor. When you view a document with AutoFormat marks, you will see the following:

This Mark	*Indicates Word*
Blue paragraph marks (¶)	Applied a style to the paragraph
Red paragraph marks (¶)	Deleted the paragraph mark
Strikethrough (Ɵ in red)	Deleted text or spaces
Underline (O in blue)	Added the underlined characters
Change bars in the left margin	Changed the formatting or text in that line

To review AutoFormat changes:

1. In the AutoFormat dialog box, click the **Review Changes** button. Word will display the Review AutoFormat Changes dialog box.
2. Review changes one by one by using the Find Next and Find Previous buttons in the Review.

Using AutoFormat to Apply Styles

- ▲ If you want to undo the last change, click the **Undo Last** button.
- ▲ If you don't want the displayed change, click the **Reject** button.
- ▲ If you want to see the document as it will appear if you select all the changes, click the **Hide Marks** button.
- ▲ If you want to have Word undo the current change and move on to the next suggested change, turn on the **Find after Next Reject** check box.
3. Click **Close** or **Cancel** to accept all of the remaining changes in the document. Then, in the AutoFormat dialog box, click either **Accept** or **Reject All**.

Changing a Style

You can change any style, including the styles provided with Word—even Word's default Normal style. When you change a style, Word automatically updates every paragraph in your document with that style. For example, to change the font and point size that Word automatically uses for a new document, you can change Word's Normal style in the NORMAL.DOT file.

Remember, if you change a style on which other styles are based, all the other styles will reflect the changes in the base style.

You can change a style in two ways:

- ▲ By changing a paragraph that has the style, then recording the new format with the same style name, using the Style dialog box or the Style list on the Formatting toolbar.
- ▲ By changing the style in the Style dialog box, using the Font, Paragraph, Tabs, Border, Language, Frame, and Numbering buttons as necessary.

Changing a Style by Recording Changes

To change an existing style (saving it with the same name) by recording changes:

1. Select a paragraph with the style you want to change.

2. Change the formats as desired. For example, if you want to add bold to a style, format the paragraph as bold text.
3. If the Formatting toolbar is displayed, use the mouse to activate the Style list, select the name of the style, then press **Enter.** Word displays a message asking you if you want to redefine the style based on the selection.
4. Click **Yes** or press **Y**.

CHECK YOURSELF

Change Word's Normal style to add ¼" of space after the paragraph.

▲ Choose the **Style** command and click the **Modify** button. Select **Normal** from the Style Name list, then click the **Format** button and click **Paragraph** to open the Paragraph dialog box. Type **.25** in the Space After box, then click **OK** or press **Enter** to return to the Modify dialog box. Click **OK** to return to the Style dialog box, then click **Close** to save the changes and close the dialog box.

Changing a Style by Using Buttons in the Style Dialog Box

To change a style by using buttons in the Style dialog box:

1. Choose **Format Style** and click the **Modify** button to display the Modify Style dialog box.
2. In the Name list, select the name of the style you want to change.
3. Click the **Format** button and choose the Character, Paragraph, Tabs, Border, Language, Frame, and Numbering buttons as necessary, then choose new options in the dialog boxes to change the style. The description of the style (beneath the list box) changes as you add and subtract formats from the style.
4. When the style is the way you want it to appear, click **OK** or press **Enter**. Word changes the format of all paragraphs with that style.
5. Click **Apply** or **Close** to close the Style dialog box.

TIP

If you want to make changes to several styles without closing the Style dialog box, type another style name in the Name box and make changes to the style. When you're through changing styles, click OK **to close the dialog box.**

Renaming a Style

There may be times when you want to give a style a name different from the one you originally assigned.

To rename a style:

1. Choose **Format Style** and click the **Modify** button to display the Modify Style dialog box.
2. In the Name list, select the style you want to rename.
3. Type the new name for the style, then click **OK** or press **Enter** to return to the Style dialog box.
4. Click **Close** to close the Style dialog box.

Setting Up a Chain of Styles to Format Sequential Paragraphs

For certain types of documents, you can use the Style for Following Paragraph option in the New or Modify dialog box to develop a sequence of styles that formats paragraphs as you type them. By default, the style name appearing in the Style for Following Paragraph box is the same as the style in the Style box; that's because Word assumes you want to apply the same format to the next paragraph when you press **Enter**.

For example, if you are writing a report with several different headings—with the paragraph after each heading always having the Normal style—you could define a *Main Heading* style, followed by Normal as the next style; a *Subhead* style, followed by the Normal style; and so forth.

To set up a chain of styles:

1. Choose **Format Style**.
2. Chose **New** (if you are defining a new style) or **Modify** (if you are modifying an existing style).
3. Select the first style you want from the list.
4. In the Style for Following Paragraph list, choose the style you want to use to format the next paragraph.
5. Click **OK** or press **Enter**.

Once you've set up a chain of styles, all you have to do is apply the first style in the sequence at the insertion point (make sure it's on a blank line at the time). Word steps through the sequence, automatically switching to the next style in the chain when you press **Enter** to begin a new paragraph.

CHECK YOURSELF

Set up a chain of styles to format a newspaper article with a *Headline* style, a *Byline* style, and a *Body* style.

▲ First define three styles: *Headline*, *Byline*, and *Body*. Choose **Format Style**. Select the *Headline* style, click **Modify**, then type **Byline** in the Next Style box, and click **OK**. Then select the *Byline* style, click **Modify**, then type **Body** in the Next Style box, and click **Define**. Finally, select the *Body* style and make sure "Body" is the name in the Next Style box. Click **OK**, and then click **Close** again to close the dialog box.

Removing Additional Formatting from Styled Paragraphs

You can apply any type of formatting after you've attached a style to a paragraph. Formatting added with a Format command overrides the style's formatting, so if you want to see only the style's formatting, you'll have to remove all formatting except for the style.

To remove formatting you've added to "styled" paragraphs and return the paragraphs to the style's format:

1. Select the paragraphs.
2. Press **Ctr+Spacebar** to remove all character formatting added after the style was applied. Press **Ctrl+Q** to remove all paragraph formatting (including tabs, borders and shading, and bullets and numbering) added after the style was applied.

Removing Additional Formatting from Styled Paragraphs

Returning Paragraphs to the Normal Style

To return paragraphs to the Normal style:

1. Select the paragraphs.
2. Apply the Normal style from the Formatting toolbar by choosing **Format Style** or by pressing **Ctrl+Shift+N**.

Deleting Styles

You can easily remove styles that you no longer use. It's a good idea to delete unused styles to prevent your style list from becoming too long.

To delete a style that you've created:

1. Choose **Format Style**.
2. In the Name list, select the style you want to delete.
3. Click **Delete**. Word displays a dialog box asking if you want to delete the style.
4. Click **Yes** or press **Y**.
5. Repeat Steps 2 through 4 to delete all the styles you don't want.
6. Click **Close** to close the dialog box.

   NOTE: You can't delete one of Word's automatic styles, such as the Normal style.

Using Styles from Another Document

When you create a style, that style is attached only to the document you're working with at the time. (Of course, if you have multiple documents based on a template, they will all have the same style unless they are individually modified.) If you're working with one document and decide you want to apply the styles you created for another document, you can easily add those styles to the current document. Be aware, though, that incoming styles take precedence, so styles copied into another document replace any styles that have the same name.

To use styles from another document:

1. Choose **Format Style**.
2. Click **Organizer** to display the Organizer dialog box as shown in Figure 8.6.
3. The styles in the current document are displayed in the In (document name) drop-down list. If you want to use styles in a different file, click the **Close File** button and then click the **Open File** button. Select a directory and a filename to specify the document containing the styles you want to use. Word displays the names of all the files in that directory that have the .DOC extension. If you want to see all the files or just template files (those with the extension .DOT), you'll need to select **All Files** or **Templates** from the List Files of Type drop-down list.
4. Select the name of the current document in the To (document name) drop-down list. If the name of the current document is not displayed, then close the present file and open the current document using the procedure described above.
5. When you have selected the file from which you want to copy styles, select the names of the styles from the list and click **Copy**. Word displays this message to remind you of the result of your action:

    ```
    Do you wish to overwrite the existing style
    entry (name of style)?
    ```

6. Click **Yes** or press **Y**.

▼ *Figure 8.6. The Organizer Dialog Box*

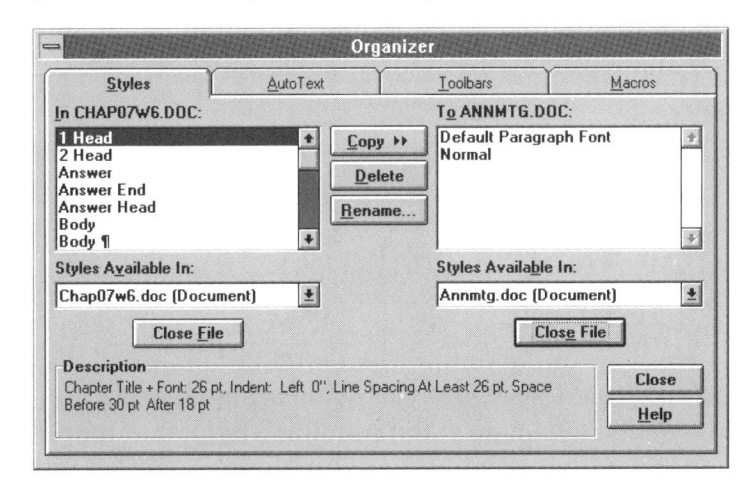

Using Styles from Another Document

7. Repeat Steps 4 and 5 to move more than one style to or from a document or template.
8. Click **Close** when you have finished.

Styles and Templates

When you create styles, they are automatically saved in the current document file. You can also tell Word to save styles in the template on which your document is based; this makes the styles available to all documents based on that template. If your document is based on the default NORMAL.DOT template, saving the styles in the template makes those styles available to all Word documents. You can add styles to the template one at a time, or add all styles associated with the document to the template at once.

Adding Individual Styles to the Template

To add individual styles to the template on which your document is based:

1. Choose **Format Style**, then choose either the **New** (if your are creating a new style) or **Modify** (if you are modifying an existing style) button.
2. In the Name box, type the name of the style you want to add to the template, or select the style from the list.

3. Turn on the **Add to Template** check box at the bottom of the dialog box.
4. Click **OK** to change the style.
5. Repeat Steps 2 through 4 to add more styles to the template if desired.
6. Click **Close** to close the Style dialog box.

Adding All Styles in the Document to the Template

If you've created several styles while your document is open, those styles are attached to the document but not to the template the document is based on. You can use the following procedure to add all the styles in the document to the template.

To add all styles attached in the document to the template:

1. Choose **Format Style**.
2. Choose **Organizer** to display the Organizer dialog box.
3. The styles in the current document are displayed in the In (document name) drop-down list. If you want to use styles in a different file, click the **Close File** button and click the **Open File** button. Select a directory and a filename to specify the document and styles you want to use. Word displays the names of all the files in that directory that have the .DOC extension. If you want to see all files or just template files (those with the extension .DOT), you'll need to select **All Files** or **Templates** from the List Files of Type drop-down list.
4. Hold down the **Shift** key and click the first style name and the last style name in the In (name of document) drop-down list.
5. Select the name of the template in the To (document name) drop-down list. If the name of the template is not displayed, then close the present file and open the current document using the procedure described above.
6. Click the **Copy** button. Word displays the following message:

    ```
    Do you wish to overwrite the existing style
    entry (name of style)?
    ```

7. Click **Yes** or press **Y**. You can also click the **Yes To All** button if you don't want to respond to each separate inquiry.

8. Click **Close** or press **Enter** to close the Organizer dialog box.

Styles and Templates

Adding All the Styles in a Template to a Document

Your document may be based on a template that contains many different styles. This makes these styles available to the document, but they are not saved in the document file. If you want to add all these styles to the document file, you can use the following procedure. You might want to do this if you want to base the document on a new template but keep all the applied template styles in the document.

To add all styles in a template to a document:

1. Choose **Format Style**.
2. Click **Organizer** to display the Organizer dialog box.
3. The styles in the current document are displayed in the In (document name) drop-down list. If you want to use styles in a different file, click the **Close File** button and click the **Open File** button. Select a directory and a filename to specify the document and styles you want to use. Word displays the names of all the files in that directory that have the .DOC extension. If you want to see all files or just template files (those with the extension .DOT), you'll need to select **All Files** or **Templates** from the List Files of Type drop-down list.
4. Hold down the **Shift** key and click the first style name and the last style list in the In (name of document) drop-down list.
5. Select the name of the template in the To (document name) drop-down list. If the name of the document you want to use is not displayed, then close the present file and open the document using the procedure described above.
6. Click the **Copy** button. Word displays the following message:

   ```
   Do you wish to overwrite the existing style
   entry (name of style)?
   ```

7. Click **Yes** or press **Y**. You can also click the **Yes To All** button if you don't want to respond to each separate inquiry.
8. Click **Close** or press **Enter**.

Printing a List of Styles

You can print the list of styles attached to a document. Word prints not only the names of the styles but also their descriptions.

To print a list of styles:

1. Open the document whose styles you want to print.
2. Choose **File Print**.
3. Select **Styles** from the Print drop-down list.
4. Click **OK** or press **Enter** to begin printing.

QUICK COMMAND SUMMARY

Command	To Do This
Format Style	Display the Style dialog box.
F4 or Edit Repeat Style	Repeat the application of a style.
View tab in Options dialog box	Open and adjust the size of the style area pane.
Ctrl+Q	Remove all formatting added after a style was applied.
File Print	Display the Print dialog box from which you can choose to print a list of styles.

PRACTICE WHAT YOU'VE LEARNED

Create two special styles for a book on poetry: a *poem* style (to format poems), with italic font, 1.75" indents on both sides, and 1½-line spacing; and a *title* style (for chapter titles), with bold and centered text and border lines 8 points above and below the text.

What You Do
1. Choose **Format Style**.

What You'll See
1. The Style dialog box.

Using Styles ▲ 189

What You Do	*What You'll See*
2. Click **New**, type **poem** in the Name box, and click the **Format** button.	2. The New Style dialog box with "poem" entered in the Name box. After you click the Format button, the list of the six formatting options is displayed.
3. Select **Font**, click the **Italic** check box, and then click **OK** to close the dialog box.	3. The Font command highlighted, then the Font dialog box displayed. After you turn on Italic and click OK, the New dialog is displayed with the word "Italic" in the Description box.
4. Select the Paragraph, type **1.75** in the Left and Right boxes, select **1.5** in the Line Spacing drop-down list, and then click **OK** to close the dialog box.	4. The Paragraph command highlighted, then the Paragraph dialog box displayed. The number 1.75 appears in the Left and Right boxes after they are entered. The Line Spacing drop-down list is displayed when activated, and the number 1.5 is highlighted when it is selected.
5. Type **title** in the Name box.	5. The New Style dialog box with "title" entered in the Name box.
6. Click the **Format** button and then select **Character** buttons, click the **Bold** check box, and then click **OK** to close the dialog box.	6. The Character command highlighted, then the Character dialog box displayed. An X appears in the Bold check box. After you click OK, the New dialog box is displayed with the word "Bold" in the Description box.

What You Do	*What You'll See*
7. Select **Paragraph**, select **Center** in the Alignment area, and click **OK** to close the dialog box.	7. The Paragraph command highlighted, then the Paragraph dialog box displayed. After you click **OK**, the Center Alignment button becomes black, and the word "Centered" appears in the Description box.
8. Click the **Borders** button.	8. The Borders button on the Formatting toolbar changes to a light gray to indicate it is in use, and the text underlined.
9. Make sure the Preset area indicates None.	9. The Borders and Shading dialog box, with a blue line around the Presets figure labeled "None" to indicate it is turned on.
10. Click the top of the sample page in the Border box.	10. A line at the top of the sample page where you clicked.
11. Click the second border type in the left column in the Line box.	11. The line with this thickness, replacing the line at the top of the sample page.
12. Click the bottom of the sample page.	12. A line at the bottom of the sample page where you clicked.

What You Do

13. Set the From Text box at 8, then click **OK** to close the dialog box.

14. Click **Close** to close the dialog box.

What You'll See

13. The number 8 displayed in the From Text box, and the sample page changed slightly to illustrate the measurement change. After you click OK, the New dialog box is displayed with the phrase "Borders formatting" in the Description box.

14. The dialog box closes, and the style added to the current style list in the Formatting toolbar.

9

Page Layout and Frames

In previous chapters, you learned how to format characters and paragraphs. A Word document also contains section and page setup formats that affect the entire document. In this chapter, you will learn how to:

▲ Divide your document into sections and apply special section formats

▲ Create multiple columns and format those columns

▲ Set margins and page orientation

▲ Put text or graphics into frames

▲ Position frames

Working with Sections

When you want part of your document to have a page layout different from the overall document layout, you can separate that part into a different section and then format that section. For example, you might want part of your document to be in two columns and part to be in single-column format, as shown in Figure 9.1.

If you don't separate your document into sections, Word considers your document to be one section.

Inserting and Deleting Section Breaks

When you want to begin a new section, you use the Break dialog box (by choosing **Insert Break**) to insert a section break. The section break ends the previous section. You then tell Word where you want the next section to begin.

▼ *Figure 9.1. A Document Divided into Sections*

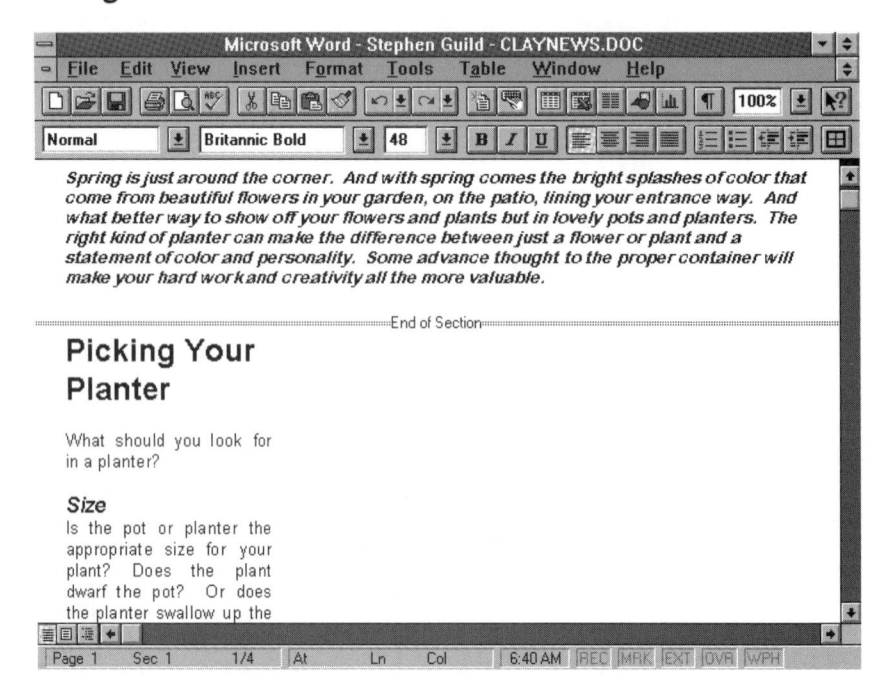

Working with Sections

To insert a section break:

1. Place the insertion point where you want to insert a section break.
2. Choose **Insert Break**.
3. In the Section Breaks area, choose one of the following options to specify where you want the next section (the text following the section break marker) to begin:

To Start the Next Section On	Choose
The next page	Next Page
The same page as the previous section	Continuous
The next even-numbered page	Even Page
The next odd-numbered page	Odd Page

   At any time, you can change where a section starts by using the Layout tab in the Page Setup dialog box.

4. Click **OK** or press **Enter**. If you are using Draft mode or Normal view and have the hidden characters displayed, a section break marker (a double dotted line) appears just above the insertion point.

The status bar tells you which section contains the insertion point. For example, "Pg 1 Sec 2 26/50" indicates that the insertion point is on Page 1 of Section 2, on the 26th page of a document that contains 50 pages.

When you have inserted a section break to tell Word where to end one section and begin the next, you're ready to format your sections. (Remember, if you don't separate your text into sections, Word considers your document to be one section; in that case, the options you choose apply to your entire document.)

TIP

If you know beforehand that your document is going to have more than one section, you can first format the entire document with most of the formatting options, then break it into sections and adjust the formatting for the individual sections.

You can always delete a section break and unite sections again. Like a paragraph mark, a section break contains all formatting for a section. So, when you delete a section break, you remove all the associated formatting, and the text becomes part of the following section.

To delete a section break and unite sections:

1. Select the section break marker (double dotted line with the words "End of Section.")
2. Press the **Delete** key.

TIP

You can quickly access the Layout tab in the File Page Setup dialog box by double-clicking the section break marker (the double dotted line). The dialog box that appears controls the placement of the following text as well as the alignment of the text preceding the marker.

CHECK YOURSELF

Why would you divide a document into sections?
▲ When you divide a document into sections, you can format different parts of the document differently. For instance, you can have different number of columns in different sections; change margins, headers, and footers in one section and not in another; and so forth.

Changing Margins

You can change page margins within a section or for the entire document.

To change margins:

1. Select the text whose margins you want to change, or position the insertion point where you want the margins to change.
2. Choose **File Page Setup** and click the **Margins** tab.

Changing Margins

3. Type or select the measurement for each page margin you want to adjust: Top, Bottom, Left, Right. The document in the Preview box changes as you adjust the margin sizes.
4. Choose one of the following in the Apply To drop-down list:

To Do This	**Select**
Apply formatting to the section containing the insertion point	This Section
Insert a section break before the insertion point	This Point Forward
Apply formatting to all sections in the document	Whole Document
Insert section breaks before and after the selection	Selected Text
Apply formatting to the selected sections	Selected Sections

5. Click **OK** or press **Enter**.

To use the ruler to change the margins:

1. Select the text whose margins you want to change, and then display the ruler.
2. Drag the left or right margin marker to the new position.

You can also use the ruler in Print Preview to change your margins.

Creating Mirrored Margins on Facing Pages

If your document will be printed double-sided (on both the fronts and backs of pages), you may want to format your pages so that the margins mirror each other. This makes inside and outside margins mirror each other. Mirrored margins are especially useful if you want a large inside margin to reserve space for binding. If you want different headers or different page number positions for even and odd pages, you'll have to create different right and left headers and footers, as you will learn in Chapter 13.

To make margins mirror each other on facing pages:

1. Choose **File Page Setup** and click the **Margins** tab.

2. Turn on the **Mirror Margins** check box.
3. Set the margins in the Top, Bottom, Inside, or Outside running list boxes to set up the page. Make sure you type a measurement for the larger inside margin in the Inside box, or type a measurement in the Gutter box.
4. Click **OK** or press **Enter**.

    NOTE: Word always makes even-numbered pages left pages and odd-numbered pages right pages, so the first page of your document will have no facing page.

CHECK YOURSELF

Create inside mirrored margins of 1.75".

▲ Choose **File Page Setup**, click the **Margins** tab, and then turn on the **Mirror Margins** check box. Type **1.75** in the Inside box, and click **OK** or press **Enter**.

Changing Page Size and Orientation

You can print on different-sized paper or change the orientation within a document so that some pages are portrait (vertical) and others are landscape (horizontal). If you want to create new page size settings and then use these as the default settings, Word can save your settings in the active template. Each new document based on that template will automatically have the revised page size and orientation.

To change paper size or orientation:

1. Select the portion of the document to which you want to apply the new settings.
2. Choose **File Page Setup** and click the **Paper Size** tab.
3. Select or type the settings you want to adjust. Under Orientation, click either **Portrait** or **Landscape**.
4. Click one of the following in the Apply To box:

Changing Page Size and Orientation

To Do This	Select
Apply formatting to the section containing the insertion point	This Section
Insert a section break before the insertion point	This Point Forward
Apply formatting to all sections in the document	Whole Document
Insert section breaks before and after the selection	Selected Text
Apply formatting to the selected sections	Selected Sections

5. If you want to make these settings the default settings, click the **Default** button and then click the **Yes** button in response to the message that appears.
6. Click the **OK** button.

Setting Vertical Alignment

You can use the Layout tab to control how Word positions text vertically on a page. You can also position text vertically by adding blank lines before and/or after lines of text. However, if you use the Layout tab, Word aligns the text for you. This technique is especially useful for creating title pages, where you want to center the text vertically as well as horizontally. (For horizontal alignment, select and center paragraphs by pressing **Ctrl+E** or by using the Centered button on the ribbon.)

To specify vertical alignment:

1. Move the insertion point into the section that you want to affect.
2. Choose **File Page Setup** and click the **Layout** tab.
3. In the Vertical Alignment box, choose one of the following options:

   Top   Aligns the first line of text with the top margin (as on any normal page)

Center   Centers the text on a page between the top and bottom margins

Justify   Adds space between paragraphs to align the first line of text with the top margin and the bottom line of text with the bottom margin

4. Click **OK** or press **Enter**.

You may need to insert page breaks or adjust the Section Start settings to control the amount of text on a page and to use these options effectively.

Creating a Default Document Format

Each time Word displays a new document, it applies its default document format to that document.

To use different settings for the default document format:

1. Choose **File Page Setup**, then choose options in the dialog box to specify the default format you want.
2. Click the **Default** button.
3. Click **Yes** in response to the message that appears.

Word records the document format in the template that you're using.

Formatting Text in Columns

In word processing, the term *column* means any text in which lines are "stacked" on top of one another. Word enables you to create several types of columns. You can use the Columns dialog box to set up columns of equal width, in which the text "flows" from the bottom of one column to the top of the next, as in a newspaper (these are sometimes called *snaking columns*). This section shows you how to work with flowing columns of text. If you want to create different types of columns, see Chapter 12 for information about tables or Chapter 7 for information about tabs.

Changing the Number of Columns

Formatting Text in Columns

Although you can set the number of columns before you type the text in a section, you'll generally find it easier to type all your information, then place it in columns. This technique makes it easier to see how the column width and the space between columns look on the pages.

To change the number of columns:

1. Move the insertion point into the section, or select the text that you want to change. If your document is not divided into sections and you don't select text, the entire document is affected.
2. Choose **Format Columns**.
3. In the Presets area, click the picture that matches the number of columns; or in the Number of Columns box, type or select the number of columns you want. If you want columns of unequal width, choose the Preset that is most like what you want; you can change it later. See "Changing the Width of Columns" later in this chapter.
4. If you want to change the default width of the columns, type a new measurement in each Width box. If you want to change the default spacing between columns, type a new measurement in each Spacing box. For example, if you want each column 1½" wide with ¼" of white space between columns, type **1.5** in each Width box and **.25** in each Spacing box.
5. If you want to insert a vertical line between columns, click the **Line Between** check box.
6. If you want columns of uneven width and spacing, turn off the **Equal Column Width** check box. As you change the measurements for each column, Word automatically calculates the width and spacing in the other columns.
7. Click one of the following in the Apply To box:

To Do This	*Select*
Insert section breaks before and after the selection (not available unless you have selected some text)	Selected Text

To Do This	Select
Insert a section break before the insertion point (not available if you have selected some text)	This Point Forward
Apply formatting to the selected section(s) only	This Section or Selected Sections
Apply formatting to the entire document	Whole Document

8. When the sample page in the dialog box looks the way you want it to appear, click **OK** or press **Enter**.

When you choose a different number of columns and choose This Point Forward in the Format Columns dialog box, Word automatically inserts a section break marker and divides your document into sections.

Don't panic if you only see one column of text on the screen after you've specified two or more columns. You can't see multiple columns in Normal view. You have to switch to Page Layout view or use Print Preview to view the columns. Figure 9.2 shows

▼ *Figure 9.2. Multiple Columns in Print Preview*

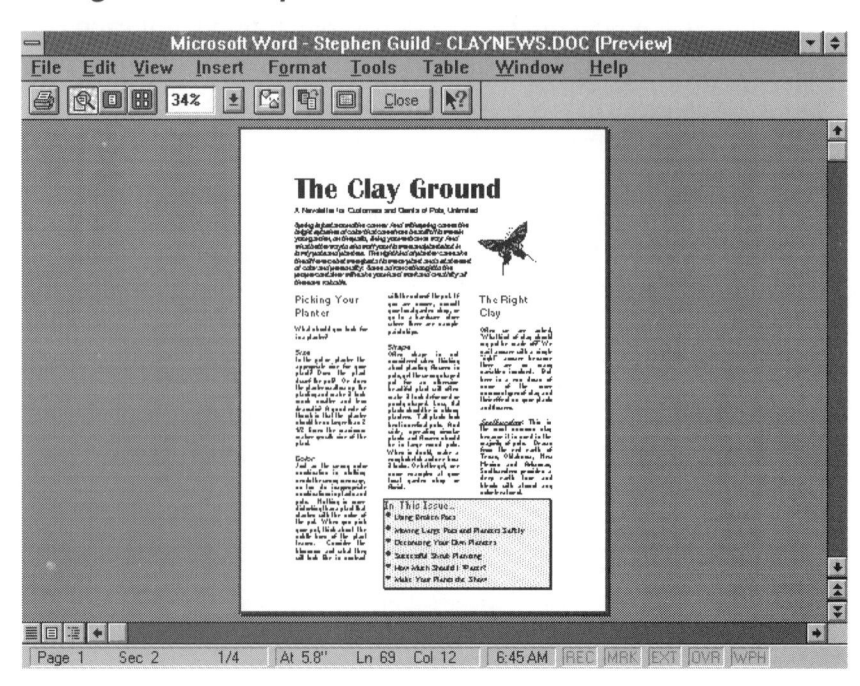

columns in Print Preview. Figure 9.3 shows columns in Page Layout view.

To switch to Page Layout view:

▲ Choose **View Page Layout** or click the **Page Layout** button at the bottom of your screen.

To switch to Print Preview:

▲ Choose **File Print Preview** or click the **Print Preview** button on the Standard toolbar.

When you use multiple columns in a document, you'll probably find it easier to edit and format text in Page Layout view, where you can see changes to columns more easily.

Changing the Width of Columns

You can change the space between columns by using the Columns dialog box or by using the ruler. Both techniques accomplish the same thing, but using the ruler is much simpler.

Formatting Text in Columns

▼ **Figure 9.3. Multiple Columns in Page Layout**

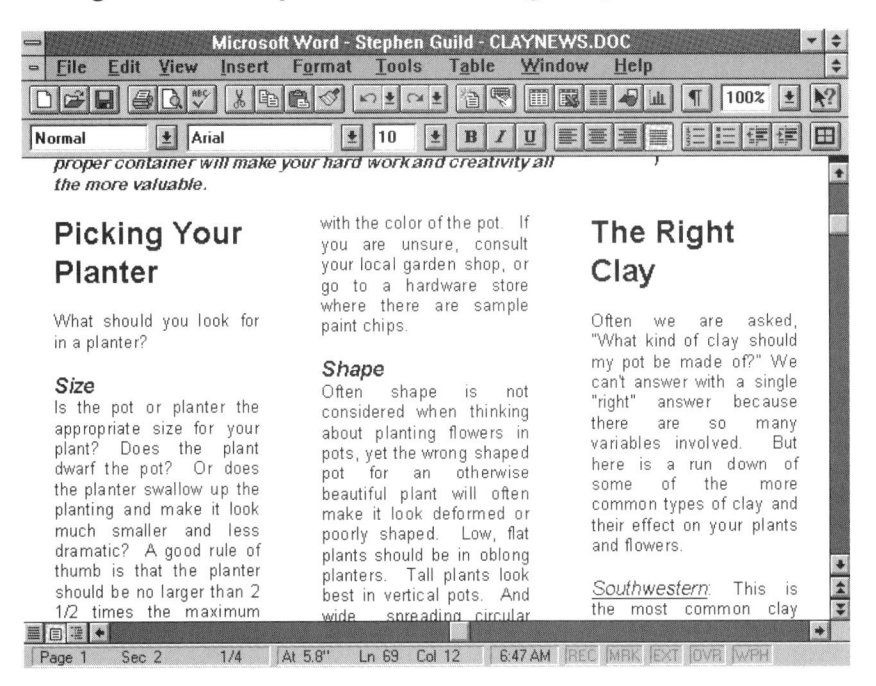

Before you use the ruler to change the width of columns in a section, you may want to switch to Page Layout view so that you can see your columns side by side and view the results of changes.

To use the ruler to change the width of columns:

1. Move the insertion point into the section in which you want to change the column width.
2. If necessary, choose **View Ruler** to display the ruler.
3. Drag column markers to new locations to change the width of the columns.

Adding and Removing Lines Between Columns

To add or remove a line between columns:

1. Move the insertion point into the section in which you want to add lines between columns.
2. Choose **Format Columns**.
3. Turn on or off the **Line Between** check box.
4. Click **OK** or press **Enter**.

The lines will display only in Print Preview mode. Figure 9.4 shows an example of lines drawn between columns.

CHECK YOURSELF

Format a page so that the top part is one column and the bottom is three columns, with lines between the columns.

▲ Place the insertion point on the page where you want the section break to occur, choose **Insert Break**, and click the **Continuous** button in the Section Break box. Then place the insertion point in the bottom section, choose **Format Columns**, type **3** in the Number of Columns box, and turn on the **Line Between** check box.

Changing Column Breaks

Word automatically breaks a column when the text reaches the bottom margin on the page. If Word's automatic column breaks

▼ *Figure 9.4. Lines Between Columns*

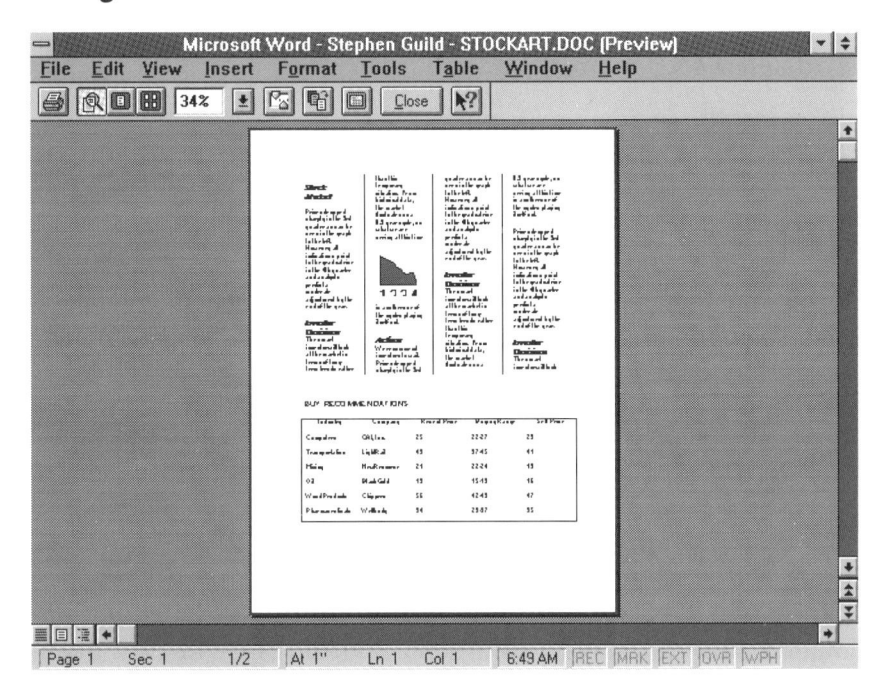

Formatting Text in Columns

don't meet your needs, you can insert your own column break marker wherever you want, from within Normal or Page Layout view.

To insert a column break:

1. Place the insertion point where you want the column break.
2. Do one of the following:
   ▲ Press **Ctrl+Shift+Enter**.
   ▲ Choose **Insert Break**, choose the **Column Break** option, then click **OK** or press **Enter**.

   Word inserts a column break marker (a dotted line).

To delete a column break that you've inserted:

1. Click the column break marker to select it, or use the direction keys to move the insertion point onto the marker.
2. Press the **Delete** key.

You can always delete a section break and unite sections again. Like a paragraph mark, a section break contains the formatting for a section. So, when you delete a section break, you remove all the associated formatting, and the text becomes part of the following section.

To delete a section break and unite sections:

1. Select the section break marker.
2. Press the **Delete** key.

TIP

If you want to balance columns at the end of a section or document, insert a continuous section break at the bottom of the last column

Using Frames

Frames are rectangular areas on a page that are used to enclose paragraphs, tables, and graphics so they can be positioned and formatted. You can move a frame to a specific place in your document, and you can easily change the size of a frame. However, you don't always "see" a frame, because you can choose to insert a frame that has no visible border lines. To create frames and to size and position them, it is best to be in Page Layout view. Figure 9.5 shows various types of frames in a document.

Creating and Deleting Frames

To create a frame:

1. Make sure that you are in Page Layout view, then choose **Insert Frame**. The insertion point changes to a cross.
2. Place the pointer where you want to anchor one corner of the frame, then drag the mouse until the frame is the approximate size you want. (Don't worry about the exact size, since you can always change that later.)

When you release the mouse button or click outside the frame, Word will draw the frame.

▼ *Figure 9.5. Some Uses for Frames*   *Using Frames*

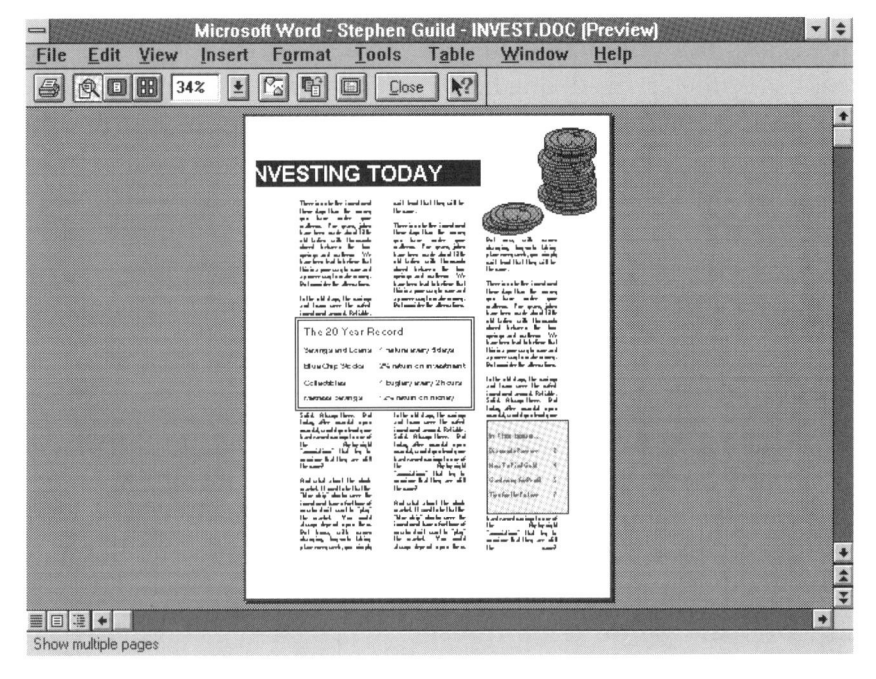

If you want to delete a frame, click the frame to select it, and then press **Delete**. Remember: when you delete a frame, you delete all text and graphics that are inside it.

Inserting Text for Graphics in a Frame

You can place text and graphics in a frame that you have created.

To insert text or graphics in a frame:

1. Select the text or graphics. Then choose **Edit Cut** or **Edit Copy**, press **Ctrl+X** or **Ctrl+C**, or use the **Cut** or **Copy** toolbar button.
2. Click the frame once to select it, then click inside the frame where you want to place the text or graphics. When the frame is selected, a shaded gray border will appear around it.
3. Choose **Edit Paste**, press **Ctrl+V**, or use the **Paste** toolbar button.

You can also choose Insert Picture to insert graphics. If you add more text or graphics than will fit in a frame, Word makes the frame longer (but not wider) to accommodate the addition. You can adjust the size of the frame by using the Frame dialog box.

Positioning Frames

You can position a frame anywhere in a document by using the mouse or the Frame dialog box. When you need to specify the *exact* position on the page where you want the frame to appear, you should use the Frame dialog box. In either case, you need to be in Page Layout view to position a frame.

Positioning a Frame with the Mouse

To position a frame using the mouse:

1. Select the frame by clicking one of the borders of the frame. Small black "handles" appear around the edge of the frame, and the mouse pointer becomes a four-headed arrow. (If you've been working inside the frame, you'll need to click outside the frame first, then click the frame once to select it.)
2. Drag the outline of the frame to the position you want. When you release the mouse button, Word draws the frame in the new position.

Positioning a Frame with the Frame Dialog Box

When you position a frame with the Frame dialog box, you can type specific measurements and specify where to measure from: the left or top edge of the page, the left or top margin, or the left or top column margin (in a multiple-column section). You can also choose relative options, such as Left, Right, Top, Bottom, or Center, and then choose what the option is relative to: the edges of the page, the margins, or the column margins (in a multiple-column section) or the surrounding paragraph (when the frame is within a paragraph).

The Frame dialog box (shown in Figure 9.6) can seem confusing until you learn how the options work together, so you should take the time to become familiar with it. This dialog box lets you control the positions of frames with precision.

▼ *Figure 9.6. Positioning a Frame with the Frame Dialog Box*

Using Frames

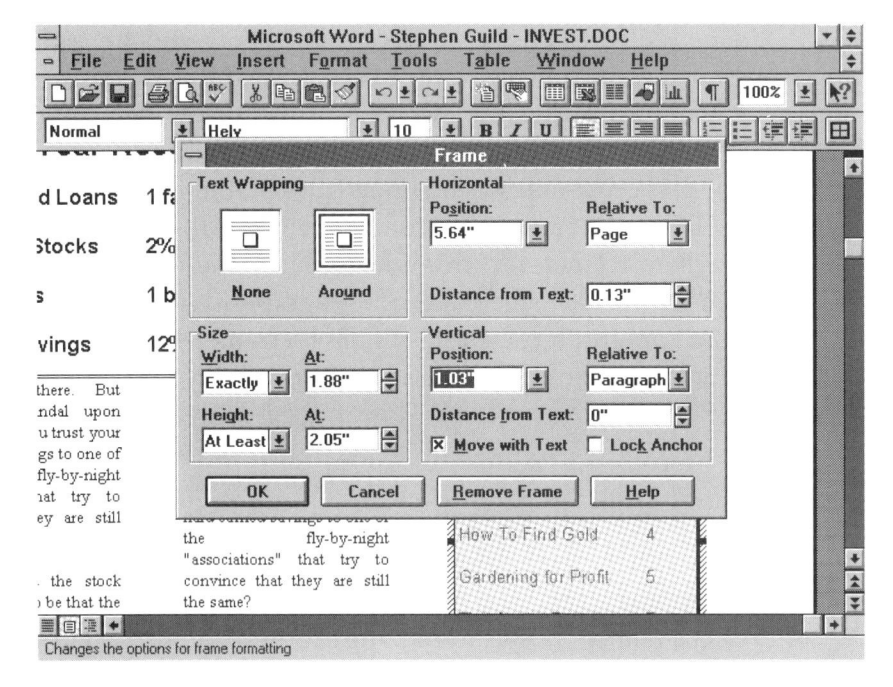

To position a frame using the Frame dialog box:

1. Click the frame. Handles appear around the edge of the frame.
2. Choose **Format Frame**.
3. To set the horizontal position, do one of the following in the Horizontal area:
    ▲ Type a specific measurement (such as **1.5**) in the Position box, then select an option from the Relative To list to specify where to measure from: **Margin** for the left margin, **Page** for the left page edge, or **Column** for the left column margin in a multiple-column format. For example, if you type **1** in the Position box and select Page in the Relative To list, the left edge of the frame will be positioned 1" from the left edge of the page.
    ▲ Select a relative position from the Position drop-down list: **Left**, **Right**, **Center**, **Inside**, or **Outside**. Then use the Relative To drop-down list box to select what that position is relative to: **Margin** for margins, **Page** for the page edges, or **Column** for the column margins in a multiple-column format. For example, if you select Right in the Position box

and select Margin in the Relative To list, the right edge of the frame will be aligned with the right margin. Use the Inside or Outside option when you want to make sure the frame is always on the inside or outside of the page, as it would appear when bound in book format.

4. To set the vertical position, do one of the following in the Vertical area:
   ▲ Type a specific measurement (such as **1.5**) in the Position box, then select an option from the Relative To list to specify where to measure from: **Margin** for the top margin, **Page** for the top page edge, or **Paragraph** for the first line of the paragraph (when positioning a frame within a surrounding paragraph of text). For example, if you type **1** in the Position box and select Page in the Relative To list, the top edge of the frame will be positioned 1" from the top edge of the page. Selecting the Paragraph option always turns on the Move with Text check box to make the frame move with the surrounding paragraph: you can't have one without the other.
   ▲ Select a relative position from the drop-down Position list: **Top**, **Bottom**, or **Center**. Then use the Relative To list to select what that position is relative to: **Margin** for margins, **Page** for the page edges, or **Paragraph** for the first line of the paragraph (when positioning a frame within a surrounding paragraph of text). For example, if you select Center from the Position list and select Margin from the Relative To list, the frame will be aligned vertically between the top and bottom margins.
5. If you need to, change the measurement in the Distance from Text box within the Horizontal box to set the amount of white space between left and right edges of the frame and the surrounding text. Or change the measurement in the Distance from Text box within the Vertical box to set the amount of white space between the top and bottom edges of the frame and surrounding text.
6. Click **OK** or press **Enter**.

There may be times when you want to lock a frame to a particular position on the page no matter what page the frame moves to.

To lock an anchor to a frame:

1. Click on the frame in Page Layout view.
2. Click the **Show/Hide** button (¶ mark) on the Standard toolbar.
3. Click on the frame. Whe you move the frame to a paragraph mark, a small anchor appears.
4. Drag the small anchor to the paragraph to which you want to lock it.
5. Choose **Format Frame** and turn on the **Lock Anchor** check box.
6. Click **OK** or press **Enter**.

Using Frames

TIP

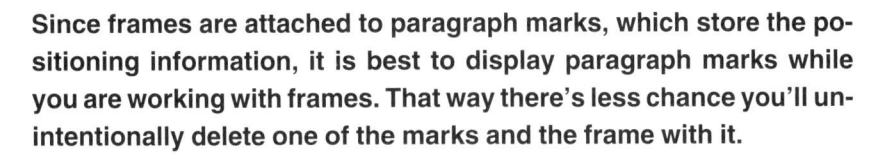

Since frames are attached to paragraph marks, which store the positioning information, it is best to display paragraph marks while you are working with frames. That way there's less chance you'll unintentionally delete one of the marks and the frame with it.

Wrapping Text Around a Frame

You can choose to wrap text around a framed paragraph, table, or graphic. To wrap text, you need to be in Page Layout view.

To wrap text around a frame:

1. Click the frame. Handles appear around the edge of the frame.
2. Choose **Format Frame**.
3. Under Text Wrapping, select **Around**, and click **OK**.

   If you don't want text to flow around the sides of the frame, select **None** under Text Wrapping.

Changing the Size of a Frame

To size a frame using the mouse:

1. Click the frame. Handles appear around the edge of the frame.
2. Drag the handles until the frame is the size you want

To size a frame using the Frame dialog box:

1. Click the frame. Handles appear around the edge of the frame.
2. Choose **Format Frame**. Word displays the Frame dialog box, as shown earlier in Figure 9.6.
3. In the Size: Width drop-down list, select **Auto** if you want the width of the frame to adjust as you increase or decrease the width of the table, graphic, or text it contains; or select **Exactly**, then type or select the width you want in the At box.
4. In the Size: Height box, select **Auto** if you want to make the height of the frame the same as the table, graphic, or text it contains; select **At Least** to set a minimum height, then type or select the height you want in the At box; or type or select **Exactly** and the height you want in the At box.
5. Click **OK** or press **Enter**.

Adding or Removing Border Lines and Shading in Frames

You can draw borders on one or all sides of a frame. You can also add different types of shading to the frame background: you can choose from a variety of patterns and can add color to the shading if you wish.

To add borders or shading to a frame:

1. Select the frame.
2. Choose **Format Borders** and shading and click on the Borders tab.
3. In the From Text box, type or select a measurement for the spacing between the border and the enclosed text or graphic.
4. To add lines or boxes, do one of the following:
    - ▲ Choose one of the options in the Presets area: **None** for no border, **Box** for a box around the frame, or **Shadow** to create a frame with a shadow effect.
    - ▲ If you don't want a border on all four sides, or if you want a different type of line for one or more sides of the frame, click the side of the diagram to specify where you want the line to appear, and then click the border type in the Line

box. If you want color for a preset border or one you choose, select the color from the Color drop-down list. Continue this approach until all borders appear the way you want.
5. If you want to include background shading, click the **Shading** tab and choose options for Shading, Foreground, and Background from the Shading tab. Click **OK** to return to the Frame Borders and Shading dialog box.
6. Click **OK** or press **Enter**.

Adding or Removing Border Lines and Shading in Frames

Smoothing Out Ragged Margins with Hyphenation

Most of the time, you'll want to use left alignment for paragraphs, which leaves a ragged right margin. If your document contains a lot of long words or if you use very wide margins or large point size, the right margin may look really rough because Word automatically shifts a whole word down to the next line when it won't fit on the original line. You can smooth out the right margin in all or part of your document with Word's hyphenation feature. The hyphenation process inserts "optional hyphens" that won't print unless they're at the end of a line. With the hyphenation feature you don't need to worry about stray hyphens ending up in unusual places. Unlike regular hyphens that you insert, optional hyphens appear only where they're needed.

TIP

It's a good idea to wait until you're finished editing the text in a document before you use Word's hyphenation feature. That way, you'll only have to hyphenate once.

To use the hyphenation feature:

1. If you don't want to hyphenate the entire document, select the text you want to hyphenate. You can select just one word if you want.
2. Choose **Tools Hyphenation**.

3. Change any or all of the following options in the dialog box:
   ▲ To tell Word to hyphenate in all cases, turn on the **Automatically Hyphenate Document** check box.
   ▲ To hyphenate uppercase words as well as lowercase words, turn on the **Hyphenate Words in CAPS** check box. (Leaving this option turned off will prevent hyphenation of titles and headings that are in all capital letters.)
   ▲ In the Hyphenation Zone box, type a positive measurement. The *hyphenation zone* is the space from the right margin into which the program will try to fit part of a word. The smaller the hyphenation zone, the more hyphens Word will try to insert.
   ▲ To limit the number of hyphens appearing consecutively in the document, indicate a number in the Limit Consecutive Hyphens To running list box. The default is No Limit.
   ▲ To confirm each hyphen before Word inserts it, choose the **Manual** button and indicate Yes or No at each instance. If you don't use Manual, Word automatically hyphenates all the words it can.
4. Click **OK** to begin hyphenation.

If there is a particular paragraph that you don't want word to hyphenate, choose the **Text Flow** tab in the Format Paragraph dialog box and turn on the **Don't Hyphenate** check box.

QUICK COMMAND SUMMARY

Command	To Do This
File Page Setup	Control margins, page size and orientation, and paper source for the printer.
Insert Break	Control page breaks, column breaks, and section breaks.
Format Columns	Control the number of columns, the space between columns, and lines between columns.

File Print Preview	Display full pages in miniature and change margins and page breaks.
Insert Frame	Change the mouse pointer to a cross for drawing a frame.
Format Frame	Control the size and position of a frame and determine whether text wraps around the frame.

PRACTICE WHAT YOU'VE LEARNED

Duplicate the figure shown in Figure 9.5, using a frame as a place holder for the graphic.

What You Do	*What You'll See*
1. Click the paragraph mark button (¶) on the ribbon to show nonprinting characters, and make sure that you are in Page Layout view.	1. A blank page and the top margin of the page when in Page Layout view.
2. Press **Enter** several times to move the paragraph mark down the page.	2. Several paragraph mark characters.
3. Choose the **Insert Frame** command or click the Insert Frame button on the Drawing toolbar.	3. The insertion point changed to a cross.
4. Draw the frame for the masthead at the top of the page.	4. A rectangle the size of the desired masthead after you have released the mouse button. There is shading around the outside edge of the frame.

What You Do	**What You'll See**
5. Change the font size to 36, change the typeface to bold, and type the masthead text.	5. The words "Investing Today" in 36-point bold font.
6. Click outside of the masthead frame at the place where you want to start the column text.	6. The masthead and the blank document work space.
7. Choose **Insert Break**, choose **Continuous** in the Section Break box, and then click **OK**.	7. The document appearance unchanged. However, you will have inserted a section that will be formatted in three columns later.
8. Place the insertion point below the section break, and type enough text to fill one page.	8. The text of the newsletter.
9. With the insertion point still in Section 2, choose **Format Columns**.	9. The Columns dialog box with the available options.
10. Set the Number of Columns at 3, click the **Line Between** check box, and click **OK**.	10. The text formatted in three columns with lines between the columns.
11. Using Insert Frame, insert a place-holder frame for the money graphic.	11. A blank frame, which will contain the graphic, at the right side of the masthead.

10

Adding Pictures and Creating Drawings

You no longer need to paste up pages when you want to add pictures to a document. Word for Windows makes it easy to integrate pictures and text. In this chapter, you will learn how to:

- ▲ Paste pictures from the Clipboard
- ▲ Import graphic files of all types, including Word's clip art
- ▲ Use Microsoft's drawing tools to create your own drawings or change imported drawings
- ▲ Resize, crop, and frame pictures

Inserting Pictures

Generally, Word distinguishes among graphics, objects, drawings, and pictures. *Graphics* and *objects* are imported elements that are either embedded in Word or linked to another application. *Drawings* are created inside of Word. *Pictures* is a general term that can apply either to drawings created inside of Word or to graphics or other objects imported from outside applications.

You can add pictures to your documents in many ways. One of the simplest ways is to copy all or part of a graphic created with a Windows program to the Clipboard, and then just paste the graphic into your Word document. You can also insert entire picture files into a document or *embed* drawings that you create with the drawing tools in Word.

Adding Pictures with the Clipboard

Anything you can copy to the Windows Clipboard can easily be pasted into Word. This makes it easy to simply copy and paste a picture from any Windows drawing program, such as Paintbrush.

Follow these steps to copy and paste a picture:

1. Open the drawing program and display the picture you want to copy.
2. Select what you want to copy (all or part of the picture), then choose **Edit Copy** from within the drawing program.
3. Open the Word document, and place the insertion point where you want to paste the picture.
4. Choose **Edit Paste** to insert the Clipboard contents.

Word recognizes the pasted contents as a picture, so you can select it and format whatever you pasted just as you can any other pasted object.

Importing Files Created in Other Programs

Word can import graphics files saved in the following formats:

Inserting Pictures

- Windows bitmaps (BMP extension)
- Windows metafiles (WMF extension)
- Tagged image file format (TIF extension)
- Encapsulated PostScript (EPS extension)
- PC Paintbrush (PCX extension)
- Computer graphics metafile (CGM extension)
- HP graphics language (HPGL extension)
- Lotus 1-2-3 graphics (PIC extension)
- Microgaphics Designer/Draw (DRW extension)
- WordPerfect graphics (WPG extension)
- Corel Draw (CDR extension)
- Macintosh PICT (PCT extension)

Word comes with a complete set of clip art that you can use in your documents. These clip art files, which are all Windows metafiles (WMF files), are installed in the CLIPART subdirectory beneath the WINWORD directory when you load Word for the first time. Figure 10.1 shows one of the clip art files in miniature in the Picture dialog box (accessed from the Insert menu).

▼ *Figure 10.1. Previewing a Clip Art File*

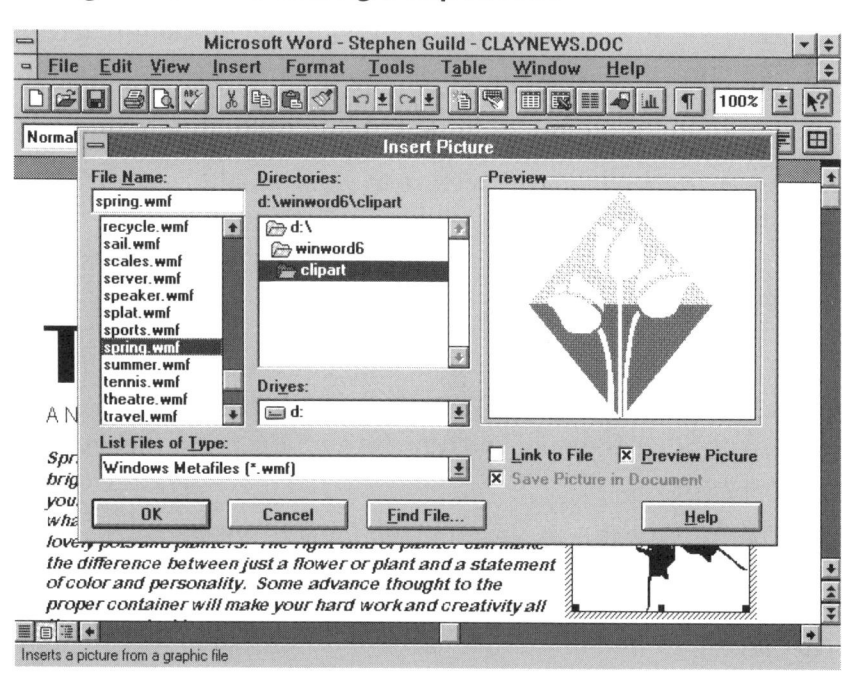

When you import a graphics file, you can choose whether to link the imported picture to its original file. If you choose not to link, Word stores a copy of the picture in the Word document. If you choose to link, Word pastes a field that tells the program where to find the graphics file. Linking allows you to update pictures in their original files and keep them current in the Word document; it also keeps your Word file down to a reasonable size because Word doesn't actually store the picture in the document. However, linking does mean that you must keep the picture file in the original location (where it was when you inserted the field into Word) or that you must remember to change the field in Word if you move the picture file. Chapter 18 will tell you more about linking and about creating and updating fields.

To import a file created in another program:

1. In your Word document, position the insertion point where you want to insert the picture.
2. Choose **Insert Picture**.
3. Make selections in the Drives, Directories, and File Name boxes as necessary.
4. If you want to see a miniature of the picture, click the **Preview Picture** check box. A picture appears in the right side of the dialog box, as shown in Figure 10.1. (You can use the Preview Picture check box to look at the contents of files until you see the picture you want.)
5. If you want to link the picture to its original file, turn on the **Link to File** check box.
6. If you want to reduce the size of your Word file, uncheck the Save Picture in Document box.
7. Click **OK** to insert the picture. (If you have turned on the Show Field Codes box in the Tools Options View tab and you have turned on the Link to File check box, you'll see the codes that link the file. To see the picture, turn off the Show Field Codes box.)

The odds are that the inserted picture will not be the exact size you want when you first insert it. To control the size and other formatting aspects, see "Working with Pictures in Word" later in this chapter.

Creating Drawings in Your Documents

Inserting Pictures

Word for Windows has a built-in drawing program that can only be used from within Word to embed a drawing. You can use Microsoft's drawing tools to create your own simple drawings, to modify the graphics that come with Word (the clip art), or to change drawings created with other applications. Whenever you draw objects, you must be in Page Layout view.

Using the Drawing Tools

Whenever you click the Drawing button on the Standard toolbar, Word displays a set of drawing tools, as shown in Figure 10.2. When you want to use a tool, you just click the tool, then drag or click with the mouse pointer. A brief explanation of the tool appears in the Status Bar when you move the mouse pointer to its button.

▼ *Figure 10.2. Drawing in a Document Window*

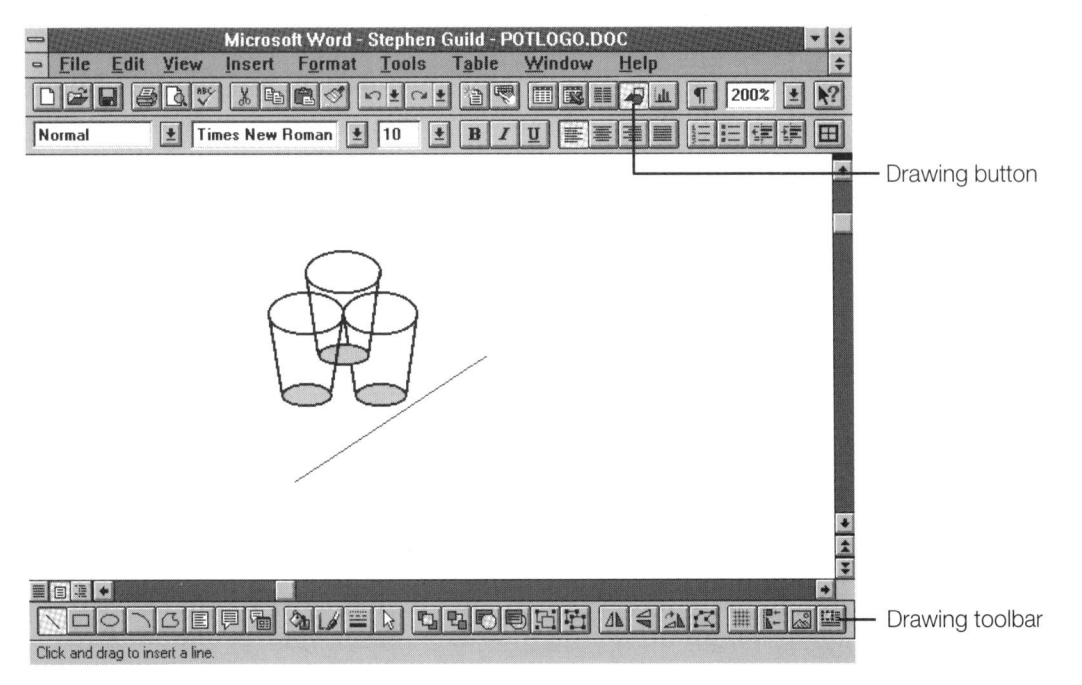

Each part of a picture (even a line) that you draw with a tool becomes a separate object in that drawing. You can select and change each object separately, or you can group objects and treat the group as a single object. Figure 10.2 shows several objects created by the drawing tools.

To create a drawing:

1. Position the insertion point where you want to insert the drawing.
2. Do one of the following:
   - ▲ Click the **Drawing** button (the one with the circle, square, and triangle) on the Standard toolbar.
   - ▲ Click the right mouse button in the "white space" of any toolbar, and select **Drawing**.
   - ▲ Choose **View Toolbars** and select **Drawing**.
3. Do one of the following:

To Draw	Do This
A straight line	Click the **Line** button and drag the mouse.
A rectangle	Click the **Rectangle** button and drag the mouse.
A square	Hold down the **Shift** key, click the **Rectangle** button, and drag the mouse.
An ellipse	Click the **Ellipse** button and drag the mouse.
A circle	Hold down the **Shift** key, click the **Ellipse** button, and drag the mouse.
An arc	Click the **Arc** button and drag the mouse.
A freeform shape	Click on the **Freeform** button, click to create straight line segments, and drag to create freeform shapes. Double-click to complete an open shape.

CHECK YOURSELF

Use Microsoft's drawing tools to draw a triangle, a circle, and a square in your document.

▲ Click the **Drawing** button on the Standard toolbar. Next, click the **Freeform Object** button. Click one point to fix a position, then drag out three lines, releasing the mouse button at the three points to create the triangle. Click the ellipse tool, hold down the **Shift** key, and drag out a circle. Finally, select the rectangle tool, hold down **Shift**, and drag out a square.

Editing a Drawing

After you've created and inserted a drawing into your document, it's easy to edit the drawing.

To edit a drawing:

▲ Double-click the drawing in your Word document. The Drawing toolbar window will appear automatically.

Selecting Objects

Before you can change an object, you must select the object.

To select an object:

1. Click the **Select Drawing Objects** button.
2. Do one of the following:
   ▲ To select one object, click the object.
   ▲ To select multiple objects, hold down **Shift** as you click each object, or point to one corner of the area around the object and drag out a selection rectangle that encloses all the objects that you want to select. (You may be wondering, What selection rectangle? If you point to a blank area, hold down the left mouse button and drag; the rectangle with dashed lines appears.)

▲ To select all the components of a freeform shape, click the shape, and then click the **Reshape** button on the Drawing toolbar.

Black square handles appear around a selected object. If you're selecting one object and you click the wrong object by mistake, just click another spot to "deselect" the object. If you're selecting multiple objects and you want to "deselect" one object, hold down **Shift** as you click the object again.

Moving Objects

To move an object or a group of objects:

1. Select the object or the group of objects, as described above. Move the pointer until it becomes a cross with four arrowheads.
2. Drag the object(s) to a new location. To constrain movement to a straight line, hold down **Shift** as you drag.

CHECK YOURSELF

Using a selection rectangle, select the three objects you created in the previous "Check Yourself," and drag them to a new location.
▲ Imagine an invisible frame around your objects, and point to one corner of that frame. Drag to the other corner to enclose all the objects. If the selection rectangle doesn't enclose all the objects, just release the mouse button and start over. After handles appear around the group of objects, move the mouse until the point becomes a cross with four arrowheads within the handles, and drag the object to a new location.

Resizing Objects

To change the size of an object:

1. Select the object.

2. Point to one of the handles, and then drag the object outline to a new size. If you hold down the shift key while you drag one of the corners, the drawing will retain its proportions.

Editing a Drawing

Layering Objects

Objects can be stacked on top of other objects. To layer objects initially, just drag one object on top of another. You can change which objects overlay others by bringing objects to the front or by sending them to the back of the stack. Figure 10.2 shows stacked objects.

To change the layering order of overlapping objects in a drawing:

1. Select the object or objects. (Click any visible piece of an object.)
2. Do one of the following:

To	*Click*
Bring the object in front of the text	The **Bring in Front of Text** button
Send the object behind the text layer	The **Send Behind Text** button
Bring the object to the front of a stack of objects	The **Bring to Front** button
Send the object to the back of a stack of objects	The **Send to Back** button

Rotating and Flipping Objects

You can rotate objects 360 degrees right (clockwise). You can also flip objects horizontally or vertically. To rotate or flip multiple objects at the same time, you must group the objects first.

To rotate or flip objects:

1. Select the object or group of objects.
2. Do one of the following:

▲ To flip the object or group horizontally, choose the **Flip Horizontal** button.
▲ To flip the object or group vertically, choose the **Flip Vertical** button.
▲ To rotate the object or group, click the **Rotate Right** button.

Changing Fill Pattern and Color

You can choose whether an object is filled with a color and a pattern by choosing **Format Drawing Object** and, in the Fill tab, making the appropriate choices, as shown in Figure 10.3.

To change the fill pattern, color, and color pattern of an object:

1. Choose **Format Drawing Object** and click on the **Fill** tab.
2. Select one of the colors in the Color box. You can also use the **Fill Color** button on the Drawing toolbar.
3. Select one of the patterns or % of "screen" in the Patterns box.
4. Select one of the colors or % of gray in the Pattern Color box.

▼ *Figure 10.3. Choosing a New Color from the Fill Tab*

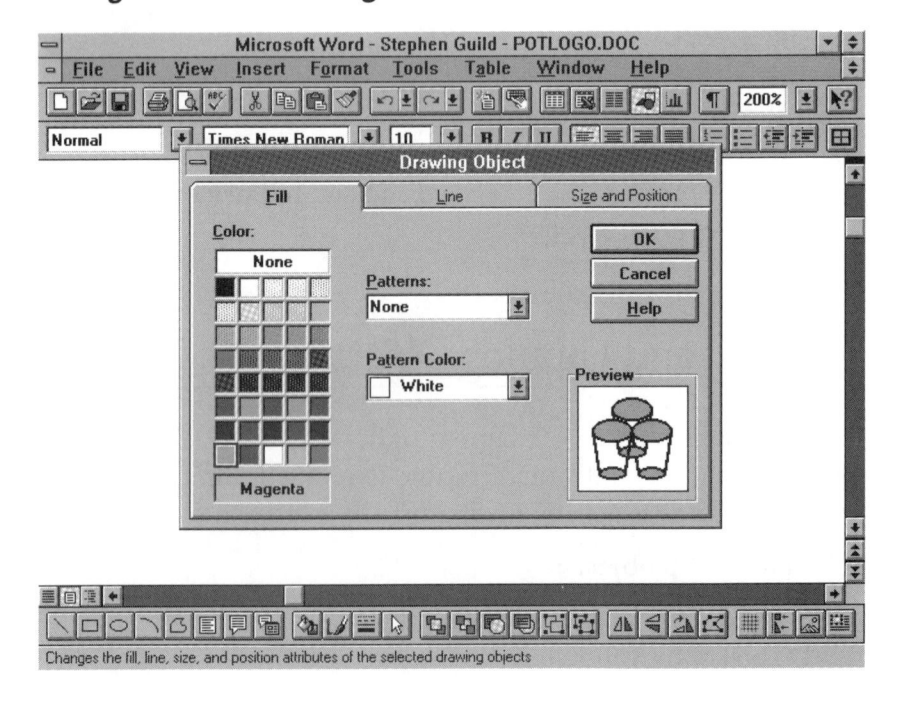

Changing Line Color and Style

Editing a Drawing

You can change the color and style of the drawing object lines. You can add arrowheads and change the thickness, style, length, and other characteristics of lines. You can also access the Format Drawing Object dialog box through the Line Style button.

To change the line color or style:

1. Select the line you want to change.
2. Choose **Format Drawing Object** and click on the **Line** tab.
3. Select one of the styles in the Style drop-down list.
4. Select one of the colors in the Color drop-down list. You can also use the **Line Color** button on the Drawing toolbar.
5. Select the other options for line weight, arrowhead style, width, length, and whether you want the drawing to have a shadowed or rounded corner.

CHECK YOURSELF

Change the color of one of the triangles in your drawing.
   ▲ Click the triangle, then click the **Fill** button on the Drawing toolbar and select a new color.

Grouping and Ungrouping Objects

When you group objects, you can treat the group as a single entity (to move, resize, rotate, flip, color, and so on). Grouped objects remain associated until you ungroup them (unlike objects in a multiple selection, which lose their association as soon as you select something else). If you want to change one object within a group, you'll need to ungroup the objects first.

To group objects:

1. Select all the objects you want to group.
2. Click the **Group** button. Handles appear around all the objects to show that the objects are grouped.

To ungroup a set of grouped objects:

1. Select the group you want to separate.
2. Click the **Ungroup** button.

> **TIP**
>
> Most of the WMF files included in Word's clip art contain grouped objects. In fact, many contain groups within groups, so if you want to modify an object in a clip art file, you may need to ungroup several times before you can select an individual object.

Changing the Magnification of a Drawing

Use the **View Zoom** command or the **Zoom Control** button on the Standard toolbar to change the magnification of a drawing. This doesn't change the actual size of the objects in the drawing but projects them larger so you can more easily work on them.

Using a Grid and Guide Lines to Align Objects

You can use an invisible grid to align and position objects in your picture. The grid has 12 lines per inch. When the invisible grid is turned on, any object that you create, move, or resize will snap to the nearest grid intersection.

To turn on the grid:

▲ Click on the **Snap to Grid** button on the Drawing toolbar.

You can position a horizontal or vertical guideline anywhere you like, then use that guideline to align and position objects precisely. When an object gets close to a guide, its edge or center automatically snaps to the guide. As you drag a guideline, Drawing displays the distance from the top left corner of the drawing area.

To align drawings:

1. Select the drawings you want to align.
2. Click the **Align Drawing Objects** button.

3. Click on the appropriate choices in the Align dialog box, then click **OK** or press **Enter**.

To hide the guide lines, click the **Align Drawing Objects** button again.

Editing a Drawing

Adding and Changing Text

To create text in a drawing:

1. Click the **Text Box** button and draw a text box.
2. Enter the text.
3. Format the text for character, paragraph, styles, borders, and all other formatting.

The text box is a separate element in the drawing. You can move it around like any other object and scale and crop as you wish.

To edit existing text:

1. Double-click the text you want to change.
2. Change the text.
3. Press **Esc**, or click away from the text.

Adding Callouts

You may want to call attention to an area of interest in an illustration or picture by using a line and a text box. Using the Drawing toolbar, you can create "callouts" with one-, two-, or three-segment lines with specific angles and distances from text boxes. You can also add borders to text boxes.

To create a callout:

1. Click the **Callout** button on the Drawing toolbar.
2. Place the pointer where you want the callout line to start, and then drag to where you want the text box to start.
3. Type the callout text.

To change a callout:

1. Click the **Format Callout** button on the Drawing toolbar.
2. Select the type of callout you want in the Type area.

3. Do one or more of the following:
   ▲ If you want to change the distance between the callout text and the callout line, select a measurement in the Gap box.
   ▲ If you want to change the angle of the callout line, select angle degrees or **Any** in the Angle box.
   ▲ If you want to change the amount of space between the top of a callout text and the start of the callout line, select **Top**, **Center**, or **Bottom** in the Drop box, or type a measurement.
   ▲ If you want to change the length of the first segment, select **Best Fit** in the Length box, or type a measurement.
   ▲ If you want to apply a border around the callout text, turn on the **Text Border** check box.
   ▲ If you want the starting position of the callout line to change automatically from left to right, turn on the **Auto Attach** check box.
   ▲ If you want to add a vertical line beside the text, turn on the **Add Accent Bar** check box.
4. Click **OK** or press **Enter**.

Undoing Drawing Actions

To reverse your last drawing action:

▲ Choose **Edit Undo**.

CHECK YOURSELF

Add your name to your picture.
   ▲ Click the text tool, click on a blank spot in your drawing, then type your name.

Working with Pictures in Word

After you've added a picture to your Word document, you can use various Word methods to change the picture's format to suit your document. The following sections tell you how.

Scaling and Cropping Pictures

Working with Pictures in Word

You can use Word commands to change the size of a picture or frame. You can change the size of a picture in two ways:

▲ *Scaling* changes the relative size of a picture while you retain the entire picture. Scaling is similar to using the reduction and enlargement features on a copy machine—that is, scaling shrinks and enlarges the picture.

▲ *Cropping* cuts out portions of a picture.

To scale (change the size of) a picture:

1. Click the picture to select it. Handles appear at the edges of the picture.
2. Do one of the following:
   ▲ Point to the handle on the side you want to move, then drag to a new position. The percentage of the original size of the picture appears in the status bar and changes as you move the mouse.
   ▲ Choose **Format Picture**, type or select scaling percentages in the Width % and Height % boxes in the Scaling area, and then click **OK**. 100% equals the original size of the picture. (Examples: to make the picture 50% taller, type **150** in the Height box; to make the picture 25% narrower, type **75** in the Width box.) Figure 10.4 illustrates how to use the Picture dialog box to scale a picture.

You'll notice that when you change the scaling percentage, you're also changing the size measurements in the dialog box. You can change these measurements instead of the scaling percentages, and the scaling will change automatically.

When you want to cut out a portion of a picture rather than just change its size, you'll crop the picture.

To crop a picture with the mouse:

1. Select the picture. Word draws handles at the edges of the picture.
2. Do one of the following:
   ▲ Hold down **Shift** and drag the handles to change the size of the picture frame until the picture is cropped the way you want it.

▼ **Figure 10.4. Scaling a Picture with the Picture Dialog Box**

▲ Choose **Format Picture**; type or select decimal cropping measurements in the Top, Left, Bottom, and Right boxes in the Crop From area; then click **OK**. (Example: if you want to take ¹⁄₁₀" off the right side, type **.10in** or **.10"** in the Right box.)

Returning Pictures to Their Original Sizes

To return a picture to its original size:

1. Select the picture or frame.
2. Choose **Format Picture**.
3. Click the **Reset** button, or type **100** in the Height and Width boxes and **0** in all the cropping boxes.
4. Click **OK** or press **Enter**.

TIP

To speed up Word, you can control whether pictures are displayed fully or as empty boxes. When you don't need to see the pictures,

choose Tools Options, **select the** View **tab, then turn on the** Picture Placeholders **check box. When you need to see the pictures, repeat the step, but turn the check box off.**

Working with Pictures in Word

Adding or Changing Border Lines Around Pictures

Pictures inserted from the Windows Clipboard have invisible frames or border lines around them. You can use Format Borders and Shading to add various types of border lines. The simplest way to create a border is to select a line style and click Box in the Border tab. See Chapter 9 for complete instructions on adding and changing borders.

CHECK YOURSELF

Add one of Word's clip art pictures to your Word document, then resize the picture to 50% and add a border around it.

▲ Use **Insert Picture** to select a picture from the CLIPART directory. (Use the **Preview** button to see the picture before inserting it, if you like.) Click the picture in your document to select it, choose **Format Picture**, type **50** in both the Width and Height boxes in the scaling area, then click **OK**. With the picture still selected, choose **Format Borders and Shading** and click the **Box** option in the Presets area, then click **OK**.

Positioning Pictures and Frames

In Word, paragraphs can have two kinds of positions: free-floating and fixed. Paragraphs with free-floating positions move as changes are made to the text. Paragraphs with fixed positions stay in their assigned positions, and surrounding free-floating text automatically flows around the positioned paragraphs. You can't see the proper positions of text in Normal view—you have to switch to Print Preview or Page Layout view for that. Figure 10.5 shows a picture fixed in a position so that text flows around it.

▼ **Figure 10.5. Text Flowing Around a Fixed Picture**

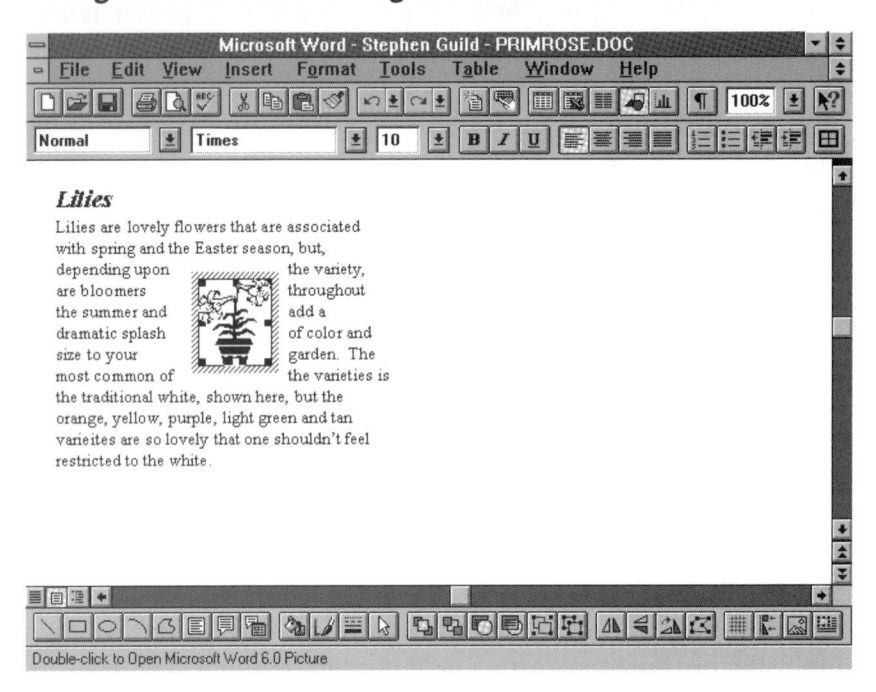

Because Word considers a picture to be a single character, it places the bottom of the picture frame on the baseline for text characters—in effect creating a very tall line—just as Word would do for a large font size. Because a picture is a character, you can use the Character dialog box to make a picture a superscript or subscript, offsetting it from the baseline. For the same reason, you can put several pictures on the same line.

If you inserted a picture or frame immediately before a paragraph mark (¶), the picture is the only character in that paragraph. You can precisely position a picture paragraph on a page using precise measurements or relative positions (top, bottom, center, for example) using the Format Frame command. See "Using Frames" in Chapter 9 for more information about using the Frame dialog box. To arrange pictures side by side with text or other pictures, you might want to create a table. For more information about tables, see Chapter 12.

To position a picture:

1. Choose **Format Drawing Object** or click the **Line** style button, then click **More**. Word will display the Drawing Default dialog box.

2. Click the **Size and Position** tab and make the appropriate choices.
3. Click **OK** or press **Enter**.

If you want to anchor your drawing to a paragraph or a particular position, turn on the **Lock Anchor** check box in the Size and Position tab. For more information about anchoring pictures and frames, see Chapter 9.

Working with Pictures in Word

TIP

If you have a picture that you want to use repeatedly, such as a business logo, you can save that picture along with its attached formatting as an AutoText entry, then insert it into your documents whenever you need it. For more information on using AutoText entries, see Chapter 4.

Copying, Moving, and Deleting Pictures

To copy, move, or delete a picture:

1. Select the picture.
2. Do one of the following:

To	*Do This*
Copy the picture	Use **Edit Copy** and **Edit Paste**.
Move the picture	Use **Edit Cut** and **Edit Paste**.
Delete the picture	Press **Delete**.

Adding a Caption to a Picture

You may want to add a caption to a picture and make sure it stays with the picture. Figure 10.6 shows a picture with a caption. The procedure described here is intended for captions that are unique or longer than those used to label figures, tables, and the like. For more information about using these types of captions, see Chapter 17.

▼ *Figure 10.6. A Picture with a Caption in the Same Paragraph*

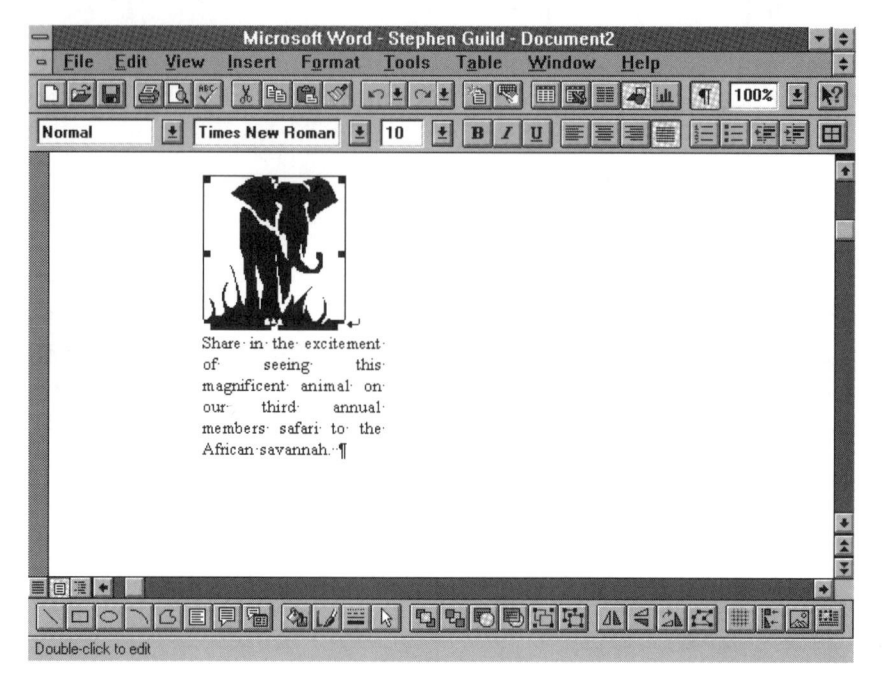

To add a single caption for a picture:

1. Place the insertion point immediately after the picture (but in front of the paragraph mark).
2. Press **Shift+Enter** to enter a newline character. This begins a new line but keeps the picture and the paragraph in the same paragraph.
3. Type the text of the caption.

You can format the caption just as you would format any characters. Keep in mind that if you use the Paragraph dialog box you'll change the format of the picture as well as the caption because they're in the same paragraph.

Using WordArt to Add Special Effects

You may want to make a report, newsletter, flyer, or other document a little more interesting or eye-catching. WordArt will help you create and change text with many different special effects. After the WordArt object has been created, it can be scaled and positioned like any other Word graphic.

Using WordArt to Add Special Effects

To create a special effect using WordArt:

1. Place the insertion point where you want the special text effect to appear.
2. Chose **Insert Object** and click the **Create New** tab.
3. Select **Microsoft WordArt** 2.0 from the Object Type list.
4. After the Word displays the WordArt toolbar, menu bar, and text bar, type the text you want to format in the text entry window.
5. If you want to add a symbol to the text, click on the **Insert Symbol** button and select a symbol from the Symbol dialog box.
6. Click on the appropriate toolbar buttons to format the text the way you want. You can select a variety of shapes and lines to fit your text into, as well as the font and font size.
7. Choose **Update Display** to see the results of your choices in the document.
8. When you have finished creating the text effect, click in the Word document. If you want to edit the text, double-click it and make your changes.

QUICK COMMAND SUMMARY

Command	To Do This
Edit Copy or Edit Cut; Edit Paste	Copy or cut pictures from other Windows programs and insert them into Word, or copy or move a picture from one location in a Word document to another.
Insert Picture	Insert pictures from a variety of programs, including Word's clip art files, into a Word document.
Insert Object	Create and insert an object, using an application that supports Object Linking and

Command	To Do This
	Embedding (OLE). In this chapter, you used the Microsoft Draw application to create and embed a picture in your document.
Drawing toolbar and commands	Create and edit pictures embedded in Windows applications.
Format Picture or Shift+drag handle	Change the size of (scale) a selected picture in a Word document.
Format Picture or drag handle	Crop a selected picture in a Word document.
Format Borders and Shading	Add border lines around a picture.
Delete key	Delete a selected picture from a Word document.

PRACTICE WHAT YOU'VE LEARNED

In a Word document, import the BOOKS.WMF file from the WINWORD/CLIPART directory (or, if you changed the default directory, wherever you keep the clip art files that came with Word). Change the color of the open book to yellow, the other book to turquoise, and the quill to red. Label each book with a callout letter, using A through C for the set. Finally, exit to your document.

What You Do
1. Use **Insert Picture** to find and insert BOOKS.WMF.

What You'll See
1. The Insert Picture dialog box with the list of clip art files provided with Word in the File Name list. Once you have selected the BOOKS.WMF file, you will see the graphic, if Preview Picture is turned on. After you click OK, the graphic is inserted in the document.

What You Do	*What You'll See*
2. Double-click the inserted picture to start the Picture editing tools.	2. The picture in an editing container in a separate window entitled Picture in (name of document). Word displays the Drawing toolbar and a Picture dialog box.
3. Click the open book to select it, then click the Fill color button and click yellow. Repeat this step again to change the closed book to turquoise and the quill to red.	3. Handles around the open book you selected. When you click yellow, the book becomes yellow, and then the other objects become turquoise and red as you do the same to them.
4. Click the **Callout** button, and drag the cross to form a callout box and line from the yellow book. Size the callout box, and press **Shift+A** to type an uppercase *A*. Repeat this step two more times to add the letters *B* and *C* to the other book and quill. You may have to use the Format Callout button to adjust the callout boxes for size, position, and line angle once you have created them.	4. The arrow changed to a cross. When you drag, a callout line and box appear. Black handles appear around the callout box, and the arrow turns to a four-sided arrow when you click the callout box to size it. The letter *A*, *B*, or *C* is displayed in the callout box after you type it. If you need to adjust the callout boxes, the Format Callout dialog box appears after you click the Format Callout button on the Drawing toolbar.
5. Click **Close Picture** to return to the document.	5. The picture in the document.

11

Charts and Equations

This chapter will show you how to use the Microsoft Graph application and the Microsoft Equation Editor application to add charts and mathematical symbols to your documents. Both of these applications come with Word. In this chapter, you will learn how to:

- ▲ Type or copy data for a chart
- ▲ Select a chart type and other formatting options
- ▲ Add mathematical equations to your documents

Creating Charts

When you want to add a chart to your document, you can copy and paste a chart from any Windows charting program into your Word document, or you can embed a chart using the charting portion of Microsoft Excel or using Microsoft Graph (the charting program included with Word). This chapter focuses on Microsoft Graph.

To begin a chart with Microsoft Graph:

1. Place the insertion point where you want the chart to appear in your Word document.
2. Choose **Insert Object**.
3. Double-click **Microsoft Graph** in the list box. Word opens a Microsoft Graph window on top of your document.

You can also begin a chart by clicking the **Insert Chart** button on the Standard toolbar.

The Microsoft Graph application window contains two windows of its own—a Datasheet window and a Chart window—as shown in Figure 11.1. You can maximize each window or rearrange the windows for your convenience, as shown in Figure 11.2.

When you create a chart using Microsoft Graph in this way, you're actually creating a link from Word to the Microsoft Graph application. For more information on linking, see Chapter 18.

After you have entered data and formatted the chart (as explained in the following sections), choose Exit and Return to (name of document) from the Microsoft Graph File menu. When the dialog box appears, choose Yes to update the chart and add it to your Word document. The chart will be inserted into your document with gray diagonal marks. These will remain on top of the object until you close the document for the first time. Thereafter, if you want to change the chart in any way, just double-click the chart to open Microsoft Graph again.

Charts and Equations ▲ 243

▼ **Figure 11.1. The Microsoft Graph Window on Top of Word**

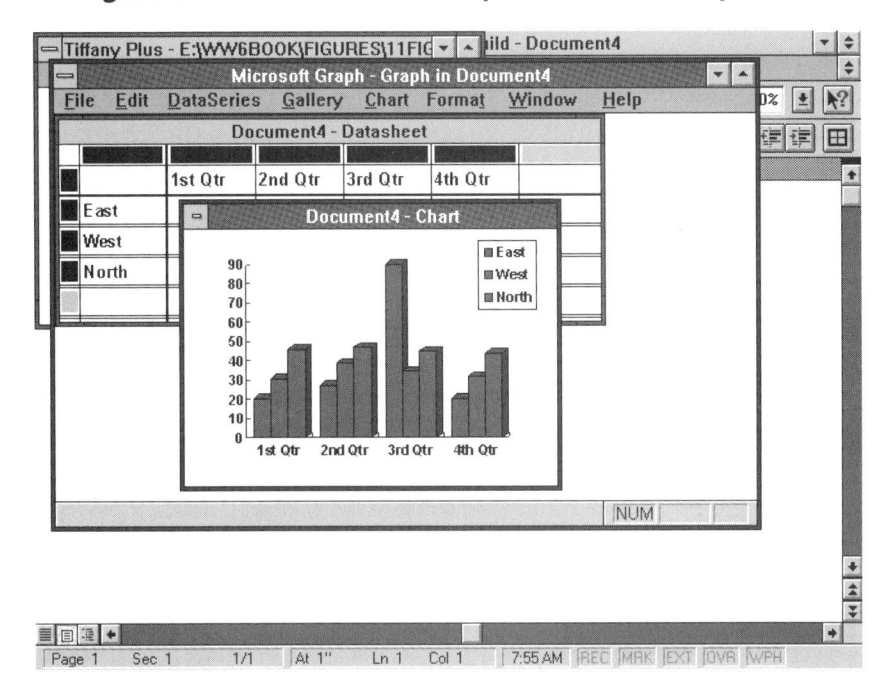

Creating Charts

▼ **Figure 11.2. The Datasheet and Chart Windows Rearranged**

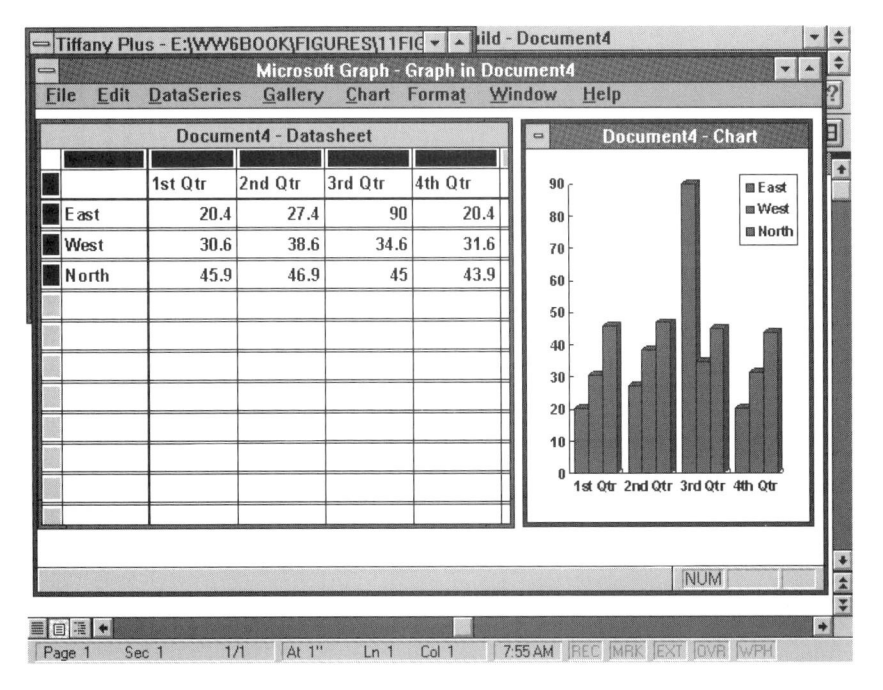

Entering Data for a Chart

You can enter the data for a chart in three ways: by typing the data in the Datasheet window, by copying it from a Word document, or by copying it from another Windows application to the Windows Clipboard and pasting it into the Datasheet window. Generally, it's easiest to type the data in the Datasheet window. If you've ever used a spreadsheet application before, entering and formatting data will be familiar to you.

When Microsoft Graph opens, you'll notice that data is already in the Datasheet window and a chart is in the Chart window. This sample data is intended as a guide to help you set up your datasheet properly. You can replace the data simply by typing your own numbers and text.

To enter chart data:

1. If you have a lot of data to type, first maximize the Datasheet window by clicking on the maximize button in the upper right corner of the window.
2. Click the first cell.
3. Type the data you want to put into the cell.
4. Use the arrow keys to move to the next cell, then type data in that cell.
5. Repeat Step 4 until you've filled in your datasheet. You'll notice that the Chart window changes as you add data.
6. If necessary, select any cells that have superfluous data, and then press **Delete** and click **OK** in the dialog box that appears. This deletes the data in the selected cells.

TIP

Don't type commas, dollar signs, or any other characters with numbers. Instead, use the Number command on the Format menu to set a consistent format for numbers, including dates. You'll find that this method of formatting is much faster and won't confuse the program when you perform calculations.

If you want to copy and paste into the Datasheet window, the copied chart data must conform to the following rules:

Creating Charts

▲ Data items (*data points* in charting terminology) must be in separate cells in a spreadsheet program or in a Word table, or be separated by tabs in regular text.
▲ If you want to label the data in the chart, put the labels in the first row and/or the first column. By default, Microsoft Graph interprets each row as a *data series* and puts the labels in the first column in the chart legend. However, you can change this by using the Series as Columns command in the DataSeries menu.

The copied data will lose its formatting (bold, underline, italic, dollar signs, commas, and so forth) when it is pasted into the datasheet.

To create a chart by copying the data to the Windows Clipboard:

1. Select the data you want to copy to the Clipboard, then choose **Edit Copy**.
2. If necessary, place the insertion point in your Word document and choose **Insert Object**. Then double-click **Microsoft Graph** in the list to open the Microsoft Graph application or click the **Insert Chart** button on the Standard toolbar.
3. If you're going to paste a lot of data, maximize the Datasheet window by clicking on the maximize button in the upper right corner of the window. This allows you to see all of your data.
4. Click the datasheet cell that you want as the upper left corner of the block of cells you're going to paste. Word will automatically fill cells to the right and down with the pasted data, overwriting any information that is currently in those cells.

Formatting Rows and Columns in a Datasheet

It's not really necessary to make the datasheet look nice because only the chart will actually appear in your Word document. However, you may want to insert or delete rows or columns, or make a column wider or narrower, so that you can read all the data in the cells.

To add or delete rows or columns:

1. Select the same number of rows or columns you want to add, or select the rows or columns you want to delete.
2. Do one of the following:
   ▲ To insert the same number of rows or columns that you've selected, choose **Edit Insert Row/Col**.
   ▲ To delete the selected rows or columns, choose **Edit Delete Row/Col**.

To change the width of a column:

1. Click any cell in the column.
2. Choose **Format Column Width**.
3. Type a new number in the Column Width box, then click **OK**.

Changing the Format for Numbers

You can control whether numbers appear with decimal points, with currency symbols, as dates, with minus signs in front of or parentheses around negative numbers, and so forth. By default Microsoft Graph uses the General format, which leaves the data in the format in which you type it: left-aligning data that includes any characters other than numbers, or right-aligning numbers.

To change the format of numbers:

1. Select the numbers you want to change, or select empty columns or rows to set the format in advance.
2. Choose **Number** from the Format menu.
3. Double-click the format you want in the list. Date formats appear near the bottom of the list.

Editing Data in a Cell

When you need to change a simple number or word that you've typed in a cell, you can just click the cell and type the data again.

If the data in a cell is fairly complex and you don't want to retype all of it, follow these steps:

1. Double-click the cell to make the Cell Data dialog box appear.
2. Edit the data in the dialog box as necessary (just click, select, add, or delete as you would anywhere else), then click **OK**.

Charts and Equations ▲ 247

Choosing a Chart Type

Creating Charts

By default, Microsoft Graph draws a column chart. However, there are several chart types to choose from.

To choose another chart type:

1. Choose a chart type from the Gallery menu to display a dialog box with more options. Figure 11.3 shows the Chart Gallery dialog box that displays different line chart types.
2. Click the option you want, then click **OK**.

CHECK YOURSELF

Create a simple pie chart with the following data:

    Apples   10
    Oranges   12
    Bananas   20

▲ First, click the **Insert Chart** button, or choose **Insert Object** and double-click **Microsoft Graph** in the list. Next, type

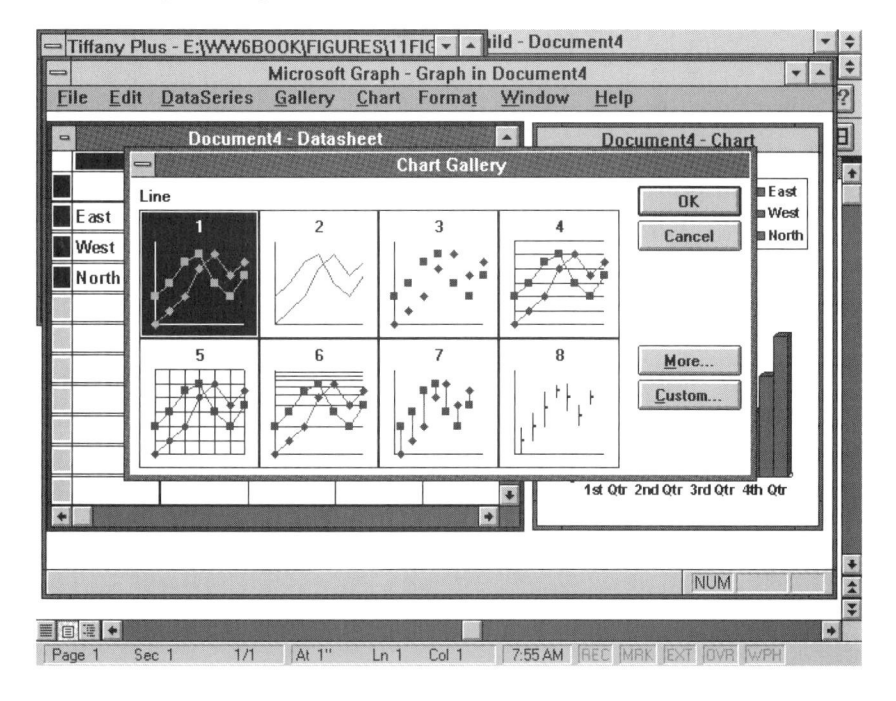

▼ Figure 11.3. Choosing a Line Chart Type in the Chart Gallery Dialog Box

the data shown above in the Datasheet window, using the arrow keys to move from cell to cell. Delete the other information. Finally, select **Pie** from the Gallery menu, and click **OK** in the dialog box to accept the default pie chart option.

Formatting the Chart

You can change the following aspects of a chart by using Microsoft Graph:

▲ Border lines, colors, or patterns used for data series in column, bar, area, and pie charts
▲ Symbols, line styles, and colors used for data series in line and scatter charts
▲ Line styles, colors, tick marks, and label fonts on an axis
▲ Border lines, colors, patterns, and fonts used in a legend

You can also import a chart into Microsoft Draw and then use the drawing tools to change or add bits and pieces of a chart, as described in Chapter 10.

Selecting Parts of a Chart

A chart consists of a variety of objects, often grouped into subsets—such as data series, axis labels, or the chart legend—which can be selected.

To select part of a chart:

▲ Point to the part and click. Handles appear around the selected part.

For example, to select a data series (such as all the columns that represent a particular store's sales throughout a year), you would point to any data point (column) in the data series and click once to make handles appear around all the columns in the data series.

Changing Aspects of the Selected Part

Creating Charts

As described in the first part of this section, you can change many aspects of a chart. The options that Microsoft Graph shows you depend on which part of a chart you have selected. Figure 11.4 shows the dialog box you will see if you select a data series. Figure 11.5 shows the dialog box you will see if you select an axis.

To change aspects of the selected part of a chart:

1. Double-click the part of the chart you want to change to display a dialog box listing your options. The dialog box contains different options for each part, so you may want to experiment by double-clicking different parts and studying the dialog box to see just what you can change.
2. Choose options in the dialog box to change line styles, colors, patterns, and many other options, depending on which part of the chart you've selected. Look at the sample in the lower right corner of the dialog box for a preview of the changes you're making.
3. Click **OK** or press **Enter**.

▼ *Figure 11.4. Changing the Pattern in a Data Series*

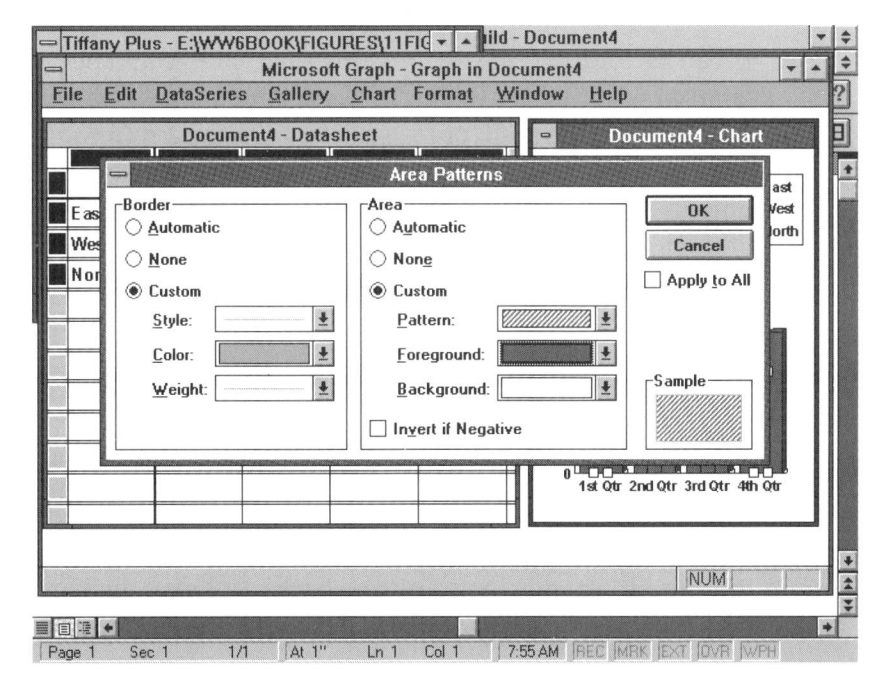

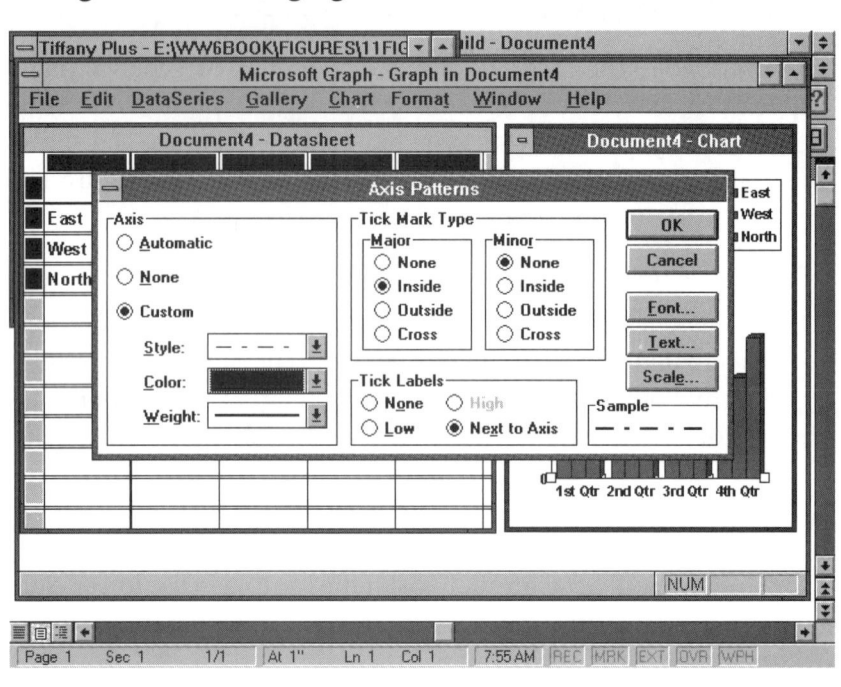

▼ *Figure 11.5. Changing the Tick Marks in an Axis*

CHECK YOURSELF

Choose a new pattern for one slice of the pie chart you created earlier.

▲ If you've returned to your document, double-click the pie chart to start Microsoft Graph. Next, double-click one slice of the pie. In the dialog box, select a new pattern from the Pattern drop-down list, and then click **OK**. Choose **Exit and Return to** (name of document) from the File menu, and click **Yes** when Microsoft Graph asks if you want to update the chart in your document.

Changing the Size or Position of a Chart

After you've used Exit and Return to update your chart and return to your Word document, Word considers the chart to be an imported graphic. To change the size of a chart, just select the chart and use the Format Picture dialog box to change its size. For more information about formatting imported graphics, see Chapter 10. You can also fix the position of a chart on a page and flow text around it by putting the chart into a frame. For more details, see "Using Frames" in Chapter 9.

Creating Charts

Building Equations

You can add complex mathematical equations to your documents using Equation Editor, a separate program that comes with Word for Windows. When you work with Equation Editor, you can insert special characters wherever you need them by selecting a picture of an equation from the drop-down graphical menus on the Equation Editor toolbar at the bottom of the window (see Figure 11.6).

The top row of the toolbar contains symbols such as operators or Greek letters that you insert into an equation. The bottom row of the toolbar has a variety of "templates" with tiny square placeholders for numbers. The menus let you choose additional formatting options. You can move the Equation Editor toolbar off the

▼ **Figure 11.6. The Equation Toolbar in a Word Document**

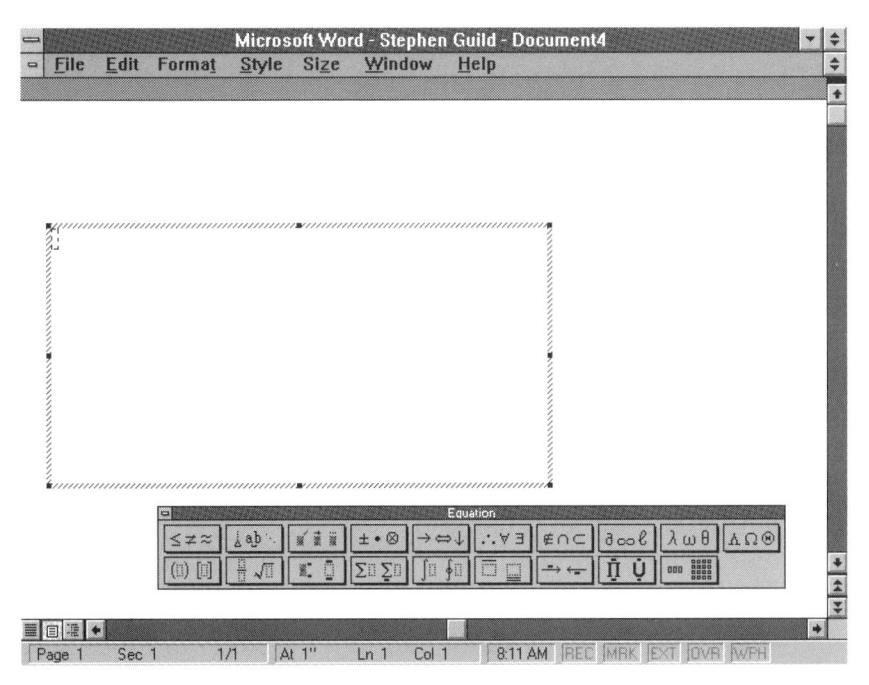

Equation editor window and onto your document window by clicking on the blank area of the toolbar and dragging it onto your document window. See Chapter 1 for more information about toolbars.

Keep in mind that Equation Editor just adds special characters and symbols to your document—you can't actually perform calculations by selecting the equations you create. Equation Editor is fairly self-explanatory: the easiest way to learn how its features work is to jump in and explore. You can always use Word's online Help to get additional information.

Inserting an Equation

Like the Microsoft Draw application, Equation Editor supports Object Linking and Embedding (OLE), which allows you to create and insert an object (in this case, an equation) by using another program from within Word.

To create an equation using Equation Editor:

1. Place the insertion point where you want the equation to appear in your Word document.
2. Choose **Insert Object**.
3. Double-click **Microsoft Equation 2.0** in the list box. Word opens an Equation Editor window on top of your document.
4. In the Equation Editor toolbar, click the picture on the bottom row of buttons for the equation template you want to insert. A graphical menu appears, displaying more options for that type.
5. Click the option you want from the graphical menu to insert an equation template.
6. If you've inserted a template with placeholder squares, click the placeholder squares and type numbers in them as necessary.
7. When mathematical symbols are needed, choose from the options on the top row of buttons.
8. Repeat Steps 4 through 7 until your equation is complete.
9. When you're ready to return to your document, choose **File Exit**. When asked if you want to update the document, choose **Yes**.

Switching Between Equation and Text Modes

Building Equations

You can always switch back to your document when you want to quit using special symbols and return to writing regular text. However, there will be times when you'll want to include a brief nonmathematical phrase in an expression. You can use Equation Editor's Text style mode to do this.

To switch to typing regular text:

1. In the Equation Editor window, position the insertion point where you want to insert the text. Be sure to click outside of any placeholder squares.
2. Choose **Style Text**, or press **Ctrl+Shift+E**.
3. Type the text.
4. To return to typing mathematical symbols (Math style), choose **Style Math**, or press **Ctrl+Shift+=**.

CHECK YOURSELF

Using Equation Editor, insert the fraction ½ in your document.

▲ Choose **Insert Object** and double-click Microsoft **Equation** 2.0 in the list. In the Equation Editor window, click the fraction picture in the equation bar (two stacked rectangles separated by a horizontal bar) to insert the template. Click the top placeholder rectangle of the inserted template and type **1** to replace the placeholder, then click the bottom placeholder and type **2** to complete the fraction. Click in the document window to get back to your document.

Editing an Equation

To edit an equation that you've inserted into a Word document using Equation Editor:

1. Double-click the equation to start Equation Editor.
2. Select and edit the parts of the equation, as necessary. Choose commands on the Edit menu and on other menus to edit the equation.

3. Click in the document window when you're ready to return to your document. The equation will be inserted into your document with gray diagonal marks. These will remain on top of the object until you close the document for the first time. Thereafter, if you want to change the equation in any way, just double-click the equation to open the Equation Editor again.

When you're working with tiny subscripts and superscripts or parts of fractions, you may find it handy to use the commands on the View menu to "zoom" the equation so you can see it better. The *Microsoft Word for Windows Users Guide* contains more detailed information about using the Equation Editor. And remember, the Help menu in the equation editor is always available

QUICK COMMAND SUMMARY

Command	To Do This
Insert Object	Start Microsoft Graph, Equation Editor, or another application that supports OLE.
Edit Copy and Edit Paste	Copy chart data to the Windows Clipboard and paste it into the Microsoft Graph Datasheet window.
Microsoft Graph commands	Create a chart in Microsoft Graph and embed that chart in your Word document.
Equation Editor commands	Create an equation in Equation Editor and embed that equation in your Word document.

PRACTICE WHAT YOU'VE LEARNED

In a Word document, create a bar chart that compares sales figures for three stores over two years.

What You Do

1. Place the insertion point where you want to insert the chart.

2. Choose **Insert Object**, and double-click **Microsoft Graph** in the list to open Microsoft Graph.

3. In the Datasheet window, type the following in the cells:

	1991	1992
Store 1	1000	1500
Store 2	3000	3200
Store 3	2500	2700

4. Select any cells containing superfluous data, press the **Clear Data** button and click **OK** in the dialog box that appears.

5. From the Gallery menu, select **Bar**, and then click **OK** in the dialog box to select the first format for a bar chart.

6. Choose **Exit** and **Return to** (name of document) from the Microsoft Graph File menu, and then click **Yes** when asked if you want to update.

What You'll See

1. The insertion point marker in the document window.

2. The Object dialog box with Microsoft Graph selected in the Object Type list. After you double-click the selection, the Microsoft Graph window appears on top of Word.

3. The Datasheet window will become active. As you enter the data, the datasheet displays the new data.

4. No text in the select cells.

5. The Gallery menu and then the Bar dialog box. In the set of eight bar chart types, number 1 is highlighted. After you click **OK**, the bar chart appears in the Graph window.

6. The Graph File menu and then a dialog box asking if you want to update or not. After you click **Yes**, the complete graph appears in your Word document.

12

Setting Up Tables and Forms

Word makes it easy to structure, edit, and format information that you want to arrange in rows and columns. In Word, information organized this way is called a *table*. In this chapter, you will learn how to:

- ▲ Create a blank table
- ▲ Create a table from selected text
- ▲ Enter text and graphics in a table
- ▲ Format and edit tables
- ▲ Perform calculations within a Word document
- ▲ Create forms with fields

Some Table Examples

Tables offer several benefits for organizing and formatting information in your documents. When you use a table to format information, Word automatically adjusts the height of a row as you add new information. You can also format the dimensions of columns and rows yourself, and you can move selected rows and columns to different locations within a table. These features are extremely useful if you want to create and edit lists that have complex row-and-column structures. Figures 12.1 and 12.2 show a few possible uses for tables created in Word.

Inserting a Blank Table

Word adds a table at the location of the insertion point. Word automatically divides the space between margins into equal columns—or, if the insertion point is in a narrow column—as on a

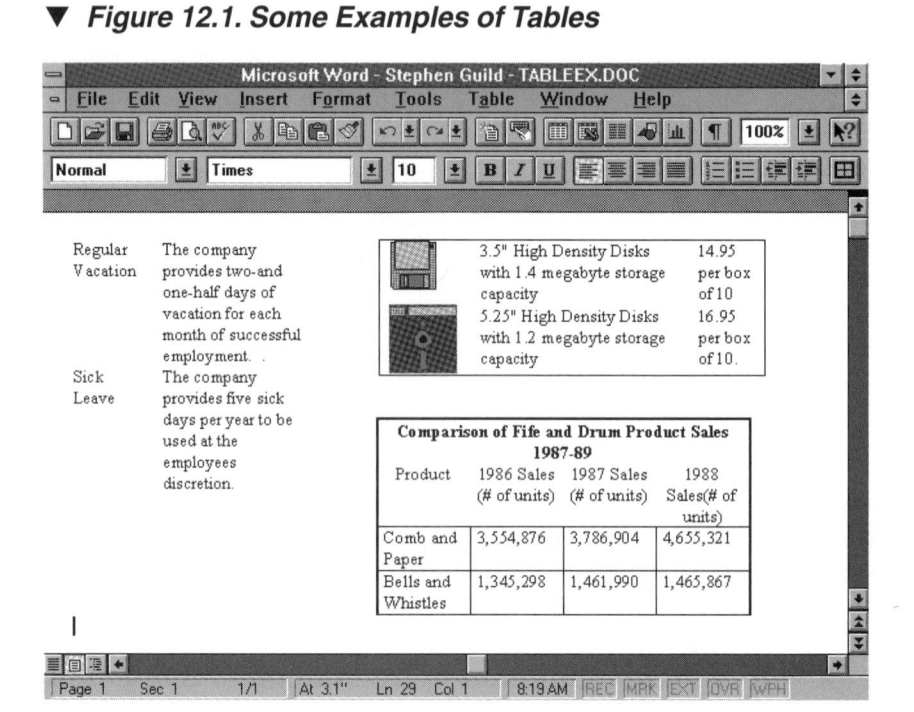

▼ **Figure 12.1. Some Examples of Tables**

▼ **Figure 12.2. A Five-Column Table with One Column Selected**

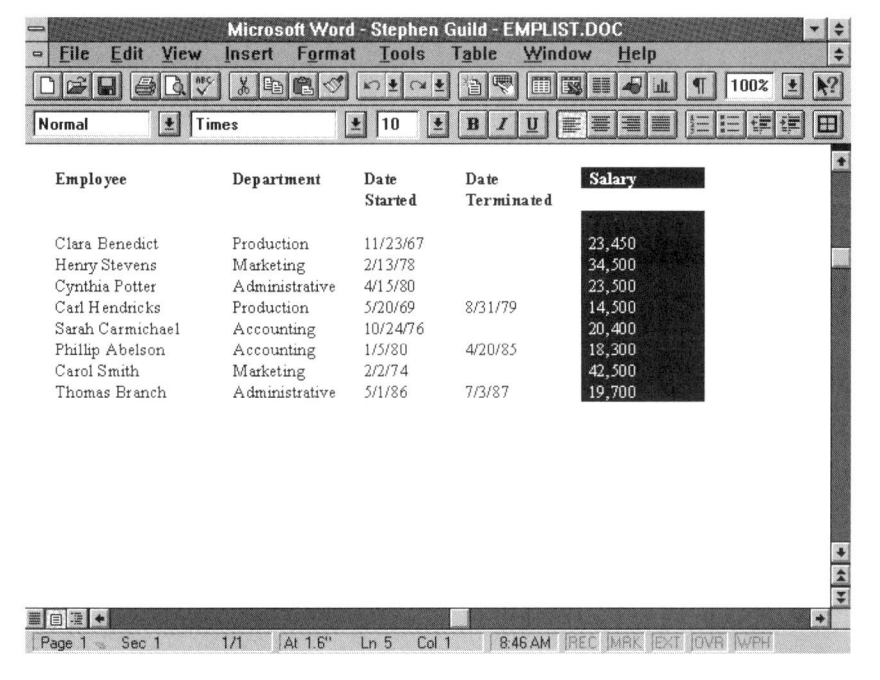

Inserting a Blank Table

two-column page—Word divides the text space in that column only. If you want to insert a table into a document that's divided into columns but you want the table to occupy the full width between page margins, you create a separate section for your table. (See Chapter 9 for more information on dividing a document into sections.)

You can insert a table into your document using the Insert Table command or the Insert Table button.

To insert a blank table into your document using the Insert Table command:

1. Place the insertion point where you want to insert a table. Make sure no text is selected in your document.
2. Choose the **Insert Table** command on the Table menu.
3. Type the number of columns you want in the Number of Columns box.
4. Type the number of rows you want in the Number of Rows box.

5. Word automatically sets the initial column width, based on the space between margins and the number of columns. You can make the columns narrower by typing a new measurement in the Column Width box or by clicking the up or down arrow. However, you can always change the column width later, so in most cases you'll want to leave this option alone. To specify different widths, see "Adjusting the Width of Columns" later in this chapter. You can always change or add formatting to a table, so you can ignore the format if you like until you fill in the table cells.
6. Click **OK** or press **Enter** to close the dialog box and draw the table.

To insert a blank table into your document using the Insert Table button:

1. Place the insertion point where you want to insert a table. Make sure no text is selected in your document.
2. Click the **Insert Table** button on the Standard toolbar.
3. Hold down the mouse button and move the pointer to shade the number of columns and rows you want. When you use the mouse, the maximum is 16 rows and 10 columns.
4. Release the mouse button. Word automatically sets the initial column width, based on the space between margins and the number of columns. You can adjust the width of the columns later by using the Cell Height and Width command on the Table menu, as described in "Adjusting the Width of Columns" later in this chapter.

Using the Table Wizard

You may want to use one of Word's preset table formats that are part of the Wizards. The Table Wizard creates and formats a table with headings, text, labels, lines, and other formatting. All you have to do is choose from the options that Word provides in the Wizard box. You can always change a table that has been created this way.

To create a table using the Table Wizard:

1. Choose **File New**.

2. Select **Table Wizard** from the Template list.
3. Double-click **Table Wizard**, or click **OK** or press **Enter**. Word opens the Wizard box and takes your through the steps for creating the table.
4. When you've completed the table, Click the **Finish** button. Word will display the finished table in a new document window.

Using the Table Wizard

CHECK YOURSELF

Create a table with three columns and seven rows.

▲ Choose **Table Insert Table**, type **3** in the Number of Columns box and **7** in the Number of Rows box, and then click **OK**.

Displaying or Removing Table Gridlines and Cell Text Markers

When you create a table, you'll see gridlines outlining the table cells. These dotted lines are especially helpful when you haven't added borders to a table. You can also see cell text markers—special characters that mark the end of text in cells. A cell text marker is an X in some form; the specific character depends on the font used in the cell, and the position of the marker depends on the alignment assigned to paragraphs in the cells.

Neither the gridlines nor the cell text markers will appear when you print your document. If you find them distracting, you can remove them by using the following procedures.

To turn table gridlines off:

▲ Choose **Table Gridlines**.

To display table gridlines:

▲ Turn on **Table Gridlines** again.

To display or remove cell text markers:

▲ Choose **Tools Options** and click the **View** tab. Turn on or off **All** in the Nonprinting Characters check box. You can also remove or display cell markers by clicking the ¶ button on the Standard toolbar.

Figure 12.3 shows a table displayed with gridlines and cell text markers.

Creating a Table from Selected Text

You may find it easier first to type the words or numbers you want your table to contain, then tell Word to put the text into a table. You can even put entire paragraphs of text into table cells.

Most often, you'll probably want to separate items with commas or tabs and press **Enter** to end each row with a paragraph mark. Word reads each comma or tab as a separator (delimiter) between columns. If you have two commas or two tabs next to each other, you'll end up with a blank cell in that spot. Don't try to align

▼ **Figure 12.3. A Table Displayed with Gridlines and Cell Text Markers**

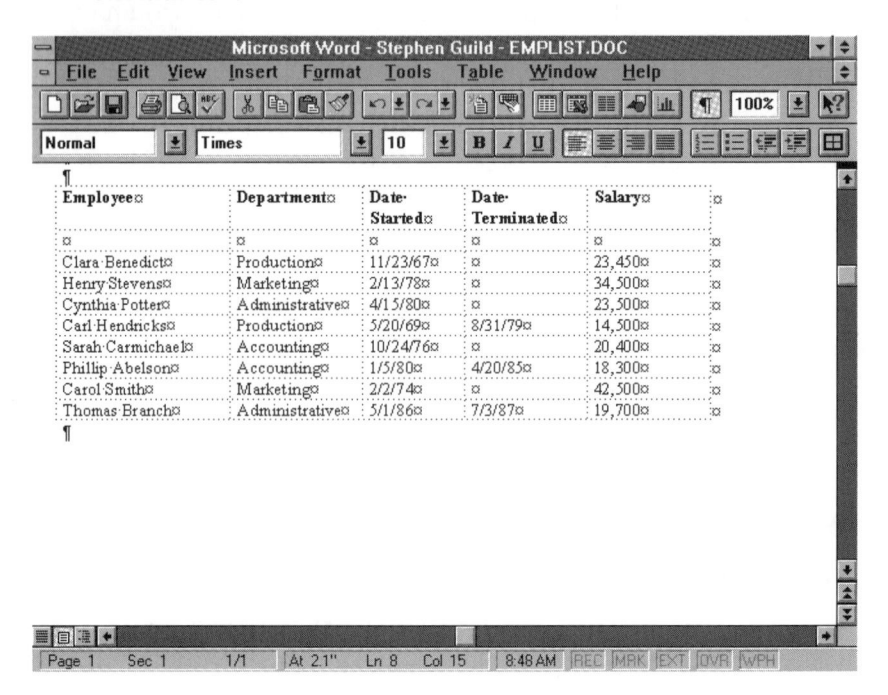

columns by adding extra tabs or spaces, and don't use commas to set off thousands in numbers—your table won't look right.

Take a look at Figure 12.4 to see how these different options work.

You can also import information from another file into a Word table and even link that information to its source file so that Word can automatically update the Word table. If you use data from another file, you must be sure that the information to be placed into table cells is separated by commas, tabs, or paragraph marks; these are the only separators that Word understands. Also, make sure there are no extra commas, tabs, or paragraph marks, because each comma or tab causes Word to insert one column.

To create a table from selected text:

1. Type the words or numbers you want to put into a table, or use **Edit Copy** and **Edit Past**e to get that information from another file.
2. Select the text for the table.
3. Choose **Table Insert Table** or choose **Table Convert Text to Table**.

Creating a Table from Selected Text

▼ *Figure 12.4. Examples of Text Converted into Word*

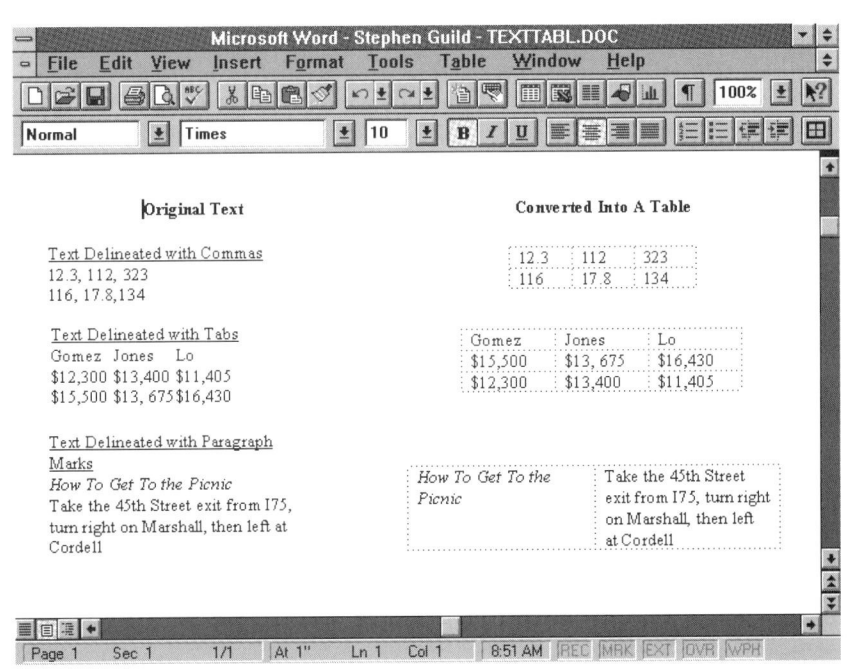

4. If you want to change the column width or row height, or make any other changes to the table, use the individual commands on the Table menu.
5. If at this time you want to specify individual column widths, align or indent rows, or draw borders around cells, click **Format**. You can always change or add formatting to a table, so you can ignore the format until later.
6. Click **OK** or press **Enter** to close the dialog box and draw the table.

TIP

If you've inserted a table as the first item in your file and you now want to insert new information in front of the table, place the insertion point in the first cell in the table and press Ctrl+Shift+Enter. **Then place the insertion point in front of the new paragraph mark and type or paste the text.**

Entering Information in Table Cells

All of Word's editing commands work in tables just as they do in the rest of your document. You enter, edit, and format text and graphics in a table in the same way as you would anywhere else. The only difference is that the text in a table is contained in individual cells; you must move the insertion point to the cell you want to affect before you can enter or edit text in that cell.

Moving the Insertion Point in Tables

To use the mouse to move the insertion point to a cell:

▲ Click the cell you want to work in.

Entering Information in Table Cells

To use the keyboard to move the insertion point to a cell:

To Move	Press
To next cell	Tab
To preceding cell	Shift+Tab
To first cell in current row	Alt+Home
To last cell in current row	Alt+End
To first cell in current column	Alt+Page Up
To last cell in current column	Alt+Page Dn

To move the insertion point within a cell, use the arrow keys or point and click with the mouse, just as you would outside of a table.

Inserting or Editing Text or Graphics

When the insertion point is in a cell, just type, choose commands to paste text or graphics, or edit text as you normally would. The following is an exception.

To enter a tab character in a table cell:

▲ Press **Ctrl+Tab**.

Word wraps the text you type when it reaches the cell margin to maintain the width of the column, and it adjusts the height of the row as you add new text. Pressing Enter adds a new paragraph to the cell and increases the height of all cells in the row.

Selecting Table Contents

A table has an invisible selection bar at the top of each column and at the left side of each cell. When the mouse pointer is in the selection bar at the top of a column, it becomes a downward-pointing arrow. When the mouse pointer is in the selection bar at the left side of a cell, it becomes a slanted arrow, just as it does at the side of a paragraph in regular text.

Selecting text in a table cell is generally the same as selecting text anywhere in a document. In a table, however, you can't select individual lines of text by clicking in the selection bar to the left of a line—this just selects the contents of the cell. To select lines, drag the mouse to highlight the text; or set the insertion point, move to the end of the text, then hold down the **Shift** key while you click the mouse button.

When you select a cell, you select all the text in that cell. Then you can choose editing or formatting commands to change the text. For example, you could select a column of cells and make all the text in those cells bold.

To select individual cells, rows, or columns:

Do This	To Select
Click the left inside edge of the cell	An individual cell
Click the selection bar on the left outside edge of the table	A table row
Move the mouse to the column and click	A table column

Formatting Tables

In a table, you can change the width of columns, the number of rows and columns, the types of borders, and so forth using Word's Table and Format menus. You can edit or format the text in the table cells using the Format menu commands, just as you would anywhere else in the document.

Using the Ruler in Tables

When you choose View Ruler while the insertion point is in a table, you can adjust the column width, cell indentations, and table margins. The paragraph and indentation markers work the same as with text outside a table. (See Chapter 7 for more information about using the ruler.)

To adjust the column width with the ruler, you use the small squares containing cross-hatch marks. Figure 12.5 shows the ruler settings in a table.

Formatting Tables

▼ *Figure 12.5. Using the Ruler to Format Paragraphs in Cells and Change Margins in Tables*

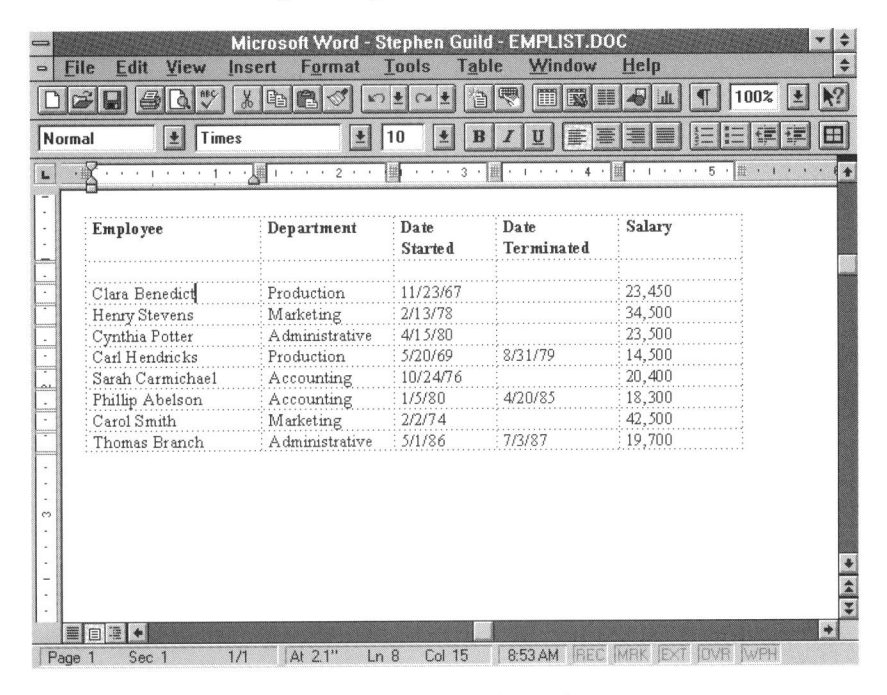

To change the column width using the ruler:

▲ Click the square column width marker and drag the marker to the position you want.

The ruler can display margins, indents, and tabs. In addition, you can set tabs and change margins, indents, and column widths. See Chapter 7 for more information about formatting paragraphs.

You can also drag the left indent marker to indent selected rows in the table or drag a column marker to make cells wider or narrower. These tasks are explained under "Adjusting the Width of Columns" and "Indenting Rows" later in this chapter.

Formatting Paragraphs in Table Cells

Here are a few facts you should keep in mind when formatting paragraphs in table cells:

▲ **Indenting and aligning paragraphs.** Paragraphs in cells are indented and aligned relative to the cell margins. For example, justifying a paragraph in a cell aligns the text with the margins of the cell that contains the paragraph.
▲ **Setting tabs in tables.** You can set tabs in tables to align or set spacing of text, and you can even use tabs to create mini-tables within table cells.
▲ **Aligning numbers that contain decimal points.** To align a column of numbers containing decimal points, select the column, then set a decimal tab to align the numbers in the column. There's no need to use Ctrl+Tab to insert tab characters in the cells; setting a decimal tab with the ruler or the Paragraph dialog box will make the numbers in a table column line up at decimal points. See Chapter 7 for more information about setting tabs.

To include more white space around your text in tables, do one of the following:

▲ Add blank lines before and after paragraphs by pressing **Enter**.
▲ Use the ruler or the **Indents and Spacing** tab in the Format Paragraph dialog box to put space before and after paragraphs in a cell or to indent the paragraphs from the cell margins.
▲ In the Column tab in the Table Cell Width and Height dialog box, type a measurement in the Space Between Columns box to put more space between the text in table cells.

Adjusting the Width of Columns

You can specify different widths for all columns before or after you insert a table. You can change the width of any individual column using the Column tab in the Cell Width and Height dialog box.

To specify different widths for columns:

1. Do one of the following:
   ▲ If you're inserting a table for the first time, choose **Insert Table**, type the number of columns and rows, then type or choose the width of the column.

▲ If you're changing the width of columns in an existing table, select the columns, then choose **Table Cell Height and Width** and choose the **Column** tab.
2. Click **Previous Column** or **Next Column** until you see the number of the column you want to change. For example, if you want to change the width of the third column, make sure the dialog box reads "Width of Column 3."
3. Type a measurement for that column. Word assumes measurements are in inches unless you've changed the default unit of measurement in the General tab of the Tools Options dialog box.
4. Repeat Steps 2 and 3 until you've changed the widths of all columns you want to affect.
5. Click **OK** or press **Enter** to close the dialog box and redraw the table.

Formatting Tables

To change the width of columns in an existing table with the ruler and the mouse:

1. Select the column(s) whose width you want to change.
2. If necessary, choose **View Ruler**. Figure 12.5 shows a table with the ruler displayed.
3. On the horizontal ruler, drag the column markers to a new location to widen or narrow the selected columns.

To change the width of the columns with the mouse:

1. Select the column(s) whose width you want to change.
2. If necessary, turn on **Table Gridlines**.
3. Position the mouse pointer on the gridline of the cells you want to change. The arrow changes to two vertical lines with arrows pointing left and right (<-||->).
4. Drag the column gridlines to a new location to widen or narrow the selected column(s).

Adjusting the Height of Rows

You can specify different heights for rows after you insert a table.

To specify different heights for rows:

1. Select the row(s), then choose **Table Cell Height and Width** and choose the **Row** tab.

2. Choose **Previous Row** or **Next Row** until you see the number of the row you want to change. For example, if you want to change the width of the fourth row, make sure the dialog box reads "Height of Row 4."
3. In the Height of Rows drop-down list, choose one of the following:

To Do This	Choose
Adjust the row height to fit text or graphics in any cell in the row	Auto
Specify a minimum row height	At Least and then select or type a number in the At box.
Specify a minimum row height	Exactly and then select or type a number in the At box.

4. Click **OK** or press **Enter** to close the dialog box and redraw the table.

If you want a row to break across two pages, turn on the **Allow Row to Break Across Pages** check box.

To change the height of rows in an existing table with the ruler and the mouse:

1. Select the row(s) whose height you want to change.
2. If necessary, choose **View Ruler**. Figure 12.5 shows a table with the ruler displayed.
3. On the vertical ruler, drag the row markers (the heavy lines) to a new location to increase or decrease the height of the selected rows.

CHECK YOURSELF

In a table that you've created, change the width of the columns to 2" and the height of the rows to .55".

▲ Select the entire table and choose **Table Cell Height and Width**. Choose the **Column** tab and type **2** in the Width of Column box. Choose the **Row** tab and type **.55** in the Height of Row box, then click **OK**.

Indenting Rows

Formatting Tables

You can use the Row tab or the ruler to indent rows in a table, repositioning the entire table or just a few rows. Rows are indented from the left margin of the document. Figure 12.6 shows an example of a table with indented rows.

To indent rows with the Row Height dialog box:

1. Select the row or rows you want to indent.
2. Choose **Table Cell Height and Width** and choose the **Row** tab.
3. Type a measurement in the Indent From Left box.
4. Click **OK** or press **Enter**.

To indent rows with the ruler:

1. Choose **View Ruler**.
2. Select the row or rows you want to indent.
3. Drag the paragraph indent marker to the exact position you want.

▼ *Figure 12.6. A Table with Indented Rows*

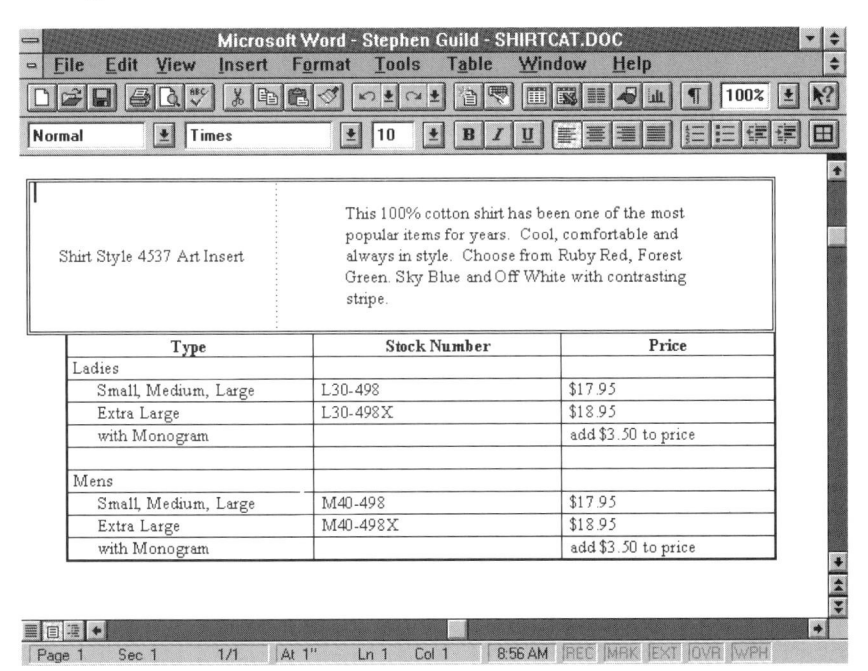

Aligning Rows

You can align table rows with the left or right document margin, or you can center rows between the two margins.

To align rows in a table:

1. Select the rows to align.
2. Choose **Table Cell Height and Width** and choose the **Row** tab.
3. Choose the **Left**, **Center**, or **Right** option.
4. Click **OK** or press **Enter**.

Adding Borders to a Table

You can add borders of different thicknesses around individual cells, groups of cells, or entire tables. You might want to insert lines between rows and columns, just between columns, or just around the outside of the table. Or you might even want to outline just one cell to make it stand out. You can add or change borders around cells anytime you like.

To add borders to cells or change borders around cells in a table:

1. Select the cells you want to affect, then choose **Format Borders and Shading**.
2. In the Presets area, do one of the following:
   - ▲ If you want the same border around the cells you've selected, click **Box**.
   - ▲ If you want a shadow effect, click **Shadow**.
   - ▲ If you want to format different sides of the cell with different borders, or some sides with and some without borders, choose **None**.
3. In the Table Borders and Shading dialog box, click the portion of the selection of cells that you want to affect, and then choose the border style that you want from the Line box. Repeat this step for each side you want to format.
4. Choose **Shading** if you want shading in the selected cells.
5. Click **OK** or press **Enter** to redraw the table.

To remove borders that you've added to a table, just select the cells you want to affect, choose the appropriate position option in

Adding Borders to a Table

the Table Borders and Shading dialog box, then select **None** from the drop-down list in the Borders tab.

Using the Borders toolbar will make formatting table a little easier. To display the Borders toolbar, click the **Borders** button on the Standard toolbar. See Chapter 7 for more information about formatting with borders.

CHECK YOURSELF

Put a border around an entire table and shade one of the cells.

▲ Select the entire table, then choose **Format Borders and Shading** and click the **Borders** tab. Choose the type of border you want in the Line area, click **Box** in the Presets area, and then click **OK** or press **Enter**. Select one cell, then choose **Format Borders and Shading** again. Choose the **Shading** tab, select the type of shading from the Shading list, and then click **OK** or press **Enter**.

Formatting a Table Using AutoFormat

If you want to use one of Word's preset table formats, use the AutoFormat feature. When you choose a specific format for a table, Word applies all of the formatting—lines, fonts, styles—to the table and text and then displays the finished product in your document. You can change any or all of Word's formatting afterward.

To apply automatic formatting to a table:

1. Create a table.
2. Enter the text and then select the table.
3. Choose **Table AutoFormat** on the Table menu.
4. In the AutoFormat dialog box, choose one of the styles of formatting from the Format list. Word will display an example of the style you select. If you want another style, just click its name on the list.

5. Turn on the check boxes for the formats you want to apply and any special formats.
6. Click **OK** or press **Enter**.

Positioning a Table on a Page Precisely

If you want to move a table to a specific location on a page (such as 2" from the left margin and 3" from the top margin), select the entire table, then place it in a frame you've created using Insert Frame. Then you can use the mouse to move the frame, as described under "Positioning Frames" in Chapter 9, or by using the Frame dialog box to specify the exact position of the frame. The surrounding text automatically adjusts to flow around the positioned table. Figure 12.7 shows a table that has been positioned in this way.

▼ **Figure 12.7. A Table with Surrounding Text Flowing Around It**

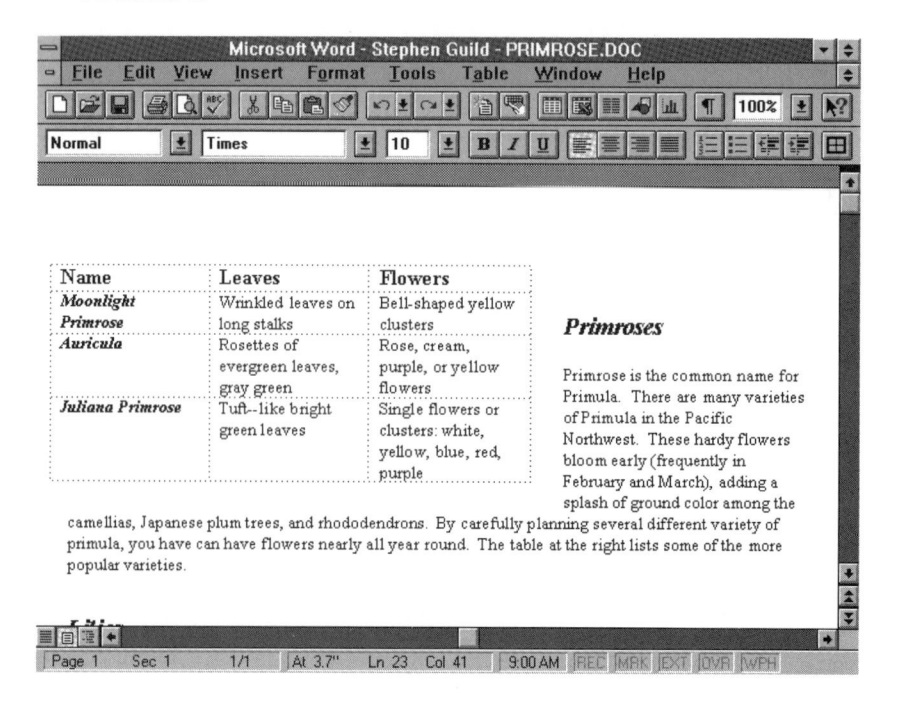

Merging Table Cells

Merging Table Cells

You may want to have one wide cell over two or more narrower ones, as shown in Figure 12.8. To create this effect, you merge two or more table cells in a row; this "dissolves" the boundaries of adjoining cells to create one wide cell.

To merge table cells:

1. Select the cells you want to merge. The cells must be in the same row; Word cannot merge cells stacked on top of each other in a column.
2. Choose **Table Merge Cells**.

Word dissolves the boundaries between cells and creates one large cell. (If the Merge Cells button is dimmed, make sure that you have selected only adjacent table cells in a row and not any text surrounding the table.)

To split a merged table cell back into individual cells:

1. Select the merged cell.
2. Choose **Table Split Cells**.

▼ *Figure 12.8. Merging Cells to Create a Wider Cell*

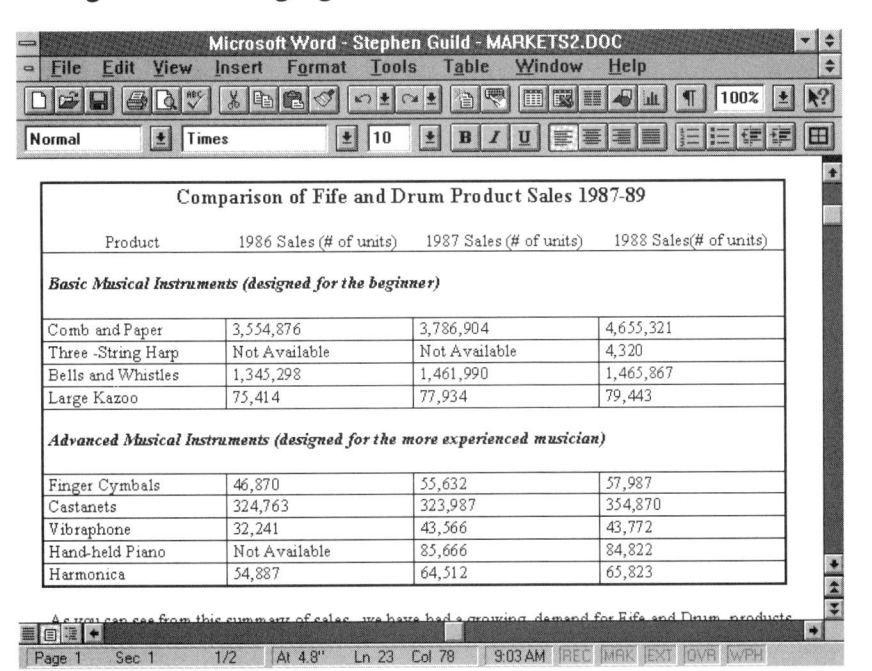

TIP

If you think you might use a certain table format (for example, five rows and three columns with thin vertical lines dividing columns and a shadow outline around the whole table), create and format an empty table. Then save that table as an AutoText entry that you can use over and over. For more information about using AutoText entries, see Chapter 4.

Adding Individual Cells and Rows and Columns to Tables

You can add an individual cell, a few cells, or entire rows and columns to a table.

To add cells to a table:

1. Select the cell or group of cells in the table where you want to insert new cells. Make sure you select the same number of cells as the number you want to insert.
2. Choose the **Table** command and then choose one of the following:
   ▲ If you select two or more cells, choose **Insert Cells**.
   ▲ If you select an entire column, choose **Insert Column**.
   ▲ If you select a single cell or an entire row, choose **Insert Row**.
3. In the Insert Cells dialog box, choose one of the following options:

To Do This	Choose
Insert new cells to the left of the selected cells	Shift Cells Right
Insert new cells above the selected cells	Shift Cells Down

4. Click **OK** or press **Enter**. Word redraws the table with new cells.

Adding Individual Cells and Rows and Columns to Tables

To add a row or column to a table:

1. Move the insertion point into the row or column preceding the one you want to insert. If you want to insert more than one row or column, select the number of rows or columns you want to insert. For example, to insert three rows, select three rows in your table. The new rows or columns will be inserted in front of the first selected row or column.
2. Choose **Table Insert Cells**.
3. Choose one of the following options:

To Do This	Choose
Insert a whole row or rows of cells	Insert Entire Row
Insert a whole column or columns of cells	Insert Entire Column

4. Click **OK** or press **Enter**. Word redraws the table with new rows or columns.

To add a column to the right side of a table:

1. Move the mouse pointer to the right of the table until it becomes a downward-pointing arrow.
2. Choose **Table Insert Row**.

TIP

To quickly add a row at the bottom of a table, move the insertion point into the last cell in the last row, then press Tab.

Deleting Individual Cells and Rows and Columns from Tables

You can delete an individual cell, a few cells, or entire rows and columns. If you just want to delete the text in a row or column of cells, select the cells, then choose **Edit Cut** or press **Delete**. The following procedures remove cells and whole rows and columns, as well as the text in those columns.

To delete cells from a table:

1. Select the cell or group of cells that you want to delete.
2. Choose the **Table** command, then choose one of the following:
   - ▲ If you select two or more cells, choose **Delete Cells**.
   - ▲ If you select an entire column, choose **Delete Column**.
   - ▲ If you select a single cell or an entire row, choose **Delete Row**.
3. In the Delete Cells dialog box, choose one of the following options:

To Do This	*Choose*
Delete the cell(s) and move all remaining cells to the left of the insertion point	Shift Cells Left
Delete the cell(s) and move all remaining cells to the right of the insertion point	Shift Cells Up

4. Click **OK** or press **Enter**. Word redraws the table.

To delete a row or column from a table:

1. Move the insertion point into the row or column that precedes the one you want to delete. If you want to delete more than one row or column, select the number of rows or columns you want to delete. For example, to delete three rows, select three rows in your table.
2. Choose **Table Delete Cells**.
3. Choose one of the following options:

To Do This	*Choose*
Delete a whole row or rows of cells	Delete Entire Row
Delete a whole column or columns of cells	Delete Entire Column

4. Click **OK** or press **Enter**. Word redraws the table.

To delete a column from the right side of a table:

1. Move the mouse pointer to the right of the table until it becomes a downward-pointing arrow.
2. Choose **Table Row**.

To delete an entire table:

▲ Select all the cells or choose **Table Select Table**, then choose **Table Delete Columns**.

Splitting One Table into Two

To split one table into two tables:

1. Place the insertion point in the cell that precedes the location where you want to split the table.
2. Choose **Table Split Table** or press **Ctrl+Shift+Enter**. Word inserts a paragraph mark, separating the table into two.

   If you want to rejoin the split table, delete the paragraph mark.

Placing a Page Break in a Table

To place a page break within a table:

1. Place the insertion point in the cell that precedes the location where you want the page break to occur.
2. Press **Ctrl+Enter**. Word inserts a page break and a paragraph mark, separating the table into two.

   If you want to rejoin the table and remove the page break, delete the paragraph mark and the page break mark.

Copying and Moving the Contents of Cells

You can copy or move the contents of cells within the same table or between tables by using the Edit Copy, Edit Cut, and Edit Paste Cells commands.

When pasting cells, Word pastes the same number of cells in the same pattern. In other words, if you copy a block of cells arranged in two columns and three rows, Word will paste the contents of those cells in two columns and three rows, beginning with the cell containing the insertion point and replacing any information in the paste area. If the paste area doesn't contain enough cells to hold the copied cells, Word displays a message telling you the areas are different sizes.

To copy or move the contents of table cells:

1. Select the cells whose contents you want to copy.
2. Choose **Edit Copy** (to copy the contents of the cells) or **Edit Cut** (to move the contents of the cells).
3. Select the cells into which you want to paste the contents, or place the insertion point in the first cell into which you want to paste (the upper left cell of the paste area).
4. Choose **Edit Paste Cells**.

You can also paste table cells outside a table; in this case, Word creates a new table with the dimensions and format of the pasted cells.

Converting a Table into Normal Text

Just as you can convert normal text into a table, you can also reverse the process and convert a table into normal text.

To convert a table into normal text:

1. Select the table.
2. Choose **Table Convert Table to Text**.
3. Select an option to choose the character that separates the contents of each cell:
   - ▲ Paragraphs (paragraph marks)
   - ▲ Tabs
   - ▲ Commas
   - ▲ Other (another character such as a question mark, ampersand, etc.). If you choose Other, be careful not to pick a character that you are also using as text in your table.
4. Click **OK** or press **Enter**.

Calculating in Tables

Calculating in Tables

Although Word is not a spreadsheet program, you can use it to perform some calculations within tables. You can add, subtract, multiply, divide, and do other calculations within a table by using the Table Formula command. Word inserts field expressions to perform the calculations and places the results in the table cells you indicate.

To sum a row or column:

1. Place the insertion point where you want the sum to appear.
2. Choose **Table Formula**. Word proposes a formula in the dialog box. If this is appropriate, click **OK**.
3. If you want another formula, you will need to build it by using the Paste Function drop-down box and perhaps bookmark names.
4. Make sure the expression you want is in the Formula box. You can choose to format the number at this time by selecting from the Number Format drop-down list.

When you follow these steps you are building an expression field that will automatically perform calculations in your table. Just as in a spreadsheet, you can refer to specific cells or ranges of cells in a Word table by inserting a field and specifying the row and column numbers this way: *RnCn*. For example, a cell in the first row and the first column is R1C1. To specify a range of cells, you separate the cell references with a colon: R1C1:R5C3. You must enclose the references in parentheses. Figure 12.9 shows a table that uses fields to calculate.

You can perform other calculations in the table by using a combination of the functions and expressions. Your *Microsoft Word for Windows User's Guide* as well as the online Help can provide additional information about calculating in tables.

CHECK YOURSELF

In a table that has one column and four rows, calculate the total of the following numbers in the fourth row: 45, −3, 8

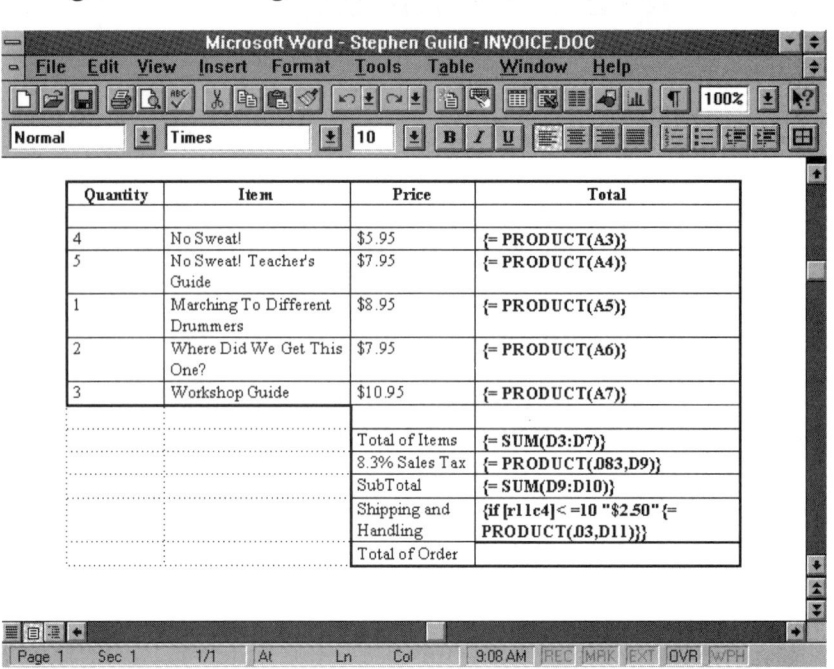

▼ **Figure 12.9. Using Fields to Calculate in a Table**

Quantity	Item	Price	Total
4	No Sweat!	$5.95	{=PRODUCT(A3)}
5	No Sweat! Teacher's Guide	$7.95	{=PRODUCT(A4)}
1	Marching To Different Drummers	$8.95	{=PRODUCT(A5)}
2	Where Did We Get This One?	$7.95	{=PRODUCT(A6)}
3	Workshop Guide	$10.95	{=PRODUCT(A7)}
		Total of Items	{=SUM(D3:D7)}
		8.3% Sales Tax	{=PRODUCT(.083,D9)}
		SubTotal	{=SUM(D9:D10)}
		Shipping and Handling	{if [r1 1c4]< =10 "$2.50" {=PRODUCT(.03,D11)}}
		Total of Order	

▲ Place the insertion point in cell A1, and in cells A1 to A3 type the specified numbers. Place the insertion point in cell A4 and choose **Table Formula**. The formula =SUM(ABOVE) should appear in the Formula box. Click **OK** or press **Enter**.

Using Tables to Create Forms

You can use Word's table features to create elaborate forms. Remember that you can format characters and paragraphs in tables any way you like, adding borders, italics, underlines, and more. You can use special fonts and graphics to create check boxes and special effects, and you can even add instructions formatted as hidden text.

With Word, you can design a variety of forms, from the simple to the complex, and include form fields that others can fill out on-line. You can include text, check box, and drop-down form fields that allow others to select from lists of names or numbers. This section provides the basics for creating and formatting forms, but you should consult the *Microsoft Word for Windows User's Guide* and the online Help for more detailed information.

Using Tables to Create Forms

Creating a Form

There are several basic steps in creating a form:

▲ Create a new template.
▲ Lay out the form using tables or paragraphs.
▲ For online forms, add form fields and define options.
▲ Protect and save the template.

To create a form:

1. Choose **File New**, click the Template button, then click **OK** or press **Enter**.
2. Lay out the form using tables or text.
3. Place the insertion point where you want users to type or select information.
4. Choose **Insert Form Field**.
5. If you want to display the Form Fields toolbar, click the **Show Toolbar** button. You can also display the toolbar by choosing View Toolbars and turning on the Forms check box.
6. In the Type area, do one of the following:

To Create	*Choose*
Fields users complete with text only	Text
Fields users check	Check Box
Fields users select from a group of options in a drop-down list	Drop-Down

7. Click the **Options** button and choose the properties of the form field, then click **OK**.
8. If you want to add text to help users with the form field, click **Add Help Text** button and complete the box that Word displays.
9. Repeat Steps 3 through 7 for each form field you want to insert.

10. Choose **Tools Protect Document** and click **Forms**.
11. Choose **File Save** and then close the template.

Formatting Form Fields

Once you have set up your form, you are ready to format the form fields. You can specify options for text, check box, and drop-down form fields as shown in Figure 12.10. Remember, though, that the form field won't become active until you choose Tools Protect Document and click the Forms button.

The Forms toolbar will take you to many of these dialog boxes when you clicking on the appropriate buttons. Figure 12.11 shows the toolbar. You can move and use this toolbar as you do any other toolbar in Word. For more information about toolbars, see Chapter 1.

You can choose from six different types of text form fields: regular text, number, date, current date, current time, and calculations. Each of these form fields needs to be formatted in a slightly different way.

▼ *Figure 12.10. Creating a Form Drop-Down List*

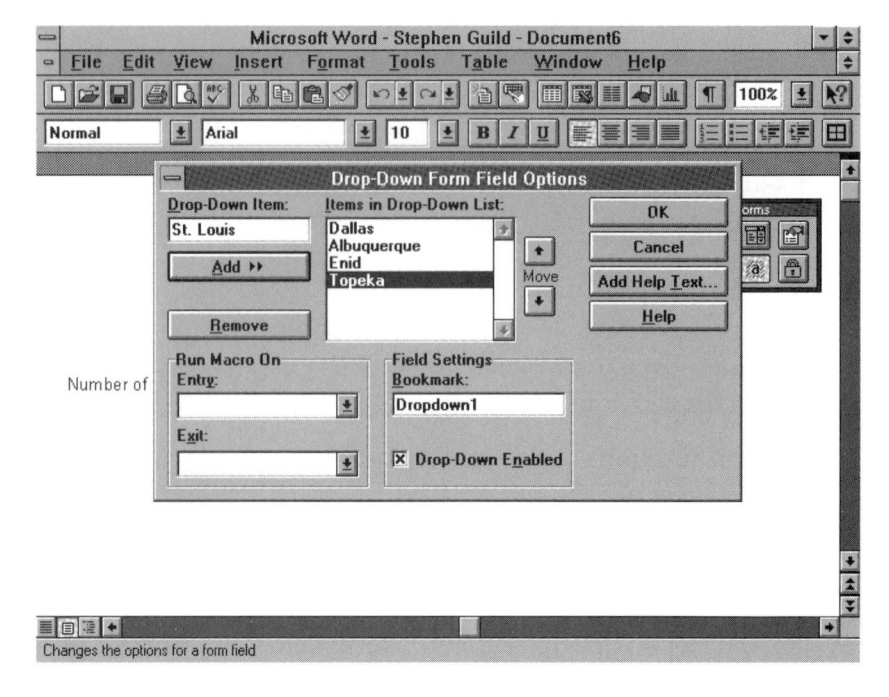

▼ **Figure 12.11. Inserting a Form Field**

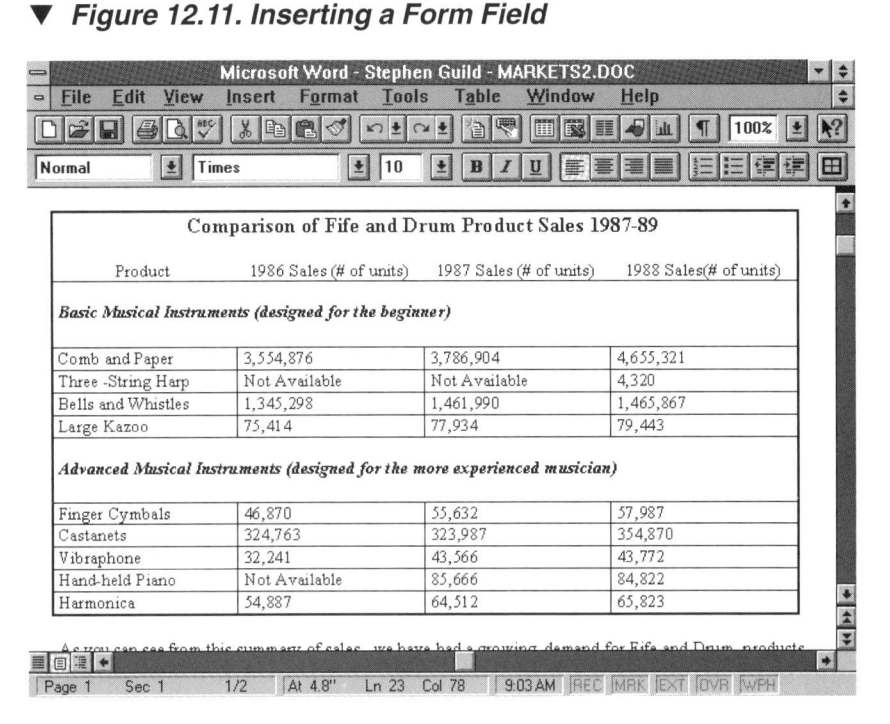

Using Tables to Create Forms

Using Text Form Fields

To format a text form field:

1. Click in the appropriate form field and click the **Form Field Options** button on the toolbar, or double-click the shaded text form field.
2. The Text Form Field Options dialog box will be displayed.
3. Make the appropriate choices, then click **OK** or press **Enter**.

Using Check Box Form Fields

To format a check box form field:

1. Click in the appropriate form field and click the **Form Field Options** button on the toolbar, or double-click the shaded check box field.
2. The Check Box Form Field Options dialog box will be displayed.
3. Make the appropriate choices, then click **OK** or press **Enter**.

Adding or Changing Drop-Down Items

To format a drop-down list:

1. Click in the appropriate form field and click the **Form Field Options** button on the toolbar, or double-click the drop-down form field.
2. The Drop-Down Form Field Options dialog box will be displayed.
3. If you want to add an item to the list, type the text in the Drop-Down Item box, then click the **Add** button.
4. If you want to delete an item from the list, select the item, then click the **Remove** button.
5. If you want to change the order of items in a list, use the up or down arrow in the Move area.
6. Repeat the appropriate steps for more additions or changes, then click **OK** or press **Enter**.

Activating and Protecting a Form Field

To activate and protect a form field:

1. Choose **Tools Protect Document**.
2. Click the **Forms** button.
3. Click **OK** or press **Enter**.

QUICK COMMAND SUMMARY

Command	To Do This
Table Insert Table	Display the Insert Table dialog box.
View category in the Options dialog box	Display the available view options.
Edit Copy	Copy information to be placed in a table.
Edit Paste	Paste information into a table.
Table Convert Text to Table or Table Convert Table to Text	Converts text to a table or a table to text format.
Ctrl+Shift+Enter	Place a paragraph mark in front of a table.

Command	To Do This
Tab	Move the insertion point right one cell.
Shift+Tab	Move the insertion point left one cell.
Alt+Home	Move the insertion point to the first cell in the current row.
Alt+End	Move the insertion point to the last cell in the current row.
Alt+Page Up	Move the insertion point to the top cell in the current column.
Alt+Page Dn	Move the insertion point to the bottom cell in the current column.
Ctrl+Tab	Enter a tab character in a table cell.
Tab	Select the next cell's contents in a table.
Shift+Home	Select the previous cell's contents in a table.
Shift+End	Select the next cell's contents in a table.
Table Select Row	Select a row of cells.
Table Select Column	Select a column of cells.
Table Cell Height and Width	Display the Cell Height and Width dialog box with the Row and Column tabs.
Format Borders and Shading	Display the Table Borders and Shading dialog box with the Borders and Shading tabs.
Table Merge Cells	Merge two or more selected cells.
Table Split Cells	Split two or more cells that have previously been merged into individual cells.

Command	To Do This
Table Insert Cells	Display the Insert Cells dialog box.
Table Delete Cells	Display the Delete Cells dialog box.
Table Split Table or Ctrl+Shift+Enter	Split a table.
Ctrl+Enter	Place a page break in a table.
Edit Paste Cells	Paste the cells you have copied (using Edit Copy) into a table.
Table Formula	Calculate the results of a column or row of figures and display the result in the cell containing the insertion point.
Insert Form Field	Display the Form Fields dialog box with the text, check box, and drop-down options.

PRACTICE WHAT YOU'VE LEARNED

NOTE: To make it easier to follow the procedures below, turn on the Table gridlines and make sure the Formatting toolbar is displayed.

Create the table shown below:

Comparison of Average Rates of Return			
Savings Account	Certificate of Deposit	Common Stock	Real Estate
5%	7.65%	9%	10.9%
5%	7.98%	9.5%	12.3%
6.55%	8.12%	10.2%	18.6%

What You Do	*What You'll See*
1. Position the insertion point in your document and then click the **Insert Table** button on the Standard toolbar. Drag the mouse until "5X5 Table" appears, then release the mouse button.	1. The insertion point in the document window. After you click the Insert Table button, the grid appears and enlarges as you drag the mouse. The words "5X5 Table" appear at the bottom of the grid. When the mouse button is released, the table corresponding to that size appears in the document window.
2. Select columns 2 through 5, and click the **Centered** button on the Formatting toolbar.	2. The black highlight that fills the selected columns. The highlighted columns will have centered formatting.
3. Choose **Table Cell Height and Width** and the column tab, and then type **1.5** in the Width of Columns 2-5 box and click **OK**.	3. The Column tab in the Cell Height and Width dialog box. After you click OK, the width of the selected columns changes to 1.5".
4. Click the first column, choose **Table Cell Height and Width** and the column tab, type **1** in the Width of Columns box, and then click **OK** to close the dialog box.	4. The Column tab in the Cell Height and Width dialog box. After you click OK, the width of the selected column changes to 1".
5. Select the entire first row and choose **Table Merge Cells**.	5. The first row highlighted. After you choose Table Merge Cells, the gridlines between the first row cells disappear.
6. Select Column 1, Row 2.	6. The black highlight in the cell.

What You Do

7. Choose **Format Borders and Shading**, click the **Shading** tab select 50% in the Fill list, and then click **OK**.

8. Choose **Table Select Table** to select the entire table.

9. Choose **Format Borders and Shading**, click the **Borders** tab, and click **Box**. Then click the 1½-point double line in the Line box.

10. Place the insertion point in Row 1. Click the **Centered**, **Bold**, and **Italic** buttons on the Formatting toolbar. Then click the **Font Size** box and select 14 from the drop-down list.

11. Type the table title, as shown, in Row 1. Use the Row tab in the Table Cell Height and Width dialog box to adjust the height of the merged cell. Click **OK**.

12. Type the remaining table text.

What You'll See

7. The Shading tab in the Borders and Shading dialog box. After you select 50% and OK, the cell is shaded.

8. The black highlight in the entire table.

9. The Borders tab in the Format Borders and Shading dialog box. When you click Box, the Box button will have a line around it. When you click the 1½-point double lines, the example is highlighted.

10. The formatting buttons shaded and the formatting applied to the cell. When you click the Font Size box, the drop-down list appears, and 14 is highlighted when you click it.

11. The title text, "Comparison of Average Rates of Return." The Row tab appears when you click on it in the Cell Height and Width dialog box, and then the cell height changes after you click OK.

12. The text of the table filling out the table.

13

Headers, Footers, and Footnotes

Headers and footers add identifying information about your printed documents. Header text appears at the top of a page, while footer text appears at the bottom. Headers and footers can be used to print page numbers as well as other information. This chapter shows you how to use headers, footers, and other features to add finishing touches to your documents or templates. In this chapter, you will learn how to:

- ▲ **Add page numbers**
- ▲ **Add headers and footers**
- ▲ **Add footnotes**

Adding Page Numbers

Word doesn't add page numbers to your document unless you say so—then you can specify exactly where and how you want the page numbers to be printed. Word has two commands that affect page numbers: Insert Page Numbers, which adds only page numbers to pages; and View Header and Footer, which lets you add text, time, date, and page number to the top or bottom of each page. Note that you can't use both commands to add a page number to the same area of a document.

When you add page numbers, Word adds a {page} field that is updated with the correct number when you print.

To add page numbers with Insert Page Numbers:

1. Move the insertion point into the section you want to affect. If your file isn't divided into sections, your choices will affect the entire document.
2. Choose **Insert Page Numbers**.
3. Choose a **Top of Page** or **Bottom of Page** vertical position in the Position drop-down list.
4. Choose a **Left**, **Center**, or **Right**—or **Inside** or **Outside** (with facing pages)—horizontal position in the Alignment drop-down list.
5. If you want to specify the number type (the default is 1, 2, 3, and so on) or the starting page number (the default is 1), click the **Format** button, and select a type from the Number Format drop-down list. Then choose the **Continue from Previous Section** option for continuous numbering throughout a document, or type a starting number in the Start At box for the first page number of the section.
6. If you want to include chapter numbers with the page numbers, click the **Include Chapter Numbers** check box and choose which style governs your chapter headings and what type of separator you want.
7. Click **OK** to return to the Page Numbers dialog box.
8. If you don't want the first page of your document numbered, turn **off** the **Show Number on First Page** check box.
9. Click **OK** or press **Enter**.

You won't see page numbers in Normal view—you have to switch to Page Layout view or Print Preview. In Page Layout view, you'll see the {page} field if you've turned on the Hidden Text check box in the Tools Options View tab; you'll see the page numbers if Hidden Text is turned off. In Print Preview, you'll always see the page numbers, although you may need to use the magnifier pointer with the mouse to identify them.

Adding Page Numbers

CHECK YOURSELF

Add page numbers centered in the top margin of a document.
▲ Choose **Insert Page Numbers**, choose the **Top of Page** and **Center** options, and then click **OK**.

Adding Headers or Footers

When you want to print text at the top of each page, you add a *header* (also known as a running head). When you want to print text at the bottom of each page, you add a *footer* (or running foot). In Word, headers and footers "belong" to sections: this allows you to have a different header or footer in each section or to use the same header or footer throughout your document. Headers and footers can contain date, time, and page number fields that Word fills in when you print the document.

If you are in any view other than Page Layout view, Word switches to Page Layout view and moves the insertion point into the header or footer box.

Setting Up a Header or Footer

Word offers you many options for headers and footers. For example, instead of having the same header and footer on each page, you may want to create different headers or footers for even and odd pages in your document, as shown in Figure 13.1.

You can also create a unique header or footer just for the first page of a document or section. If you don't want a header or foot-

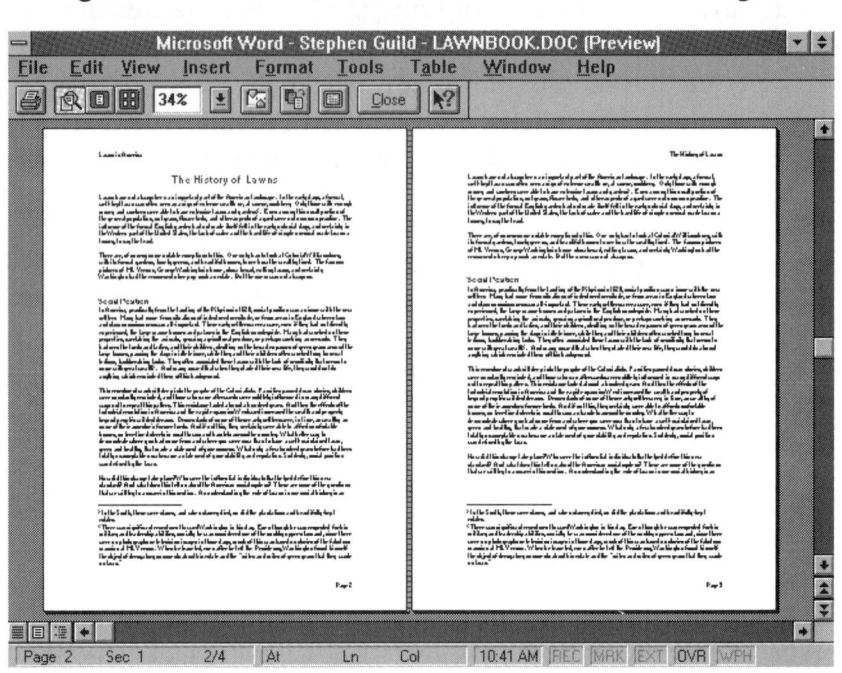

▼ **Figure 13.1. Different Headers on Odd and Even Pages**

er to appear on the first page, specify a unique first-page header or footer but don't type any text for that header or footer.

By default, Word uses Arabic numerals (1, 2, 3, and so forth) for page numbers in headers and footers, but you can choose to use roman numerals or letters instead.

To add a header or footer:

1. Move the insertion point into the section you want to affect. If your document is not divided into sections, Word adds headers or footers to the entire document.
2. Choose **View Header and Footer**. Word displays the Header and Footer toolbar. Figure 13.2 illustrates the buttons on the Header and Footer toolbar.
3. To switch between the header and footer boxes, click the **Switch Between Header and Footer** button (the far left-hand button) on the toolbar.
4. If you want different headers and footers for specific pages, click the **Page Setup** button (the "open book" button) and click the **Layout** tab. Choose one or both of the following options in the Headers and Footers area:

Adding Headers or Footers

▼ *Figure 13.2. Setting Up a Footer Using the Header and Footer Toolbar*

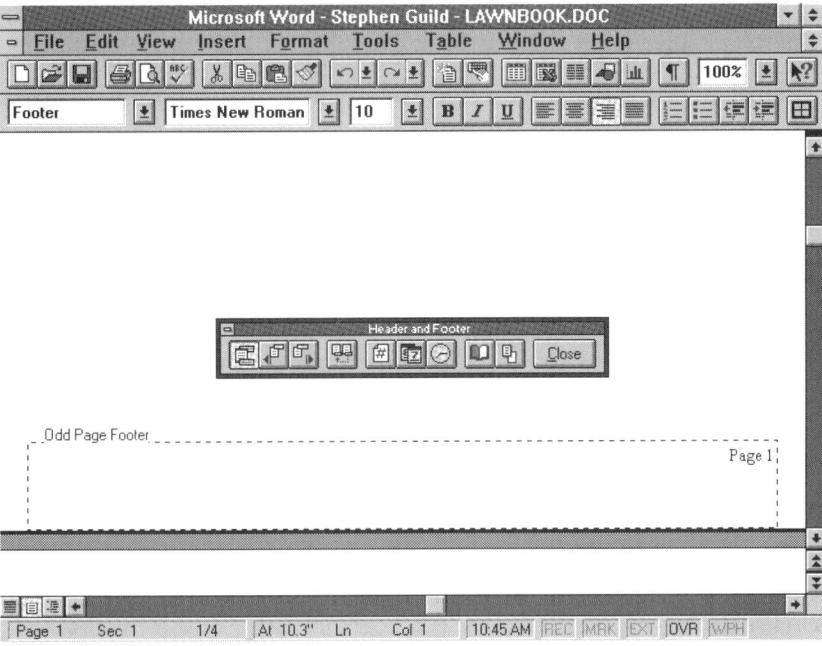

- ▲ To create different headers for odd and even pages, turn on the **Different Odd and Even** check box.
- ▲ To create a different header (or no header) for the first page for your section, turn on the **Different First Page** check box.

5. If you want to set a new position for the header or footer relative to the edges of the page, choose the **Margins** tab and type a measurement (such as **.75**) in the From Edge: Header box or in the From Edge: Footer box. The measurement for headers is from the top edge of the page to the top of the header; the measurement for footers is from the bottom edge of the page to the bottom of the footer.
6. Click **OK** to return to the Header and Footer toolbar.

To change the starting page number (the default is 1) or the number type (the default is 1, 2, 3, and so on):

1. Choose the **Insert Page Numbers** command and click the **Format** button to display the Page Numbers dialog box.
2. Select a type from the Number Format drop-down list.

3. Choose the **Continue from Previous Section** option for continuous numbering throughout a document, or type a starting number in the Start At box for the first page number of the section.
4. Click **OK** to return to the Page Numbers dialog box, then click **OK** or press **Enter** to return to the Header and Footer toolbar.

Typing and Formatting a Header or Footer

After you've told Word where you want the header or footer to appear, you're ready to type and format text to create it. Headers and footers can contain just a couple of characters, whole paragraphs of text, or graphics—anything that you can put in your document you can put in a header or footer.

If your document is divided into sections and you don't want the same header or footer to appear throughout the document, you can click the **Link to Previous** button (the one with two pages) and a message will appear asking you if you want to link to the previous section.

You use the appropriate buttons on the Header and Footer toolbar to add page numbers, current date, and current time to a header or footer.

To create a header or footer:

1. Choose **View Header and Footer**. Word displays the Header and Footer toolbar.
2. To switch between the header and footer boxes, click the **Switch Between Header and Footer** button (the far right-hand button) on the toolbar.
3. Type or paste the text you want to appear in the header or footer.
4. If you want a different header or footer on that page, click the **Link to Previous** (the one with two pages) button and a message will appear asking you if you want to link to the previous section.
5. To add page numbers, the date of printing, or the time of printing to your header or footer, position the insertion point, then do the following:

Adding Headers or Footers

To Add	Do This
Page numbers	Click the # button on the Header and Footer toolbar to add a {page} field.
Current date	Click the date button (the button that looks vaguely like a desk calendar) on the Header and Footer toolbar to add a {date} field.
Current time	Click the time button (the button that looks like a clock) on the Header and Footer toolbar to add a {time} field.

These fields will be updated when you print your file. (If you want to add a specific date or time to your header or footer, just type the date or time you want; don't use these fields.)

6. Format the text as desired. You can use the ruler and the commands in the Format menu to format headers and footers, choosing different alignments, borders, or character formatting (such as bold or italic).
7. Click the **Close** button or click in the document to close the Header and Footer toolbar to return to your main document text.

Word automatically attaches a default style named Header to headers and a default style named Footer to footers, but you can apply different styles if you like. You can also modify the Header and Footer styles with the Styles dialog box. (See "Changing a Style" in Chapter 8 for more information about modifying styles.)

To edit or reformat a header or footer in Page Layout view, just select the header or footer on the page.

CHECK YOURSELF

Add headers to all pages except the first page of a document.
  ▲ Choose the **Layout** tab in File Page Setup, turn on the **Different First Page** check box, and then, on the second page of your document, type your header text.

Adding Footnotes or Endnotes

Every footnote or endnote has two parts: the *reference mark* (that little number or mark in text that tells you to look for a footnote or endnote) and the *text*. The default position is at the bottom of the page for footnotes and at the end of the document for endnotes. Both are, by default, numbered continuously throughout the document.

To insert a footnote:

1. Place the insertion point where you want the footnote reference (usually a superscript number) to appear.
2. Choose **Insert Footnote**.
3. Click the **Footnote** button in the Insert area.
4. The AutoNumber option is already chosen for you to insert numbered footnotes. If you want a footnote reference mark other than a number, type the character you want to use instead in the Custom Mark box, or click the **Custom** button, then the **Symbol** button, and click a symbol in the Symbol dialog box. For example, if you want to mark your footnote with an asterisk, type * in the Custom Mark box or choose from the Symbol dialog box.
5. If you want to change the position of footnotes, click the **Options** button to display the Note Options dialog box, then click the **All Footnotes** tab and choose a new position from the Place At drop-down list.
6. Footnotes will be numbered consecutively throughout the document unless you do one of the following:
   - ▲ Turn on the **Restart Each Section** box to make footnotes start at 1 in each section of your document.
   - ▲ Turn on the **Restart Each Page** to make footnotes start at 1 on each new page in your document.
     If you want to change the starting number either in a new section or on a new page, type a new starting number in the Start At box.
7. Click **OK** to return to the Footnote and Endnote dialog box.
8. Click **OK**. In Normal view, Word inserts a footnote reference mark and opens the footnote pane at the bottom of the document window. In Page Layout view, Word scrolls to the footnote area.

Adding Footnotes or Endnotes

9. Type and format the text for your footnote. You can use the ruler and the commands on the Format menu to format footnotes.
10. To add more footnotes in Normal view, press **F6** or click the document text, then repeat Steps 1 through 8. When you're finished, click the **Close** button in the footnote pane. To add more footnotes in Page Layout view, repeat Steps 1 through 8.

Figure 13.3 illustrates how to add footnotes to a document in Normal view.

To insert an endnote:

1. Place the insertion point where you want the endnote reference (usually a superscript number) to appear.
2. Choose **Insert Footnote**.
3. Click **Endnote** in the Insert area.
4. The AutoNumber option in the Numbering box is already chosen for you to insert lowercase letter endnotes. If you want an endnote reference mark other than a letter, type the character you want to use instead in the Custom Mark box, or click the **Custom** button then the Symbol button, and click a symbol in

▼ *Figure 13.3. Footnotes in Page Layout View*

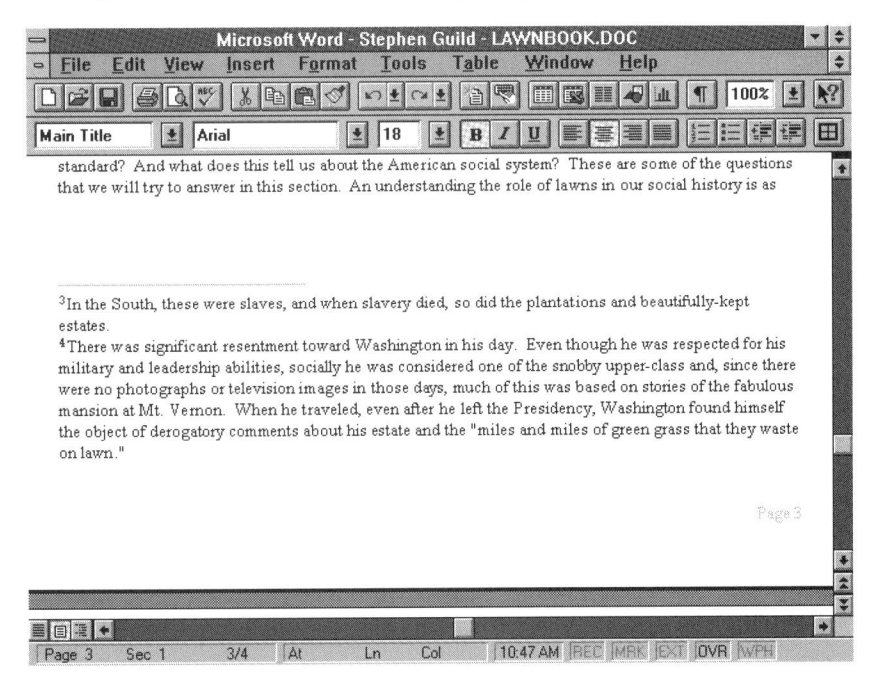

the Symbol dialog box. For example, if you want to mark your endnote with an asterisk, type * in the Custom Mark box or choose from the Symbol dialog box.
5. If you want to change the position of endnotes, click the **Options** button to display the Note Options dialog box, then click the **All Endnotes** tab and choose a new position from the Place At list.
6. Endnotes will be marked consecutively throughout the document unless you turn on the Restart Each Section box to make endnotes start at i in each section of your document. Make sure you've selected End of Section in the Place At list. If you want to change the starting mark either in a new section or on a new page, type a new starting mark in the Start At box.
7. Click **OK** to return to the Footnote and Endnote dialog box.
8. Click **OK**. In Normal view, Word inserts an endnote reference mark and opens the endnote pane at the bottom of the document window. In Page Layout view, Word scrolls to the endnote area.
9. Type and format the text for your endnote. You can use the ruler and the commands on the Format menu to format endnotes.
10. To add more endnotes in Normal view, press **F6** or click the document text, then repeat Steps 1 through 8. Click the **Close** button in the endnote pane.

CHECK YOURSELF

Add a numbered footnote in Page Layout view.
▲ Choose **Insert Footnote** and click **OK**, then type the text in the footnote area.

Changing the Styles of Separator Characters for Footnotes or Endnotes

Word automatically attaches a style named Footnote Reference to the footnote reference mark and a style named Footnote Text to the footnote text, but if you like you can apply different styles or modify the styles with the Styles dialog box. See Chapter 8 for more information about changing styles.

Adding Footnotes or Endnotes

To separate footnotes from text on a page, Word uses a 2" line as a *footnote separator*, as shown in Figure 13.3. If the text of a footnote is long and must continue on the next page, Word uses a margin-to-margin line as the *continuing separator*, the mark that separates a continued footnote from following text. You can accept or change any of these default options, and you can also add a *continuation notice* to tell readers that a footnote is continued on the next page.

To change the separator you need to be in Normal view. You cannot edit the separator in Page Layout view.

To change the separator characters for footnotes or endnotes:

1. In Normal view, choose **View Footnotes**.
2. In the drop-down list at the top of the note pane, select either **All Footnotes** or **All Endnotes**, as applicable.
3. If you want to change the separator (the short line above the footnotes or endnotes), do one of the following in the Notes box at the top of the note pane:

To Change	*Do This*
The footnote or endnote separator line	Select Footnote Separator or Endnote Separator, then change the line.
The continuing separator line	Select Footnote Continuation Separator or Endnote Continuation Separator, then change the line.

4. In the note pane, make the changes you want in the separator. If you want to delete the separator, select it, then press **Backspace** or **Delete**.
5. Click the **Close** button in the note pane to return to the document.

Adding Continuation Notices to Footnotes or Endnotes

When you have a footnote or endnote that is too long for the page, you can insert a continuation notice that tells the reader to go to the next page.

To create a continuation notice for footnotes or endnotes:

1. In Normal view, choose **View Footnotes**.
2. In the drop-down list at the top of the note pane, select either **All Footnotes** or **All Endnotes** depending on which you are working with.
3. To add a notice that notes continue on the next page, select **Footnote Continuation Notice** or **Endnote Continuation Notice** in the drop-down list at the top of the note pane.
4. In the note pane, type the text you want to use as a continuation notice.
5. Click the **Close** button in the note pane to return to the document.

Converting Footnotes and Endnotes

You may decide that you want to convert one or more footnotes to endnotes or vice versa. Or you may decide that you want all notes to be of one kind or the other.

To convert individual notes:

1. In Normal view, choose **View Footnotes**.
2. In the drop-down list at the top of the note pane, select the **All Footnotes** or **All Endnotes** tab.
3. Select the note or notes you want to convert.
4. Point to the selected notes and click the right mouse button.
5. Choose **Convert to Footnote** or **Convert to Endnote**.

To convert all notes:

1. Choose **Insert Footnote**.
2. Click the **Options** button, then click the **Convert** button.
3. Choose the conversion option you want, then click **OK** or press **Enter**.
4. Click **OK** or press **Enter** again, and then click **Close**.

Jumping to Footnotes or Endnotes

You can use the F5 key or the Edit Go To command to jump to the footnote reference mark you want. If the footnote or endnote window is open at the bottom of the screen in Normal view, the text scrolls to display the text of the selected reference mark.

To jump to a footnote reference mark, use the following procedure:

1. Press **F5** or choose **Edit Go To** to display the Go To dialog box.
2. Select **Footnote** or **Endnote** from the Go To What list, and type the footnote or endnote number in the Enter Footnote Number or Enter Endnote Number box.
3. Click **Close** when you have finished.

Editing Footnotes or Endnotes

You can change the footnote or endnote text or the reference mark for the footnote or endnote.

To edit the text of a footnote or endnote in Normal view:

1. Choose **View Footnotes** or click the footnote or endnote number in the text to display the footnote or endnote pane at the bottom of the document window.
2. In the pane, scroll to the text you want to edit.
3. Edit the text in the pane.
4. When you're finished, click the **Close** button.

To edit the text of a footnote or endnote in Page Layout view, simply scroll to the footnote or endnote and edit the text.

You can change a footnote or endnote reference character that you've specified. For example, you might want to change from an ampersand to an asterisk or change to an automatically numbered footnote or endnote.

To edit a footnote or endnote reference mark:

1. Select the reference mark in the document.
2. Choose **Insert Footnote**.
3. If you want to specify a new character, type the new character in the Custom Mark box or choose a new symbol in the Symbol dialog box. If you want to change to an automatically numbered reference, click the **AutoNumber** button.
4. Click **OK**.

Adding Footnotes or Endnotes

If you change to an automatically numbered reference, Word renumbers footnotes or endnotes throughout the document.

Changing the Placement of Footnotes or Endnotes

Normally a footnote appears at the bottom of the page where its reference mark occurs and an endnote at the end of the section, but you can tell Word where you want footnotes and endnotes to appear in your document.

To change the placement of footnotes and endnotes:

1. Select Insert **Footnotes** and click the **Options** button.
2. Click the **All Footnotes** or **All Endnotes** tab.
3. Select the location where you want the footnote or endnote to appear in the Place At box.
4. Click **Close**.

Preventing Endnotes from Printing at the Ends of Specific Sections

Use the following procedure if your document is divided into sections and you've chosen the Restart Each Section option in the Note Options dialog box but you don't want footnotes to print at the end of a particular section. This situation may occur when you've used section formatting to make parts of the document look different, but the division into sections doesn't reflect a logical division of the text.

To prevent endnotes from printing at the end of a section:

1. Move the insertion point into the section.
2. Choose **File Page Setup** and click the **Layout** tab.
3. Turn on the **Suppress Endnotes** check box.
4. Click **OK**. Word will print the endnotes at the end of the next section in which endnotes are not suppressed.

Deleting Footnotes or Endnotes

To delete a footnote or endnote:

1. Select the footnote or endnote reference mark.
2. Press **Delete** or choose **Edit Cut**. Word automatically deletes the note text and renumbers the footnotes or endnotes as appropriate.

Adding Footnotes or Endnotes

QUICK COMMAND SUMMARY

Command	To Do This
Insert Page Numbers	Add only page numbers to the top or bottom margin of a document.
View Header/Footer	Add text, page numbers, dates, and times to the top or bottom margin of a document.
Insert Footnote	Add and format footnotes.
View Footnotes	Display footnotes in normal view.
File Page Setup, Layout tab	Suppress footnotes in a section.
Edit Go To or F5 key	Jump to a footnote.

PRACTICE WHAT YOU'VE LEARNED

In any Word document, add a header with the title at the left margin, the date in the center, and the page number at the right margin, like this:

Annual Report   8/3/89   Page 2

Then add a footer that contains the centered company name, like this:

The Company, Inc.

What You Do

1. Choose **View Header and Footer**.

2. Type **Annual Report**, press **Tab**, click the date button, press **Tab**, type **Page**, press the **spacebar**, then click the **page Number** button.

3. Click the **Switch Between Header and Footer** button on the Header and Footer toolbar.

4. Press **Tab** to move the insertion point to the center, then type **The Company, Inc.**

5. Click the **Close** button to close the Header and Footer toolbar.

What You'll See

1. The Header and Footer toolbar with the various buttons that control header and footer formatting. Your document changes to Page Layout view. A Header box with dotted lines appears.

2. The text "Annual Report," the date, and the text "Page" and page number 1.

3. The Footer box with dotted lines.

4. The insertion point moves to the center of the Footer box and the text "The Company, Inc." appears.

5. The document returns to the view it was in before the header and footer were inserted.

14

Pagination and Printing

When you've finished editing and formatting a document, you'll want to check the page breaks, then print all or part of your file. In this chapter, you will learn how to:

- ▲ Control background pagination
- ▲ Force Word to repaginate
- ▲ Insert, delete, and prevent page breaks
- ▲ Print all or part of your document
- ▲ Print associated information such as AutoText entries, styles, annotations, and summary information
- ▲ Print envelopes
- ▲ Troubleshoot printing problems

Controlling Pagination

Whenever your text fills a page, Word adds a "soft" or "automatic" page break, which appears as a dotted line in Normal view, as shown in Figure 14.1. Normally, you'll want to leave this "background pagination" feature on while you work. However, if your computer system is very slow and has limited memory, you can speed it up slightly by turning off background pagination.

To control background pagination:

1. Make sure you're in Normal view. Choose **Tools Options** and click the **General** tab.
2. Turn on or turn off the **Background Repagination** check box.
3. Click **OK**.

Keep in mind that, if you've turned off background repagination, the page numbers Word displays in the status bar won't necessarily match your printed output. You'll need to turn on the Background Repagination check box whenever you want to see

▼ *Figure 14.1. Hard and Soft Page Breaks*

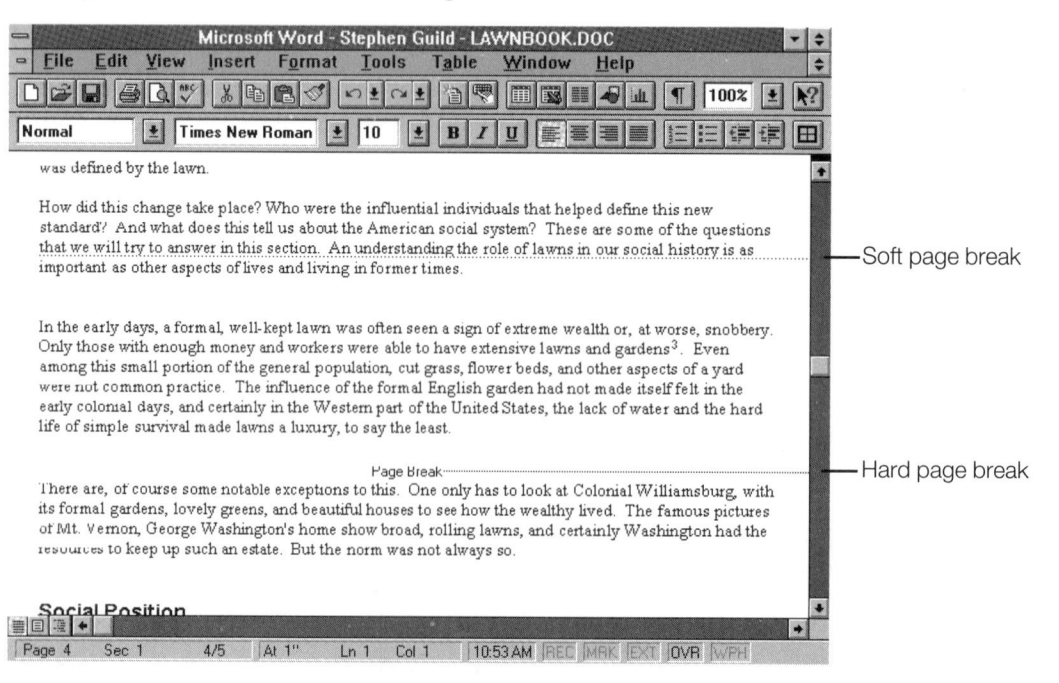

page breaks in the correct positions and current page numbers in the status bar.

TIP

Page breaks that appear in odd places might be caused by a Paragraph dialog box setting—such as Page Break Before, Keep With Next Paragraph, or Keep Lines Together; or by a Footnote setting of Bottom of Page or Below Text, a Section Break setting where the section begins on Next Page or a page break marker is accidentally formatted as hidden text.

If, at the time Word repaginates, you are displaying text that you've formatted as hidden, the hidden text will affect the pagination. If you don't plan to print hidden text, choose the **View** tab in **Tools Options** and turn off the **Hidden Text** check box before checking page breaks.

Inserting Page Breaks

To insert your own manual, or "hard," page break, use one of the following procedures:

1. Place the insertion point where you want to insert a page break.
2. Press **Ctrl+Enter**.

or

1. Place the insertion point where you want to insert a page break.
2. Choose **Insert Break** and click the **Page Break** button.
3. Click **OK**. Word inserts a hard page break marker—a dotted line with the dots very close together, as shown in Figure 14.1.

Deleting a Page Break That You Have Inserted

You can't delete a soft page break calculated by Word, but you can delete one that you've inserted.

To delete a hard page break:

1. In Normal view, select the page break marker.
2. Press **Delete**.

TIP

To quickly remove all page breaks that you've inserted in a document, place the insertion point at the top of the document, then choose Edit Replace. **In the Find What box, type** ^m **(the code for a page break character), or click the** Special **button and select** Manual Page Break. **Make sure the Replace With box is blank, then click the** Replace All **button. (NOTE: Make sure to type the caret (^) in the Find What box: the caret doesn't stand for the Ctrl key as it does in many other programs.) You can also use the ^m code with Edit Find to quickly locate page breaks that you've inserted.**

Controlling Page Breaks Within and Between Paragraphs

By default, Word automatically prevents widows and orphans—single lines of text separated from the rest of their paragraphs. However, you can change the setting anytime you like.

To prevent or allow widows and orphans:

1. Select the whole document or those paragraphs you want to affect.
2. Choose **Format Paragraph** and click the **Text Flow** tab.
3. Turn on or turn off the **Widow/Orphan Control** check box.
4. Click **OK**.

Using the same dialog box you can make sure that Word doesn't split one paragraph between pages or split related paragraphs across pages, and you can tell Word to put a page break before a specific paragraph to make sure it falls at the top of a page. For more information, see "Controlling Page Breaks in Paragraphs" in Chapter 7.

Jumping to a Specific Page

Jumping to a Specific Page

When you have paginated your document and you want to go to a certain page number, you can quickly jump to that page.

To jump to a page:

1. Press **F5** or choose **Edit Go To**. Word displays the Go To dialog box.
2. Choose **Page** from the Go To What list, and type the page number you want to jump to. If you have more than one section, type **p** followed by the page number, then **s** followed by the section number. For example, type **p5s2** to specify page 5 in section 2.
3. Press **Enter**.

Preparing to Print

Before you print, you may want to complete these tasks:

▲ Choose **File Page Setup** and check the margin, page size and orientation, and paper source settings. These settings override any settings shown in the Print Setup dialog box (which you access by choosing File Print Printer or by clicking the Printer button in the Print dialog box).

▲ Choose **File Print Printer** and check the printer selection. Selecting a different printer can change fonts and other settings.

▲ Check pages using Print Preview and Page Layout View.

Basic Printing

If you have multiple files open, Word prints the file that contains the insertion point. You can use Find File to mark multiple files for printing. See Chapter 2 for more information.

To print all pages in a Word file:

1. If necessary, open the document or template you want to print, or move the insertion point to the window whose contents you want to print.
2. Do one of the following:
    - ▲ To use the default settings in the Print dialog box and begin printing immediately, click the **Printer** button on the Standard toolbar.
    - ▲ Choose **File Print**, choose options in the dialog box, then click **OK**.
3. If your file contains fields that should be updated before printing, click **Printer** to display the Print tab in the options dialog box, turn on the **Update Fields** check box, then click **OK** to return to the Print dialog box.
4. Click **OK** to begin printing.

The Print dialog box is shown in Figure 14.2. The text at the top of the dialog box indicates the printer Word will use. If this text is "None," click **Printer** to display a dialog box that allows you to select a printer, or click **Cancel** and then install a printer using the

▼ *Figure 14.2. Preparing to Print Two Copies of a Page*

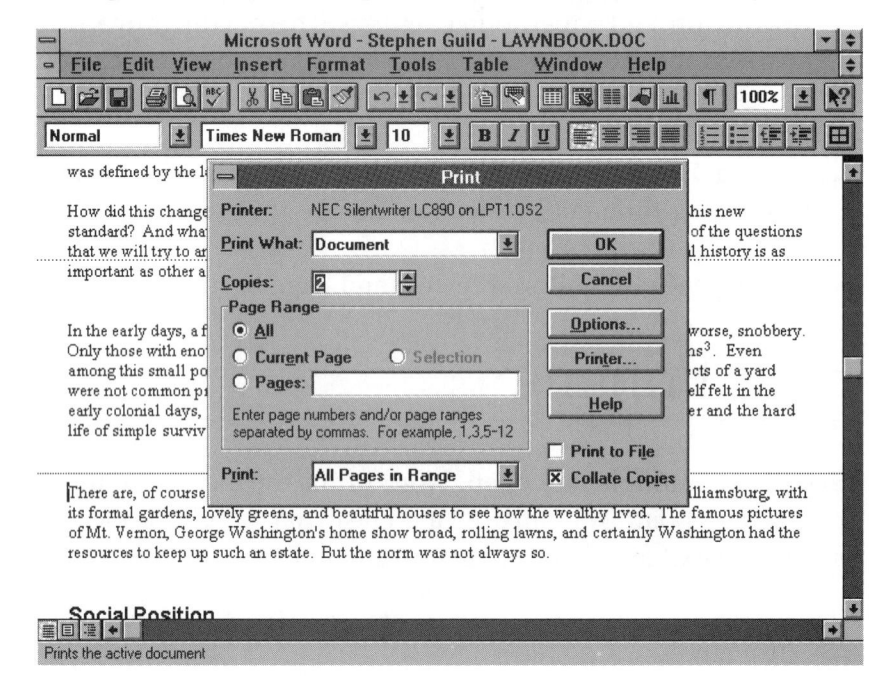

Basic Printing

Windows Control Panel. See your Windows documentation for more information.

Don't be alarmed if printing doesn't begin instantly—Word takes a few seconds to format pages and communicate with the printer. If the file doesn't print after a few seconds, read "What If It Doesn't Print?" later in this chapter for suggestions on finding and correcting the problem.

Canceling Printing

If you need to cancel printing at any time:

▲ Press **Esc**.

The printer might not stop immediately because it continues to print whatever is in its memory until it receives the "Stop!" message from Word. If the paper is jammed or another emergency situation has developed, press the online printer button (if your printer has one) to take the printer offline or, in a dire emergency, turn off the printer. (Turning off some printers causes them to lose information; if that happens you'll have to resend your file to the printer.)

Printing a Draft Copy

When you don't care about the document's layout, page breaks, or anything else except the words, you can print a draft copy of your document. Draft printing is fast because Word doesn't print graphics, use microspace justification, or perform other time-consuming printing tasks. For draft copies, Word prints an empty frame where a graphic belongs.

To print a draft copy:

1. Choose **File Print** and click the **Options** button. Note that the dialog box that is displayed is the same as the Printing tab in Tools Options.
2. Turn on the **Draft Output** check box, then click **OK** to return to the Print dialog box.
3. Click **OK** to begin printing.

Printing More than One Copy

To print more than one copy of your document:
1. Choose **File Print**.
2. Type or select the number of copies you want in the Copies box.
3. If you want Word to collate the copies (print all pages of one copy before printing the next copy) and put a blank sheet of paper between copies, turn on the **Collate Copies** check box.
4. Click **OK** or press **Enter**.

Printing Part of Your Document

You can use the Print dialog box to tell Word to print a range of pages or to print only the text you have selected at the time.

To print only part of your document:
1. Select the part of your document you want to print.
2. Choose **File Print**.
3. In the Range box, choose an option to tell Word what you want to print:

To Print	*Do This*
The entire document	Choose All.
Selected text only	Choose Selection. (This option is grayed in the diaog box unless you've selected text.)
The page containing the insertion point	Choose Current Page.
A specified range of pages	In the Pages box, type the numbers of the first and last pages you want to print. Separate them with a hyphen.
Several individual pages	In the Pages box, type the numbers of the pages you want to print. Separate them with commas.
An entire section	In the Pages box, type **s** and the section number.

Basic Printing

For example, to print pages 5 through 10, type **5-10** in the Pages box. To print several pages, type **1**, **5**, **10**. To print one page, type the same page number in both boxes. You can specify pages in sections this way: **p3s2** (page 3 in section 2). Or you can specify a single section this way: **s5** (section 5).

4. Click **OK** to begin printing.

CHECK YOURSELF

Print one paragraph from a document.
- ▲ Turn on your printer, select one paragraph in a document, then choose **File Print**. Choose the **Selection** option, then click **OK** to begin printing.

Printing Information Associated with a Document

You can use the Print dialog box to print the following items: a summary information sheet containing information you entered about the file, annotations, an AutoText entry, a list of styles, and a list of key assignments.

To print summary information and/or annotations:

1. Choose **File Print**.
2. Do one of the following:
   - ▲ If you want to print only the summary information or annotations, select **Summary Info** or **Annotations** from the Print drop-down list.
   - ▲ If you want to print summary information and/or annotations in addition to your document, click **Options** to display another dialog box, turn on the **Summary Info** and/or **Annotations** check boxes, then click **OK** to get back to the Print dialog box.
3. Click **OK** or press **Enter**. Word first prints the document or template text, then prints the summary information and/or annotations on separate pages.

To print a list of styles, Autotext entries, or key assignments contained in a document:

1. Choose **File Print**.
2. From the Print drop-down list (shown in Figure 14.3), select the item you want to print:

Select	*To Print*
Styles	The styles contained in a document or template.
AutoText Entries	The AutoText entries from a document or template and from NORMAL.DOT.
Key Assignments	The names of macros and commands, their key assignments for a template, and the description text.

3. Click **OK** to begin printing.
4. Repeat Steps 1 through 3 to print other items as necessary.

▼ *Figure 14.3. Preparing to Print a List of Styles*

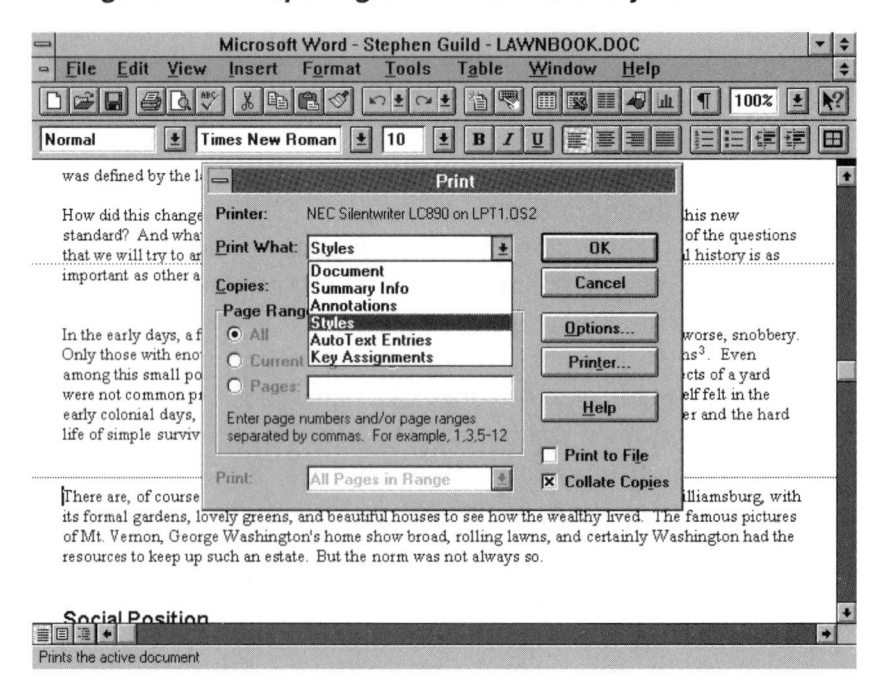

To print hidden text or drawing objects contained in a document:

1. Choose **File Print**.
2. Choose the **Options** button and turn on the **Hidden Text** or **Drawing Objects** check box.

Basic Printing

CHECK YOURSELF

Print a list of styles used with a document.
- ▲ Open the document and choose **File Print**. Select **Styles** from the Print drop-down list, then click **OK** to print the list.

Printing in Reverse Order

If your printer stacks the pages face up as they emerge, you may want to print the pages in your file in reverse order. This approach will save you the work of shuffling the pages into the correct order.

To print in reverse order:

1. Choose **File Print**.
2. Click **Options** to display the Print tab .
3. Turn on the **Reverse Print Order** check box.
4. Click **OK** or press **Enter** to return to the Print dialog box.

Printing Field Codes and Hidden Text

If your document contains fields, you need to decide whether to print the results of fields or the field codes themselves. Also, if your document contains text that is formatted as hidden, you need to decide whether to print the hidden text. Hidden text is displayed and printed with a dotted underline. It does not matter whether field codes or hidden text are displayed on the screen—the printing of results or codes is controlled by settings in the Options dialog box (displayed from the Print menu).

To specify whether to print field results or field codes:

1. Choose **File Print**.
2. Click **Options** to display the Print tab.
3. Do one of the following:
   ▲ If you want to print field codes, turn on the **Field Codes** check box.
   ▲ If you want to print the results of fields, turn on the **Update Fields** check box and turn off the **Field Codes** check box.
4. If you want to print hidden text, turn on the **Hidden Text** check box. Otherwise, make sure the check box is turned off.
5. Click **OK**.

Printing to a File

If you don't have the correct printer connected to your computer, you may want to print your Word document to a file. Printing to a file saves the Word document in its printed format. This lets you take the file to a computer that does not have Word for Windows and still print the file from DOS.

To print to a file:

1. Choose **File Print**.
2. Turn on the **Print to File** check box near the bottom of the dialog box.
3. Click **OK**. Word displays a dialog box so you can specify the name of the output file.
4. Type a filename for the file, then click **OK**. Word will display messages as it prints to the file, just as it would when printing to a printer.

To print a file that has been saved in this way, use the Print command from the DOS command line. See your operating system manual for more information.

Printing Envelopes

If your printer can handle envelopes, you can quickly set up and print envelopes with delivery and return addresses, special text

Printing Envelopes

and graphics, and even machine-readable codes. If you want to print envelopes with different addresses, you'll need to use Word's Mail Merge Helper. See Chapter 15 for more information about merging to produce envelopes.

To format and print an envelope with a single address:

1. If you already have a document containing more than one possible mailing address, open that document and select the address to which you want to mail.
2. Choose **Tools Envelopes and Labels**, and click the **Envelopes** tab. Word displays the dialog box shown in Figure 14.4.
3. If necessary, type or edit the addresses in the Delivery Address box and the Return Address box. If you type in a new return address, Word will ask you (after you complete these steps) if you want this to be the default return address. If you answer Yes, Word will change the Mailing Address box in the Tools Options User Info tab. If your envelopes are preprinted with the return address, turn on the Omit check box.

▼ *Figure 14.4. Preparing to Print an Envelope*

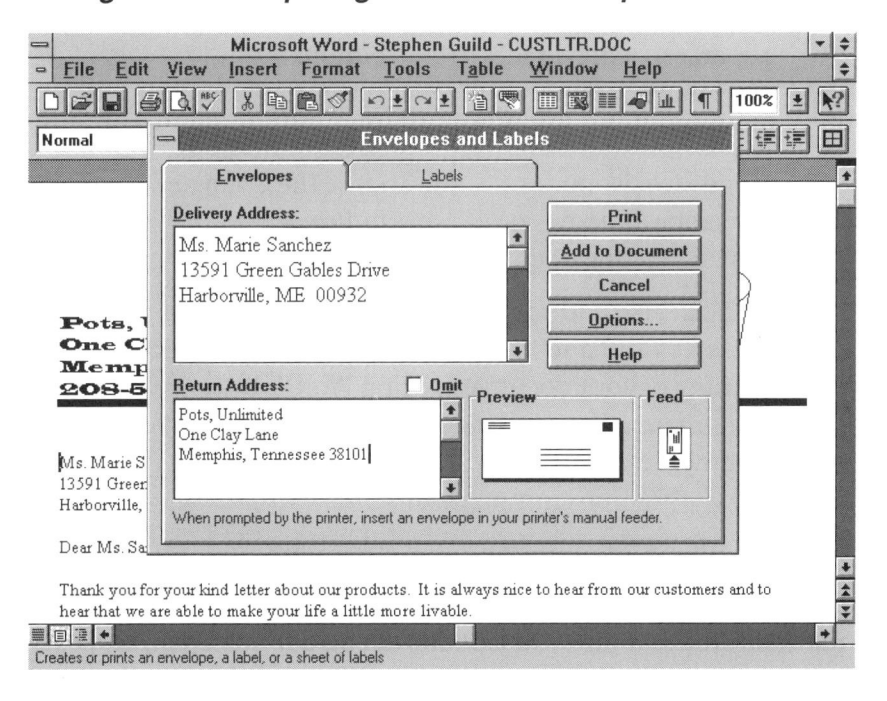

4. Choose **Options** and the **Envelope Options** tab. Select the envelope size you're using from the Envelope Size drop-down list.
5. If you want to change the font and position of either the delivery or return address, use the **Font** button and the **From Left** and **From Top** boxes.
6. If you want special bar codes printed on the envelope, click the appropriate check boxes in the If Mailed in the USA box.
7. Click the **Printing Options** tab, and choose how the envelope will be fed into the printer in the Feed Method area and Feed From box. Individual printers feed envelopes in different ways, so be sure to check your printer manual for more information about how the printer handles envelopes.
8. Click **OK** or press **Enter** to return to the Envelopes and Labels dialog box.
9. Do one of the following

To	*Do This*
Print the envelope	Insert the envelope in the printer and choose the Print button.
Add the envelope as a separate section at the beginning of the document	Choose the Add to Document button.
Change an existing envelope already attached to the document	Choose the Change Document button.

You can also add special text and graphics if you follow the above steps and add the text and graphics in the section at the beginning of your document, using Word's Insert Picture command or using the drawing tools that come with Word to create a graphic.

TIP

Click in the Preview **area to open the Envelopes dialog box; click in the** Feed **area and the Print Options dialog box will open; and click in the** Label **area and the Label Options dialog box will open.**

Printing Labels

You can print mailing labels for a single address using the Tools Envelopes and Labels command. If you want to print labels with several different addresses, you'll need to use Word's Mail Merge Helper. See Chapter 15 for more information about merging to produce mailing labels.

To print one label or a sheet of labels with a single address:

1. Choose **Tools Envelopes and Labels** and click the **Labels** tab.
2. If you want to print a delivery address on the label, use the proposed address in the Address box or type in another address.
3. If you want to print a return address on the label, turn on the **Use Return Address** check box or type in another address.
4. To print a single label, click the **Single Label** button and choose the number of columns and rows on the label sheet.
5. To print a full page of the same address on the same sheet of labels, click the **Full Page of the Same Label** button.
6. Choose the **Options** button, and in the Label Options dialog box indicate the printer information, label product, and product number.
7. To set the height and width of the label as well as other information necessary for printing, choose the **Details** button and make the appropriate choices.
8. Click **OK** or press **Enter** to return to the Labels Options dialog box, then click **OK** or press **Enter** to return to the Labels tab.
9. To print a label or sheet of labels, insert the sheet of labels into the printer and choose **Print**.

If you want to save the sheet of labels as a table in a Word document, choose the **New Document** button. Word will create a new document with the label information.

What If It Doesn't Print?

If Word displays a message indicating that your document is printing but your printer is producing no pages, don't lose your temper.

It takes Word a few seconds to format pages and communicate with the printer. The time required depends on the length of your document and the speed of your computer. However, if you've waited a moment or two and the document still isn't printing or Word has displayed an error message, go through the steps in the following checklist. We can't foresee all problems, but if you follow all these steps in order, chances are that you'll find and fix your problem.

To uncover and correct printing problems:

1. Make sure the printer is plugged in and turned on.
2. Make sure the printer cable is securely plugged into the correct printer and the computer ports.
3. Make sure the printer buttons (such as Online and Ready) are "on" if they should be.
4. Make sure the paper is positioned properly in the printer.
5. Make sure all parts of the printer (covers, ribbon or cartridge, paper trays, and so on) are in place.
6. Choose **File Print** and check the dialog box settings to make sure they're correct.
7. Turn the printer off, wait a few seconds, then turn it back on and try to print again, using **File Print**.
8. If you're using PostScript codes in your document, create another copy of the document, remove the PostScript codes, and try printing the copy. An error in a PostScript code can prevent a document from printing.
9. Make sure the printer "connections" shown in the Windows Control Panel are set to the correct port.
10. Check the Word printer manual to make sure the driver file that's installed is the correct one for your brand and model of printer.

If you've gone through every step in this list and your document still doesn't print, call your printer manufacturer or the Microsoft Product Support number.

QUICK COMMAND SUMMARY

Command	To Do This
Tools Options, General tab	Turn background pagination on or off.
Ctrl+Enter, or Insert Break, Page Break button	Insert a hard page break.
Delete key	Delete a selected page break marker.
Format Paragraph	Control page breaks within and between paragraphs.
Tools Options, Print tab	Prevent or allow widows and orphans, and tell Word whether an envelope feeder is attached to the printer.
Edit Go To, or F5	Jump to a specific page.
File Print	Print documents and related information.
Printer button on the Standard toolbar	Print the entire document without displaying a dialog box.
Esc key	Cancel printing.
Tools Options, User Info tab	Set up a return address for use with envelopes.
Tools and labels	Format and print an envelope or a single label or sheet of labels with a single address.

PRACTICE WHAT YOU'VE LEARNED

Create a letter with an address and two pages, then change the page break. Save the letter. Next, print two copies of the letter, along with summary information. Finally, print an envelope for the letter.

What You Do

1. In Normal view, type the letter, including the address at the top.

2. When a dotted line appears, you've begun the second page. Position the insertion point somewhere above the page break marker, and press **Ctrl+Enter** to insert a page break.

3. Use **File Save** to save the file with a filename, and complete the Summary Information dialog box.

4. Turn on your printer, if necessary, then choose **File Print**.

5. Type **2** in the Copies box.

6. Click **Options** and turn on the **Summary Info** check box in the Print tab. Click **OK**.

What You'll See

1. At the lower left-hand corner of your document, the Normal view button highlighted. The text of your letter will appear after you have typed it.

2. A dotted line after the first full page. After you press **Ctrl+Enter**, a new, heavier page break marker with the words "Page Break" appears, and the automatic page break marker added by Word will disappear.

3. The Save As dialog box. After you click OK, the Summary Info dialog box appears. After filling in the dialog box, the name of the file appears in the document window title bar.

4. The Print dialog box.

5. The number 2 in the Copies box.

6. The Print tab in the Options dialog box, and a check beside Summary Info in the Include with Document area. After you click **OK**, you will return to the Print dialog box.

What You Do	*What You'll See*
7. Click **OK** to print the letter and summary information.	7. The Printing message indicating which page is printing. The letter and summary information sheet will be printed.
8. Place an envelope in your printer's envelope or manual feeder.	8. The document window unchanged.
9. If necessary, choose **Tools Options**, then use the User Info tab to specify your address. Click **OK**.	9. The User Info tab in the Tools Options dialog box. Any changes you make to your name or address will be displayed. After you click OK, the letter in the document window will be displayed again.
10. Choose the **Envelope** tab in the Tools Envelopes and Labels dialog box.	10. The Envelopes tab in the Envelopes and Labels dialog box.
11. If necessary, type or edit the address shown in the Delivery Address and Return Address dialog box, and select a new envelope size.	11. The changes in the addresses and any change in envelope size.
12. Click **Print** to print the envelope.	12. The Printing message indicating the page that is printing. The finished envelope will be printed.

15

Creating Form Letters and Address Labels

You can use Word to create form letters, invoices, and other documents that need to be merged with a list of names, addresses, and other information you supply. In this chapter, you will learn how to:

▲ Create a data source document

▲ Create a main document

▲ Merge data into a main document to create form letters

▲ Sort data alphabetically or numerically

▲ Merge data to create address labels and envelopes

Merging Basics

To create form letters and other form documents, you follow three basic steps:

▲ Create a main document containing text that remains the same and fields that contain names, addresses, and other variable information.
▲ Create a data source document containing names, addresses, and other variable information to insert into the main document.
▲ Merge and print the individual forms.

Figure 15.1 illustrates a simple data source document and main document and the form letters that result from a merge.

▼ *Figure 15.1. Merging a Data Document and a Main Document*

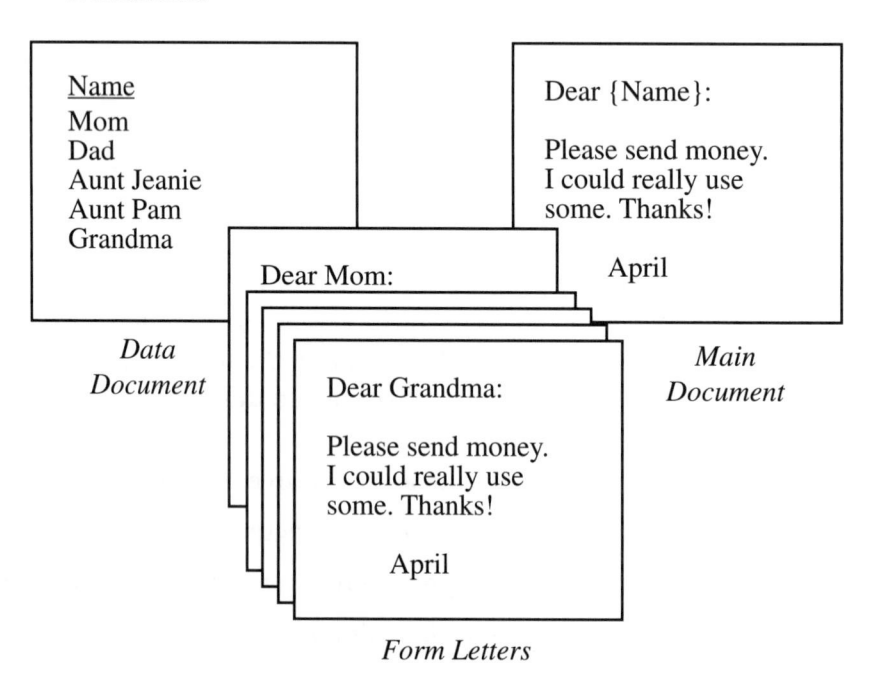

Data Document

Name
Mom
Dad
Aunt Jeanie
Aunt Pam
Grandma

Main Document

Dear {Name}:

Please send money. I could really use some. Thanks!

April

Dear Mom:

Dear Grandma:

Please send money. I could really use some. Thanks!

April

Form Letters

CHECK YOURSELF

What is the relationship between a data source document and a main document?
- ▲ A data source document contains the data that will be placed into fields in the main document to create form letters.

Using Word's Mail Merge

Word's Mail Merge Helper provides a step-by step process that you can use to create form letters, labels, and envelopes. Merging also has some advanced uses, such as catalogues. You can explore them once you get the basic steps down.

To use Mail Merge Helper:

1. Choose **Tools Mail Merge**. Word displays the Mail Merge Helper dialog box, as shown in Figure 15.2.
2. Go through the Mail Merge Helper steps described in the following sections.

▼ **Figure 15.2. The Mail Merge Helper Dialog Box**

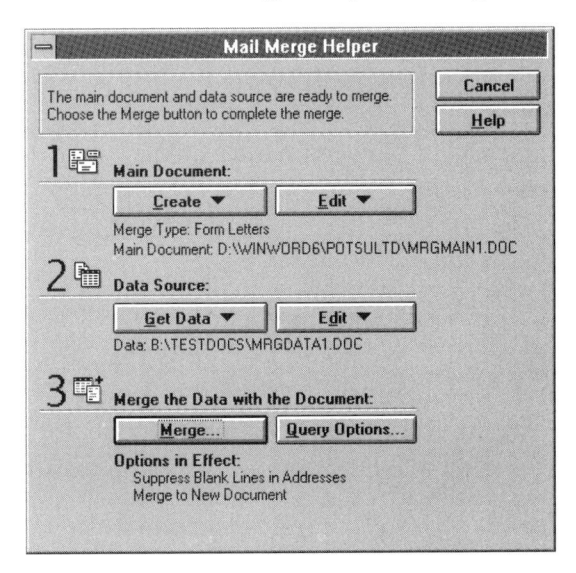

Using Mail Merge to Create a Main Document

A main document contains two elements:

▲ The boilerplate text, which remains the same in each letter
▲ Fields that tell Word where to find the variable information to insert into the main document (from the data source document)

As with any other Word document, you can enter and format the standard text of a main document by using an existing document, or you can create a new one.

Mail Merge Helper provides a series of dialog boxes to help you create main documents.

To create a main document:

1. Open the document you want to use as the main document.
2. Choose **Tools Mail Merge**.
3. In the Main Document area, click the **Create** button and select **Form Letters**, **Mailing Labels**, **Envelopes**, or **Catalog**.
4. Click the **Active Window** button. If you want Word to open a new document window, choose **New Main Document**.
5. If you want to enter text at this point, choose the **Edit** button and select the main document name. If you change your mind, you can click **Create** and either change the document type or select a new document.
6. Do one of the following:
   ▲ Type the text of your main document.
   ▲ Continue using the Mail Merge Helper by creating the database. For more information on creating a database, see the next section.

When you move to the main document, the Mail Merge toolbar will be displayed, as shown in Figure 15.3. You can control most of the mail merge functions from this toolbar, which will always appear when you are in your main document (unless you have closed the toolbar). For more information about using toolbars, see Chapter 1.

▼ ***Figure 15.3. Creating a Main Document***

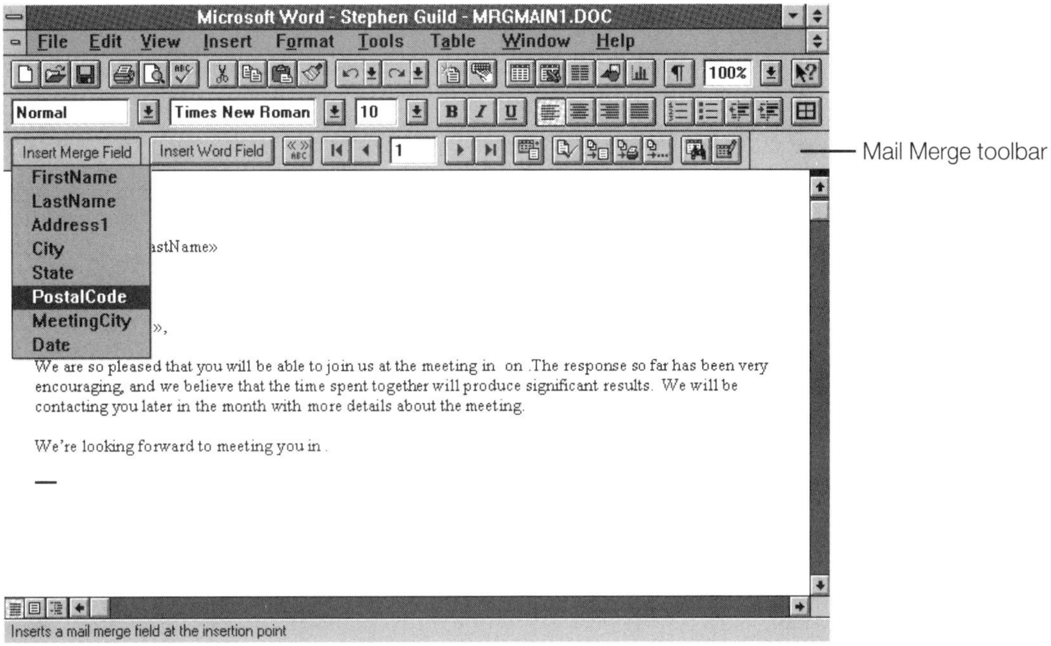

To continue with the Mail Merge process, click the **Mail Merge Helper** button on the toolbar or choose **Tools Mail Merge** again.

Using Mail Merge to Create a Data Document

A data source document contains two elements, as shown in Figure 15.4:

- ▲ A row of field names, called a header record
- ▲ Data records containing field entries, in the same order as the fields in the header record

To create a data source:

1. In the Data Source area of the Mail Merge Helper, click **Get Data**, then choose **Create Data Source**. Word opens a dialog box with field names commonly used in form letters, label, envelopes or catalogs, as shown in Figure 15.5.

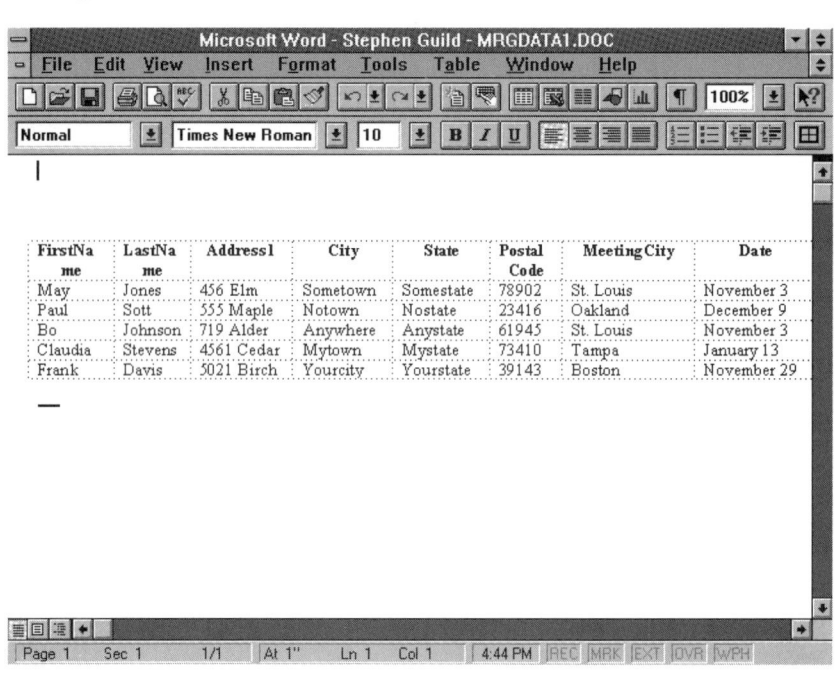

▼ *Figure 15.4. Data Document in a Table*

FirstName	LastName	Address1	City	State	Postal Code	Meeting City	Date
May	Jones	456 Elm	Sometown	Somestate	78902	St. Louis	November 3
Paul	Sott	555 Maple	Notown	Nostate	23416	Oakland	December 9
Bo	Johnson	719 Alder	Anywhere	Anystate	61945	St. Louis	November 3
Claudia	Stevens	4561 Cedar	Mytown	Mystate	73410	Tampa	January 13
Frank	Davis	5021 Birch	Yourcity	Yourstate	39143	Boston	November 29

2. From the Field Names in Header Row list select any field name you *don't* want to use in your data source document, and click the **Remove Field Name** button. Continue doing this for each name you want to remove from the list.

   ▲ If you want to add a field name, type the field name in the Field Name box, and click the **Add Field Name** button. A field name can be up to 40 characters long. The first character in the field name must be a letter, and you cannot include

▼ *Figure 15.5. The Data Form Dialog Box*

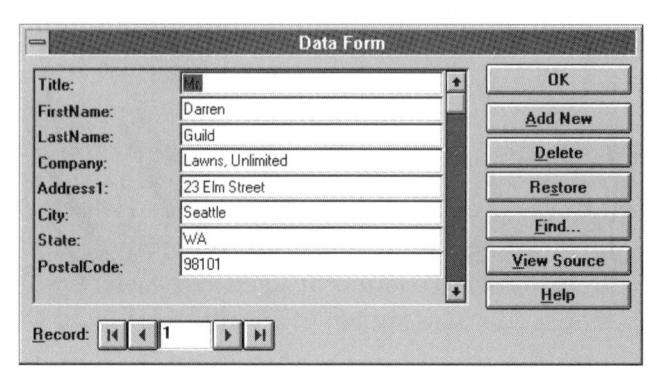

spaces in a field name. If you want space between words in a field name, type an underline character where you would normally use a space—for example, **Number_of_Items**).

▲ If you want to rename a field, select the field name and click the **Remove Field Name** button. Type a new field name in the Field Name box, and then click the **Add Field Name** button. This will return the new field name to the list.

3. If necessary, rearrange the order of the field names by using the up and down arrows in the Move area.
4. Click **OK**, then type a data source name in the File Name box and make any changes to the Directories and Drives boxes.

Using Word's Mail Merge

Entering New Records in the Data Source Document

You are now ready to enter individual records in the data source document.

1. If you are already using Mail Merge Helper, click the **Edit Data Source** button; otherwise choose **Tools Mail Merge**. In the Data Source area, click **Edit** and select the name of the data source document you want to edit.
2. In the Data Form dialog box, as shown in Figure 15.4, fill in the individual boxes of each data record. (Remember, whatever you type will appear in the merge field for that record, but you can always edit an individual record later.) Leave the box blank if you have no information.

To	*Do This*
Add a new record and boxes	Click the Add New button and complete the data field.
Remove a record	Click the Delete button.
Undo any changes made while using that record	Click the Restore button.
Search for a specific record	Click the Find button and choose options in the dialog box

3. To move back and forth among the records, use the Record running-list box.
4. If you want to look at the data source document, click **View Source**. Word will take you to the data source document with the header row and the individual records, as shown in Figure 15.5. This is the document Word will use to perform the merge. You can make changes in this document at any time.

You can also copy and paste data from other Windows documents to use in Word merges. The fields in imported information must be separated by tabs or commas, or placed into a table so that Word can correctly separate the data into fields.

Because Word treats graphics as characters, you can also include graphics in data records. Word inserts the graphics in the form letters when they are merged. However, this must be done through the data source document table, not in the Data Record dialog box. See Chapter 10 for more information on using graphics.

Editing a Data Source Document

You can make changes and corrections in the data source document at any time. You can either use the Mail Merge Helper or open the data source document and use the Database toolbar button.

To edit a data source document:

1. Open the data source document.
2. On the Database toolbar, click the **Data Form** button (if you want to change several records), or click the **Find Record** button and complete the Find in Field dialog box (if you want to change only one record).
3. Make the changes in the individual records.
4. Click **OK** or press **Enter**.

You can also make changes directly in the data source document table by editing a specific cell.

Adding or Deleting Records

You can add or delete a record using the toolbar or the Mail Merge Helper.

Entering New Records in the Data Source Document

To add or delete a record using the toolbar:

1. Open the data source document.
2. Place the insertion point in the data table where you want to add or delete a record.
3. Click the **Add New Record** button or the **Delete Record** button, depending on which you want to do.
4. If adding, enter text in the row added to the data source table.
5. When you have finished adding or deleting, save the data source document.

To add or delete a record using Mail Merge Helper:

1. Choose **Tools Mail Merge**.
2. Click **Edit** in the Data Source section.
3. Select the data record you want to delete in the Data Form dialog box.
4. Click the **Delete** button. Be careful when you do this because you won't be able to undo a deletion. The Restore button only restores an individual record to the form it was in before you made changes to it.
5. Click **OK** or press **Enter**.

Sorting Data in Mail Merge Helper

When you have a list of names or numbers, such as a mailing list, you don't have to arrange them yourself—you can have Word sort the list.

To sort a Mail Merge data source document:

1. Choose **Tools Mail Merge**. Make sure that your main document is the active window and the data source document is listed in the Data Source area of Mail Merge Helper.
2. In the Merge the Data with the Document area, click the **Query Options** button and click on the **Sort Records** tab, as shown in Figure 15.6.
3. Do one or more of the following:
    ▲ Select a field number or name in the drop-down list in the Sort By section.

▼ *Figure 15.6. Sorting a Document Using the Sort Records Tool*

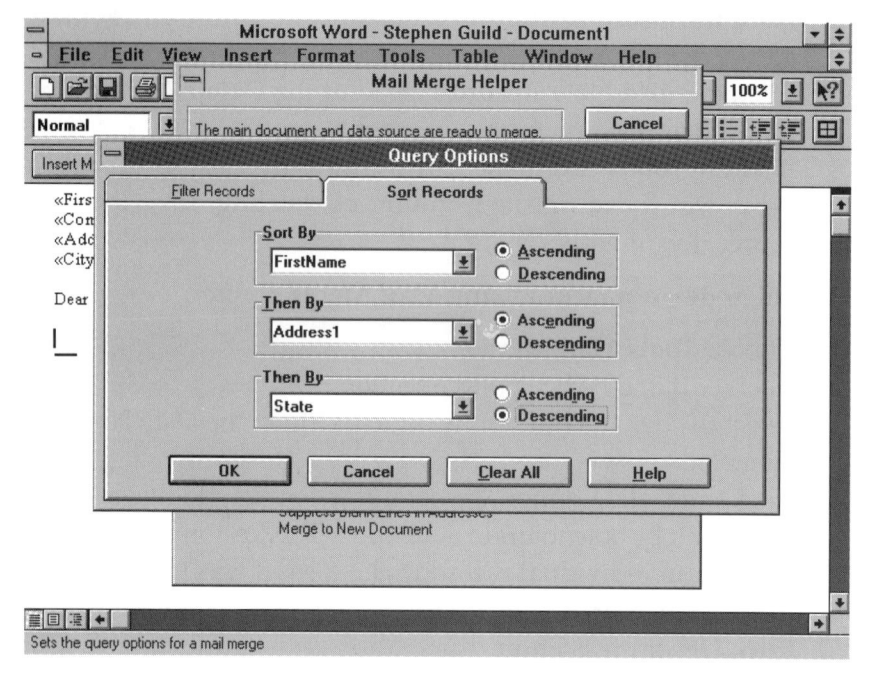

- ▲ Click either the **Ascending** or **Descending** button: Ascending to sort from A to Z or from 0 to 9; Descending to sort from Z to A or from 9 to 0.
- ▲ If you want to sort by a second field, complete the Then By section in the same manner as the Sort By section. Repeat once more in the second Then By section if you want to sort on a third field.
4. Word performs the sort and returns to the Mail Merge Helper box.

Sorting Data in Tables and Columns

In tables or in text where items are separated by tabs or commas, you can choose to use any "field" (column or comma-separated item) as a sort key. Word rearranges all rows in the table on the basis of the sort key. For example, in the following table, you could do an alphabetic sort using the first field (the column of names) as a sort key, or you could do a numeric sort using the second field (the column of salary figures) as a sort key:

Name	Salary
Gorgios	54,500
Alessandra	51,350
Callahan	52,448
Foster	67,112

Sorting Data in Mail Merge Helper

You can also sort entire paragraphs of data, such as a list of names in which each line ends with a paragraph mark. When sorting paragraphs of information, Word uses the first word in the paragraph to put the items in order.

TIP

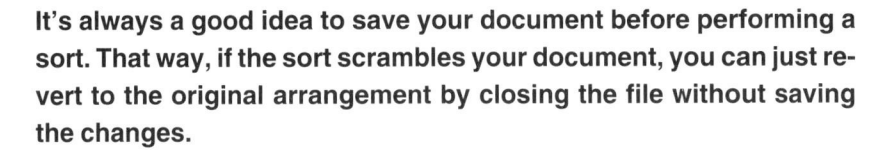

It's always a good idea to save your document before performing a sort. That way, if the sort scrambles your document, you can just revert to the original arrangement by closing the file without saving the changes.

To sort a list using tab or comma separators:

1. Select all of the text you want to sort. Be sure not to select items, such as column headings, that you don't want included in the sort. (If you want to rearrange *only* the items in a specific column, leaving the rest of the columns in place, you can also select just that column. However, you'll rarely find a use for this, and it will really scramble most documents.)
2. Choose **Table Sort**.
3. Do one or more of the following:
    ▲ If the list has a heading you don't want sorted, click the **Header Row** button in the My List Has box. Make sure the first line of data is your header information.
    ▲ Select a field number or name in the drop-down list in the Sort By section.
    ▲ Select the type of information to be sorted (Text, Number, Date) in the Type drop-down list, and then click either the **Ascending** or **Descending** button: Ascending to sort from A to Z or from 0 to 9; Descending to sort from Z to A or from 9 to 0.

▲ If you want to sort by a second field, complete the Then By section in the same manner as the Sort By section. Repeat once more in the second Then By section if you want to sort on a third field.

▲ If you want to change the field separator, click the **Options** button; then click the appropriate button in the Separate Field At box or type a separator of your choice in the box.

▲ If you selected only one column and you want to rearrange only the items in that column, leaving all other items in the same position, click the **Options** button and turn on the **Sort Column Only** check box. You will rarely, if ever, want to use this option.

▲ To make uppercase letters precede lowercase letters, click the **Options** button and turn on the **Case Sensitive** check box, then click **OK**.

4. Click **OK** or press **Enter**.

If you don't like the results of your sort, choose **Edit Undo** immediately. Figure 15.7 illustrates how to set up the Sort dialog box to sort on the zip code field of a data source document.

▼ *Figure 15.7. Sorting a Data Document by the Postal Code Field*

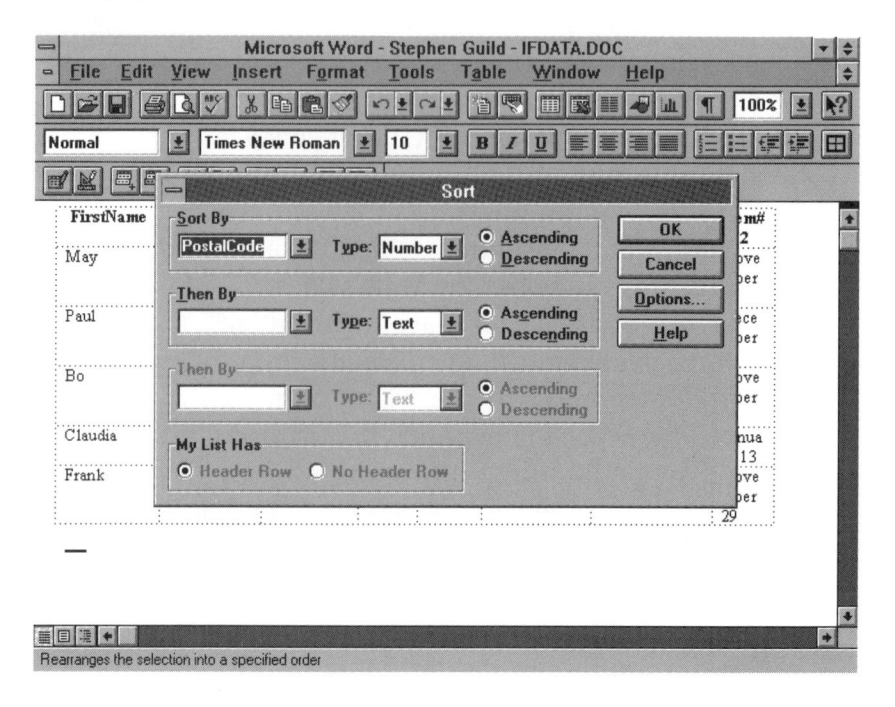

TIP

Here's a tip for simplifying the print merge process. When you set up a data document, separate first and last names, articles (a, an, the), and titles (Mr., Ms., Dr.) into different columns. This gives you more flexibility in sorting and in including information in your form letters. For example, if you put "The Sofa Store" in a Company_ Name field and then sort the list, The Sofa Store will be sorted according to the letter T, when you really want it sorted according to S. By placing "The" in a separate column, you keep your list in the appropriate order.

To sort in a table:

1. Select the rows or list items you want to sort.
2. Choose **Table Sort**.
3. Do one or more of the following:
   - ▲ If the list has a heading you don't want sorted, click the **Header Row** button in the My List Has box. Make sure the first line of data is your header information.
   - ▲ Select a field number or name in the drop-down list in the Sort By section.
   - ▲ Select the type of information to be sorted (Text, Number, Date) in the Type drop-down list, and then click either the **Ascending** or **Descending** button: Ascending to sort from A to Z or from 0 to 9; Descending to sort from Z to A or from 9 to 0.
   - ▲ If you want to sort by a second field, complete the Then By section in the same manner as the Sort By section. Repeat once more in the second Then By section if you want to sort on a third field.
   - ▲ If you want to change the field separator, click the **Options** button; then click the appropriate button in the Separate Field At box or type a separator of your choice in the box.
   - ▲ If you selected only one column and you want to rearrange only the items in that column, leaving all other items in the same position, click the **Options** button and turn on the **Sort Column Only** check box. You will rarely, if ever, want to use this option.

▲ To make uppercase letters precede lowercase letters, click the **Options** button and turn on the **Case Sensitive** check box, then click **OK**.

4. Click **OK** or press **Enter**.

To undo a sort:

▲ Click the **Undo** button on the Standard toolbar, or press **Ctrl+Z** or **Alt+Backspace**.

Making Data Queries

You can further refine your merges by using Word's data query capability. When you do a data query, you are selecting certain data records that you want to use in your merge. For instance, say that you want to send a letter only to customers in certain western states. Your query might specify that zip codes lower than 61000 not be included. If you wanted to send the letter to those states and to customers in Maine, you could specify the western state zip codes and those for Maine as well. There are many other ways to filter data records and to refine your merge. The *Microsoft Word for Windows User's Guide* and online Help provide additional information.

To develop a Mail Merge query:

1. Choose **Tools Mail Merge**. Make sure that your main document is the active window and the data source document is listed in the Data Source area of Mail Merge Helper.
2. Click the **Query Options** button in the Merge Data with Document area, and click on the **Filter Records** tab.
3. Select a field name from the Field drop-down list.
4. Select one of the expressions from the Comparison drop-down list.
5. Type information to compare with the field. In our example above, the Field would be ZIP; Comparison would be Greater Than or Equal; and Compare To would be 61000. Figure 15.8 illustrates this query in the Filter Records tab.
6. If you want to include another comparison, then select **And** or **Or** from the drop-down list to the left of the Field boxes. (In our example that includes Maine, so we would select And.)

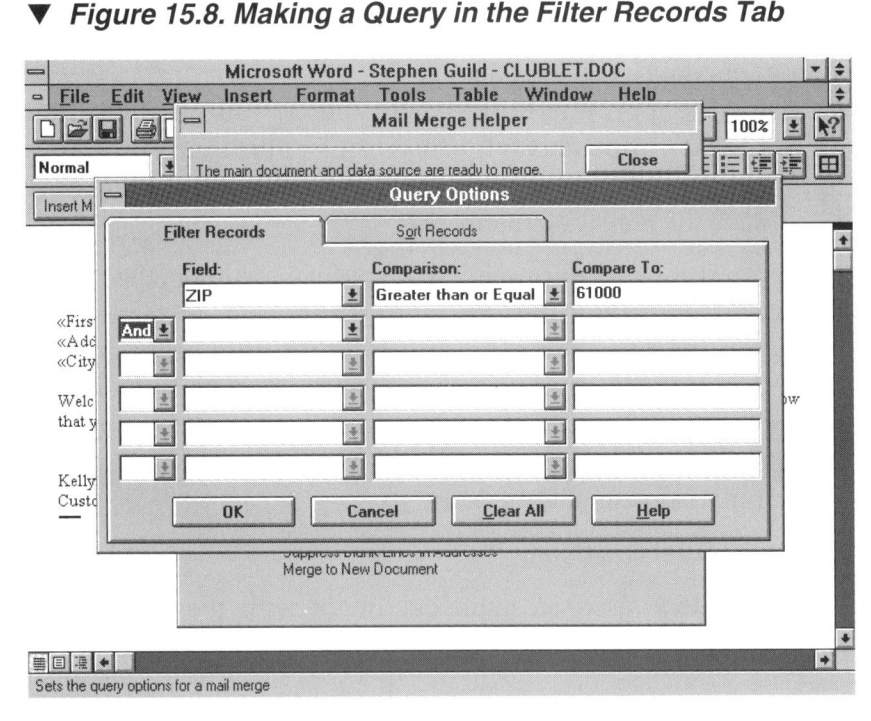

▼ **Figure 15.8. Making a Query in the Filter Records Tab**

Sorting Data in Mail Merge Helper

7. When you have finished with all of the filter statements, click **OK** or press **Enter**.

   If the query process seems a little confusing at first, you may want to write your statement on paper and test it out before entering it in Word.

Inserting Merge Fields

When you have finished creating your main document and setting up a data source document, you are ready to insert the data fields into your main document. These fields tell Word to place information from the individual records into your letter, label, or envelope. They are different from the Word fields, which are explained under "Using Word Fields in Merging" later in this chapter.

To insert merge fields into the main document using the toolbar:

1. Make the main document the active window.
2. Type or change the text in your main document.

3. Place the insertion point where you want to insert information from the data source, then click the **Insert Merge Field** button on the Mail Merge toolbar.
4. Select the appropriate merge field name. Be sure that you type spaces and any punctuation between or after fields.
5. When you have inserted all the merge fields, choose **File Save** to save the main document.

If you want the information that you're inserting in the field to be formatted a certain way, format the entire field. Formatting the records in the data source document has no effect because Word doesn't keep that formatting when it merges the information with the form letters. For example, if you want the customer's last name to appear in bold in the form letters, make the Last Name field bold in your main document, this way:

Dear {Title} {LastName}

Figure 15.9 shows a main document with the merge field names inserted into the document.

▼ **Figure 15.9. A Simple Main Document (Form Letter)**

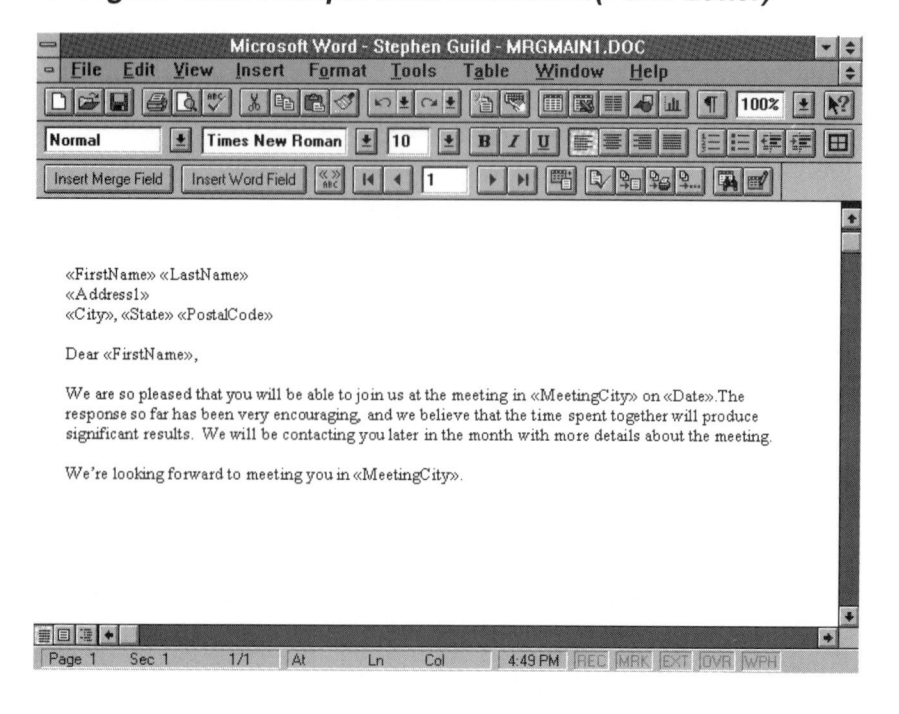

```
«FirstName» «LastName»
«Address1»
«City», «State» «PostalCode»

Dear «FirstName»,

We are so pleased that you will be able to join us at the meeting in «MeetingCity» on «Date». The
response so far has been very encouraging, and we believe that the time spent together will produce
significant results. We will be contacting you later in the month with more details about the meeting.

We're looking forward to meeting you in «MeetingCity».
```

Deleting Merge Fields

Deleting Merge Fields

You can add or delete a field using the toolbar or the Mail Merge Helper.

To delete a merge field in the main document:

1. Open the main document.
2. Select the field you want to delete.
3. Use **Edit Cut** or the **Delete** key.
4. When you have finished all the deletions, save the main document.

To delete a merge field in the data source document:

1. Open the data source document and click in the document.
2. Click the **Manage Fields** button.
3. In the Manage Fields dialog box, select the name of the field you want to delete from the Field Names in Header Row list, then click **Remove**.
4. If you want to add a new field, type the name of the field in the Field Name box and click **Add**.
5. If you want to rename the field, type the new name, click the **Rename** button, then click **OK**.
6. Click **OK** or press **Enter**.

If your data is in a table, you can simply delete the column containing the field name in the header row by highlighting the column and then choosing Table Delete Column.

Checking for Errors in the Data Records

You can check for errors in your data records while you working with your main document.

To check for errors in the data source document:

1. Make sure that your main document is the active window and the data source document is listed in the Data Source area of Mail Merge Helper.

2. In the main document, click the **Check for Errors** button on the toolbar.
3. In the Checking and Reporting Errors dialog box, do one of the following:
   ▲ Simulate the merge and have any errors listed in a new document.
   ▲ Start the merge and stop at any error.
   ▲ Complete the merge and have any errors listed in a new document.

In most cases you will want to check the entire file, but there may be times when you want to check only individual records.

To view individual data records inserted in the main document:

1. Make sure that your main document is the active window and the data source document is listed in the Data Source area of Mail Merge Helper.
2. Click the **View Merged Data** button on the Mail Merge toolbar. Word will display information from the first data record in the fields. If you change the data record number on the toolbar by typing a number in the Record Number box or by using the First Record, Previous Record, Next Record, or Last Record button (the ones with the arrows), the main document will display the data for that particular record.

Merging Data with the Main Document

You are now ready to merge the data source document with the main document. You can do this by using the Mail Merge Helper or the Merge toolbar in the main document.

To merge data using the Mail Merge Helper:

1. Make sure that your main document is the active window and the data source document is listed in the Data Source area of Mail Merge Helper.
2. Click the **Mail Merge** button.
3. In the Merge dialog box, shown in Figure 15.10, do one or more of the following:

▼ *Figure 15.10. The Merge Dialog Box*

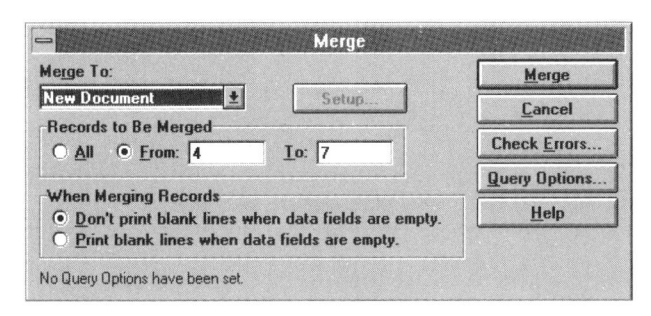

Merging Data with the Main Document

- ▲ If you want to merge the data and the main document into a new document, select **New Document** in the Merge To drop-down list; if you want to print the merged data and document, choose **Printer**.
- ▲ If you want only certain records to be merged, type the record numbers in the From and To boxes.
- ▲ Click one of the buttons in the When Merging Records box. This will determine whether or not blank lines will be printed.
- ▲ If you want to check for errors at this point, click the **Check Errors** button. See "Checking for Errors in the Data Records" earlier in this chapter.
- ▲ If you want to include queries in your merge, click the **Query Options** button and make appropriate choices. See "Making Data Queries" earlier in this chapter for more information.

4. Click **Merge** to merge the data with the main document.

To merge data using the Merge toolbar:

1. Make sure that your main document is the active window and the data source document is listed in the Data Source area of Mail Merge Helper.
2. In the Merge toolbar, do one of the following:
   - ▲ If you want to use the Merge dialog box as described above, click the **Mail Merge** button and complete the dialog box.
   - ▲ If you want to merge the data and main document into a new document, click the **Merge to New Document** button.
   - ▲ If you want to print the merged data and document, click the **Merge to Printer** button.

▲ If you want to check for errors, click the **Check Errors** button. See "Checking for Errors in the Data Records" earlier in this chapter.

Using a Range of Records from the Data Source Document

If you don't want to print form letters for all records in the data source document, you can specify a range of records in the Merge dialog box. For example, to print records 5 through 10, type **5** in the From box and **10** in the To box. To print only record 3, type **3** in the From box and **3** in the To box. Click **OK** to begin the merge process.

Using Word Fields in Merging

You can refine your merging process by using the Word fields that are included as part of the Mail Merge Helper. When inserted into a document, these fields can call up information, ask for special comments, or eliminate or sort out records that don't match certain criteria. Word has made your task a lot easier with the Insert Word Field button. The field is already set up, and all you have to do is insert the bookmarks and other information.

Although using some of these fields may at first seem complicated because you must follow a strict format, you'll find it's worth the effort. In this section, we will cover the ASK and IF...THEN... ELSE... fields, since they are most commonly used. For more information about fields in general, see Chapter 18. You can always get additional assistance from the *Microsoft Word for Windows User's Guide* and the online Help.

The following Word fields are available on the Mail Merge toolbar when you click the Insert Word Field button:

Use This Field	**To**
ASK	Request information from a user before filling in a field (specifies a bookmark for multiple insertions).

Using Word Fields in Merging

Use This Field	To
FILL IN	Request information from a user before filling in a field (when you want to print information only once).
IF...THEN...ELSE...	Instruct Word that if a field doesn't meet certain conditions, other data should be inserted.
MERGE RECORD #	Print the data record number.
MERGE SEQUENCE #	Count the number of records that were successfully merged.
NEXT RECORD	Go to the next data record.
NEXT RECORD IF	Go to the next record only if data doesn't meet certain criteria.
SET BOOKMARK	Insert an assigned value for a bookmark name.
SKIP RECORD IF	Skip over a record if it doesn't meet the criteria.

Creating a Main Document That Asks for Information

You can use the ASK instruction in a main document to request information to put into fields, immediately before printing a form letter. The basic form of the ASK instruction is

```
{ask bookmark_name "text?"}
```

where "bookmark_name" is the name of the bookmark to fill in with the information you type, and " 'text' " is the information you want Word to print in a dialog box as a prompt. Figure 15.11 shows an ASK instruction that fills in a *location* bookmark during a print merge process. You can even use multiple ASK instructions.

▼ *Figure 15.11. Using an ASK Instruction to Prompt for Data*

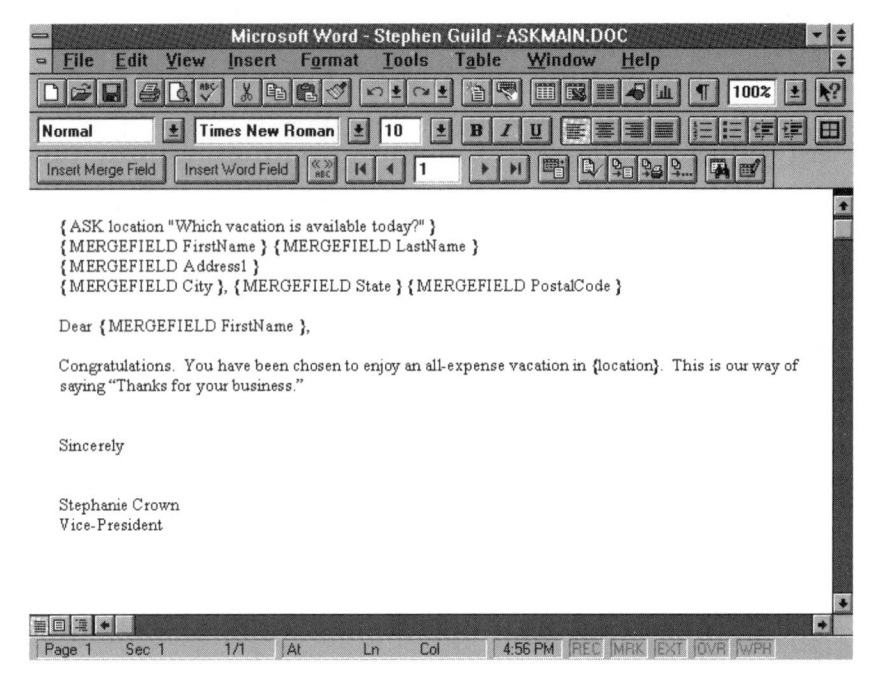

```
{ ASK location "Which vacation is available today?" }
{ MERGEFIELD FirstName } { MERGEFIELD LastName }
{ MERGEFIELD Address1 }
{ MERGEFIELD City }, { MERGEFIELD State } { MERGEFIELD PostalCode }

Dear { MERGEFIELD FirstName },

Congratulations. You have been chosen to enjoy an all-expense vacation in {location}. This is our way of saying "Thanks for your business."


Sincerely


Stephanie Crown
Vice-President
```

Note that the bookmark you name in an ASK instruction must actually be present in your main document. Since it's not normally a field in your data source document, you may need to insert it by pressing **Ctrl+F9** to enclose the bookmark in field characters, then typing the bookmark name. See Chapter 4 for more information on bookmarks.

Inserting an ASK Instruction into a Main Document

To insert an ASK instruction into a main document:

1. Create a main document using the instructions given earlier in this chapter. Be sure the bookmark you want to use is in your document.
2. Place the insertion point at the top of the main document.
3. Click the **Insert Merge Field** button.
4. Click **Ask** in the drop-down list. Word displays the Insert Word Field: Ask dialog box.

Using Word Fields in Merging

5. In the Bookmark list box, type or select the name of the bookmark you're going to fill in. For example, if you wanted to fill in the *location* bookmark field in each form letter with the information provided by the ASK instruction, you would type **location** as the bookmark.
6. In the Prompt box, type the text you want to appear in the dialog box. For example, you might want to type **Which vacation is available today?** to prompt for information for the *location* field.
7. If you want text other than the Prompt to be inserted, type that text in the Default Bookmark Text box.
8. Save your main document.

When you merge the documents, Word will display the text in each ASK instruction for each form letter it creates. Type the information requested in the dialog box, and press **Enter**.

Including IF Clauses for Variable Conditions

If you want to print a field's contents in a form letter only when certain conditions are met, you must use IF instructions.

You can use several variations of IF instructions when you want Word to check the contents of a field in your data source document before inserting text in a form letter. Figure 15.12 shows a sample document that uses IF instructions. These instructions are explained in greater detail in the following sections.

You can use an IF instruction in three ways:

▲ To test whether a field exists in the data source document
▲ To test whether text in a field matches text you specify in the IF clause
▲ To test whether numbers in a field match numbers you specify in the IF clause

To insert an IF instruction in your main document:

1. Create a main document using the instructions given earlier in this chapter.
2. Place the insertion point at the top of the main document.
3. Click the **Insert Merge Field** button.
4. Click **If...Then...Else...** in the drop-down list.

▼ ***Figure 15.12. A Main Document with If Instructions***

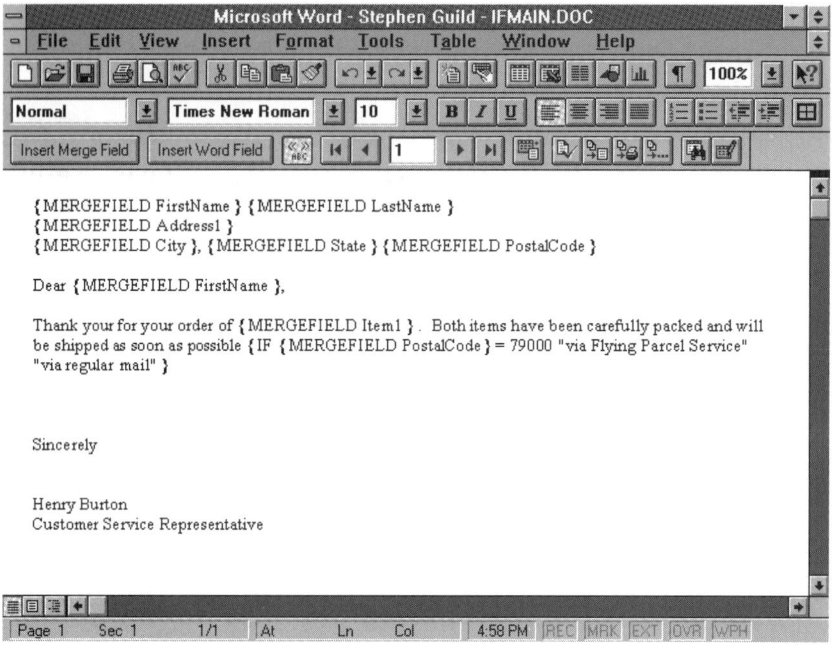
Microsoft Word - Stephen Guild - IFMAIN.DOC
File Edit View Insert Format Tools Table Window Help
100%
Normal
Times New Roman
10
Insert Merge Field
Insert Word Field
1
{MERGEFIELD FirstName } {MERGEFIELD LastName }
{MERGEFIELD Address1 }
{MERGEFIELD City }, {MERGEFIELD State } {MERGEFIELD PostalCode }
Dear {MERGEFIELD FirstName },
Thank your for your order of {MERGEFIELD Item1 }. Both items have been carefully packed and will be shipped as soon as possible {IF {MERGEFIELD PostalCode } = 79000 "via Flying Parcel Service" "via regular mail" }
Sincerely
Henry Burton
Customer Service Representative
Page 1 Sec 1 1/1 At Ln Col 4:58 PM REC MRK EXT OVR WPH

You can set up an incredible variety of IF and IF...THEN... ELSE... expressions. See your *Microsoft Word for Windows User's Guide* and the online Help for more examples.

CHECK YOURSELF

What elements go into a letter main document?

▲ The boilerplate text that you want to stay the same from letter to letter, and fields into which Word will insert the information from the data source document to personalize the letters.

Printing Merges

When you've created both the main document and the data document, you're ready to create and print your form letters. You can send all your form letters to a file so that you can review and edit them before printing, or you can send the form letters directly to the printer.

Printing Merges

Word prints merged documents in the same order as the records in your data document. If you don't want to print a letter for every record, you can specify a range of record numbers in the Merge dialog box.

You can also sort records or copy records to another file to create a data document that contains only the records you want. If you want to print in a certain order, you can sort your records. For example, you might want to sort according to zip code to make mailing easier. For more information about sorting, see "Sorting Data in Tables and Columns".

You can refine your printing by using the Query button. For more information on queries, see "Making Data Queries" earlier in this chapter.

You can correct any errors by using the Check for Errors button. For more information about correcting errors, see "Checking for Errors in the Data Records" earlier in this chapter.

You can print out your documents or print them to a file so you can work with them later. If you want to merge the data into a single document without printing, click the **Merge to New Document** button. Word will create a new document that you can view and save as a separate document if you wish. If you want to print your merged document, click the **Merge to Printer** button.

Merging to Create Form Letters

When you have finished creating the main document and have prepared the data source document the way you want it, you are ready to create the actual merged form letters. You can collect all the letters in a single file for review, or you can print the letters directly in their final form. If you wish, you can view each letter individually.

To create form letters in a file to review:

1. Open the main document. Make sure that your main document is the active window and the data source document is listed in the Data Source area of Mail Merge Helper.
2. Click the **Merge to New Document** button (an arrow pointing to a sheet of paper) in the Mail Merge toolbar.
3. Check the form letters, then save and/or print the file.

Word opens a single file containing the form letters separated by sections. If you have any special instructions in Word Fields, you'll be prompted for responses during the merge.

To print form letters:

1. Open the main document. Make sure that your main document is the active window and the data source document is listed in the Data Source section of Mail Merge Helper.
2. Click the **Merge to Printer** button (an arrow pointing to a printer) in the Mail Merge toolbar. Word displays the Print dialog box.
3. Choose any options you want (such as the number of copies) and click **OK**. Word begins printing the form letters.

To view form letters individually:

1. Open the main document. Make sure that your main document is the active window and the data source document is listed in the Data Source area of Mail Merge Helper.
2. Click the **View Merged Data** button and use the left or right arrow beside the Record Number box to select individual records. The screen will display the information from each record.

Merging to Create Sheets of Address Labels

To create and print sheets of address labels, you must first create a main document that will contain the labels and a data source document that contains all the information to be printed on the labels. You then ask Word to do the merge for you. Mail Merge Helper will lead you through this process. You need to use Avery brand or similar address labels and know the Avery product number or equivalent, since you will have to tell Word what you are using.

To create sheets of mailing labels:

1. Choose **Tools Mail Merge**. Make sure that you're not in an existing data source document at the time.

2. In the Main Document area, click **Create** and select **Mailing Labels**.
3. Click the **New Main Document** button. In cases where you want Word to use an existing document, choose **Active Window**.
4. In the Data Source area, click the **Get Data** button. Then follow the steps for creating a data source as described under "Using Mail Merge to Create a Data Document" earlier this chapter (or use an existing data document).
5. Click **Setup** in the Main Document area. Word will display the Label Options dialog box, as shown in Figure 15.13.
6. Do one of the following:
   ▲ In the Printer Information box, click **Laser** or **Dot Matrix** and the printer tray that contains the labels.
   ▲ Select the name of a label from the Label Products drop-down list and a number from the Product Number list. Review the Label Info box for other information about your selection.
7. If you want to customize a label, click **Details** and type measurements in the appropriate boxes in the dialog box:

Merging to Create Sheets of Address Labels

▼ **Figure 15.13. Creating Address Labels**

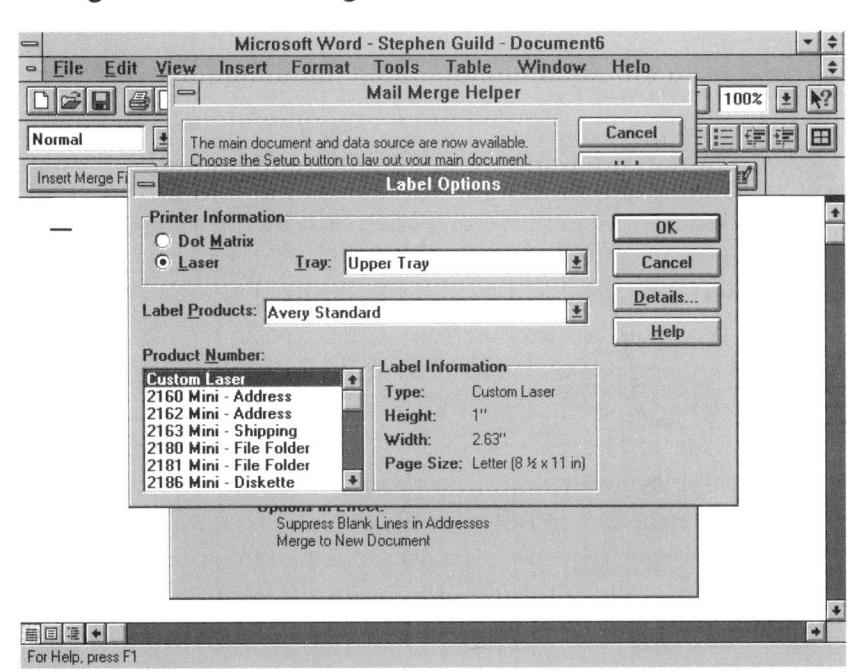

Type a Measurement In	To Set
Top Margin	The measurement from the top of the label page to the top of the first row of labels
Side Margin	The measurement from the left edge of the label page to the edge of the first column of labels
Vertical Pitch	The measurement from the top of each label to the top of the next label in a column
Horizontal Pitch	The measurement from the left edge of each label to the left edge of the next label in the row.
Height Label	The height of the label from top edge to bottom edge
Width Label	The width of the label from left edge to right edge
Number Across	The number of labels in a row across the page
Number Down	The number of labels in a column down the page

8. Click **OK** or press **Enter** to return to the Label Options dialog box. Review the Label Information box, then click **OK** or press **Enter**.
9. In the Create Labels dialog box, click **Insert Merge Fields** and select the field names that you want to use in the label.
10. If you want postal bar codes on the labels, click the **Insert Postal Bar Code** button and complete the Merge Field with ZIP Code and the Merge Field with Street Address boxes. Click **OK** or press **Enter**.
11. Click **Merge** and complete the **Merge** dialog box.
12. In the Merge To drop-down list, do one of the following:
    ▲ Choose **New Document** if you want Word to set up your main document like the sheet of labels you specified.

Merging to Create Sheets of Address Labels

▲ Choose **Printer** and the Print Dialog box will appear. Choose any options you want (such as the number of copies) and click **OK**. Word begins printing the labels.

13. When you have finished, click **OK** or press **Enter**.

To print labels:

1. Open the main document. Make sure that your main document is the active window and the data source document is listed in the Data Source section of Mail Merge Helper.
2. Click the **Merge to Printer** (an arrow pointing to a printer) button in the Mail Merge toolbar. Word displays the Print dialog box.
3. Choose any options you want (such as the number of copies), and click **OK**. Word begins printing the labels.

If you click the View Merged Data button, you will notice that after the first label there is a field named {NEXT}. This tells Word to go on to the next record until it comes to the end of the data file. The number of records in the data file will correspond with the number of records in your data base.

If you want to repeat labels, then you need to insert a {NEXT} field where you want the next label to start. For instance, if you had only three records in your database and you wanted to repeat the same three records more than once on your label sheet, you would need to delete the {NEXT} field and then insert a {NEXT} field at the point where you wanted the second data record to start. You would follow the same steps where you wanted the third data record to start. Your printer would then repeat the same label on the label sheet until it came to the {NEXT} field, then it would print the second label, and so on.

TIP

When you print labels, it is always a good idea to run a sheet of labels or plain paper first to see if the alignment is correct.

Once you've created and saved your main document, you can use it to print labels again. If you change information in your data source document, Word will automatically update your address labels.

Creating and Printing Addresses on Envelopes

You can use Mail Merge in Word to print envelopes using merge fields and your data source document. The process for setting this up is basically the same as for mailing labels and form letters. If you want to print one address directly on an envelope, see "Printing Envelopes" in Chapter 14.

To set up a main document for envelopes:

1. Open the main document. Make sure that your main document is the active window and the data source document is listed in the Data Source section of Mail Merge Helper.
2. Choose **Tools Mail Merge**.
3. In the Main Document section, click **Create** and select **Envelopes**.
4. Click the **New Main Document** button. In cases where you want Word to use an existing document, choose **Active Window**.
5. In the Data Source area, click the **Get Data** button. Then follow the steps for creating a data source as described under "Using Mail Merge to Create a Data Document" earlier in this chapter, (or use an existing data document).
6. Click **Setup** in the Main Document area. Word will display the Envelope Options dialog box.
7. Select the envelope size you're using from the Envelope Size drop-down list.
8. If you want to change the font and position of either the delivery or the return address, use the Font button and the From Left and From Top boxes.
9. If you want special bar codes printed on the envelope, click the appropriate check boxes in the If Mailed in the USA area.
10. Choose the **Printing Options** tab. Choose how the envelope will be fed into the printer in the Feed Method area and Feed From drop-down list. Individual printers feed envelopes in different ways, so be sure to check your printer manual for more information about the way your printer handles envelopes.

11. Click **OK** or press **Enter**. Word will display the Envelope Address dialog box. Click **Insert Merge Fields** and select the field names that you want to use from the drop-down list.
12. If you want the postal bar codes on the envelopes, click the **Insert Postal Bar Code** button and complete the Merge Field with ZIP Code and Merge Field with Street Address boxes. Click **OK** or press **Enter** to return to the Mail Merge Helper dialog box.
13. Click **Merge** and complete the Merge dialog box.
14. In the Merge To drop-down list, do one of the following:
    ▲ Choose **New Document** if you want Word to set up your main document like the envelope you specified.
    ▲ Choose **Printer** and the Print dialog box will appear. Choose any options you want (such as the number of copies) and click **OK**. Word begins printing the envelopes.
15. When you have finished, click **OK** or press **Enter**.

To print envelopes:

1. Open the main document. Make sure that your main document is the active window and the data source document is listed in the Data Source area of Mail Merge Helper.
2. Click the **Merge to Printer** (an arrow pointing to a printer) button in the Mail Merge toolbar. Word displays the Print dialog box.
3. Choose any options you want (such as the number of copies) and click **OK**. Word begins printing the form letters.

Creating and Printing Addresses on Envelopes

Removing Merges from Main Documents

There may be times when you want to remove a mail merge from your main document temporarily or permanently.

To remove a merge from a main document:

1. Make sure your main document is the active window.
2. Choose **Tools Mail Merge**.
3. Click the **Create Main Document** button and select **Restore to Normal Word Document**.

4. Word will display a message advising you that all of the mail merge will be removed from the main document. You can later use the Mail Merge Helper to create another merge for the main document.

QUICK COMMAND SUMMARY

Command	To Do This
Tools Mail Merge	Create a main document, a data source document, and merge the two.
Tools Mail Merge, Main Document: Create	Create a form letter, mailing labels, envelopes, or catalog main document.
Tools Mail Merge, Main Document: Edit	Display a form letter, mailing labels, envelopes, or catalog main document for editing.
Tools Mail Merge, Data Source: Get Data	Create or open a data source document for a main document.
Tools Mail Merge, Data Source: Edit	Display the Data Form dialog box or data source document for editing.
Tools Mail Merge, Merge the Data with the Document: Merge	Merge the data source document with the main document.
Tools Mail Merge, Merge the Data with the Document: Query Options	Display the Query Options dialog box with the Filter Records or Sort Records tab.
Table Sort	Sort items in a table or list.

PRACTICE WHAT YOU'VE LEARNED

Create a main document and a data document that, when merged, generate form letters asking Larry Jones to send you $10, Jeanine Barker to send you $20, and Ruby Tuesday to send you $15. Include addresses in your form letters.

Creating Form Letters and Address Labels ▲ 359

What You Do	*What You'll See*
1. Choose **Tools Mail Merge**.	1. The Mail Merge Helper dialog box.
2. Click the **Create** button in the Main Document area.	2. A drop-down list with Form Letters, Mailing Labels, Envelopes and Catalogue listed.
3. Select **Form Letters**, then click the **New Main Document** button.	3. An information box with several choices. When you choose New Main Document, a new document window opens.
4. Type the following text: **Dear ,** **Could you please send me ?**	4. The text you enter.
5. Click the **Mail Merge Helper** button on the Mail Merge toolbar.	5. The Mail Merge Helper dialog box.
6. Click the **Get Data** button, then click **Create Data Source** in the Data Source section.	6. The Create Data Source dialog box.
7. Select in succession all the field names except First Name, LastName, Address1, City, State, and Postal Code; click the **Remove Field Name** button after each selection. Type **Amount** in the Field Name box and click **Add Field Name**.	7. The field names FirstName, LastName, Addresss1, City, State, Zip, and Amount.
8. Click **OK**. Type a filename in the File Name box in the Save Data Source dialog box, and click **OK**.	8. The Save Data Source dialog box.

What You Do

9. Click the **Edit Data Source** button in the information box.

10. Fill in the data records for Larry Jones, Jeanine Barker and Ruby Tuesday with the information below.

Larry Jones	123 Main	Tulsa	OK	74133	$10
Jeanine Barker	456 Main	Kansas City	KS	79122	$20
Ruby Tuesday	987 Oak	Seattle	WA	98155	$15

Click **OK**.

11. Using the **Insert Merge Field** button, insert the fields from the list. Insert FirstName after Dear and Amount before the question mark.

12. Click the **Merge to New Document** button to see your form letters in a new document.

What You'll See

9. The Data Form dialog box.

10. The individual data records with the information. Word returns you to the main document.

11. The Main Document in the active window. When you press the Insert Merge Field button, a list of the fields you selected drops down. After you click each one, it appears in the document where you have positioned the insertion point.

12. The individual letters with the appropriate data.

16

Outlining and Numbering

When you're creating a long document, such as a screenplay for Hollywood or a proposal for the office, you'll need to structure and number your document so that you can easily refer to the appropriate sections. In this chapter, you will learn how to:

- ▲ Create and edit an outline in Outline view
- ▲ Number outlines using outline format, legal format, or a format you create
- ▲ Create numbered lists and bulleted lists
- ▲ Number lines

Working with Outlines

A Word outline is not a separate document—Word's Outline view is another way to view your document. Take a look at Figure 16.1, which shows a document created in Outline view, and Figure 16.2, which shows the same document in Normal view. Whether you are the kind of person who takes the time to organize a document well beforehand or one who simply writes and then reorganizes later, you'll find that Outline view can help you produce a complex document more easily.

To switch to Outline view from Normal view:

▲ Choose **View Outline** or click the **Outline View** button at the bottom left corner of your screen. Word puts a dot next to the command and displays the Outlining toolbar, shown in Figure 16.3.

To switch back to Normal view:

▲ Choose **View Normal** or click the **Normal View** button at the bottom left corner of your screen.

▼ *Figure 16.1. A Document Created in Outline View*

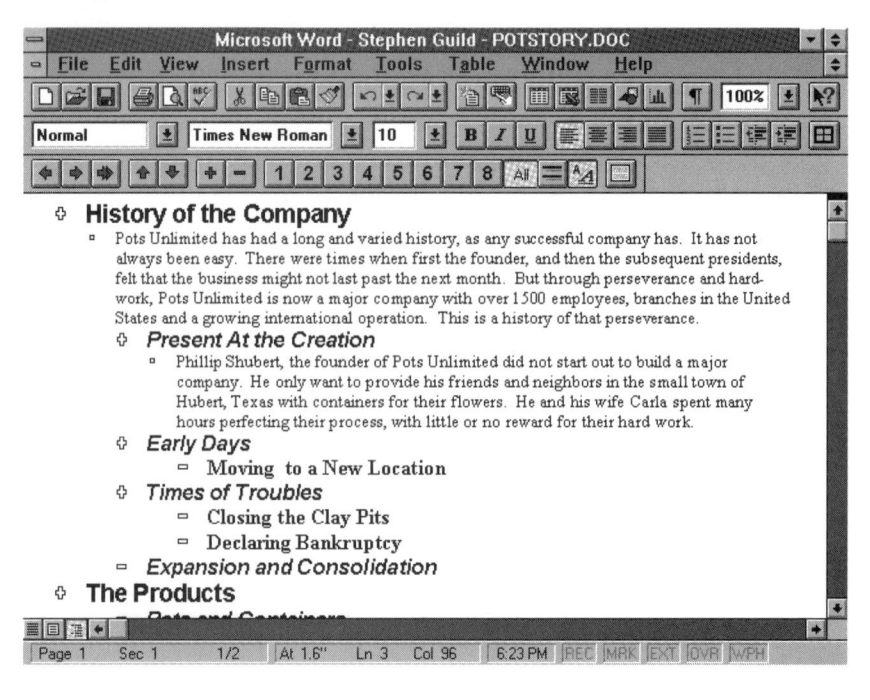

Outlining and Numbering ▲ 363

▼ *Figure 16.2. An Outline Displayed in Normal View*

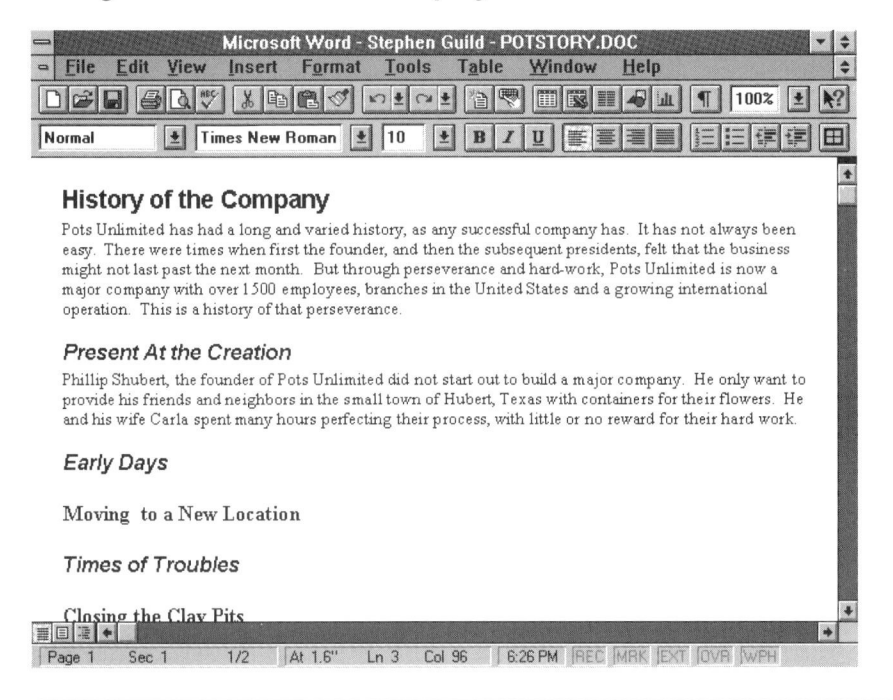

Working with Outlines

▼ *Figure 16.3. Using Outline View*

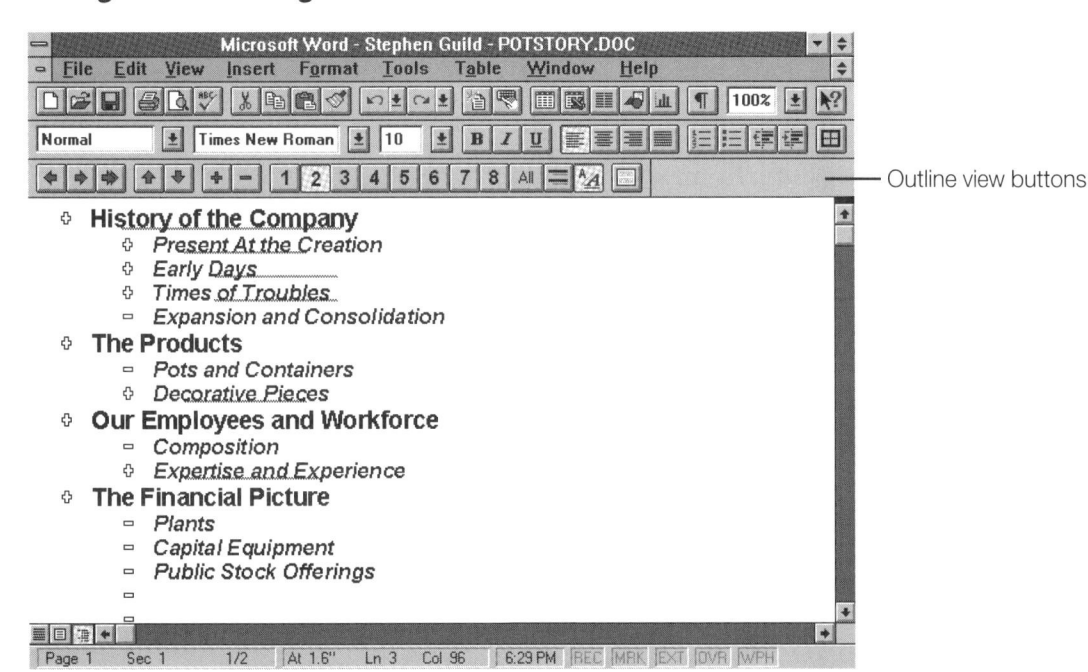

— Outline view buttons

Creating an Outline

The easiest way to use Word's outlining feature is to create an outline before you type the text for your document. In Outline view, the text in your document falls into two categories: headings and body text. Headings are the titles of sections; they are arranged according to levels that indicate their relative importance in the document. Paragraphs in a section are the body text. Word marks headings with hollow plus signs and rectangles and marks body text with hollow squares.

When you create an outline in Outline view, Word assigns outline styles to your text. These styles, named Heading 1, Heading 2, Heading 3, and so forth, are part of Word's default style sheet, NORMAL.DOT. When you use these heading styles, Word can easily create a table of contents by collecting section titles that have heading styles. (For more information about styles and how to apply or change them, see Chapter 8. For information about creating a table of contents, see Chapter 17.)

To create an outline:

1. Choose **View Outline** or click the **Outline View** button at the bottom left corner of your screen. Word displays the Outlining toolbar at the top of the screen, as shown in Figure 16.3.
2. Type the outline heading paragraphs, assigning levels as you type:
   - ▲ To make a paragraph one level lower than the preceding paragraph, click the -> button on the Outlining toolbar, drag the heading marker (the hollow plus sign or rectangle) to the right, or press **Alt+Shift+Right arrow**.
   - ▲ To make a paragraph one level higher than the preceding paragraph, click the <- button on the Outlining toolbar, drag the heading marker (the hollow plus sign or rectangle) to the left, or press **Alt+Shift+Left arrow**.
   - ▲ To make the paragraph the same level as the preceding paragraph, just type the text.
   - ▲ To type body text, click the ->> button in the Outlining toolbar, then type. (You'll generally find it more convenient to switch back to Normal view if you need to work extensively on the body text of your document.)

You can always change the heading levels and rearrange the outline later. You'll learn how to do that in the following section.

Working with Outlines

Viewing Different Heading Levels in Your Outline

You can collapse or expand all or part of an outline to view different levels of text. Collapsing and expanding doesn't remove text from or add text to a document—it just displays or hides specific levels of headings in the Outline view screen.

To collapse all the subheadings and body text beneath a specific heading:

▲ To collapse the text, point to the heading marker (the pointer becomes a cross with four arrows), then double-click; click the − (minus) button on the Outlining toolbar; or move the insertion point into the heading and then press − (the minus key) on the numeric keypad. Word draws a dotted line to indicate that a heading has hidden text beneath it, as shown in Figure 16.4.

▼ *Figure 16.4. Collapsed Headings in Outline View*

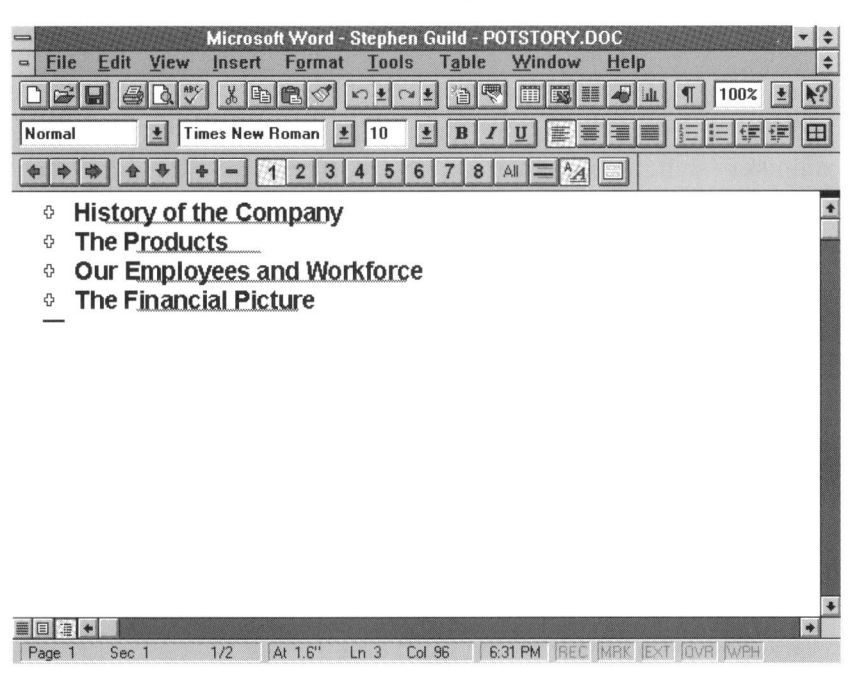

To show only the first line of body text:

▲ Press **Alt+Shift+L**.

To expand all the subheadings and body text beneath a specific heading:

▲ Point to the heading marker, then double-click; click the + (plus) button on the Outlining toolbar; or move the insertion point into the heading and press + (the plus key) on the numeric keypad.

To display specific levels of your outline:

▲ Click a level number button on the Outlining toolbar, or hold down **Alt** and **Shift** while you press a number key in the top row of the main keypad to indicate the level number you want. Word hides all headings and text beneath that level. For example, click **3** or press **Alt+Shift+3** to see only levels 1 through 3.

To display all levels of your outline:

▲ Click the **All** button on the Outlining toolbar. Word displays all headings and text in the document.

Editing an Outline

In Outline view you can always edit the text, change the levels of headings in your document, or rearrange your headings. Just remember—when you edit an outline, you're editing the entire document, not just a separate outline file.

Selecting text in Outline view is much like selecting in Normal view, with the following exceptions:

▲ You can select text within a single paragraph, but if you extend the selection to the space between two paragraphs, both paragraphs are selected automatically.

▲ If you double-click beside a heading while the pointer is in the selection bar, you select the heading and all subtext.

To change a heading level, click the <-, ->, or ->> button; press the **Alt+Shift+arrow key** combination as described under "Creating an Outline" earlier in this chapter; or point to the heading marker and drag the heading right or left.

TIP

To select the entire document in outline view, move the mouse to the selection bar and triple-click the left mouse button.

Rearranging a Document by Rearranging Its Outline

You can change the order of headings in Outline view and rearrange your document at the same time. In Outline view, when you move a heading whose text is collapsed, Word relocates that heading, all of its subordinate headings, and all of its associated text in your document.

To make rearranging easier and faster, collapse text beneath headings to make sure that text stays with related headings. Moving text in Outline view does not change heading levels.

To move headings and rearrange your document, use one of the following procedures:

1. Point to the marker in front of the heading you want to move, then drag the heading to a new position. A horizontal line moves with the mouse pointer.
2. When the horizontal line is in the new location, release the mouse button to relocate the heading.

Or

1. Select the headings.
2. To move the selected headings a short distance, click the up or down arrow button on the Outlining toolbar, or press **Alt+Shift+Up arrow** or **Down arrow** until the text is where you want it. To move the selected headings a sizable distance in a long outline, use the **Edit Cut** and **Edit Paste** commands. (See Chapter 3 for more information about cutting and pasting text.)

Converting a Nonoutline Document into an Outline

If you didn't use Outline view to create an outline, you can still display your document in Outline view. This won't be of much use to you unless you have formatted your headings using Word's Heading styles from the default style sheet or unless you want to reformat your headings using these styles. If your text contains no Heading styles, Word can't distinguish between the levels of text, and it will display everything as body text in Outline view.

To turn your document into an outline, you can use the procedures described earlier in "Editing an Outline" to change heading levels. This causes Word to replace the styles assigned to your text with the Heading styles from the default style sheet.

You could also create an outline by applying styles to your headings in this way:

1. Select the paragraph that you want to be an outline heading.
2. Press **Ctrl+Shift+S**. Word selects the current style in the Style box.
3. Type the heading style you want. For example, if you wanted to make the selected text a first-level heading, you would type **heading 1**. If you wanted to make it a second-level heading, you'd type **heading 2**, and so forth.
4. Press **Enter** to apply the style.

You may want to use the **F4** key or choose **Edit Repeat** to format several headings at the same level without having to retype the style name.

TIP

Using Edit Replace, you can easily change a document that has non-outline styles (styles other than Heading 1, Heading 2, etc.) attached to its heads into a document you can work with as an outline. Click in the Find What box, and choose the Format **button to put the name of the current style in the description box underneath. Click in the** Replace With **box, and choose** Format **again to put the name of the appropriate level Heading style in the description box. Click** Replace All, **and Word will change all of the heads of one style into the other. Continue doing this for all of your headings. When you've finished your outlining, you can reverse the process and change the heads back to their original styles.**

Using Outline View to Navigate

Working with Outlines

You can use Outline view as a tool to get around in a large document in which the headings have Heading styles (attached through outlining or with style commands). You simply collapse the text beneath headings to see the structure of your document, then select the appropriate heading in the outline, and then expand the text or switch to Normal view. If you want to refer to a particular section, copy words or phrases, or check for terms or other data, you can locate the section quickly if you know its heading.

To navigate quickly in a document that contains Heading styles:

1. If you're working in Normal view, choose **View Outline** or click the **Outline View** button at the bottom left corner of your screen.
2. Collapse the outline to its major headings by clicking **1** or **2** on the Outlining toolbar or by pressing **Alt+Shift+1** or **Alt+Shift+2**.
3. Select the heading to which you want to move the insertion point.
4. If desired, choose **View Normal** or click the **Normal View** button at the bottom left corner of your screen to switch back to Normal view.

Numbering Outlines

You can use the Heading Numbering dialog box in the Format command to number headings in Outline view. This is different from adding numbers or bullets to paragraphs outside of outlines (see "Numbering Paragraphs" later in this chapter for more information). This dialog box inserts fields that are updated during printing. You can choose among traditional outline format (roman numerals and letters), legal numbering, and sequential numbering. A traditional outline format is shown in Figure 16.5; a legal numbering format is shown in Figure 16.6.

If you don't like any of the provided formats, you can create your own custom numbering style by choosing the Modify button and making the appropriate choices in the Modify Heading Numbering dialog box. For example, you might want to add a dif-

▼ *Figure 16.5. Traditional Outline Numbering*

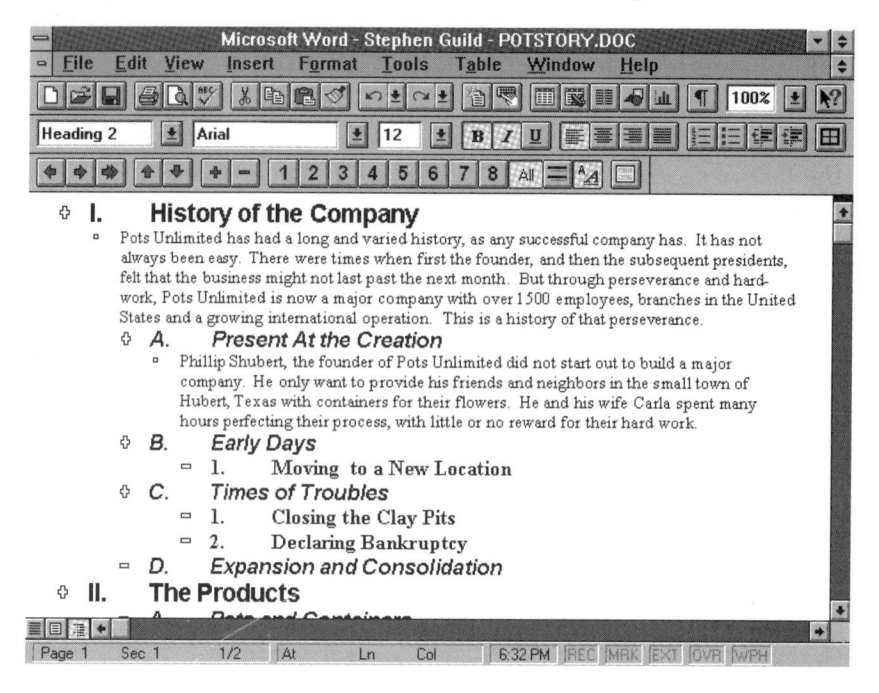

I. History of the Company

Pots Unlimited has had a long and varied history, as any successful company has. It has not always been easy. There were times when first the founder, and then the subsequent presidents, felt that the business might not last past the next month. But through perseverance and hardwork, Pots Unlimited is now a major company with over 1500 employees, branches in the United States and a growing international operation. This is a history of that perseverance.

- **A.** *Present At the Creation*
  - Phillip Shubert, the founder of Pots Unlimited did not start out to build a major company. He only want to provide his friends and neighbors in the small town of Hubert, Texas with containers for their flowers. He and his wife Carla spent many hours perfecting their process, with little or no reward for their hard work.
- **B.** *Early Days*
  - 1. Moving to a New Location
- **C.** *Times of Troubles*
  - 1. Closing the Clay Pits
  - 2. Declaring Bankruptcy
- **D.** *Expansion and Consolidation*

II. The Products

▼ *Figure 16.6. Legal Numbering*

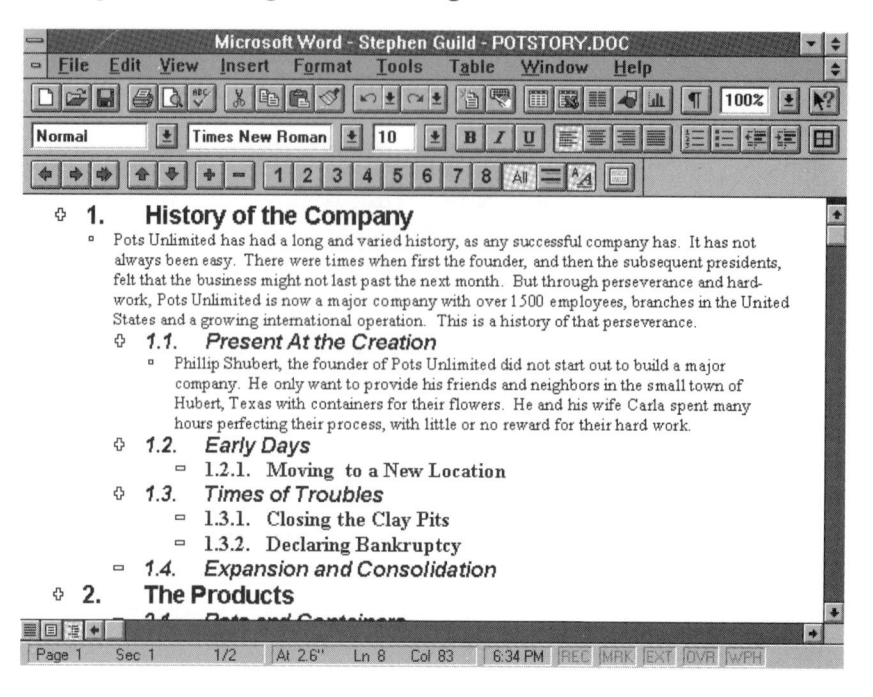

1. History of the Company

Pots Unlimited has had a long and varied history, as any successful company has. It has not always been easy. There were times when first the founder, and then the subsequent presidents, felt that the business might not last past the next month. But through perseverance and hardwork, Pots Unlimited is now a major company with over 1500 employees, branches in the United States and a growing international operation. This is a history of that perseverance.

- **1.1.** *Present At the Creation*
  - Phillip Shubert, the founder of Pots Unlimited did not start out to build a major company. He only want to provide his friends and neighbors in the small town of Hubert, Texas with containers for their flowers. He and his wife Carla spent many hours perfecting their process, with little or no reward for their hard work.
- **1.2.** *Early Days*
  - 1.2.1. Moving to a New Location
- **1.3.** *Times of Troubles*
  - 1.3.1. Closing the Clay Pits
  - 1.3.2. Declaring Bankruptcy
- **1.4.** *Expansion and Consolidation*

2. The Products

ferent character before numbers, such as #1 or @1, and then have Word copy that format to number headings throughout the document. Or you might want to change the alignment of the text or the distance of the outline number from the text. The Level and Preview areas will show you the results of your choices. When you have made all the changes you want, click **OK** or press **Enter**.

Working with Outlines

To change outline number headings:

1. In Outline view, choose **Format Heading Numbering**.
2. Select a format from one of the six numbering styles, or click **Modify** to create your own.
3. Make the appropriate choices in the Modify Heading Numbering dialog box, then click **OK** or press **Enter.** Word inserts numbers and tab characters in front of the displayed paragraphs.

To remove outline numbers:

1. Click in the section from which you want to remove numbers.
2. Choose **Format Heading Numbering**.
3. Click **Remove**.

Printing an Outline

Word prints only the headings that are displayed in Outline view, so make sure all levels you want to print are displayed.

To print an outline:

1. Expand or collapse headings as necessary to display the levels of text you want to print.
2. Click the **Print** button on the Standard toolbar or use **File Print** to print your outline.

CHECK YOURSELF

What's the connection between Outline view and Heading styles?
▲ Outline view uses the Heading 1, Heading 2, Heading 3 (and so forth) styles to format headings. If your document contains headings formatted with these styles, Word can easily recognize the heading hierarchy in Outline view.

Numbering Paragraphs

You can easily number any kind of paragraphs with Word, creating numbered lists or just adding structure to your document so you can easily refer to the location of a paragraph. If you want to use the last-saved number style and the hanging indent measurements, you can simply select the text paragraphs and click the Numbering List button on the Standard toolbar. If you want to choose a new number format or alter the indent measurement, you'll need to use the Bullets and Numbering dialog box. This new formatting will be retained by the toolbar button until you change it again using the Bullets and Numbering dialog box. Word numbers only those paragraphs that contain text, not those that create blank lines.

To number paragraphs using one of the provided formats:

1. Select the paragraphs you want to number.
2. Choose **Format Bullets and Numbering** and click the **Numbered** tab.
3. If you want the paragraphs to have a hanging indent (the most common format for numbered lists), make sure the **Hanging Indent** check box is turned on.
4. Select a format from one of the six numbering styles. If you want to create your own, click **Modify** and make the appropriate choices in the Modify Numbered List dialog box.
5. Click **OK** or press **Enter**. Word inserts numbers at the beginnings of the paragraphs.

Removing Paragraph Numbers

To remove numbers from paragraphs in your document:

1. Select the paragraphs from which you want to remove numbers.
2. Choose the **Numbered** tab in the Format Bullets and Numbering dialog box.
3. Click **Remove**.

Adding Numbers to a List Using the Standard Toolbar

Numbering Paragraphs

You can easily number a list by using the Numbering button on the Standard toolbar. When you use the toolbar button, you only have one style of numbering available. If you want another style, use the Format Bullets and Numbering command as described above.

To create a numbered list using the toolbar button:

1. Select the text to which you want to add numbers.
2. Click the **Numbering** button on the Standard toolbar.

Often you need to interrupt numbered list for other text, but you want the numbers to continue in sequence further on in the document.

To interrupt a list:

1. Place the insertion point where you want to remove number.
2. Click the right mouse button to display the mini-menu of commands.
3. Choose **Skip Numbering**.

There may be times when you want to stop numbering a list, but you want the list to continue with the same format.

To stop numbering:

1. Place the insertion point where you want to stop numbering.
2. Click the right mouse button to display the mini-menu of commands.
3. Choose **Stop Numbering**.

CHECK YOURSELF

Add or update numbers in a numbered list.
▲ Select the paragraphs, then click the **Numbering** button on the toolbar.

Adding Bullets to Paragraphs

With Word you can add bullets to any kind of paragraphs. Word adds bullets only to paragraphs that contain text, not to those that create blank lines. If you want to use the last-saved bullet character and the hanging indent measurements, you can simply select paragraphs and click the **Bullets** button on the Standard toolbar. This new formatting will be retained by the toolbar button until you change it using the Bullets and Numbering dialog box.

To add bullets to paragraphs using the Format Bullets and Numbering dialog box:

1. Select the paragraphs to which you want to add bullets.
2. Choose **Format Bullets and Numbering** and click the **Bulleted** tab.
3. If you want the paragraphs to have a hanging indent (the most common format for bulleted lists), make sure the **Hanging Indent** check box is turned on.
4. Select a format from one of the six bullet styles. If you want to create your own, click **Modify** and make the appropriate choices in the Modify Bulleted List dialog box.
5. Click **OK** or press **Enter**. Word inserts bullets at the beginnings of the paragraphs.

Figure 16.7 shows a bulleted list created in this way.

To add bullets or to change bullets in paragraphs, just repeat one of the procedures listed above. The bullet symbol and indent spacing that you specify in the Bullets and Numbering dialog box will also be used when you click the Bulleted List button on the toolbar.

Removing Bullets from Paragraphs

To remove bullets from paragraphs in your document:

1. Select the paragraphs from which you want to remove bullets.
2. Choose the **Bulleted** tab in the Format Bullets and Numbering dialog box.
3. Click **Remove**.

▼ **Figure 16.7. A Bulleted List Created with the Bulleted List Button**

Adding Bullets to Paragraphs

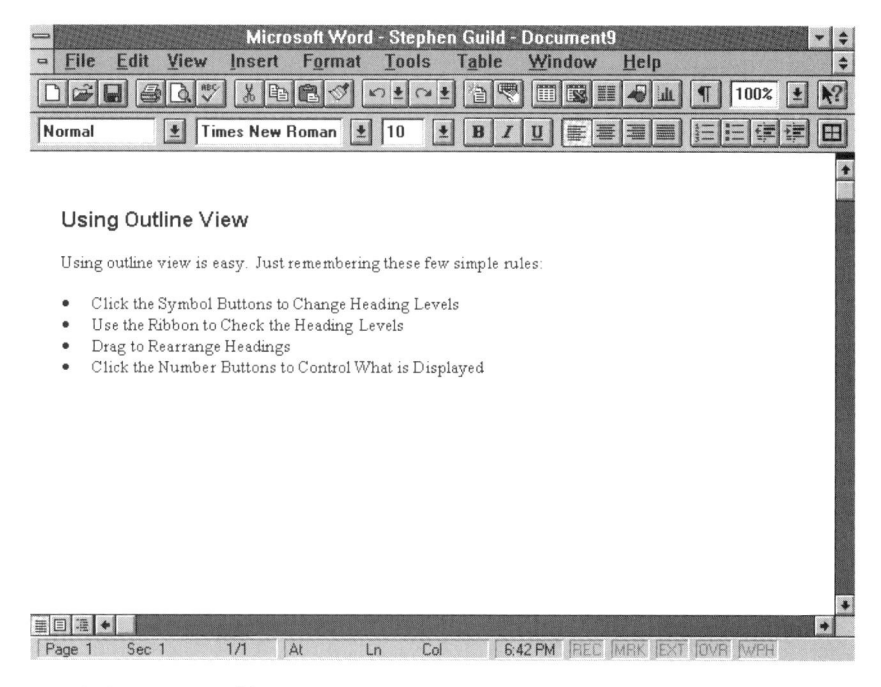

Adding Bullets to a List Using the Standard Toolbar

You can easily make a bulleted list by using the Bullets button on the Standard toolbar. When you use the toolbar button, you only have one style of bullets available. If you want another style, use the Format Bullets and Numbering command as described above.

To add bullets to paragraphs quickly using the Standard toolbar:

1. Select the paragraphs to which you want to add bullets.
2. Click the **Bullets** button on the Standard toolbar.

You can skip or stop bullets by using the mouse and the mini-menu of commands. See "Adding Numbers to a List Using the Standard Toolbar" earlier in this chapter.

CHECK YOURSELF

Add bullets to selected paragraphs.
- ▲ Select the paragraphs, then click the **Bullets** button on the Standard toolbar.

Creating a Multilevel List

If you have a document that contains an outline or other type of multilevel list, you can choose to format only those paragraphs as a multilevel list.

To create a multilevel list:

1. Select the paragraphs you want to make into a multilevel list.
2. Choose **Format Bullets and Numbering** and click the **Multilevel** tab.
3. Select a format from one of the six multilevel styles. If you want to create your own, click **Modify** and make the appropriate choices in the Modify Multilevel List dialog box.
4. Click **OK** or press **Enter**. Word formats the selected paragraphs as a multilevel list.

Numbering Lines

You can add line numbers to your document when you need to count lines at a glance or make text easier to find on a page. Line numbers are commonly used in legal documents and military specifications.

When you use line numbering in Word, you assign a number to each line in a section, including blank lines that you've added by pressing **Enter**. The numbers appear only when the document is printed or when you choose **File Print Preview**.

You can decide how many lines you want to number—each line, every other line, or every fifth line, for example. You can also turn off line numbering in selected paragraphs, such as headings and figures. Figure 16.8 shows a page with numbered lines in Print Preview.

Numbering Lines

▼ *Figure 16.8. Line Numbers in Print Preview*

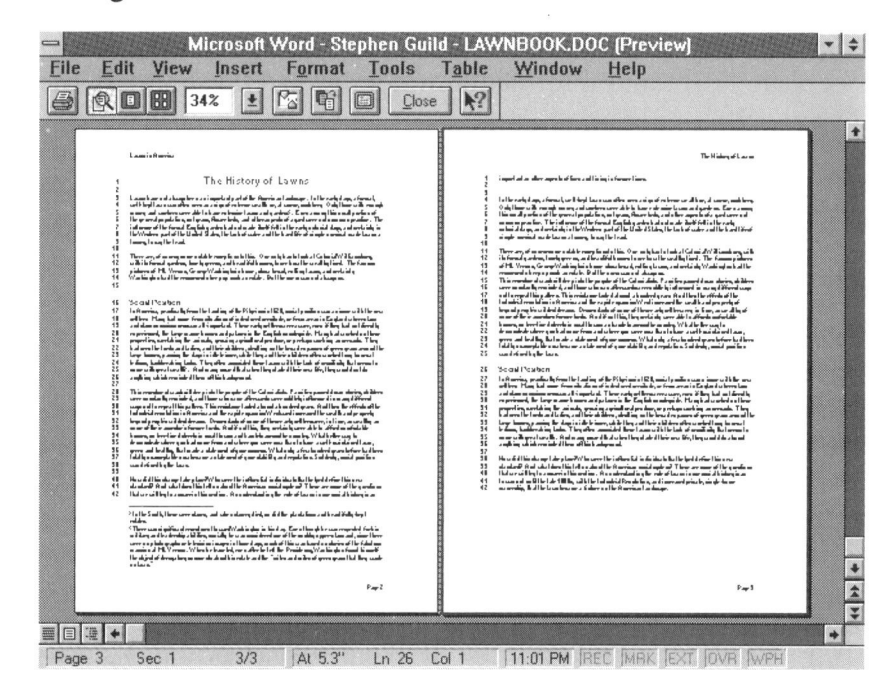

To add line numbers:

1. Select the section(s) to which you want to add line numbers, or select the entire document.
2. Choose the **Layout** tab in the File Page Setup dialog box.
3. Click the **Line Numbers** button.
4. Turn on the **Add Line Numbering** check box.
5. If you want to start numbering lines with a number other than 1, type the starting number in the Start At box.
6. If you want to change the distance between the text and the line numbers, type a new measurement in the From Text box.
7. If you want to print line numbers at intervals (every third or fifth line, for example), type the interval you want in the Count By box (for example, type **5** to print a number beside every fifth line).
8. To determine when line numbering should be restarted, choose an option in the Numbering box. Select **Restart Each Page** to start each page with line number 1, select **Restart Each Section** to start each section with line number 1, or select **Continuous** to number each line in sequence throughout the document.
9. Click **OK** or press **Enter**.

If you don't see line numbers in your document after you've specified them, don't panic. You can't see line numbers in Normal view. You have to switch to Page Layout view or Print Preview to see them. For more information about using Print Preview, see Chapter 9.

Removing Line Numbers

You can remove line numbers from all or part of a document.

To remove line numbers from an entire document:

1. Select the section(s) from which you want to remove line numbers.
2. Choose the **Layout** tab in the File Page Setup dialog box.
3. Click the **Line Numbers** button.
4. Turn off the **Add Line Numbering** check box, and then click **OK** to return to the Page Setup dialog box.
5. Click **OK** or press **Enter**.

To remove line numbers from selected paragraphs in a document:

1. Select the paragraphs from which you want to remove line numbers.
2. Choose the **Text Flow** tab in the Format Paragraph dialog box.
3. Turn on the **Suppress Line Numbers** check box in the Line Numbers box.

Jumping to a Specific Line Number

Once you have added line numbers, you can use the following procedure to jump to a specific line number.

To jump to a line number:

1. Press **F5** or choose **Edit Go To**.
2. Do one of the following:
    - ▲ To jump to a line number in the current page or section, type **l** (lowercase L) followed by the line number. (For example, type **l55** for line 55.)
    - ▲ To jump to a line number on a different page or in a different section, type **p** for page or **s** for section, followed by the

Numbering Lines

page or section number, then type **l** (lowercase *L*) followed by a line number. (For example, type **p2l20** for page 2, line 20; or type **s3l20** for section 3, line 20.)
▲ To jump to a relative line number, type **l** (lowercase *L*) followed by a **+** or **−** (plus or minus) sign and a number. (For example, type **l−50** to jump back 50 lines, or **l+50** to jump forward 50 lines.)
▲ Select **Line** in the list box and then type the page and/or section number or relative position you want.
3. Press **Enter**.

CHECK YOURSELF

Add line numbers to an entire document, then remove line numbers from one paragraph.
▲ Select the entire document, choose **File Page Setup** and click the **Layout** tab. Click **Line Numbers**, and turn on the **Add Line Numbers** check box. To remove line numbers from one paragraph, select the paragraph, choose **Format Paragraph**, and turn on the **Suppress Line Numbers** check box.

QUICK COMMAND SUMMARY

Command	To Do This
View Outline	Switch to Outline view.
View Normal	Switch back to Normal view.
Buttons in Outline view	Create or change heading levels in an outline, move headings, and display different levels of outline headings.
Format Bullets and Numbering	Add, change, or remove numbers from outline headings.
Tools Bullets and Numbering, or Bullets or Numbering button on the toolbar	Add, change, or remove bullets or numbers from paragraphs.

Command	To Do This
File Page Setup, Layout tab	Add or remove line numbers from sections.
Format Paragraph	Remove line numbers from selected paragraphs.

PRACTICE WHAT YOU'VE LEARNED

1. Create this simple outline in Outline view:
    - I. Jumping
        - A. Pulling the Ripcord
        - B. Stepping Out
    - II. Landing
        - A. Positioning Yourself
        - B. Cushioning the Impact
2. Under I, move B in front of A so that the outline reads:
    - I. Jumping
        - A. Stepping Out
        - B. Pulling the Ripcord

What You Do	What You'll See
1. If necessary, choose **View Outline** to switch to Outline view.	1. The document window changed to outline view and the Outline toolbar at the top of the document.
2. Type **Jumping**, click the ← button or press **Alt+Shift+Left arrow** until the style box reads "Heading 1," and then press **Enter**.	2. The text "Jumping," and "Heading 1" in the style box. Heading 1 will be applied to the text after you press Enter.
3. Type **Pulling the Ripcord**, click the —> button or press **Alt+Shift+Right arrow** once (the style box should say "Heading 2"), and then press **Enter**.	3. The text "Pulling the Ripcord." The style box will read "Heading 2," which will be applied to the text.
4. Type **Stepping Out**, and then press **Enter**.	4. The text "Stepping Out." The style box will read "Heading 2."

What You Do	*What You'll See*
5. Type **Landing**, click the <— button or press **Alt+Shift+Left arrow** once (the style box should read "Heading 1"), and then press **Enter**.	5. The text "Landing." The style box will read "Heading 1," which will be applied to the text.
6. Type **Positioning Yourself**, click the —> button or press **Alt+Shift+Right arrow** once (the style box should read "Heading 2"), and then press **Enter**.	6. The text "Positioning Yourself." The style box will read "Heading 2," which will be applied to the text.
7. Type **Cushioning the Impact**, and then press **Enter**.	7. The text "Cushioning the Impact." The style box will read "Heading 2," which will be applied to the text.
8. Select all of the the text and click the **Numbering** tab in the Format Bullets and Numbering dialog box. Click the first numbering format in the numbering tab and click **OK**.	8. The Numbering tab with the first numbering format selected. After you click OK, the numbering format will be applied to the text.
9. Do one of the following: ▲ Point to the symbol in front of IB, "Stepping Out," and then drag up. When the horizontal line is before IA, "Pulling the Ripcord," release the mouse button. ▲ Click or move the insertion point to "Stepping Out," then click the up arrow once or press **Alt+Shift+Up arrow** to move the heading up one position.	9. The "Stepping Out" topic heading moved before "Pulling the Ripcord" heading to become topic IA.

17 Finishing Touches

When you have several smaller documents, you can create a final master document in Word. You can also finish a long document by creating a table of contents for the front and an index for the back. You might also want to compile lists of certain elements such as figures or tables. In this chapter, you will learn how to:

- ▲ Create a table of contents from outline entries or fields
- ▲ Create lists of figures, tables, and other document elements
- ▲ Create an index
- ▲ Create captions for figures, tables, and other items
- ▲ Cross-reference topics and text
- ▲ Create and manage master documents

Creating a Table of Contents

When you finish writing and formatting a long document, you may want to add a table of contents so readers can see the document's structure at a glance and know where to find information. Figure 17.1 shows a table of contents created by Word.

If you used Word's Outline view to create an outline for your document, or if you formatted your headings using Word's Heading 1 through 9 styles, you can create a table of contents using your document's headings—that's by far the easiest way. (For more information about outlining, see Chapter 16.) If you didn't use the heading level styles or Outline view to create your headings, you'll have to insert fields into your document to create a table of contents.

One note of caution: Word considers the table of contents or another list the first page in the document when you insert it at the top, and your first text page will be numbered as page 2. If you want your table of contents or other lists to come first but you want

▼ *Figure 17.1. A Table of Contents Created by Word*

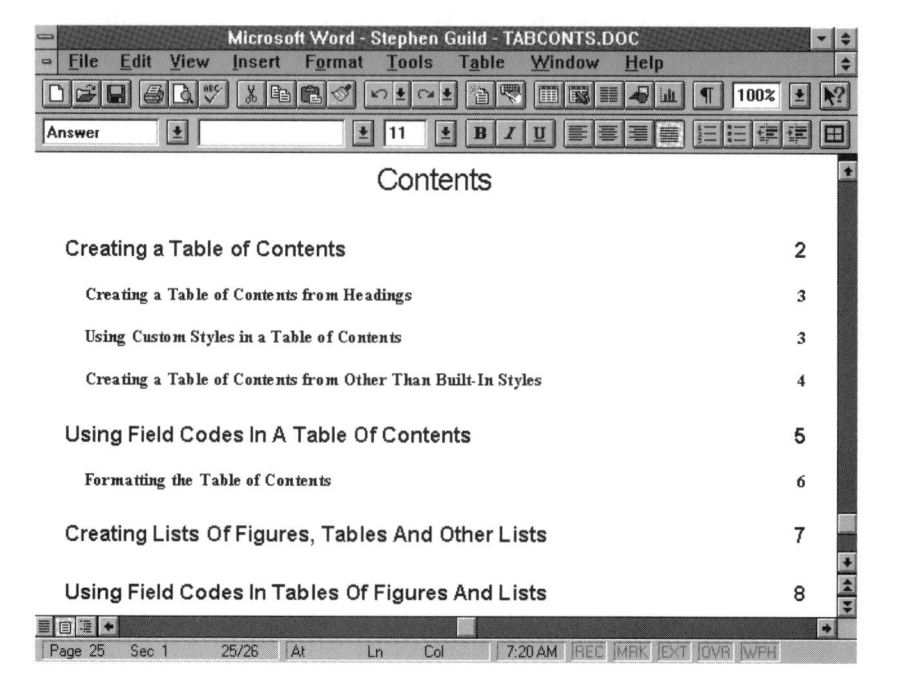

Creating a Table of Contents

the page numbering to begin on page 1 of your text, you need to do the following before you insert the table of contents.

To place a table of contents or other list at the beginning of your document and still have a "page 1":

1. Place the insertion point at the top of your document.
2. Choose **Insert Break** and click the **Next Page** button in the Section Breaks area.
3. Click **OK** or press **Enter**. Word inserts a section break at the beginning of your document. You'll see "Page 2, Sec 2" in the status bar.
4. Place the insertion point in the second section.
5. Choose **Insert Page Numbers** and click the **Format** button.
6. Type **1** in the Start At box and click **OK** or press **Enter**; then close the Page Numbers dialog box.
7. Place the insertion point in the first section and follow the steps for creating a table of contents or other list as described below.

If you have several lists at the beginning of your document, you may have to repeat this process several times, making sure that you format the first page of your document as page 1.

Creating a Table of Contents from Headings

To create a table of contents using Word's Heading styles:

1. Place the insertion point where you want the table of contents to appear (usually at the front of your document).
2. Choose **Insert Index and Tables** and click the **Table of Contents** tab.
3. To select the style you want for the table of contents, do one of the following:
   - ▲ Select one of the styles listed in the Formats list, then click the **Options** button. In the Table of Contents Options dialog box, turn on either the **Styles** or **Table Entry Fields** check box and select the style you want.
   - ▲ Select **Custom Style** and click the **Modify** button. Select the style you want to change, and then click **Modify.** See the next section for information on building custom styles.

4. If you want to use only certain heading levels in your table of contents, choose or type the ending level number in the Show Levels box. For example, if you want the table of contents to contain only heading levels 1 and 2, type **2** in the Show Levels box.
5. If you want the page numbers included in the table of contents, turn on the **Show Page Numbers** check box. Check the **Right Align Page Numbers** box if you want the page numbers to appear on the right side of the page.
6. If you want leader characters before the page numbers, choose the leader character type from the Tab leader drop-down list.
7. Click **OK** or press **Enter**. Word collects the headings from your document and formats them into a table of contents. If your document is long, this process may take a few moments.

Using Custom Styles in a Table of Contents

If you don't want to use the table of formats provided by Word, you can create your own table of contents styles.

To create custom styles in a table of contents:

1. Place the insertion point where you want the table of contents to appear (usually at the front of your document).
2. Choose **Insert Index and Tables** and click the **Table of Contents** tab.
3. Choose **Custom Style** in the Format list.
4. Click the **Modify** button.
5. In the Style dialog box select the style you want to modify and click the **Modify** button.
6. Change each of the styles as you want. (For more information about modifying styles, see Chapter 8.)
7. Click **OK** to return to the Style dialog box.
8. If the format you want appears in the Paragraph Preview area, click **Close** or **Apply** to return to the Index and Tables dialog box. If you want to change the style, click **Modify** and make additional changes following Steps 8 through 10. When the styles are the way you want them, click **OK** or press **Enter.** Word collects the headings from your document and formats them into a table of contents.

Creating a Table of Contents from Other than Built-In Styles

Creating a Table of Contents

If you don't have your headings formatted with Heading styles, you can create a table of contents by using other styles in your document. Word assigns Table of Contents (TOC) fields to those styles and compiles your table of contents from these fields.

To compile a table of contents by using styles other than the built-in Heading styles:

1. Place the insertion point where you want the table of contents to appear (usually at the front of your document).
2. Choose **Insert Index and Tables** and click the **Table of Contents** tab.
3. If you want the page numbers included in the table of contents, turn on the **Show Page Numbers** check box. Check the **Right Align Page Numbers** box if you want the page numbers to appear on the right side of the page.
4. If you want leader characters before the page numbers, choose the leader character type from the drop-down list.
5. Choose the **Options** button. Word displays the Table of Contents Options dialog box.
6. In the Available Styles box, you will see a list of the available styles in your document. Type a number from 1 to 9 in the TOC Level box to the right of each style name to indicate the level you want for that style. You don't need to number styles that you will not be including in your table of contents.
7. Click **OK** or press **Enter** to return to the Index and Tables dialog box, then click **OK** or press **Enter** to compile the table of contents.

Using Field Codes in a Table of Contents

You can also create a table of contents by inserting TC fields (different from TOC fields) in front of your headings, then collecting all the TC fields. The TC fields are formatted as hidden text; they won't print unless you instruct Word to print hidden text.

When you have inserted all the TC fields you need, you can compile the table of contents, collecting all the TC fields along with the associated page numbers.

To insert a TC field to mark a table of contents entry:

1. Place the insertion point next to the information you want to reference, usually at the end of a heading.
2. Choose **Insert Field**.
3. Select **Index and Tables** from the Categories list, then select **TC** in the Field Name list. Be sure that you select TC, not TOC. A TC field creates a table of contents entry, whereas a TOC field creates the actual table of contents.
4. After "TC" in the Field Code box, enter a space followed by a quotation mark ("). Then type or copy and paste the text you want to use as an entry in the table of contents, followed by a quotation mark, this way:

   TC "Starting the Compressor"

5. If you want your entry to be a level other than level 1, type a space, then type \l (backslash and lowercase L) followed by a level number. For example, the following entry creates a level 2 table of contents entry, which would be indented beneath the preceding entry:

   TC "Starting the Compressor" \l2

6. Press **Enter**. The field is automatically formatted as hidden text, so if you want to see it, you may need to click the ¶ button on the Standard toolbar.
7. Repeat Steps 1 through 6 until you've added all the fields you need.

To compile a table of contents from TC field entries:

1. Place the insertion point where you want the table of contents to appear.
2. Choose **Insert Index and Tables** and click the **Table of Contents** tab.
3. Click the **Options** button and turn on the **Use Table Entry Fields** check box.
4. Click **OK**, and then click **OK** again or press **Enter** to insert the table of contents.

CHECK YOURSELF

What is the connection between the Heading styles and a table of contents created by Word?
▲ When headings are formatted with the Heading styles, Word can collect the headings into a table of contents. Otherwise, you have to insert table of contents entries to create a table of contents.

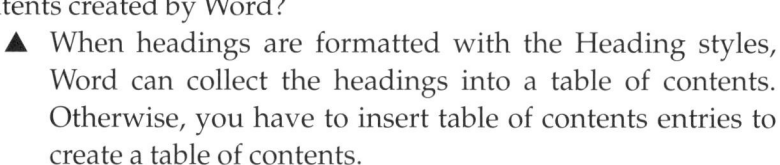

Formatting the Table of Contents

Word inserts the table of contents as a field. If you have Field Codes turned on, you'll see the TOC field. If you have Field Codes turned off, you'll see the table of contents itself.

Word automatically adds the TOC styles to table of contents entries by changing the Heading 1 style to the TOC 1 style, the Heading 2 style to the TOC 2 style, and so forth. You can edit and format the text in the table of contents just as you would edit and format any other text, and you can change the TOC styles if you don't like the default formats. See Chapter 8 for more information on changing styles.

Most of the time, you'll only use a few of Word's heading levels for actual headings in your text (for example, Headings 1 through 3). You can assign any of the remaining Heading styles to table titles, figure captions, photo descriptions—to any items you want to collect into a list. For example, you might want to assign the Heading 7 style to all table titles and the Heading 8 style to figure captions. For more information about using styles, see Chapter 8.

Creating Lists of Figures, Tables, and Other Elements

You can follow steps similar to those described in the preceding sections to create a list of figures or other elements (such as tables, charts, graphs, slides, and authorities) found in your document.

When you create a list in this way, Word keeps track of the page numbers and can update the list whenever you change the document.

To compile a list of figures or other elements:

1. Place the insertion point where you want the list to appear (usually at the front of your document).
2. Choose **Insert Index and Tables** and click the **Table of Figures** tab.
3. Choose the type of caption label you want (**Equation**, **Figure**, **Table**, or **None**) from the Caption Label drop-down list.
4. To select the style you want for the list of figures or other items, do one of the following:
   ▲ Select one of the styles in the Formats list, then click the **Options** button. In the Options dialog box, turn on either the **Style** or **Table Entry Fields** check box and select the style you want assigned to your captions. Select a letter in the Table Identifier drop-down list.
   ▲ Select **Custom Style**, click the **Modify** button. Select the style you want to change, and then click **Modify**. See "Using Custom Styles in a Table of Contents," earlier in this chapter, for information on building custom styles.
5. If you want your labels and number captions (such as "Figure 23.4") to be included with your figure captions, then turn on the **Include Label and Number** check box.
6. If you want the page numbers to be included in your list, turn on the **Show Page Numbers** check box. Check the **Right Align Page Numbers** box if you want the page numbers to appear on the right side of the page.
7. If you want leader characters before the page numbers, choose the leader character type from the Tab Leader drop-down list.
8. Click **OK** or press **Enter**. Word collects the headings from your document and formats them into a list of figures or other items.

Using Field Codes in Lists of Figures and Other Elements

You can also collect figure captions and other items into lists by using field codes.

Using Field Codes in Lists of Figures and Other Elements

Follow the instructions given earlier in this chapter under "Creating a Table of Contents from Headings," but type the number of the level you want to collect in the Table of Contents dialog box. For example, to collect only paragraphs with the Heading 7 style, type **7** in both the From and To boxes of the Table of Contents dialog box.

If you don't want to use a Heading style, you can create a list by inserting TC fields with a **\f** switch and a one-letter code to the field to tell Word what kind of item (such as a figure, table, or illustration) you're marking. For example, you might use a **\ff** code to mark figure captions for collection into a list of figures or a **\ft** code to mark table titles for a list of tables. Another difference is that you use Insert Field instead of the Insert Table Index and command to compile the list.

To create a list by inserting and collecting fields:

1. Place the insertion point close to the information you want to reference.
2. Choose **Insert Field**.
3. From the Field Type list, select **TC**.
4. In the Field Code box, type a space after TC, then type the text you want, within quotation marks. Press the spacebar followed by **\f** and press the spacebar again, then type a one-letter code to indicate the type of item.
5. Press **Enter**.
6. Repeat Steps 1 through 5 to mark all items that you want to collect into a list.
7. Place the insertion point where you want to insert the list (usually near the beginning of the document).
8. Choose **Insert Field**.
9. From the Field Type list, select **TOC**.
10. In the Field Code box, press the spacebar after toc, type **\f**, press the spacebar again, then type the one-letter code you used to mark your items. For example, if you used *f* as your one-letter code, fill in the Field Code box to look like this: **toc \ff**
11. Press **Enter** to gather all the fields and insert a list field. You can use **Field Codes** (from the View menu) to toggle between the field codes and the list.

Creating an Index

To create an index with Word:

1. Insert index entry fields throughout your document.
2. Compile the index entries to create and insert an index.

   Figure 17.2 shows an index created by Word.

Marking Index Entries

You can designate existing text on a page as an index entry, or you can type new text for an index entry as shown in Figure 17.3. Either way, the index entry field is formatted as hidden text and won't appear in your document when printed. You may need to click the ¶ button on the Standard toolbar to see these fields on the screen.

To mark an index entry:

1. If a page contains text that you want to use as an index entry, select that text.

▼ *Figure 17.2. An Index Created by Word*

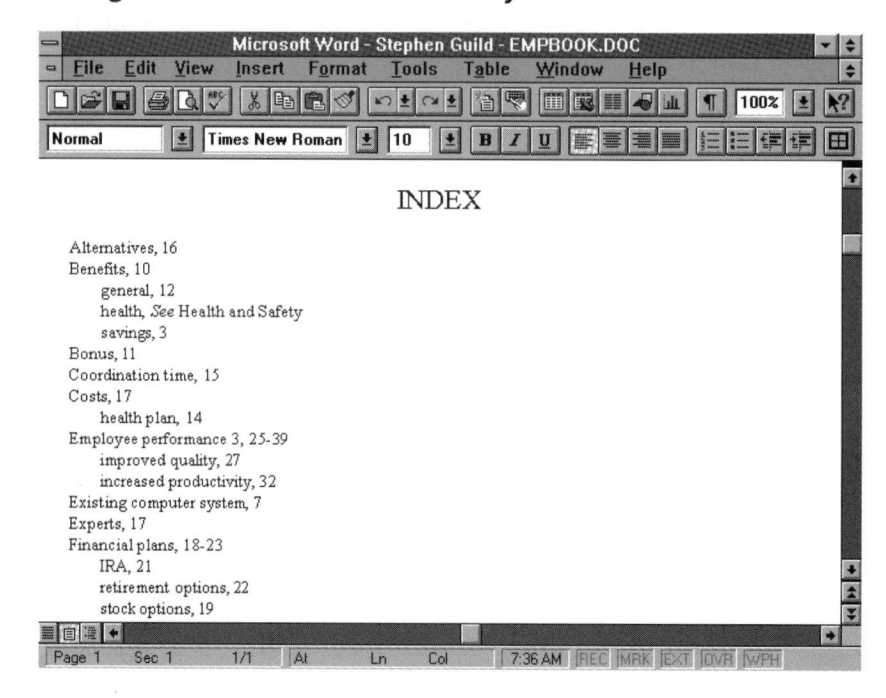

▼ *Figure 17.3. Inserting an Index Entry*

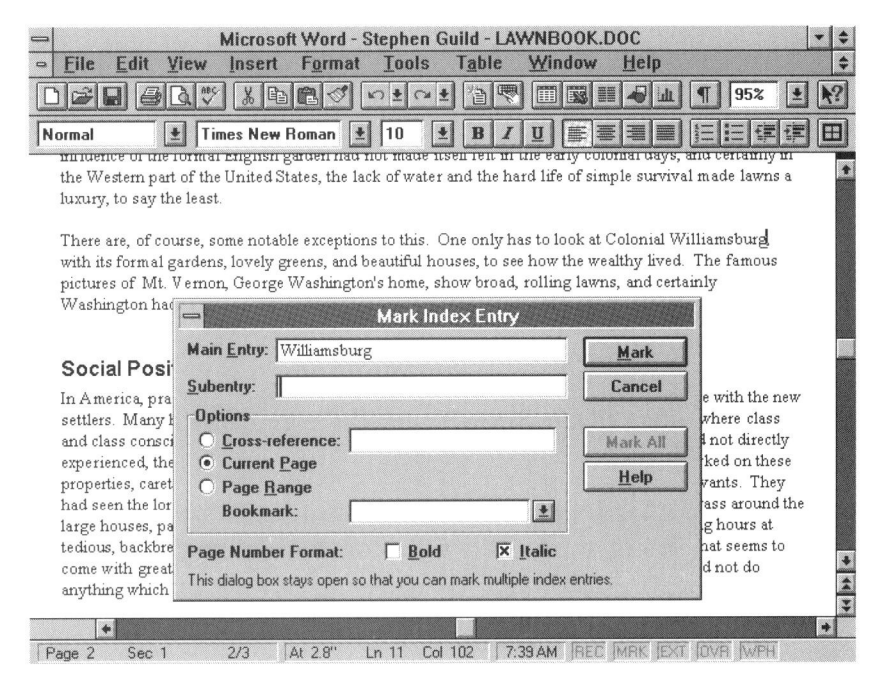

Creating an Index

2. Choose **Insert Index and Tables** and click the **Index** tab.
3. Choose the **Mark Entry** button. In the Main Entry box, edit the existing text or type new text for the index entry. This box will stay open as you make index entries throughout your document.
4. If you want a subentry, type the subentry in the Subentry box. For example, you might type **Bears** in the Main Entry box and **polar bears** as a subentry. If you want still another level of entry, type a colon and a space after the first subentry and then type the next subentry. In our example, you could type **polar bears: sightings** in the Subentry box. If you type an entry in which you want a colon to appear, type a **backslash (\)** in front of the colon so Word won't interpret it as a separator between subentries. If you select text with a colon, Word automatically adds the backslash in the dialog box.
5. If you want a cross-reference to appear instead of a page number in the index, click the **Cross-reference** button and then type the text you want to use for the cross-reference.
6. If you want to use text that has been tagged with a bookmark to specify a range of pages, select the bookmark name in the

Page Range: Bookmark box. For example, if you've named a section "Statistics" and you select Statistics here, Word will insert the page range of the Statistics text in the index for you. See Chapter 4 for more information about tagging text with bookmarks.

7. If you've selected text that occurs repeatedly, click **Mark All**. If you want bold or italic entries, turn on the appropriate check box.
8. Turn on either the **Bold** or **Italic** (or both) Page Number Format: check boxes.
9. Click **OK** or press **Enter**. Word inserts an XE field containing the index entry.
10. Repeat Steps 1 through 8 to insert all the index entry fields you need.

You can also enter the field codes for index entries directly in the text, but this is much more time-consuming than the method described above.

TIP

If you have a lot of index entries to mark, you can speed up your work by pressing Alt+Shift+X. **This will take you to the Mark Index Entries dialog box.**

CHECK YOURSELF

Designate a subentry in an index.
▲ In the Index Entry dialog box, type a colon and a space between the main entry and the subentry.

Creating Automatic Index Entries

You can create automatic index entries by creating a concordance file that contains two columns: one column with the words and phrases you want to index, and in the second column, the index entries generated from the words and phrases in the first column.

Creating an Index

To create a concordance file:

1. Choose **File New** or click the **New** button on the Standard toolbar.
2. Choose **Insert Table** and click **OK**.
3. In the first column of the table, type the text you want to index. You must type these entries exactly as they appear in the document, matching upper- and lowercase letters.
4. Press **Tab** and type the index entry exactly as it will appear in the index, matching upper- and lowercase letters, in the second column.
5. Repeat Steps 3 and 4 for additional entries.
6. Choose **File Save** and type a filename in the File Name box.

Figure 17.4 shows a concordance table.

To mark index entries automatically:

1. Open the document you want to index.
2. Choose **Insert Index and Tables** and click the **Index** tab.
3. Click the **AutoMark** button.

▼ *Figure 17.4. A Concordance File for Automatic Index Entries*

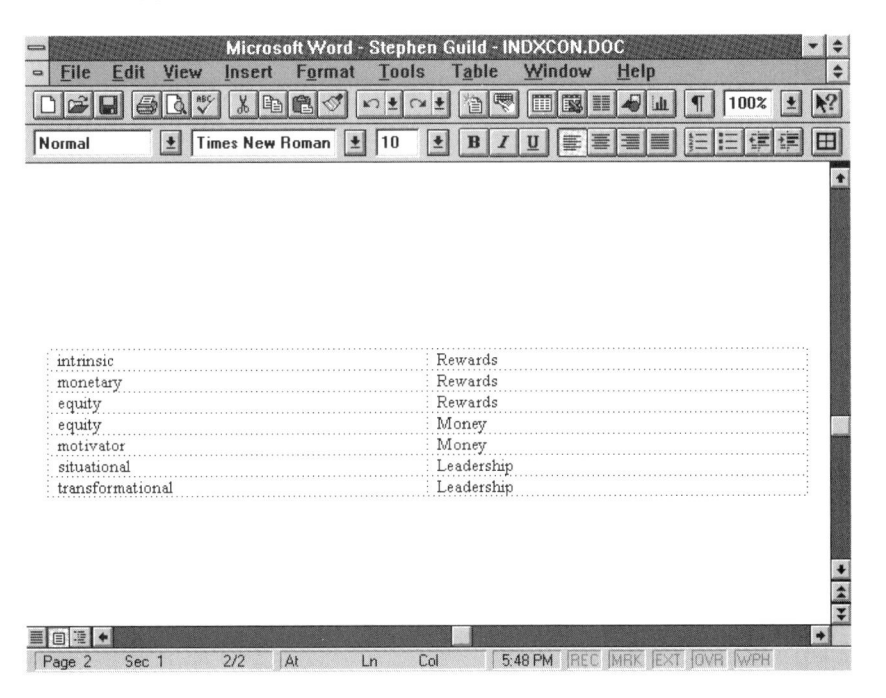

intrinsic	Rewards
monetary	Rewards
equity	Rewards
equity	Money
motivator	Money
situational	Leadership
transformational	Leadership

4. Type or select the name of the concordance file in the File Name box.
5. Click **OK** or press **Enter**. Word will mark the index entries which correspond with the text you have entered in the concordance file.

Compiling Index Entry Fields to Create the Index

When you've inserted index entry fields throughout your document, you're ready to create the final index. You can choose to create a normal index, where the subentries are indented as shown in Figure 17.2, or you can create a run-in index, where subentries continue on the same line after the main entry, separated by semicolons, this way:

Ponies: Shetland, 34; Welsh, 53

If you want to insert a space or print a letter between letter groups in an index, you can also choose a heading separator, the character that separates one letter group from another.

To compile the index:

1. Place the insertion point where you want the index to appear (usually at the back of your document).
2. Choose **Insert Index and Tables** and click the **Index** tab.
3. In the Type area, choose **Indented** if you want the entries to appear below the main entry, or choose **Run-in** if you want them on the same line as the main entry.
4. If you want the page numbers to appear on the right side of the page, turn on the **Right Align Page Numbers** check box, and, if you want a leader character, select one from the Tab Leader drop-down list.
5. If you want the index in more than one column, type or select the number of columns in the Columns box.
6. Click **OK** or press **Enter** to compile the index.

An existing index is not automatically updated when you add or change material. So, if you make changes to your document after compiling an index, you'll have to update the index to be sure it's accurate. See "Updating a Table of Contents or an Index" later in this chapter for instructions.

Formatting Indexes

Creating an Index

Word uses the Index styles (Index 1, Index 2, Index 3, and so forth) to format an index. You can alter the index by selecting and changing each line, or you can change the style Word uses for each index level. You can also change the Index Heading style, which Word uses to format the characters (if any) that separate the letter groups in an index. For example, you might want to make the letters italic or change the font or point size. You change index heading styles in the same way as table styles.

Updating a Table of Contents or an Index

When you change a document, Word doesn't automatically update the table of contents, any lists you created with a TOC field, or the index. If you've made changes to your document, you need to compile the table of contents, lists, and index again to make sure they have the correct page numbers and include all appropriate items.

Tables of contents, lists, and indexes are contained within fields, so you'll use the same process you would use to update any field.

To update a table of contents, list, or index field:

1. Place the insertion point anywhere within the table, list, or index to update. (If necessary, click the Show/Hide ¶ button to display the field codes.)
2. Press **F9** to update. Word will rebuild the table.

CHECK YOURSELF

What does the F9 key do?
  ▲ It updates the field containing the insertion point.

Creating a Table of Authorities

You can compile a table of authorities, which lists the locations of citations (references to cases, statutes, and rules) in briefs or other legal documents, in much the same way as you do an index. You must first mark the citations and then gather them in a single table with the references and page numbers. You can format the table of authorities in the same way you can a table of contents or a list of figures or other items. For more information about creating, formatting, and compiling tables of authorities, refer to your *Microsoft Word for Windows User's Guide*.

Adding Captions and Labels to Figures and Tables

You can add captions to your document to identify figures, tables, and other items. These are different from explanatory captions that are incorporated into graphics and pictures. For more information about such explanatory captions, see Chapter 10.

Word will insert the label and number and additional caption text, if you like. You can even automate the process so that when certain items are inserted into the text, Word will also insert a caption and label and number it sequentially.

To create a caption for an inserted item:

1. Select the item.
2. Choose **Insert Caption**.
3. If the caption label is the way you want it, proceed to step 5.
4. If you want to make changes, do one of the following in the Caption dialog box:

To	*Do This*
Add more text	Type the text in the Caption box.
Change the label	Select a new label in the Label box.
Add a new label	Click the New Label button.

To	Do This
Position a caption	Select Below Selected Item or Above Selected Item.
Change the number format	Click the Numbering button.

5. Click **OK** or press **Enter**.

Adding Captions and Labels to Figures and Tables

Changing the Formatting and Numbering of Captions

To change the number format for captions:

1. Select the item with the caption you want to change.
2. Choose **Insert Caption**.
3. Click the **Numbering** button.
4. Select the numbering format you want from the Format drop-down list.
5. Click **Close**.

To include a chapter number in a caption:

1. Format the chapter heading you are using with the Heading 1 style.
2. Choose **Format Heading Numbering**, select the numbering style you want, then click **OK** or press **Enter**.
3. Select the item in whose caption number you want to include the chapter number.
4. Choose **Insert Caption**.
5. Click the **Numbering** button.
6. Turn on the **Include Chapter Number** check box.
7. Select **Heading 1** in the Chapter starts with Style box.
8. Select a separator character in the Use Separator box, then click **OK**.
9. If you want to add a new label, click **New Label**.
10. Click **OK** or press **Enter**.

Revising Captions

After you have created and inserted your captions, you may find that you need to change them (other than by updating as described as earlier). If you need to revise caption text, such as a title, just retype it. If you need to change one or all labels, follow the steps outlined below.

To change a label in a single caption:

1. Select the item with the caption you want to change.
2. Press the backspace or delete key to delete the caption.
3. Choose **Insert Caption**.
4. If you want to change a label, select the type of label you want from the Label drop-down list and click **OK**.
5. If you want to add a new label, click the **New Label** button, type the new label in the Label box, then click **OK**.

To change labels in captions of the same type:

1. Select the item with the caption you want to change.
2. Choose **Insert Caption**.
3. If you want to change a label, select the type of label you want from the Label drop-down list and click **OK**.
4. If you want to add a new label, click the **New Label** button, type the new label in the Label box, then click **OK**.
5. Click **OK**.

Adding Captions Automatically

Instead of creating a new caption with each occurrence of a table, figure, or other item, you can have Word insert captions for similar items automatically. You should select the types of items to which you want to apply captions while you are creating the document; otherwise, you'll need to insert captions individually as described earlier.

To add captions automatically:

1. Select the table, graphic, or frame.
2. Choose **Insert Caption**.
3. Click the **AutoCaption** button.
4. In the Add Caption When Inserting box, turn on the check box to the left of the item to which you are applying a caption. You can add captions to more than one type of item. So, for exam-

ple, if you want tables, drawings, and graphs all to have the label "Figure," make sure that each time you turn on a check box in the AutoCaption dialog box you also select a label and position before you select the next box.

5. Select the label you want to use in the Use Label drop-down list.
6. Select the location where you want the caption to appear in the Position drop-down list.
7. If you want to change the numbering format, click the **Numbering** button, select the number format you want, then click **OK**. Repeat Steps 3 through 7 for each item to which you want to add a caption.
8. If you want to add a new label, click the **New Label** button, type the new label in the Label box, then click **OK**.
9. Click **OK** or press **Enter**.
10. Insert the item.

Adding Captions and Labels to Figures and Tables

Creating Cross-References

In longer documents, you may want to include references to help the reader find related topics or sections easily. In Word, you can create cross-references to headings, footnotes and endnotes, captions, and items that have been marked with bookmarks. If a reference changes, Word updates the cross-reference entry.

To create a cross-reference in the same document:

1. Place the insertion point where you want the cross-reference to occur in the document, and type the introductory text (such as **For more information see**).
2. Choose **Insert Cross-Reference**.
3. Select the type of item you want to refer to (heading, footnote, figure, etc.) from the Reference Type list.
4. Select the type of information about that item you want to insert in the document:

Choose	To Insert
Heading Text	The text of the heading you want to appear in the cross-reference

Choose	To Insert
Page Number	The number of a page you want to reference
Heading Number	The number of a heading you want to reference

5. Select the specific item you want to refer to in the For Which Heading list.
6. Click the **Insert** button. Repeat Steps 3 through 6 to insert other cross-references. You can work outside of the dialog box to enter other text and format your cross-references.
7. Click **Close** when you have finished with all cross-references.

You can include more than one reference in a cross-reference. For instance, if you wanted your cross-reference to read "For more information see Chapter 6, 'Preserving an African Habitat,' on page 73," you would type the descriptive text **For more information see** and then insert the chapter, heading, and page number information using the Insert Cross-Reference command.

Cross-Referencing Another Document

You can cross-reference text in other documents by using a master document that includes two or more different documents. For more information about master documents, see "Creating Master Documents" later in this chapter.

To cross-reference another document:

1. Open or create a master document.
2. Choose **View Master Document**.
3. Place the insertion point outside the subdocuments.
4. Follow the steps for creating a cross-reference as explained above.

Updating Cross-References

After you've created cross-references, you can change the items that are referenced, and Word will update the cross-references.

To update cross-references:

1. Choose **Edit Select All** and press **F9**.
2. Choose **File Print** or the **Print** button on the Standard toolbar, if you want to print the document. Word updates all cross-references automatically when it prints.
3. Select an individual cross-reference and press **F9**.

If you want to delete a cross-reference, select the reference information (such as a chapter number) and press **Delete** or **Alt+Backspace**. Word will alert you the next time you update, so you can change the cross-reference.

Creating Cross-References

Creating Master Documents

When you must produce a large document—a book, a catalogue, a multipart report—that is divided into separate subdocuments (chapters, sections), Word makes it easy for you to compile all the separate parts into one master document. You can set up a new master document before you begin entering text in the subdocuments, convert an existing document into a master document, or insert existing subdocuments into a single master document.

To create a new master document:

1. Choose **File New** or click the **New File** button on the Standard toolbar.
2. Choose **View Master Document**. The Outlining and Master Document toolbars are displayed. You can use and move these toolbars as you can all the others in Word. (For more information about using toolbars, see Chapter 1.)
3. Type the outline for the master document. Since you are in Outline view, Word treats the master document like an outline and uses the same heading styles. (For more information about outlining, see Chapter 16.)
4. Select the headings and text you want to divide into subdocuments. Be sure that the first heading in the selected text is the one that you want to begin each new subdocument. For instance, in a book with chapter titles, the chapter title style should be the first one in the outline.

5. Click the **Create Subdocument** button. A box is drawn around each subdocument, and a subdocument icon appears in the upper left corner of each subdocument.
6. Choose **File Save** (or **File Save As** if you're using a previously saved document), and type or select a name for the master document.
7. Click **OK** or press **Enter**.

To convert an existing document into a master document:

1. Open the existing document.
2. Choose **View Master Document** and, using the Outlining toolbar, arrange the headings in the outline the way you want.
3. Select the headings and text you want to divide into subdocuments. Be sure that the first heading in the text you've selected is the one that you want to begin each new subdocument. For instance, in a book with chapter titles, the chapter title style should be the first text in each subdocument.
4. Click the **Create Subdocument** button. A box is drawn around each subdocument, and a subdocument icon appears in the upper left corner of each subdocument.
5. Choose **File Save** (or **File Save As** if you're using a previously saved document), and type or select a name for the master document
6. Click **OK** or press **Enter**.

To insert an existing Word document into a master document:

1. Choose **File New** or click the **New File** button on the Standard toolbar to set up a new master document or open a previously saved master document.
2. Place the insertion point where you want to add the existing document.
3. Click the **Insert Subdocument** button on the toolbar.
4. In the File Name box, select the name of the file (including the directory and drive) you want to add.
5. Click **OK** or press **Enter**.

Opening Subdocuments from the Master Document

Creating Master Documents

When you are working in a master document, you may need to open one of the subdocuments and make changes or additions. After you make your changes, you can save the subdocument and the changes will automatically appear in your master document.

To open and change a subdocument from the master document:

1. Open the master document.
2. Locate the beginning of the subdocument you want to edit, and double-click on the **Subdocument** icon in the upper left corner of the subdocument as shown in Figure 17.5. The subdocument file will open.
3. Make any changes, then save the subdocument.

▼ *Figure 17.5. A Document in Master Document View*

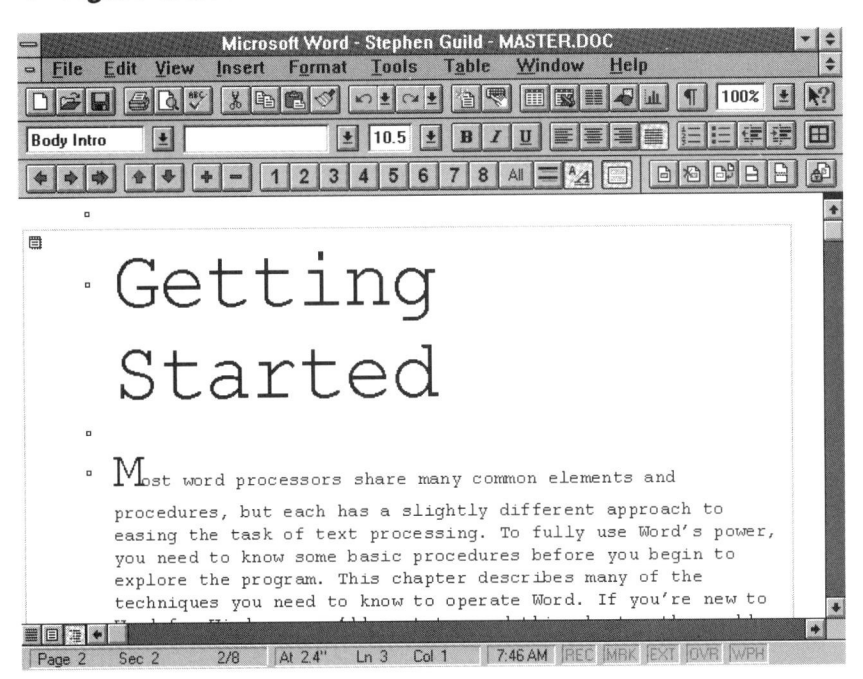

Renaming a Subdocument

You can also give your subdocument a new filename from the master document.

To rename a subdocument:

1. Open the master document.
2. Locate the beginning of the subdocument you want to rename, and double-click on the **Subdocument** icon in the upper left corner of the subdocument. The subdocument file will open.
3. Choose **File Save As** and type a new filename.
4. Click **OK** or press **Enter**.

Rearranging a Master Document

Word makes it easy to change the order of subdocuments within a master document. You can move subdocuments around, spilt subdocuments, and merge one subdocument with another.

To rearrange a master document:

1. Open the master document.
2. In Master Document view, locate the beginning of the subdocument you want to move.
3. Click on the **Subdocument** icon in the upper left corner of the subdocument, and drag the icon and the selected text to the new position. If you want to move only certain paragraphs, select the text and move it to the new position.

To split a subdocument:

1. Open the master document.
2. Place the insertion point where you want the split to occur.
3. Click on the **Split Subdocument** button on the Master Document toolbar.
4. Choose **File Save** or click the **Save** button. Word will save both your master document and the subdocument.

To merge subdocuments:

1. Open the master document.
2. In Master Document view, locate the beginning of the first subdocument you want to merge.

3. Click on the **Subdocument** icon in the upper left corner of the subdocument.
4. Locate the beginning of the next subdocument you want to merge. Hold down the **Shift** key, and click on the **Subdocument** icon. Repeat this step for each subdocument you want to merge.
5. Click the **Merge Subdocument** button on the Master Document toolbar.
6. Choose **File Save** or click the **Save** button. Word will save both your master document and the merged subdocuments. The merged subdocuments will have the filename of the first merged subdocument.

Creating Master Documents

Removing Subdocuments from Master Documents

If you've made a mistake or changed your mind, you can remove subdocuments that you've inserted into a master document. There may also be times when you want to remove a subdocument from the master document while keeping its contents in the master document.

To remove a subdocument and its contents from a master document:

1. Open the master document.
2. In Master Document view, locate the beginning of the first subdocument you want to remove.
3. Click on the **Subdocument** icon and press **Backspace** or **Delete**.

To remove a subdocument and keep its contents in the master document:

1. Open the master document.
2. In Master Document view, locate the beginning of the first subdocument you want to remove.
3. Click on the **Subdocument** icon, then click the **Remove Subdocument** button.

Formatting Master Documents

You can format a master document in the same way you would any other Word document. You can create a template, define styles, and apply formatting to any part of the master document or its subdocuments.

You can change headers, page number, margins, and column layout at the beginning of each subdocument and at section breaks within the subdocument. You can also create a table of contents and a list, of figures or other items, as well as an index.

Information on all of these operations can be found elsewhere in this book:

▲ For more information on templates, see Chapter 2.
▲ For more information on formatting paragraphs, see Chapter 7.
▲ For more information on styles, see Chapter 8.
▲ For more information on page layout, see Chapter 9.
▲ For more information on headers and footers, see Chapter 13.
▲ For more information on tables of contents, lists, and indexes, see previous sections in this chapter.

QUICK COMMAND SUMMARY

Command	To Do This
Insert Index and Tables, Index tab	Insert and format index entries and create indexes in a document.
Insert Index and Tables, Table of Contents tab	Create and format a table of contents in a document.
Insert Index and Tables, Table of Figures tab	Create and format a table of figures in a document.
Insert Index and Tables, Table of Authorities tab	Create and format a table of authorities in a document.
Insert Field	Insert a table of contents, table of authorities, table of figures, or index entry field; insert a field to create a table of contents or index.

PRACTICE WHAT YOU'VE LEARNED

Create a document using Heading 1 and Heading 2 styles for a few headings, and insert a few index entries into the document. Finally, compile a table of contents and an index for the document.

What You Do	*What You'll See*
1. Create a new document (or open a copy of an old one).	1. A blank document window.
2. If necessary, type a few paragraphs of text titles and other text. Select a title and select the Heading 1 style from the Formatting toolbar. Select another title and select the Heading 2 style from the Formatting toolbar. Repeat to add the heading styles to several titles.	2. The text you enter. For each of the titles you select and apply a heading style to, the heading style (Heading 1, Heading 2, etc.) will appear in the Style box.
3. Place the insertion point in a paragraph, choose **Insert Index and Tables**, and click the **Index** tab. Click the **Mark Entry** button, then type text for the index entry and click **OK**. Repeat this step to add index entries in a few more spots.	3. The Index tab in the Index and Tables dialog box. After you click the Mark Entry button, the Mark Index Entry dialog box will open. After you type the text and click OK, the index entry will be made.
4. Place the insertion point at the beginning of the document, choose **Insert Table of Contents**, click the **Table of Contents** tab, and click **OK** to compile and insert the index. (The Headings option is already chosen for you.)	4. The Table of Contents tab in the Index and Tables dialog box. After you click OK, the table of contents will appear at the beginning of the document.

What You Do

5. Place the insertion point at the end of the document, choose **Insert Index and Tables**, click the **Index** tab, and then click **OK** to compile and insert the index.

What You'll See

5. The Index tab in the Index and Tables dialog box. After you click **OK**, the index will appear at the end of the document.

18

Macros, Fields, and Linking

Have you ever wished that you could automate word-processing tasks that you repeat frequently? Word lets you save time by using macros and fields to automate selected tasks. In this chapter, you will learn how to:

- ▲ Record and run macros
- ▲ Assign macros to menus and keys
- ▲ Insert fields
- ▲ Format, edit, and update fields

Saving Time with Macros

You are already familiar with many macros in Word, such as the Bullets button on the Standard toolbar, which automatically sets tabs to produce hanging indents and inserts bullets next to paragraphs. With Word, you can record actions like these one time as a macro. Then, you can click the mouse button or press a key combination and watch Word do all of the steps for you.

A *macro* is a set of commands, keystrokes, and other instructions that automate repetitive or complex Word tasks. In fact, Word's commands are all macros. You can easily record your own macros to do exactly what you want. Macros can perform very simple actions, like inserting a specific set of characters, or they can contain complex instructions with programming elements, such as structure and control statements and variables.

If you want your macro to be easily accessible, you can add it to a menu so you can choose it like any other command. If you're a dedicated keyboard user, you can assign a key combination to the macro so you can run it without taking your fingers off the keyboard.

Creating Your Own Macros

There are two ways to create a macro:

▲ By recording keystrokes and commands
▲ By typing representations for keystrokes, commands, and instructions, using Word's macro language

Because recording a macro is much easier than using the macro language, this chapter concentrates on the recording method. The easiest way to learn the macro language is to record several steps, then check the macro text using the procedure outlined in "Troubleshooting and Correcting Macros" later in this chapter. You can also check your *Microsoft Word for Windows User's Guide* for more information about using the macro language.

Creating Your Own Macros

To create your macro:

1. Plan the steps that you want the macro to perform, and choose a name for your macro.
2. Turn on the macro recorder. Name the macro, perform the steps, then turn off the macro recorder.
3. Test the macro to see if it works.
4. If necessary, record the macro again, or revise the steps that you planned.

Planning a Macro

Before you record a macro, think about what you want the macro to do. Keep in mind that every action you perform is recorded. Doing a little planning up front saves time because you improve your odds of recording the macro correctly the first time instead of having to edit and rerecord later.

Here are some general guidelines for planning macros:

▲ Use keystrokes or key combinations, not the mouse, to select text or scroll in a macro. (When you use the mouse, the macro can't know where you want to begin or end your selection.)

▲ It's okay to use key combinations to select or scroll if the keys select specific blocks of text (such as a paragraph or the whole document) or if they scroll to a definite location that remains the same in every document, such as the beginning or end of a document. In general, though, you'll probably find it's easier if you plan to select text before running a macro that affects it.

▲ Don't plan for the macro to initiate a time-consuming process, such as printing or merging form letters. This takes control out of your hands. Instead, make the last step in the macro display the appropriate dialog box. Then you can turn on the printer, check other settings, and begin the process when you're ready.

You might want to write a short description of the steps you want the macro to perform, creating a script you can follow. It's also a good idea to rehearse the steps you've planned for your macro before you begin recording, just to make sure you haven't left anything out.

You must also choose a name for your macro. A macro name must begin with a letter; it can consist of letters and numbers (no punctuation, spaces, or formatting). The name should be descriptive so that you can remember what the macro does. Following are some examples of macro names: print2copies; bolditalic; letter-inverts; docformat.

A macro name must be unique. You may want to display the Macro Run dialog box to check the list of existing macros in your template and make sure the name you want to assign hasn't already been used. If you accidentally try to save a macro with the same name as another, Word tells you that the name has already been used.

Recording a Macro

Recording a macro is like videotaping your actions. Whatever you do is recorded, exactly as you do it. After you've recorded the macro, you can run it to reproduce your actions, just as you would play a videotape. Word responds to the macro just as if you were performing the actions yourself.

To record a macro:

1. Choose **Tools Macro**, and click the **Record** button or double-click **REC** in the status bar and follow Steps 4 through 7.
2. Type a name for the macro in the Record Macro Name box.
3. In the Description box, type a short description of the macro to remind yourself of what the macro does.
4. In the Make Macros Available To: drop-down list, choose one of the following:

To Do This	*Choose*
Include the macro in each available template	All Active Templates
Include the macro only in the NORMAL.DOT template	Normal.dot
Use Word Commands only	Word Commands

Creating Your Own Macros

5. Assign the macro to a toolbar, or a menu, or to shortcut keys using the keyboard. Depending on your choice, Word will display the appropriate tab in the Customize dialog box.
6. Complete the tab and click **Close**. The mouse pointer will now have a recording tape graphic attached to it and a small toolbar with a Pause and a Stop Recording button on it will appear in the document window.
7. Perform the actions you want to record. There's no hurry. The recorder records only when you press the keys or use the mouse, so take the time you need to think or refer to your notes.
8. When you've performed all the steps, click the **Stop Recorder** button. Your macro will be saved.

Next, you'll want to run your macro to test it.

Running a Macro

To run a macro, you can use one of three different procedures, depending on whether you've assigned the macro to a toolbar, a menu, or a shortcut key combination. The macro instructions are carried out at the insertion point, so be sure to move the insertion point or select text as necessary before you start the macro.

TIP

If you're running a macro for the first time, be sure to save your document first. (In fact, it's always a good safety measure to save your work before you run a macro.) That way, if the macro does something unexpected that garbles the text, you can close the document without saving it, discarding the changes made by the macro. You could also create a test document to use for macro-testing purposes.

Choosing a Macro from a List

To run a macro not assigned to a toolbar, to a menu, or to a key combination:

1. Choose **Tools Macro**.
2. Do one of the following:
   ▲ Select the macro name from the Macro Name list, then click **Run**.
   ▲ Double-click the macro name in the list.

Running a Macro from a Menu

If you've assigned the macro to a menu, you can run the macro in this way:

▲ Choose the macro name from the menu, as shown in Figure 18.1.

Press **Esc** if you need to interrupt or cancel a macro after you've started it.

▼ *Figure 18.1. A Macro Assigned to a Menu*

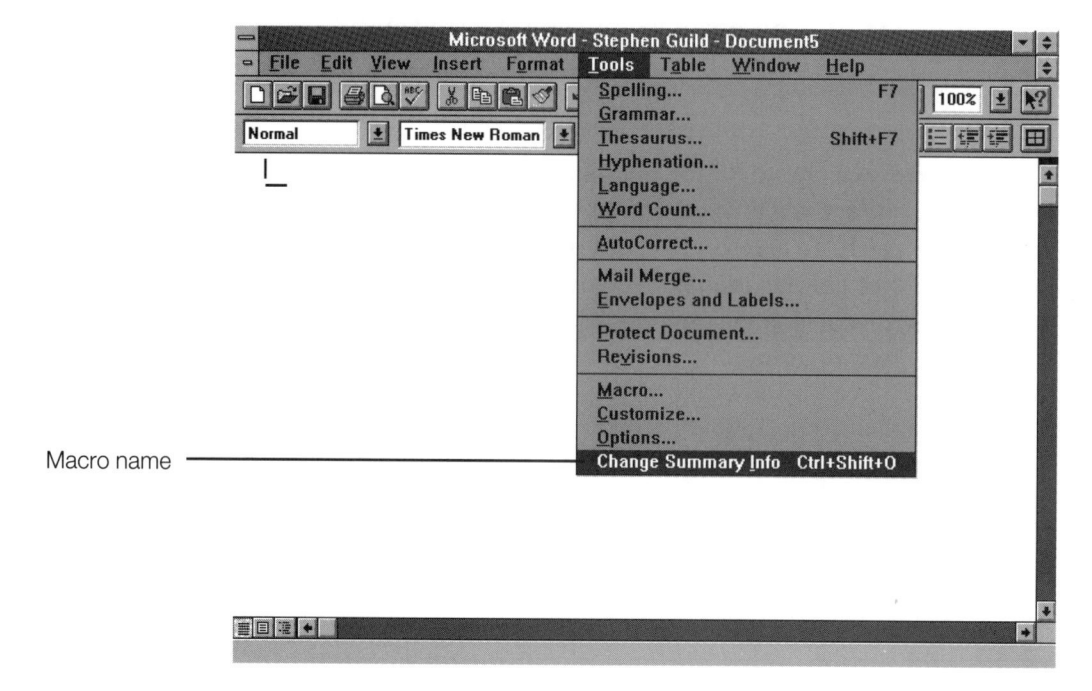

Macro name

Running a Macro Using Its Key Combination

Running a Macro

If the macro you want to run has an assigned key combination, you can run the macro without choosing a command first. If the macro is also assigned to a menu, Word displays its key combination along with its name on the menu, as shown in Figure 18.2.

To run a macro when you know its key combination:

1. Move the insertion point or select text as necessary.
2. Press the key combination.

Assigning Macros to Toolbars, Menus, or Keys

You can assign a macro to a toolbar, a menu, and/or a key combination. You don't have to do any of these because you can always

▼ *Figure 18.2. A Macro's Key Combination with the Macro Name*

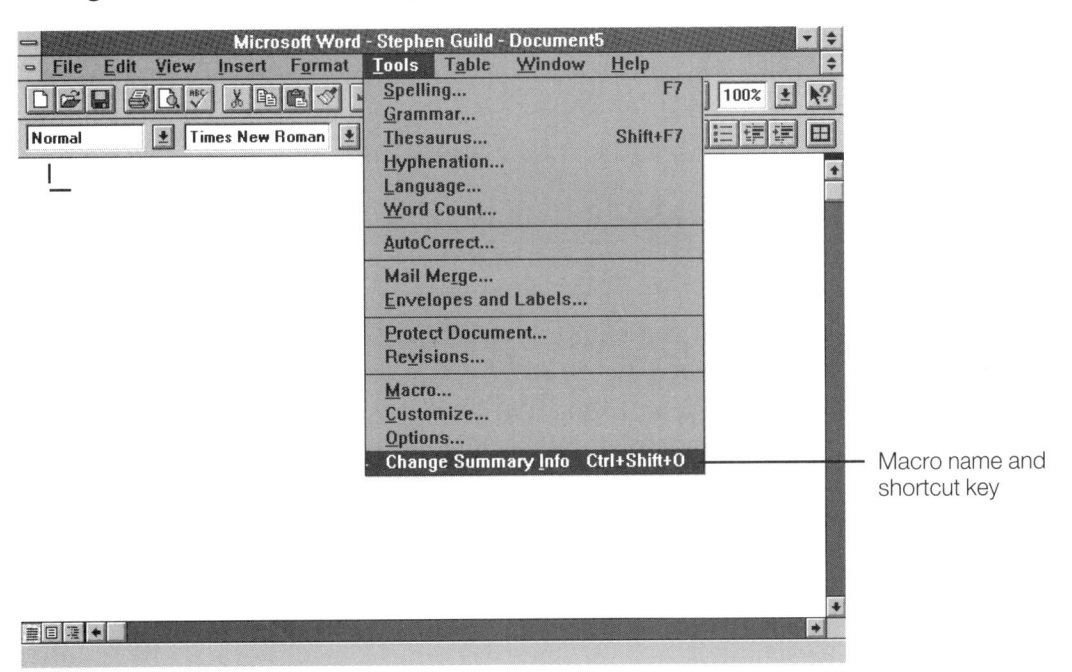

Macro name and shortcut key

run a macro by selecting the macro name in the Macro Name list box as described earlier.

Assigning Macros to a Toolbar

Assigning macros to toolbars makes them easily accessible and easy to use with the mouse. You may have to rearrange or edit the toolbar to make room for macros if you have many to add. For more information about toolbars, see Chapter 1.

To assign a macro to a toolbar:

1. Choose **Tools Customize** and click the **Toolbars** tab.
2. Select **Macros** in the Categories list, and then select a macro in the Macros list box.
3. Click the macro name and hold down the mouse button as you drag a blank square placeholder button to the toolbar you want to use. A Custom Button dialog box appears. Click one of the symbols or choose a text button.
4. Click **OK** or press **Enter**, and then click **OK** or press **Enter.**

To remove a toolbar button:

1. Choose **Tools Customize** and click the **Toolbar** tab.
2. Click and drag the button you want to remove from the toolbar.

Assigning Macros to Menus

When you assign a macro to a menu, it displays and behaves just like a Word command. When you assign a macro to a menu, you need to designate the letter in the macro name that you'll use to choose the command from the keyboard. Placing an ampersand (&) in front of a letter in the name causes an underline to appear under that letter when the name appears on a menu (for example, &Zap creates the menu command Zap). You can change the underlined letter by putting the ampersand in front of any other letter in the macro name. Make sure that it doesn't duplicate the underlined letter in any other command on that menu.

Macros, Fields, and Linking ▲ 419

To assign a macro to a menu:

1. Choose **Tools Customize** and click the **Menus** tab.
2. Select **Macros** in the Categories list, and then select a macro in the Macros list box.
3. Select the menu name from the Change What Menu drop-down list.
4. Select the place on the menu you want in the Position on Menu drop-down list.
5. Type the name you are giving the macro.
6. Click **Add**, then click **Close** or press **Enter**.

Figure 18.3 illustrates adding a macro named "twocopies" to the File menu.

You can take a macro off a menu as easily as you added it.

To remove or rename a macro from a menu:

1. Choose **Tools Customize** and click the **Menu** tab.
2. Select **Macros** in the Categories list, and then select a macro in the Macros list box.
3. Select the menu name from the Change What Menu drop-down list.
4. Select the place on the menu you want in the Position on Menus drop-down list.
5. Do one of the following:

Assigning Macros to Toolbars, Menus, or Keys

▼ *Figure 18.3. Adding a Macro to the File Menu*

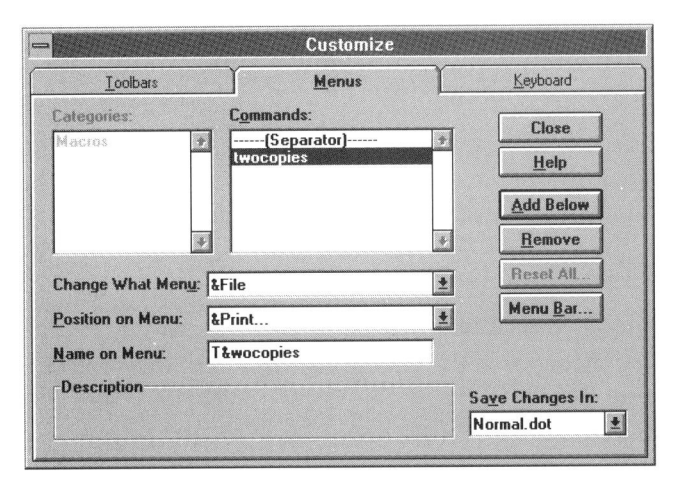

▲ Click **Remove** to remove the selected macro from the menu.
▲ Click **Rename** if you want to rename the macro.
▲ Click **Reset All** if you want to remove all menu changes from the NORMAL.DOT.
6. Click **Close** or press **Enter**.

CHECK YOURSELF

Assign a macro named "twocopies" to the File menu.
▲ Record a macro named "twocopies," choose the **Menu** category in the Options dialog box, and then select the name of the macro and the menu you want to assign it to.

Assigning Macros to Keys

If you want to use the keyboard to run macros, you can assign a macro to a key combination so it automatically runs that macro.

You can assign a macro to a combination of the Ctrl and Shift keys and any alphanumeric key, any function key, or the Insert or Delete key. Because each macro's key combination must be unique, you must choose a combination of keys that is currently "unassigned." The best way to do this is through trial and error, using the procedure described next. Word tells you if a key combination is already assigned to something else. To improve your chances of picking a unique combination, we suggest using one of the following combinations:

▲ **Ctrl+Shift+**another key
▲ **Ctrl+**number key (either from the top row of keys on the main keyboard or from the numeric keypad with Num Lock on)

To assign a macro to keys:

1. Choose **Tools Customize** and click the **Keyboard** tab.
2. Select **Macros** in the Categories list, and then select a macro in the Macros list box.
3. Click in the **Press New Shortcut Key** box. Press a combination of the **Ctrl** and **Shift** keys and an alphanumeric key, a function

Macros, Fields, and Linking ▲ 421

key, or the **Insert** or **Delete** key. The keys you press appear in the box. If the key combination is not currently in use, Word displays "[unassigned]". Any other key combinations for that macro are listed in the Current Keys drop-down list.

4. Click **Add** to assign the key combination to the macro.
5. Click **Close** or press **Enter**.

Assigning Macros to Toolbars, Menus, or Keys

You can check key assignments at any time by selecting the macro name in the Macros box and the Keyboard category in the Options dialog box. If the macro is also assigned to a menu, the keys appear alongside the name in the menu.

Your key assignments are not necessarily permanent; you can change them at any time.

To "unassign" a key assignment:

1. Choose **Tools Customize** and click the **Keyboard** tab.
2. Select **Macros** in the Categories list, and then select a macro in the Macros list box.
3. Select the menu name from the Change What Menu drop-down list.
4. Click **Remove**.
5. Click **OK** or press **Enter**.

If key assignments have become confusing and you would like to return to Word's default assignments, you can use the following procedure.

To restore key combinations to the original Word settings:

1. Choose the **Tools Cutomize** and click the **Keyboard** tab.
2. Choose **Reset All**.
3. Click **Close** or press **Enter**.

CHECK YOURSELF

Find an unassigned shortcut key combination for the "twocopies" macro and assign the key combination to it.

▲ Choose the **Keyboard** tab in the Customize dialog box, and experiment with the Shortcut Keys boxes until you find an unused combination. Then, select "twocopies" from the Macros list and click **Add**.

Using Word's Supplied Macros

The macros that come with Word are stored in the NORMAL.DOT template.

To display a list of the supplied macros:

1. Choose **Tools Customize** and click the **Menus** tab. The dialog box displays all of Word's macros, most of which are commands that you see on the menus.
2. Click **All Commands** in the Categories list. Word will list all of the names. To see what a macro does, select its name in the list, then read the text Word displays in the Description box.
3. To close the dialog box without running the macro, click **Close**.

You can run Word's supplied macros "as is" or assign them to different menus or keys using the procedures described earlier in this chapter.

Troubleshooting and Correcting Macros

If your macro is fairly simple but you've made a mistake in recording it, the easiest way to fix it is to record the macro again.

If you've recorded a complex macro and it's not working properly, you can step through the macro instructions in various ways to see just what's wrong and then correct the macro text. Figure 18.4 shows the text of a macro.

For more information about this and other topics relating to macros, see the *Microsoft Word for Windows User's Guide*.

Renaming a Macro

To change the name of a macro that you created:

1. Choose **Tools Macro**.
2. Click the **Organizer** button and then the **Macros** tab.

▼ *Figure 18.4. Troubleshooting a Macro in the Macro Edit Window*

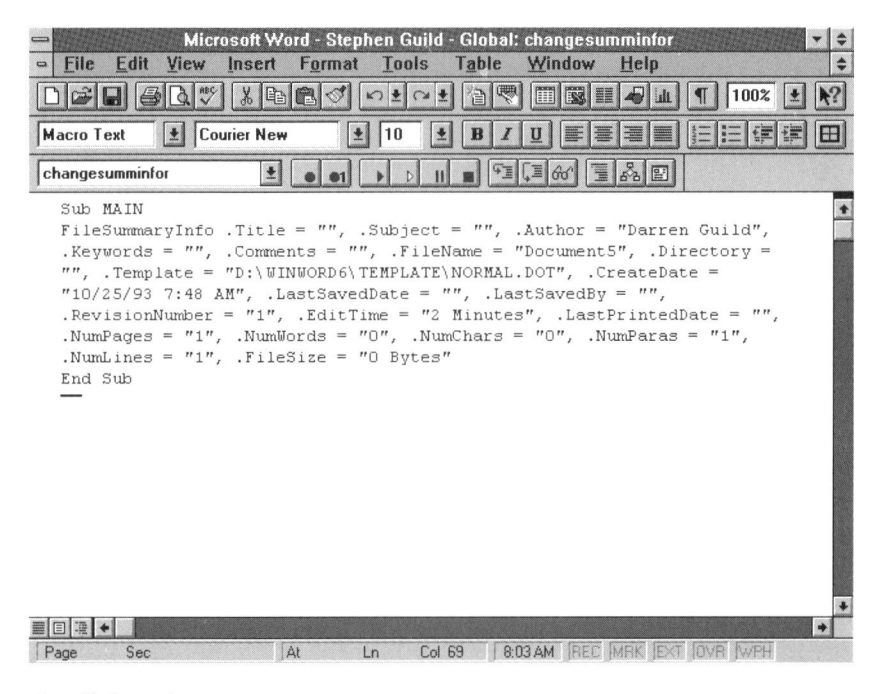

Trouble-shooting and Correcting Macros

```
Sub MAIN
FileSummaryInfo .Title = "", .Subject = "", .Author = "Darren Guild",
.Keywords = "", .Comments = "", .FileName = "Document5", .Directory =
"", .Template = "D:\WINWORD6\TEMPLATE\NORMAL.DOT", .CreateDate =
"10/25/93 7:48 AM", .LastSavedDate = "", .LastSavedBy = "",
.RevisionNumber = "1", .EditTime = "2 Minutes", .LastPrintedDate = "",
.NumPages = "1", .NumWords = "0", .NumChars = "0", .NumParas = "1",
.NumLines = "1", .FileSize = "0 Bytes"
End Sub
```

3. Select the macro you want to rename.
4. Click **Rename**. Type a new name in the dialog box.
5. Click **OK** to return to the Macro dialog box.
6. Click **Close** or press **Enter**.

Copying and Moving Macros

You can copy and move macros to different templates by using the Organizer dialog box, which is similar to the one used with styles and AutoText entries. (For more information about the use of the Organizer dialog with styles, see Chapter 8. For more information about the use of the Organizer dialog with AutoText entries, see Chapter 4.)

To copy or move macros:

1. Choose **Tools Macro**.
2. Click the **Organizer** button and then the **Macros** tab.
3. The macros in the current document are displayed in the In (document name) drop-down list. If you want to use the same

macros in a different template, click the **Close File** button and click the **Open File** button. Select a directory and a filename to specify the document containing the macros you want to copy or move. Word displays the names of all the files in that directory that have the .DOT extension.
4. Select the name of the template in which you want to copy of move the macros in the To (document name) drop-down list. If the name of the document you want to use is not displayed, then close the present file and open the document using the procedure described above.
5. Select the names of the macros you want to copy or move and then click the **Copy** button. You can also choose to Delete or Rename a macro at this point.
6. When you have finished, click **Close**.

Deleting a Macro

When you no longer need a macro that you created, you can get rid of it to free up disk space and computer memory.

NOTE: If you're using the Macro Edit window to correct a macro when you decide to delete it, close the Macro Edit window before you use the following procedure.

To delete a macro:

1. Choose **Tools Macro**.
2. Select the macro name from the Macro Name list.
3. Click **Delete**.
4. Click **OK** or press **Enter**.

Using Fields

In other parts of this book, you have used information that occurs in fields (for example, merge fields, bullets, pictures, and objects), so you already know that fields can speed up and simplify your work.

A *field* is a special set of codes that instruct Word to insert information into a document. You can insert almost anything into a document—text, pictures, tables, charts, indexes, tables of contents, numbers, dates, times, page numbers, and so on. Some common uses of fields are to:

Using Fields

- Merge large amounts of data into a standard format.
- Create cross-references to another part of a document.
- Include information from other parts of a document as well as from other documents.
- Assemble indexes and tables of contents.

Fields typically consist of three parts:

- **Field characters**, the symbols { and } that Word inserts to show the beginning and end of the field. The symbols look identical to braces, but you cannot insert them by pressing the brace keys.
- **Field type**, a name identifying the action you want the field to perform. The field type is the first item in the field after the beginning field character. A field type can consist of a field name (such as ASK, INCLUDE, QUOTE), an equal sign (=), or a bookmark name.
- **Instructions**, which describe how you want the action performed. Instructions can consist of arguments, bookmark names, expressions, text, and switches.

More detailed information about field codes, expressions, switches, and other formatting in fields can be found in the *Microsoft Word for Windows User's Guide* and in the online Help.

Inserting Fields

You can insert fields into Word documents by using the Field dialog box (displayed when you choose Insert Field) or by pressing **Ctrl+F9**.

To insert a field with the Field dialog box:

1. Place the insertion point where you want the field to appear.
2. Choose **Insert Field**. Word displays the Field dialog box shown in Figure 18.5.
3. Select a field type from the Categories list. Word displays the text for that field type in the Field Codes box and the description in the Description box.

▼ *Figure 18.5. The Field Dialog Box*

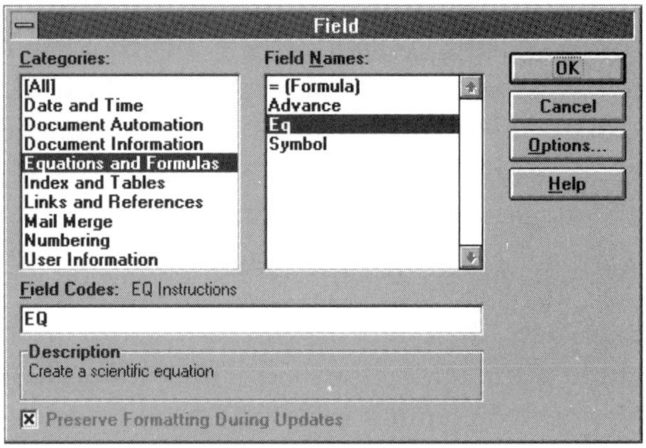

4. If you want to change the format of the result, click the **Options** button, select formatting instructions in the form of switches in the Field Options dialog box, then click the **Add to Field** button. Continue do this until you have inserted all the necessary formatting instructions.
5. Type any additional instructions (such as mathematical expressions) needed in the Field Codes box.
6. Click **OK** or press **Enter** to return to the Field dialog box, then click **OK** or press **Enter**.
7. Press **F9** to update the field.

To insert a field using keys:

1. Press **Ctrl+F9** to enclose the insertion point within the field characters.
2. Type the field type and its instructions.
3. When you have finished typing and formatting the field, press **F9** to update the field.
4. Press a direction key to move the insertion point out of the field.

Alternatively, you can type the contents of the field first, select the contents, then press **Ctrl+F9** to add field braces.

Displaying Codes or Results in Fields

Displaying Codes or Results in Fields

You can display fields in two ways:

▲ Show field codes: field types and instructions
▲ Show results: the visible text or graphics produced by the field codes

Figure 18.6 shows two field displays from the same document. In the top window, the field results are displayed; in the bottom window, the field codes are displayed.

You can switch from codes to results and back again by selecting the field, then pressing **Alt+F9** or choosing Toggle Field Codes on a mini-menu that appears when you place the insertion point in a field and click the right mouse button.

▼ **Figure 18.6. Showing the Results of Fields (Top) or the Field Codes (Bottom)**

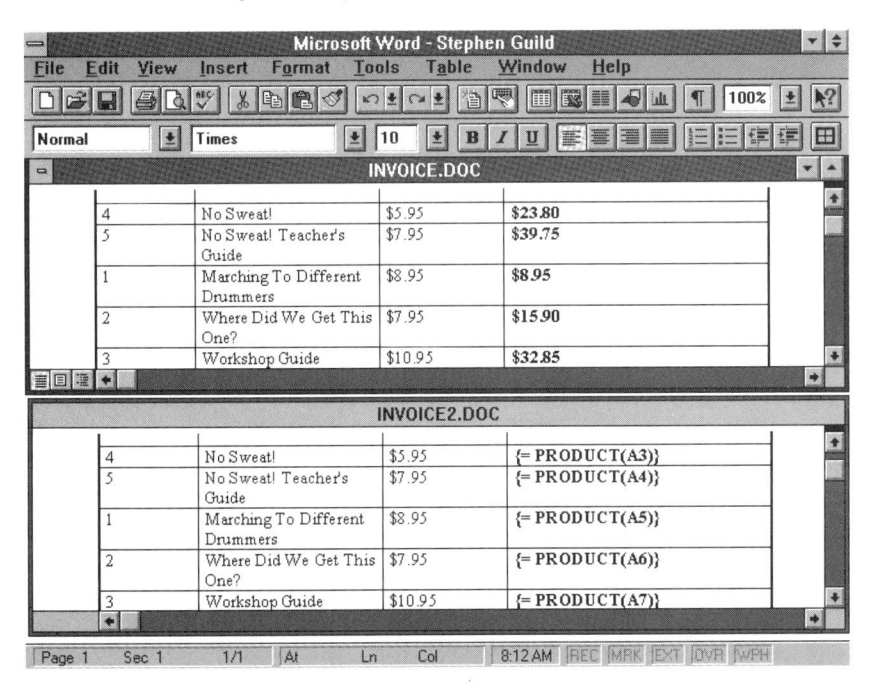

Some Word fields do not have visible results, but instead initiate actions. The XE (Index Entry), TC (TOC Entry), and RD (Referenced Document) fields are a few of these. When you display field results, these fields "disappear," although the field codes are still in the document.

Some fields are automatically formatted as hidden text, so you may need to choose the View tab in the Options dialog box and turn on the Hidden Text option to see the fields.

When you print a document, Word prints the results of all the document's fields unless you specifically tell Word to print the codes, as explained in the following section.

Printing Field Codes

If you want to print a document that contains fields but you want to print the field codes rather than the results, do this:

1. Choose **File Print**.
2. Choose **Options** to display the Print tab. (Note that this takes you to the same box as the Print tab in Tools Options.)
3. Turn on the **Field Codes** check box in the Include with Document box.
4. Click **OK** or press **Enter** to close the Print tab, and then click **OK** or press **Enter** to begin printing.

Editing and Deleting Fields

Once you have inserted a field in your document, you can edit and delete the field as you would any other text. You can select text in a field the same way you select normal text, but if you select either the beginning or the closing field character, Word automatically selects the entire field.

To edit a field:

1. Position the insertion point in the field.
2. If the result is shown, press **Alt+F9** to see the field codes.
3. Edit the text of the field as desired.
4. With the insertion point still in the field, press **F9** to update the field.

5. Press **Alt+F9** to check the results.

To delete a field:

1. Select the entire field, including the field characters.
2. Delete the text as you would any other text.

Editing and Deleting Fields

Updating Fields

You can update a field directly by selecting the field (or the entire document) and then pressing **F9** or choosing Update Fields on the mini-menu that appears when you place the insertion point in the field and click the right menu button. This does not affect fields that don't produce visible results, such as these:

▲ DATA
▲ NEXTIF
▲ NEXT
▲ RD (Referenced Document)
▲ SET
▲ SKIPIF
▲ TC (Table of Contents Entry)
▲ XE (Index Entry)

If text that you've selected contains ASK fields, Word displays dialog boxes requesting information to update the ASK fields.

Some fields are also updated when you use File Print. To be sure that all fields are updated when you print the document, choose **Options** in the Print dialog box, then turn on the **Update Fields** option before printing.

Jumping to Fields

When your document contains a number of fields, you may want to move from one field to another while you are revising or editing.

To quickly jump to fields, you can use these keys:

▲ To jump to the next field, press **F11** or **Alt+F1**.
▲ To jump to the previous field, press **Shift+F11** or **Alt+Shift+F1**.

Locking and Unlocking Fields

When several people are working with the same document and you want to prevent inadvertent changes to fields in the document, you can lock the fields. When you've locked fields, they cannot be changed unless you unlock them first.

To lock a field:

1. Select the field.
2. Press **Ctrl+F11**.

To unlock a field:

1. Select the field.
2. Press **Ctrl+Shift+F11**.

Exchanging Information with Other Applications

In addition to all the text, formatting, graphics, tables, and drawings you can include in Word documents, you can also include information from other applications that you can position and format as you like.

There are two ways to include information from other applications in Word: *embedding* and *linking*. When you embed an object, it becomes part of the Word document itself. Objects that are linked are stored in the source file, and Word keeps track of the location of the file and displays the objects in the document.

If you want to include information that becomes an integral part of the Word document and is independent of the original file, then you should embed the object. If you need to include information that is contained in another file or application and is constantly being updated or is very large, then you should link the source file to Word.

Linking in Word involves placing fields in your document to tell Word what to do with information from other applications or within Word. You can link fields with files created by other applications to include information from those files in your Word document.

You can create two kinds of links:

Exchanging Information with Other Applications

▲ Regular links, which do not automatically update information in the Word document
▲ Auto Update links, which automatically update the Word document when you save, close, or open that document

To embed an object in a Word document:

1. Place the insertion point where you want the object to appear.
2. Choose **Insert Object**.
3. Do one of the following:
   ▲ If you want to embed a new object, click the **Create New** tab and select the object you want from the Object Type list.
   ▲ If you want to embed an exisiting object, click the **Create from File** tab, and in the File Name box type or select the object you want.
4. Click **OK** or press **Enter**.
5. To return to Word, do one of the following:
   ▲ If the object was created in a separate application, choose **Exit** from that application's File menu.
   ▲ If the application temporarily replaces some of Word's menus and toolbars, click anywhere in the Word document.

Creating Regular Links

To create a regular link:

1. Open the file containing the information you want to link with Word.
2. Select the information you want to link with Word.
3. Choose **Edit Copy** to copy the information to the Clipboard.
4. Place the insertion point in the Word document where you want to paste the copied information.
5. Choose **Edit Paste Special**. (If this command is "gray" on the menu, the odds are that the information was copied from an application that does not support DDE (Dynamic Data Exchanges) in that case, you can't link.)
6. Click the **Paste Link** button.
7. Select the type of object in the As box.
8. Click **OK** or press **Enter**.

To link information to a Word file:

1. Choose **Insert Object** and click the **Create from File** tab.
2. In the File Name box, type the name of the file to which you want to link.
3. Turn on the **Link To File** check box.
4. Click **OK** or press **Enter**.

Creating Automatic Update Links

To create a link that Word will automatically update:

1. Create a regular link as described above.
2. Choose **Edit Links**.
3. Select one or more links for which you want to create automatic updates.
4. Click the **Automatic** button.
5. Click **OK** or press **Enter**.

Editing Embedded and Linked Objects

To edit an embedded object:

1. Select the object.
2. Make changes using Word's formatting dialog boxes or in a separate window (if a source application such as Microsoft Graph is used for editing).
3. Return to Word by clicking outside of the object or choosing **File Exit**.

To edit a linked object:

1. Select the object.
2. Choose the object's name from the Edit menu. For example, the Edit menu changes to "Microsoft Excel Worksheet Link" if you're editing an Excel worksheet linked to Word, and then the source application opens.

3. Make the changes you wish, and return to Word. The linked information will be updated.

There are many other ways to use embedded and linked objects in Word documents. For more information, refer to the *Microsoft Word for Windows User's Guide* and the online Help.

Editing Embedded and Linked Objects

Unlinking Fields

Fields can be unlinked at any time. After unlinking a field, you'll have to remember to update the field with the **F9** key.

To unlink a field:

1. Choose **Edit Link**s.
2. Select one or more links that you want to cancel.
3. Click the **Break** Link button.
4. Click the **Yes** button.

You can also select the field(s) and press **Ctrl+Shift+F9**.

QUICK COMMAND SUMMARY

Command	To Do This
Tools Macro	Display the Macro dialog box.
Tools Customize menu tab	Provide the options that modify the menus stored in the current template.
Tools Customize keyboard tab	Provide the options that modify the keyboard assignments stored in the current template.
Insert Field	Display the Field dialog box.
F9 key	Update the selected field.
Ctrl+F9	Add field braces around the insertion point.
Alt+F9	Turn the display of the field codes on and off.

Command	To Do This
F11 or Alt+F1	Jump to the next field.
Shift+F11, or Alt+Shift+F1	Jump to the previous field.
Ctrl+F11	Lock a field.
Ctrl+Shift+F11	Unlock a field.
Edit Copy	Copy information to the Clipboard.
Edit Paste Link	Display the Paste Link dialog box.
Edit Links	Display the Links dialog box.
Ctrl+Shift+F9	Cancel links in your document.

PRACTICE WHAT YOU'VE LEARNED

Create a macro that asks for your name, and assign an unused key combination to the macro.

What You Do

1. Choose **Tools Macro**.

2. Type **namemac** in the Macro Name box and click Record.

3. In the Record Macro dialog box, click the **Keyboard** button, press the key combination you want in the Press New Shortcut Key box, and then click **Assign** and click **Close**.

4. Choose **Insert Field**, and select **(All)** in the categories list and **Ask** in the Field Names list.

What You'll See

1. The Macro dialog box.

2. The Record Macro dialog box and the Macro Name "namemac."

3. The Record Macro dialog box and, when you press the key combination, the key names in the Press New Shortcut Key box. When you click **Assign** and **Close**, the dialog box will close and the document window will be blank except for the Macro toolbar displayed in the upper left part of the screen.

4. The Field dialog box.

What You Do

5. Type **yourname "What is your name?"** in the Field Codes box after the field name ASK.

6. Click **OK** or press **Enter**; then, when the question displays, press **Esc**.

7. Choose **Tools Macro** and choose **Stop Recording**. Click **close** to close the Macro dialog box.

What You'll See

5. The text you type in the Field Codes box.

6. A dialog box with the question "What is your name?" which will close when you press **Esc**.

7. The Macro dialog box, which will close after you choose Stop Recording.

Index

A

Active window, 72
Addition, 281
Address, changing in User Info tab, 54
Address labels, 321, 352-355
Advanced Search, 48-49
Alignment
   of rows in tables, 272
      paragraphs, 149-151
      vertical alignment, 199-200
Achoring frames, 211
Annotations, 99-103
Annotation mark
   replacing, 85
   searching for, 88
Arc, drawing, 222
Arranging windows, 74
ASK instruction, 346, 347-349
Author name, changing, 54
Authorities, table of, 398
AutoCorrect, using, 111-112
AutoFormat, using, 177-179
Automatic page break, 308-309
AutoText entries
   changing, 93
   defining, 91
   deleting, 93-94
   inserting, 92
   printing, 94
   saving, 90-91
   saving paragraph formatting as, 159
   saving drawings as, 90-91

B

Backup copies, 40
Bitmaps, 219
Block of text, selecting, 65
Bold formatting, 125-126
Bookmarks
   adding, 103-104
   defined, 103
Border lines
   adding to paragraphs, 153-154
   adding to tables, 272-273
   around frames, 212-213
   around pictures, 233
Boxes, creating for paragraphs, 153-154
Breaks
   column, 204-205
   line, 236
   page, 156
   section, 194-196
Bullets, adding to paragraphs, 374-375

C

Calculations, 281
Callouts, 229-230
Canceling
    a change, 71-72
    printing, 313
Captions
    adding to figures and tables, 398-401
    adding to pictures, 235-236
Caret character, searching and replacing, 85, 88
Case, changing text, 131-132
Centering
    paragraphs, 149-151
    text, vertically on page, 199-200
Chaining styles, 181-182
Change bars. See Revision marks.
Change, undoing, 71-72
Characters
    formatting, 121-133
    styles, creating, 171-172
Charts, 242-251
Check box, 8
Checking grammar, 115-117
Checking spelling, 108-113
Circle, drawing, 222
Circumflex, searching and replacing, 85, 88
Clicking with mouse, 4
Clip art, working with, 219-220
Clipboard, 68-69, 158, 218
Closing
    style area pane, 176
    windows, 76
    Word, 24-25
Color
    of objects in drawings, 226
    of text, changing, 128
Columns. See also Tables.
    changing column breaks, 85, 88, 204-205
    changing number of, 201-202
    in chart datasheet, 245-246
    of flowing text, 200
    selecting, 66
    width, 203-204
Command assignments, printing, 316
Command button, 7, 8, 9
Commands
    choosing with keys, 6
    choosing with mouse, 5-6
    displaying descriptions of, 24

terminology, 5-6
Comments, 99-103
Comparing versions, 98-99
Condensing text, 130
Continuation notices, 301-302
Control menus, 3, 6
Copies, printing, 314
Copying
    character formatting, 132-133
    files using Find File, 53
    paragraph formatting, 157-158
    pictures, 218, 235
    table cell contents, 245
    text, 68-70
Counting words or characters, 114-115
Creating files, 32-35
Cropping pictures, 231-232
Cross-references,. 401-403
Cube roots, 252

D

Data source document
    creating, 331-333
    defined, 328, 329, 330
    described, 330
Datasheets in charting, 244-245
Date of printing in headers or footers, 297
Default document format, 200
Default path, 53-54
Defining AutoText entries, 90
Deleting
    annotations, 102
    AutoText entries, 93-94
    bookmarks, 104
    column breaks, 205
    documents from the Find File dialog box, 52
    fields, 428-429
    footnotes, 305
    macros, 424
    page break, 309-310
    paragraph formatting, 182
    pictures, 235
    section breaks, 196, 206
    styles, 183
    table cells, 277-279
    tabs, 147-148
    text, 68
Dialog boxes, use of, 7-10
Dictionaries, using, 112-113

Display
    changing size of, 12-13
    field codes or results, 427-428, 433-434
    Formatting toolbar, 20
    gridlines and markers in tables, 261-262
    hidden text, 19
    non-printing characters, 18-19
    optional hyphens, 19
    paragraph marks, 18
    picture placeholders, 17
    scroll bars, 18
    setting preferences, 17
    space characters, 18
    status bar, 18
    tab characters, 19, 149
    table gridlines, 261-262
    text boundaries, 17
Dividing document into parts, 194-196
Division, 281
Document Control menu, 3, 60
Document format, 200
Document management system
    described, 45-47
    searching for documents, 47-50
Document windows
    arranging, 74
    closing, 76
    described, 72
    displaying same document in two, 77
    moving, 76
    moving insertion point between, 73
    splitting into panes, 77-78
    using multiple, 72
Documents
    comparing versions of, 98-99
    creating, 32-35
    defined, 31-32
    displaying statistics about, 45
Double clicking with mouse, 4
Draft copy, 313
Draft mode, 11-12
Drag-and-drop technique, 69
Dragging with mouse, 4
Drawing, in Word, 221-230
Drop-down list box, 8
Dropped capital letter, 155
Dynamic Data Exchange (DDE), 431

E
Editing marks. See Revision marks.
Ellipse, drawing, 222
Embedding drawings, 218-220
Encapsulated Postscript files, 219
Endnotes
    adding, 299-300
    deleting, 305
    editing, 303
    jumping to, 302-303
    print control, 304
    replacing reference mark, 88
    searching for reference mark, 86
End-of-file mark, 3
Enlarging display, 12-14
Entire file, selecting, 66
Envelopes, printing, 318-321, 356-357
Equations,
    creating, 251-252
    editing, 254
    inserting, 252
    switching to text mode, 253
Exiting from Word, 24-25
Expanding text, 130
Extend mode, 66

F
Facing pages, mirroring margins on, 197-198
Fields
    contents, 425
    defined, 424-425
    deleting, 429
    displaying codes or results, 427-428, 433-434
    editing, 428-429
    for table of contents, 387-389
    in main documents, 341-343, 346-350
    inserting, 425-426
    linking, 430-433
    locking, 430
    printing, 428
    updating, 429
Files
    changing default path, 53-54
    creating, 32-35
    displaying statistics about, 45
    locking for annotations, 102-103
    naming, 30
    opening, 36-37, 72-73

Files *(continued)*
   opening from File Find, 50-51
   printing, 311-315
   saving, 38-41
   searching for, 47-50
Fill pattern, changing in drawings, 226
Finding
   bookmark, 104
   formatting, 84-87
   special characters, 85-86
   text, 84-87
Flipping objects in drawing, 225-226
Fonts
   choosing, 125, 126
   types of, 123-124
Font sizes, 123-124, 125
Footers
   adding, 293-297
   defined, 293
Footnotes
   adding, 298-299
   deleting, 305
   editing, 303
   jumping to, 302-303
   print control, 304
   replacing reference mark, 88
   searching for reference mark, 86
Foreign words, marking for spell check, 112
Forms
   activating, 286
   creating, 283-284
   formatting, 284-286
   protecting, 286
Form fields
   check box, 285
   drop-down list, 286
   text, 285
Form letters. See Merging.
Formatting
   characters, 121-133
   charts, 245-246, 248, 249
   form fields, 284-286
   paragraphs, 137-159
   replacing, 87-89
   removing, character, 133
   searching for, 84-87
Formatting toolbar
   defined, 3
   displaying, 20
   use of, 20, 124-125
   used to define style, 167
Frames
   anchoring, 211
   defined, 206
   creating, 206
   deleting, 207
   inserting text and graphics in, 207
   moving, 208-210
   positioning, 208-210
   sizing, 211-212
Freeform shapes, drawing, 222

G

Gallery, use of Style, 165
Grammar checking, 115-117
Graphics,
   inserting inframe, 207
   searching and replacing, 78-81
   using, 218-237
Graphs. See Charts.
Grid, use in drawing, 228-229
Gridlines in tables, 261-262
Grouping objects in drawing, 227-228

H

Hard page break, 86, 88, 308, 309
Header record, 331-333
Headers
   adding, 293-297
   defined, 293
Help system, using, 23-24
Hidden characters
   creating, 128-129
   displaying with Standard toolbar, 128
   displaying with Tools Options, 128
   printing, 317-318
Horizontal scroll bar
   displaying, 18
   using, 60
Hyphens
   automatic hyphenation, 213-214
   displaying optional hyphens, 19
   replacing, 86
   searching for, 88

I

IF clauses, 349-350
Indenting
   paragraphs, 141-144
   rows in tables, 271
Index
   compiling, 396
   inserting entries in fields, 392-396
   updating, 397
Inserting
   annotations, 100-101
   AutoText entries, 92
   contents of Spike, 71
   equations, 252
   fields, 425-426
   frames, 206-207
   in tables, 264-266
   pictures, 218-220
   tables, 259
   text or graphics into frame, 207
   text over selected text, 66-67
Insertion point
   described, 61
   moving, 62-63
   moving between panes, 78
   moving between windows, 73
Italic formatting, 125-126

J

Jumping
   to bookmark, 104
   to fields, 450
   to footnotes, 302-303
   to line number, 378-379
   to specific page, 311
Justified paragraphs, 150-151

K

Keys
   assigning macros to, 420-421
   assigning shortcut keys to styles, 174
   choosing commands with, 5-6
   choosing dialog box options with, 9
   for moving insertion point, 62-63
   for selecting in tables, 265-266
   for selecting text, 62
   selecting text with, 65-66

   selecting window with, 73
   shortcut combinations for commands, 6
   shortcuts for aligning paragraphs, 151
   shortcuts for character formatting, 130-131
   shortcuts for indenting paragraphs, 144
   shortcuts for line spacing, 152-153
   sizing window with, 75
   splitting window with, 77-78
   terminology, 5

L

Labels, 321, 352-354, 398
Layering objects in drawing, 225
Leader characters, 148
Left-aligned paragraphs, 150-151
Line break
   controlling mark display, 19
   inserting, 236
   replacing, 88
   searching for, 86
Line color, 227
Line numbers, 157
Line spacing, controlling, 151-152
Line style, 227
Lines
   adding to paragraphs, 153-154
   adding to tables, 272-273
   around frames, 212-213
   around pictures, 233
   between columns, 204
   drawing, 222, 227
Lines of text, selecting, 64
Linking fields, 430-433
List box, using, 9
Lists of figures, 389-391
Locking fields, 430

M

Macros
   assigning to keys or menus, 420-421
   assigning to toolbars, 418
   correcting, 422-424
   creating, 414-415
   defined, 412-413
   deleting, 424
   printing, 316
   renaming, 422-423

Macros *(continued)*
 running, 415-417
 supplied with Word, 422
Magnifying
 drawing, 228
 Word display, 12-13
Mail Merge Helper, 329-330
Main document
 creating, 330-331
 described, 330
Manual page break, 308, 309
Margins
 changing, 196-197
 mirrored, 197-198
Marking
 foreign words for spell check, 112
 place in file, 103-104
 revisions, 94-98
Master documents
 creating, 403-408
 formatting, 408
Mathematical calculations, 281
Maximize button, 3, 75-76
Menus
 assigning macros to, 420-421
 using mini-menus, 22
Merging
 creating data source document, 331-335
 creating main document, 330-331
 described, 328
 styles, 186-187
 table cells, 275
 to create envelopes, 356-357
 to create form letters, 351-352
 to create mailing labels, 352-353
Microsoft Graph program, 242-251
Minimize button, 3
Mini-menus, using, 22
Mirror margins, 197-198
Modes
 described, 10
 Draft, 11-12
 switching between text and equation, 235
Mouse
 choosing commands with, 7-8
 choosing dialog box options with, 7-8
 scrolling with, 60-61
 selecting text with, 64-65
 selecting window with, 73

sizing window with, 74-75
splitting window with, 77
terminology, 4
Moving
 between annotation marks and text, 101-102
 dialog boxes, 9
 document windows, 76
 frames, 208-210
 insertion point between windows, 73
 insertion point in tables, 264-265
 insertion point in text, 61-63
 objects in drawing, 224
 pictures, 233-235
 table cell contents, 279-280
 text, 68-70
Multiple copies, 314
Multiple document windows, 72
Multiplication, 281

N
Naming files, 30
New line mark
 inserting, 236
 replacing, 88
 searching for, 86
Newspaper-type columns, 200
Nonbreaking hyphens, 86, 88
Nonbreaking spaces, 86, 88
Nonprinting characters, 19
Normal view, 3, 10
NORMAL.DOT, 7, 31-32
Notes, 99-103
Numbering
 in charts, 246
 lines, 157, 376-379
 outlines, 269-270
 paragraphs, 372-373
Numeric keyboard, 62

O
Object Linking and Embedding (OLE), 252
Opening
 documents, 72-73
 files, 72-73
 new window, 79
 style area pane, 175
Operating system, 2

Option button, 8
Optional hyphens, 19
Options in dialog boxes, 7-9
Organizer
   styles, 184-185
   macros, 423-424
   AutoText entries, 90, 91
Orientation of page, 198-199
Outlining, 362-373
Overtype mode, 67

P

Page breaks
   adding to tables, 279
   controlling, 156, 308-309
   inserting, 309
   replacing, 88
   searching for, 85
Page Layout view, described, 10-12
Page number, adding, 292-293
Page size, changing, 198-199
Pagination, controlling, 308-309
Panes
   opening and closing style area pane, 175-176
   using to view same document, 77-78
Paper size, 198-199
Paragraph formatting, 137-159
Paragraph marks
   displaying, 18
   replacing, 88
   searching for, 86
Paragraphs
   adding bullets, 374-376
   adding lines, boxes, shading, 153-154
   aligning, 149-151
   controlling page breaks in, 156
   defined, 138
   indenting, 141-144
   numbering, 372-373
   saving formatting in an AutoText entry, 159
   selecting, 138
   creating, style, 169-170
Pasting
   contents of Spike, 71
   in tables,
   into Edit Find dialog box, 84, 87
   into Edit Replace dialog box, 84, 87

pictures, 218
Pattern, changing in drawings, 226
PC Paintbrush files, 219
Pictures, 17, 86, 88
Placeholders for pictures, displaying, 17
Pointing with mouse, 4
Positioning
   charts, 250-251
   pictures and frames, 233-235
   text and graphics, 208-210
Preferences for screen display, 16-19
Print Preview
   described, 14
   using, 14-16
Printing
   address labels, 321, 355
   all pages, 311-312
   annotations, 103
   AutoText entries, 94
   canceling, 313
   envelopes, 318-3211, 356-357
   field results or codes, 428
   footnotes, 304
   from the Find File dialog box, 52
   hidden text, 317-318
   in reverse order, 317
   multiple copies, 314
   orientation of page, 198-199
   outlines, 371
   part of a document, 314-315
   preparation, 311
   styles, 188
   to a file, 318
   troubleshooting, 321-322

Q

Queries, 340-341
Quitting Word, 24-25

R

Readability checking, 115-117
Rearranging an outline, 367
Recording style formatting, 166
Recording macros. See Macros, creating.
Rectangle, drawing, 222
Reducing size of display, 12-13
Removing, character or paragraph formatting, 133, 182

Renaming
  macros, 422-423
  styles, 181
Repeating last action, 158
Replacing
  formatting, 87-89
  selected text with inserted text, 66-67
  special characters, 88
  text, 87-89
Restore button, 76
Reverse order for printing, 317
Revision marking, 94-98
Right-align paragraphs, 150-151
Rotating objects in drawing, 225-226
Rounded rectangle, drawing, 222
Rows, adding to tables, 276-277
Ruler
  clicking to display dialog boxes, 140
  defined, 3
  displaying, 139
  setting tabs with, 145
  using for paragraph formatting, 141-144
  using in tables, 266-267
Rules. See Border lines.
Running feet, adding, 294-295
Running heads, adding, 294-295
Running list box, 8, 9

S

Saving
  AutoText entries, 90-91
  files, 38-41
  paragraph formatting as a style, 159
  text in Spike, 70-71
Scaling in pictures, 231
Scroll bars, 18
Scrollable list box, 8, 9
Searching
  for bookmarks, 104
  for documents, 47-50
  for formatting, 84-87
  for revisions, 97
  for special characters, 86
  for text, 84-87
Sections
  beginning new section, 194-196
  described, 194
Selecting

  in charts, 248
  in tables, 265-266
  objects in drawing, 223-224
  paragraphs, 138
  text, 63-66
Selection bar, 64
Shading
  adding to paragraphs, 153-154
  adding to tables, 272
  in frames, 212-213
Shadow boxes, 153-154, 272
Size
  of charts, 231-232
  of frame, 212-213
  of objects in drawing, 231-232
  of page, 198-199
  of pictures, 224-225
  of windows, 73-76
Soft page break, 308-309
Sorting, 335-340
Spaces,
  displaying characters, 18
  replacing, 88
  searching for, 86
Spacing
  before or after paragraph, 151-153
  between characters, 130
  between lines in paragraph, 151-153
  of tabs, 145-147
Special effects, using WordArt for, 236-237
Spelling checker, 108-113
Spike, 70-71
Split bar, 77
Splitting
  tables, 279
  merged table cells, 275
  windows into panes, 77-78
Square, drawing, 222
Square roots, 252
Stacking objects in drawing, 225
Starting Word, 2
Statistics for documents, 45
Status bar, displaying, 18
Style Gallery, using, 165
Styles
  applying, 173, 177-178
  changing, 179-181
  character, creating, 171
  closing style area pane, 175

defining, 166, 167, 168
described, 164
deleting, 183
displaying names in window, 175-177
opening style area pane, 175
paragraph, creating, 170
printing, 188
provided with Word, 165
renaming, 181
repeating, 174
saving paragraph formatting as, 159
setting up a chain, 181-182
using AutoFormat, 177-179
use with templates, 185-187
using from another document, 184-185
Subdocuments, 403, 405-406
Subscripts, 129
Subtraction, 281
Summary Info, 43-45, 53
Superscripts, 129
Symbols, inserting, 132
Synonyms, finding, 113-114

T

Table of contents
    creating from Heading styles, 385-386
    creating from TC fields, 387-388
    updating, 397
Table Wizard, using, 260-261
Tables
    adding borders or shading, 272-273
    adding cells, 276-277
    adding page breaks, 279
    aligning rows, 272
    calculating, 281
    changing column width, 268-269
    changing row height, 269-270
    converting from text, 262-264
    converting to text, 280
    deleting cells, 277-279
    entering information in, 264-266
    examples, 263
    formatting, 266-272
    gridlines and markers, 261-262
    indenting rows, 271
    inserting, 259
    merging cells, 275
    moving and copying cell contents, 279-280
    moving from cell to cell, 264-265
    positioning, 274
    selecting in, 265-266
    splitting one table into two, 279
    splitting merged cells, 275
    using AutoFormat, 273-274
    using for data source documents, 331-332
    using to create forms, 282-286
Tabs
    changing, 147-148
    changing default tab spacing, 147
    deleting, 147-148
    displaying characters, 18, 149
    in tables, 265
    replacing, 88
    searching for, 86
    setting, 145-146
    spacing, 145-149
Tagging with bookmarks, 103-104
Templates
    creating, 32-35
    defined, 31-32
    printing assignments, 316
    saving AutoText entries in, 90-91
Text
    adding to drawing, 229
    changing case of, 131-132
    converting into tables, 262-264
    in frames, 207
    replacing, 87-89
    searching for, 84-87
    selecting, 63-66
    switching to equation mode, 253
Text boundaries, 17
Text box, 8, 9
Text markers in tables, 261-262
Thesaurus, using, 113-114
TIFF files, 219
Time of printing in headers or footers, 297
Title page, 199-200
Toolbar
    changing assignments, 20-22
    defined, 19
    displaying description of button, 20
    moving, 22
    Forms, 284
    Formatting, 124-125
Typing over text, 67, 68, 70

U

Underlined formatting, 125-126
Undoing a change, 71-72, 232
Ungroup, 227-228
Updating fields, 429

V

Version control, 98-99
Vertical scroll bar, 3
Views
    described, 10
    Normal, 10
    Page Layout, 10-11
    Print Preview, 14-16
    Outline, 362
    setting preferences for display, 17-19

W

White space, 86, 88
Whole file, selecting, 66
Widow, 310
Wildcard character, 85, 88
Window, Word, parts of, 3
Windows,
    changing size of, 73-76
    closing, 76
    displaying same document in two, 77
    moving insertion point between, 73
    splitting into panes, 77-78
    using multiple document windows, 72
Windows Metafiles, 219
Windows, Microsoft, 2
Winword command, 3
WINWORD.EXE file, 2
Wizards,
    defined, 35
    using, 35-36, 260-261
WordArt, 236-237
Word control menu, 6
Words
    checking grammar, 115
    checking spelling, 108-113
    counting, 114-115
    replacing, 87-89
    searching for, 84-87
    selecting, 64- 66
Wrapping text around frame, 211

Z

Zooming display, 12-14